Essential Business Process Modeling

Other resources from O'Reilly

Essential Business Process Modeling

Michael Havey

O'REILLY®

Beijing · Cambridge · Farnham · Köln · Paris · Sebastopol · Taipei · Tokyo

Essential Business Process Modeling
by Michael Havey

Published by O'Reilly Media, Inc.
1005 Gravenstein Highway North
Sebastopol, CA 95472.

O'Reilly books may be purchased for educational, business, or sales promotional use. Online editions are also available for most titles (*safari.oreilly.com*). For more information, contact our corporate/institutional sales department: (800) 998-9938 or *corporate@oreilly.com*.

Editors:	Andrew Odewahn/Mary O'Brien
Production Editor:	Mary Anne Weeks Mayo
Cover Designer:	MendeDesign
Interior Designer:	Marcia Friedman
Creative Director:	Michele Wetherbee
Printing History:	August 2005: First Edition.

RepKover™ This book uses RepKover™, a durable and flexible lay-flat binding.

ISBN: 0-596-00843-0

[M]

TABLE OF CONTENTS

PREFACE — ix

PART ONE CONCEPTS — 1

1   INTRODUCTION TO BUSINESS PROCESS MODELING — 3
   The Benefits of BPM — 7
   BPM Acid Test: The Process-Oriented Application — 8
   The Morass of BPM — 9
   Workflow — 16
   Roadmap — 17
   Summary — 18
   References — 19

2   PRESCRIPTION FOR A GOOD BPM ARCHITECTURE — 21
   Designing a Solution — 22
   Components of the Design — 27
   Standards — 42
   Summary — 44
   Reference — 45

3   THE SCENIC TOUR OF PROCESS THEORY — 47
   Family Tree — 48
   The Pi-Calculus — 49
   Petri Nets — 55
   State Machines and Activity Diagrams — 64
   Summary — 70
   References — 71

4   PROCESS DESIGN PATTERNS — 73
   Design Patterns and the GoF — 73
   Process Patterns and the P4 — 74
      Basic Patterns — 75
      Advanced Branch and Join Patterns — 79
      Structural Patterns — 82
      Multiple Instances Patterns — 84
      State-Based Patterns — 87
      Cancellation Patterns — 91

	Yet Another Workflow Language (YAWL)	93
	Additional Patterns	·95
	Process Coding Standards	98
	Summary	98
	References	99
PART TWO	*STANDARDS*	101
5	*BUSINESS PROCESS EXECUTION LANGUAGE (BPEL)*	103
	Anatomy of a Process	104
	BPEL Example	108
	BPEL in a Nutshell	114
	BPELJ	134
	BPEL and Patterns	140
	Summary	141
	References	142
6	*BPMI STANDARDS: BPMN AND BPML*	143
	BPMN	145
	BPML	163
	Summary	172
	Reference	173
7	*THE WORKFLOW MANAGEMENT COALITION (WFMC)*	175
	The Reference Model	176
	XPDL	180
	WAPI	193
	WfXML	197
	Summary	201
	References	201
8	*WORLD WIDE WEB CONSORTIUM (W3C): CHOREOGRAPHY*	203
	About the W3C	203
	Choreography and Orchestration	204
	WS-CDL	206
	WSCI	218
	WSCL	225
	Summary	229
	References	230
9	*OTHER BPM MODELS*	231
	OMG: Model-Driven BPM	232
	ebXML BPSS: Collaboration	237
	Microsoft XLANG: BPEL Forerunner	240
	IBM WSFL: BPEL Forerunner	243
	BPEL, XLANG, and WSFL	249
	Summary	250
	References	251

PART THREE   *EXAMPLES*   253

10   *EXAMPLE: HUMAN WORKFLOW IN INSURANCE CLAIMS PROCESSING*   255

Oracle BPEL Process Manager   257

Setting Up the Environment   259

Developing the Example   260

Testing the Example   280

Summary   283

References   284

11   *EXAMPLE: ENTERPRISE MESSAGE BROKER*   285

What Is a Message Broker?   285

Example: Employee Benefits Message Broker   288

Summary   310

KEY BPM ACRONYMNS   313

INDEX   317

Preface

To him who looks upon the world rationally,

the world in its turn presents a rational aspect.

—Hegel
Philosophy of History

THIS BOOK IS INTENDED AS A REASONED, CONCEPTUAL PRESENTATION OF THE BURGEONING BUT FREN-
ZIED WORLD OF BUSINESS PROCESS MODELING, or BPM (also known as *business process management*), at a recent point in time. Endless material about BPM can be found on the Web,
but it is a morass of vendor sales pitches, insubstantial business and technical articles, and
imprecise terminology. When BPM is introduced into a modern consulting project, it is
frequently misapplied (used to solve problems that BPM was not meant to solve) and
designed poorly (hacked, rather than coded by pattern). BPM cannot even decide what to
call itself. What happened to the wonderfully descriptive "workflow?" Seemingly interchangeable with BPM, the term "workflow" has fallen out of fashion, and is now
verboten.

But BPM—or, dare we say, workflow—is actually quite a taut, intelligible topic. It is
about modeling a business process, using standard graphical and XML representations, as
a flow of activities. Thanks to those standards (notably BPEL and BPMN, defined in
Chapters 5 and 6), the semantics of a flow are as rigorously defined as those of any
programming language: anyone can informally sketch boxes and arrows on a whiteboard
during a requirements meeting, but a BPM process is designed with execution in mind.

BPM is also closely aligned with the notion of service-oriented architecture, particularly
the emerging W3C web services stack. Whereas the traditional use of a workflow was

about the movement of work from person to person within an organization, contemporary BPM processes are built to interact as services with other systems, or even to orchestrate or choreograph other systems, including the business processes of other companies. Indeed, a business process *is* a service, one intended to be called by other systems, and these calls drive its execution. Realizing this fact is one of the first big steps in understanding BPM.

The goal of *Essential Business Process Modeling* is to demonstrate standard ways to code rigorous processes that are centerpieces of a service-oriented architecture. Along the way, this book introduces design patterns and best practices specific to BPM, as well as some underlying theory. The book aims to do three things:

- Describe the concepts of BPM, and the nature of a process and a process-oriented application.
- Isolate the major standards and describe each in detail. Most contemporary standards use XML to code a process, but some are based on graphical notation.
- Develop substantial examples using tools that are available for free and can be run on an average contemporary PC or laptop.

Audience

Essential Business Process Modeling is for software architects and developers who intend to build solutions that feature or use BPM; it provides concepts, standards, and substantial examples of the technology in action. In addition, the first four chapters will help project managers, IT managers, enterprise architects, and anyone else who seeks a high-level introduction to the subject.

Assumptions This Book Makes

This book assumes that the reader is comfortable with or has had some exposure to web services (especially Web Services Description Language, or WSDL) and XML, including XML Schema Definition (XSD) and XPath. Other prerequisites are:

Oracle SQL
    Chapter 2 includes a few SQL statements in Oracle's syntax.

Java
    Chapters 5 and 10 have a few lines of Java code embedded in BPEL.

UML (Unified Modeling Language)
    The discussion of activity diagrams in Chapter 3 assumes the reader is comfortable with UML. In addition, many of the figures in the book use UML to illustrate designs.

Eclipse

The examples in Chapters 10 and 11 require Oracle BPEL Process Designer, which runs within the Open Source Eclipse integration development environment.

Visio

The BPMN portion of the example in Chapter 11 requires the use of ITpearls' Visio stencils.

Contents of This Book

The book is organized into three parts, eleven chapters and a glossary:

Part One, *Concepts*

Covers the BPM essentials, an approach to BPM architecture, a tour of BPM theory, and a survey of process design patterns and coding practices.

Chapter 1, *Introduction to Business Process Modeling*

Examines what BPM (and is not!) and discusses its benefits.

Chapter 2, *Prescription for a Good BPM Architecture*

Develops a model BPM architecture, and discusses the main pieces of a "good" BPM application, the design of each piece, and which standards are adopted.

Chapter 3, *The Scenic Tour of Process Theory*

Provides a tour of the Pi Calculus, Petri nets, state machines, and UML activity diagrams, and why they matter. Practical software books seldom delve into theory, but theory matters more in BPM than in most software subjects.

Chapter 4, *Process Design Patterns*

Includes a detailed look at the 20 process patterns identified by some of the leading BPM theorists, a group referred to in this book as the "P4." The patterns cover common branch-and-join and synchronization scenarios. Also covered are process communication patterns, human interaction patterns, and briefly, coding best practices.

Part Two, *Standards*

Provides a detailed look at BPEL; the BPMI specifications (BPML and BPMN); the WfMC (WAPI, XPDL, WfXML, and the reference architecture); web services choreography (WSCI, WS-CDL, WSCL); and the OMG's model-driven approach (BPDM, BPRI), BPSS, XLANG, and WSFL.

Chapter 5, *Business Process Execution Language (BPEL)*

Provides a detailed look at BPEL, the leading BPM standard.

Chapter 6, *BPMI Standards: BPMN and BPML*

Examines BPMI and its two standards: BPML and BPMN.

Chapter 7, *The Workflow Management Coalition (WfMC)*

Overviews the main offerings of the WfMC: the reference model, WAPI, WfXML, and XPDL.

Chapter 8, *World Wide Web Consortium (W3C): Choreography*

Examines the W3C's work in choreography. Provides an overview of web services choreography and orchestration, and examines how they differ. A look at three choreography languages of the W3C: WSCI, WS-CDL, and WSCL.

Chapter 9, *Other BPM Models*

Discusses four process languages that are too important not to mention. Examines how XLANG and WSFL have influenced BPEL, the nature of collaboration in BPSS, and the OMG's model-driven architecture (MDA) and leading BPM models.

Part Three, *Examples*

Develops two substantial BPEL applications using Oracle BPEL Process Manager.

Chapter 10, *Example: Human Workflow in Insurance Claims Processing*

Illustrates a fully functional working example of a BPEL insurance claim processing application based on the Oracle BPEL Process Manager product, including how to incorporate human workflow into an otherwise automated process.

Chapter 11, *Example: Enterprise Message Broker*

Develops another working example, a central message broker application that manages system communications for a company's employee benefits. Shows BPMN graphical modeling with ITpearls' Process Modeler and BPEL implementation with Oracle BPEL Process Manager.

Glossary

BPM is rife with three-letter acronyms (or TLAs). Our glossary decodes some of the most important terms.

Conventions Used in This Book

The following typographical conventions are used in this book:

Italic

Indicates new terms, URLs, email addresses, filenames, file extensions, pathnames, directories, and Unix utilities.

Constant width

Indicates activities, commands, options, switches, variables, attributes, keys, functions, types, classes, namespaces, methods, modules, properties, parameters, values, objects, events, event handlers, XML tags, HTML tags, macros, the contents of files, or the output from commands.

Constant width bold

Shows commands or other text that should be typed literally by the user.

Constant width italic

Shows text that should be replaced with user-supplied values.

NOTE

This icon signifies a tip, suggestion, or general note.

WARNING

This icon indicates a warning or caution.

Using Code Examples

This book is here to help you get your job done. In general, you may use the code in this book in your programs and documentation. You do not need to contact us for permission unless you're reproducing a significant portion of the code. For example, writing a program that uses several chunks of code from this book does not require permission. Selling or distributing a CD-ROM of examples from O'Reilly books does require permission. Answering a question by citing this book and quoting example code does not require permission. Incorporating a significant amount of example code from this book into your product's documentation does require permission.

We appreciate, but do not require, attribution. An attribution usually includes the title, author, publisher, and ISBN. For example: "*Essential Business Process Modeling*, by Michael Havey, Copyright 2005 O'Reilly Media, Inc., 0-596-00843-0."

If you feel that your use of code examples falls outside fair use or the example permission given here, feel free to contact us at *permissions@oreilly.com*.

Safari Enabled

 When you see a Safari® Enabled icon on the cover of your favorite technology book, that means the book is available online through the O'Reilly Network Safari Bookshelf.

Safari offers a solution that's better than e-books. It's a virtual library that lets you easily search thousands of top technical books, cut and paste code samples, download chapters, and find quick answers when you need the most accurate, current information. Try it for free at *http://safari.oreilly.com*.

We'd Like to Hear from You

Please address comments and questions concerning this book to the publisher:

O'Reilly Media, Inc.
1005 Gravenstein Highway North
Sebastopol, CA 95472
(800) 998-9938 (in the United States or Canada)
(707) 829-0515 (international or local)
(707) 829-0104 (fax)

We have a web page for this book, where we list errata, examples, and any additional information. You can access this page at:

http://www.oreilly.com/catalog/essentialpm

To comment or ask technical questions about this book, send email to:

bookquestions@oreilly.com

For more information about our books, conferences, Resource Centers, and the O'Reilly Network, see our web site at:

http://www.oreilly.com

Acknowledgments

When I started on this book, I wondered what it would take it to finish it. Could I master the subject matter and write it the O'Reilly way? Could I, already maxed out on time with a busy day job and family life, work vigorously, keep the pace, and finish on schedule? Well, I made it, and as it turns out, I had help. Though I can't part with the image of a solitary me sitting night-after-night by laptop at kitchen table, when I think it through, I have to admit that this book would have been doomed without the help of my family, my reviewers, and my editors.

Family comes first, in more ways than one. This book is dedicated to you, Paola, for supporting and inspiring me! And to our beautiful children, Napoleon, Nina, Mason, and Ireland: when you get older please study BPM and quote me in your theses. To my mother Maureen, dear departed father Frank and brother Tim, brothers Mark and John, and sisters Liza and Susan: thank you for your cheerleading, and I do admit that this book is proof of Dr. Spock's methods.

My reviewers were drawn from a wish list that editor Andrew Odewahn asked me to put together. I chose heroes of the field. That we were actually able to get some of these guys delights me immensely. Thanks to Wil van der Aalst (larger-than-life BPM academic and patterns visionary), Nick Kavantzas (WS-CDL lead author and Oracle web services architect), and David Frankel (BPTrends editor and author of a key MDA book) for their constructive criticism. I also had two top-echelon consulting enterprise architects: Brian Waterworth from IBM, and my friend Mark Janzen from BEA. Customers rely on these individuals to make sound business and technology decisions, and I trust their criticism of my thoughts on BPM.

Finally, among the many folks at O'Reilly who contributed to this book, let me single out copy editor Nancy Kotary, illustrators Rob Romano and Leslie Borash, production editor Mary Anne Weeks Mayo, indexer Lucie Haskins and, above all, editors Andrew Odewahn and Mike Hendrickson. Andrew, a talented writer and a *writer's* editor, encouraged me and diligently spotted needed improvements in my writing. Much like a BPM runtime engine, Andrew helped guide me through the process. Mike Hendrickson was the first one from O'Reilly to contact me, and his acceptance of my proposal was not the thunderous "Congratulations!" that I had expected, but an understated "By the way, we have the go-ahead" camouflaged in the body of an email entitled "RE: Proposal." When Mike and I first spoke on the phone, I was struck by his sense of possibility and open-endedness in a book. He assured me that books often change course in mid-flight, and although I largely stuck to my original flight plan, I flew more confidently knowing the extent of the sky.

PART ONE CONCEPTS

An introduction to the concepts of BPM, including: the definition of process, the acid test for a process-oriented application, a comparison of workflow and BPM, the advantages of BPM, an overview of the major BPM vendors and standards, the ideal BPM solution architecture and its use of current standards, process theory, process design patterns, and process coding best practices.

CHAPTER ONE

Introduction to Business Process Modeling

IN THE WORLD OF SOFTWARE, THE WORD "PROCESS" HAS SEVERAL DENOTATIONS. The verb means to handle, as in processing an error, or processing a message. The noun sometimes refers to a program running in an operating system, and sometimes to a procedure, or a set of procedures, for accomplishing a goal. In each case, the connotations of the term are movement, work, and time; a process performs actions over some interval of time in order to achieve, or to progress to, some objective. This book addresses the concept of a *business* process, which we all intuitively understand as the step-by-step rules specific to the resolution of some business problem. As mentioned in the Preface, *business process modeling* (BPM), sometimes called business process management, refers to the design and execution of business processes. This book explores BPM's foundations, standards and typical uses.

This chapter examines an example problem, a travel reservation application, that models the nature of a business process and its core concepts. Stated informally in English, the process for this application is the following:

1. Get the customer's itinerary.

2. For each item on the itinerary, attempt to book with the target company. Specifically, book a flight with the airline, a room with the hotel, and a car with the car rental agency. These bookings can be made in parallel.

3. If all the bookings succeed, get payment from the customer and send the customer a confirmation. Process completes normally!

4. If at least one booking fails, cancel the successful bookings and report the problem to the customer.

5. If the user does not wish to continue, stop the process. Otherwise, return to Step 1.

For a software developer, this listing reads like an algorithm: it is a sequence of steps, with conditions, loops and—to complicate matters a little—parallelism. Indeed, a carefully conceived process is algorithmic and is often sketched, either extemporaneously on a meeting room whiteboard or deliberately and rigorously with drawing software, as a flowchart, such as the one shown in Figure 1-1.

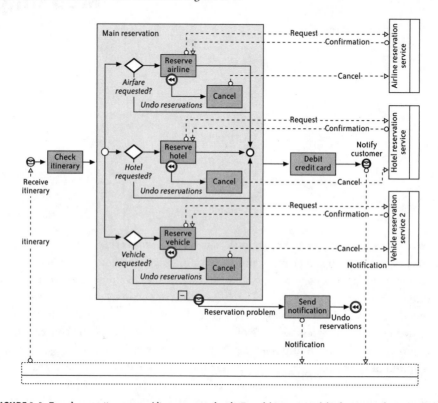

FIGURE 1-1. *Travel reservation process (diagram created with ITpearls' Process Modeler for Microsoft Visio, v. 1.1)*

Being algorithmic, a process can potentially be run by some sort of process engine. As long as the process can be expressed in a form that is syntactically and semantically unambiguous—that is, in a programming language or other interpretable form—the engine can accept it as input, set it in motion, and drive its flow of control. To be precise, the engine creates and runs *instances* of a given process *definition*. The steps of the process are called *activities* or *tasks*.

The following list summarizes the most important process modeling terms and their relationships to each other:

Process definition
  The basic algorithm or behavior of the process.

Process instance
  An occurrence of a process for specific input. Each instance of the travel reservation process, for example, is tied to a specific customer's itinerary.

Activity or task
  A step in a process, such as sending a flight request to the airline.

Automated activity or automated task
  A step in a process that is performed directly by the execution engine.

Manual activity or manual task
  A step in a process that is meant to be performed by a human process participant.

The distinction between manual and automated activities is extremely important. At one time, before the reign of software, a business process was completely manual and paper-driven: paper was passed from person to person, and was often misplaced or delayed along the way. Now, much of the process runs on autopilot.

Even so, some steps—typically managerial approvals or business exception handling—remain manual. In the case of the travel agency, when at least one itinerary booking fails, the process assigns to an agent the task of contacting the customer to adjust the itinerary. Figure 1-2 shows a page in the travel agency's portal web application that displays a list of itineraries requiring a manual fix because of a failed booking.

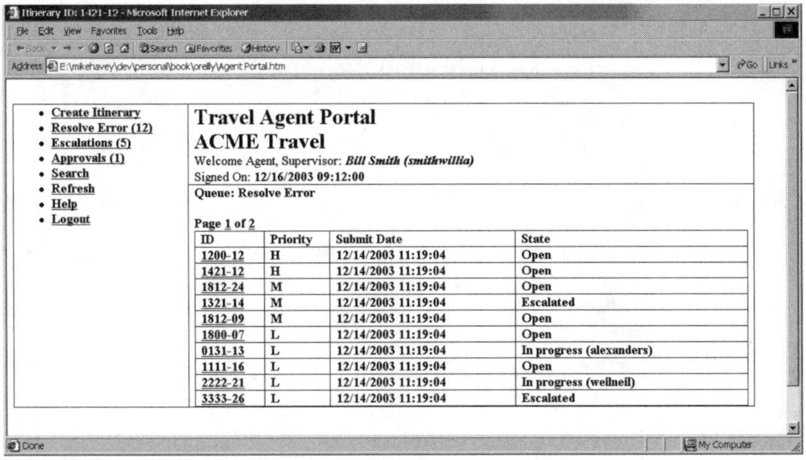

FIGURE 1-2. *Travel reservation worklist portal*

As the figure indicates, the user Bill Smith, who is an agent and a supervisor at the agency (ACME Travel), is logged into the portal. The options on the left menu include a link to create an itinerary (used when a customer calls in with a new request), as well as links to three manual activity queues: Resolve Error (which has 12 current activities), Escalations (5 activities), and Approvals (1 activity). The main frame on the right side shows a summary list of Resolve Error activities, displaying the ID, priority, submission time, and status of each activity.

A *queue* is a list of activities of a particular type assigned to a particular user or group of users. The Resolve Error queue is a list of activities, shared by all agents, to fix itineraries; any agent logged into the portal can claim an activity from the queue whose status is "open"; once claimed, the status changes to "in progress"; the activity is removed from the queue once the agent successfully handles it.

When the agent selects a task from the queue (e.g., ID 1421-12), the resultant page (shown in Figure 1-3) displays information about the customer (Paul Chang), the original itinerary (under Itinerary Details), and the reason for the booking failure (Exception), and prompts for itinerary changes (the edits Flight Change, Hotel Change, and Car Change are submitted with the Submit Change link). The page, also enables the agent to perform a manual fix to a problem in a mostly automated process.

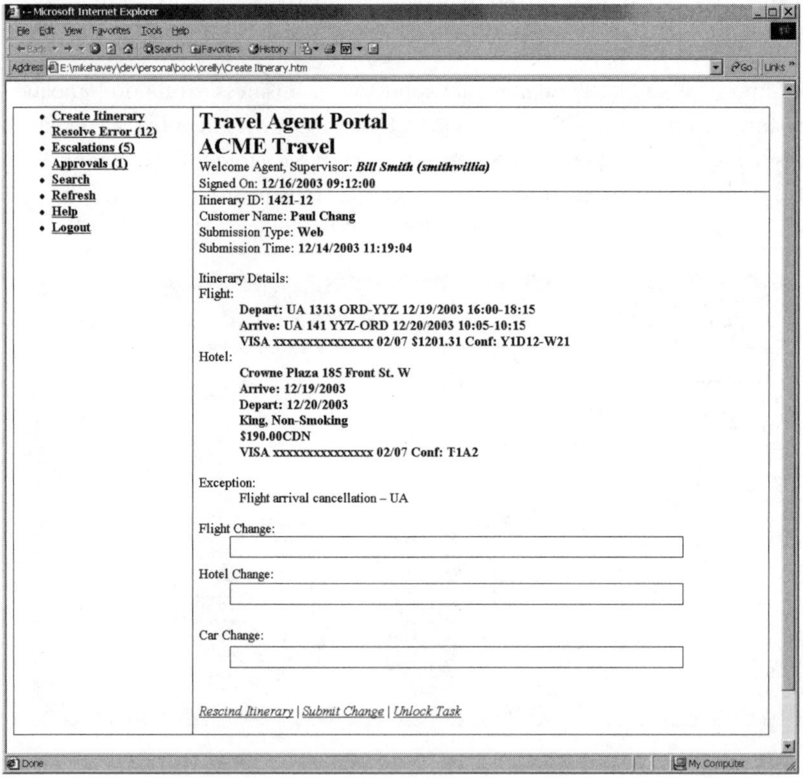

FIGURE 1-3. *Travel reservation task page*

Automated activities generally fall into two categories:

- Interactions with external systems: e.g., sending a booking request to an airline
- Arbitrary programmatic logic: e.g., calculating the priority of a manual task

The external system interface requires the process runtime engine to have significant enterprise application integration (EAI) capabilities, such as XML, B2B, web services, MOM, .NET, and J2EE interfaces. Indeed, no contemporary business process lives in isolation: it acts upon, and is triggered by, other applications, whether internal or external to the enterprise.

Arbitrary programming logic requires that the process either support embedded code or provide the ability to call code. The logic of a process is necessarily coarse-grained; the fine-grained programming is best performed in a lower-level language such as Java.

The Benefits of BPM

An organization's decision to build a BPM solution is made by its business architects, CIO, CTO, or CEO. Possible motivations for choosing BPM include the following:

Formalize existing process and spot needed improvements. Adopting BPM forces a business to think through and formalize its understanding of current processes. Along the way, those running the business invariably spot potential improvements, such as the removal of steps, automation of manual steps, or the reengineering of a part or the whole of the flow.

Facilitate automated, efficient process flow. Given that a process spans multiple activities, the less time spent *between* activities, the better. When BPM software drives the process flow, downtime between activities is almost zero, unless the software itself is down. Even better, BPM supports process parallelism, so that independent sequences of work can be performed concurrently in isolation of each other, with their results merged and synchronized later in the flow. A process controlled by some other means—for example, by phone calls, emails, or inter-office mail exchange—is bound to be significantly slower and prone to getting lost or stuck.

Increase productivity and decrease head count. Get work done faster with fewer people! Actual BPM case studies provide some interesting results: a financial services was able to reduce staff from 613 to 406 while decreasing processing time and increasing customer satisfaction; an insurance company trimmed off 40% of its staff and increased its rate of claims handling.*

Allow people to solve the hard problems. Although BPM is often about removing or decreasing human participation in a process, one of its benefits is its flexibility to use people to

---

* C. Plesums, "Introduction to Workflow," *http://www.plesums.com/image/introworkflow.html.*

help fix problems, as in Figure 1-4, where an exception in Step D is passed to a human resolver, who corrects it and resumes the process at Step E.

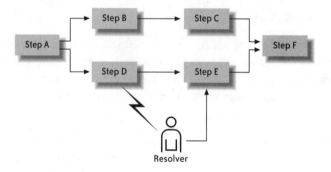

FIGURE 1-4. *Person resolves process failure*

James Raby, vice president of engineering for a claims processing outsourcer, observes that BPM doesn't necessarily eliminate people but has them "do the hard problems."* For example, if an automated step (such as a query to a legacy system) fails, a manual workaround is assigned to an operations clerk (who does the query and passes the results back to the process).

Simplify regulations and compliance issues. As the Butler Group points out, BPM helps businesses build auditable processes that help organizations comply with various regulatory requirements:

"Organizations do not really have much control over compliance. The smarter businesses will therefore look to offset the cost of compliance with the benefits of closer process control and management."†

In the financial sector, for example, the introduction of regulations such as the Patriot Act and the Basel Accord has forced companies to build new processes, or improve existing processes, to track money laundering and to buffer against risk.

BPM Acid Test: The Process-Oriented Application

Irrational exuberance about BPM might compel a vendor or customer to believe that BPM is the solution to all enterprise application problems. After all, BPM empowers the business analyst, who knows the application requirements best, to create a design or flowchart for the high-level logic. And after all, what is an enterprise application but a set of logic? The flaw in this argument is that the logic of a process is not its procedural

---

*   D. L. Margulius, "Workflow Meets BPM," *InfoWorld*, April 2002, *http://www.infoworld.com/article/02/04/18/020422febpmtca_1.html*.

†   Butler Group, "Business Process Management: A Guide to Navigating the Process Minefield," 2004, *http://www.butlergroup.com/reports/bpm/*.

implementation but its declarative dynamic behavior, or its change in state over time as events occur.

Many BPM vendors provide a graphical process editor that lets the end user design a process by dragging boxes and arrows onto a canvas. The drawing that the user creates looks like a program, but it is really a kind of state diagram for the process. A good BPM product makes it relatively easy to turn the diagram into an executable application; it is a matter of filling in the blanks. But this ease does not make the product the right choice to build all executable applications.

BPM is suited only for applications with an essential sense of state or process—that is, applications that are process-oriented. An application passes the BPM acid test if it is legitimately process-oriented. The travel agency application, for example, passes the test because it is best understood in terms of the state of the itinerary and is defined at all times by how far the itinerary has gotten. Other typical characteristics of a process-oriented application include the following:

Long-running
  From start to finish, the process spans hours, days, weeks, months, or more.

Persisted state
  Because the process is long-lived, its state is persisted to a database so that it outlasts the server hosting it.

Bursty, sleeps most of the time
  The process spends most of its time asleep, waiting for the next triggering event to occur, at which point it wakes up and performs a flurry of activities.

Orchestration of system or human communications
  The process is responsible for managing and coordinating the communications of various system or human actors.

Some process-oriented applications have only a subset of these characteristics. The processes of the Message Broker application presented in Chapter 11, for example, are short-lived and never sleep, running from start to finish in a single burst with no stopping points. But they satisfy—indeed, epitomize—the orchestral quality, and hence are perfectly suited to a BPM implementation.

The boxes and arrows of BPM are a poor fit for nonprocess-oriented applications. For example, in an automated teller machine, which lets users query their account balance, withdraw cash, deposit checks and cash, and pay bills—any sense of process is fleeting and inessential; an ATM is an online transaction processor, not a process-oriented application.

The Morass of BPM

BPM is one of the most fashionable three-letter acronyms in software today. The field is known for having many competing vendors and standards, unusually named academic underpinnings, and a diverse set of potential users, from techies to business analysts, business architects, CIOs, CTOs, and CEOs.

The topic of BPM is profoundly simple to the beginner: the business analyst designs the process, the process is run by an engine, and the engine has EAI and human interaction capabilities. In practice, a morass of concepts, terminology, standards, vendors, and philosophies confounds the intermediate-level student of BPM who knows the basics but is lost in detail—and is also responsible for building a BPM-based solution. Which product to choose? Or is the right solution the combination of several products, such as a design tool product and an execution engine product? Which standard to build on? Which version of which standard? Are the standards too immature? Are the products themselves immature?

The goal of this book is to discover through the morass a system of thought that, like all good systems, depends on a small number of concepts. The medieval philosopher William of Ockham argued:

> *Entia non sunt multiplicanda praeter necessitatem.*
> (Entities ought not to be multiplied without necessity.)

Known as Ockham's Razor, this aphorism implies that a good system is fundamentally simple. Reducing BPM to its essentials yields the following basic criteria:

- A good BPM architecture, as described in Chapter 2, is as elegant an enterprise architecture as can be. Many applications fail because they lack an intelligible initial design; BPM can prevent this.

- Some BPM standards are better than others. A good BPM solution is achieved by choosing the best pieces. The adoption of BPEL and BPMN is a recipe for success.

- Processes, like object-oriented applications, have recurring design patterns. A good BPM application exhibits, or explicitly uses, industry standard patterns. Chapter 4 describes the 20 standard process patterns conceived by the Process Four group.

The following sections survey the leading standards and vendors of BPM, as well as the dominant contributions to process theory.

Standards

BPM does not lack standards or standards bodies. Some of the most important of these include the OASIS group's BPEL standard, BPMI's BPML and BPMN standards, the various W3C choreography standards, the WfMC's reference model, the OMG's MDA specifications, and the OASIS BPSS language. This section introduces these players and standards.

First, the OASIS group's Business Process Execution Language for Web Services (BPEL4WS), sometimes shortened to BPEL (rhymes with "people"), is the BPM specification with the strongest backing (IBM, Microsoft, Oracle, BEA) and the greatest chance to win the standards war. A BPEL process is a web service with an associated process definition defined in an XML-based language. The behavior of a BPEL process is to act on, and be acted on by, other processes; put differently, a BPEL process can invoke another web service or be invoked as a web service. As illustrated in Figure 1-5, a travel agent process exposes a web service method called sendItinerary, which, when invoked, calls the requestTickets method in the airline's web service, as its process flow specifies. The airline service, another BPEL process, is programmed to respond to a ticket request by invoking the sendTickets method of the calling process. BPEL for Java (BPELJ) is a BPEL extension that supports Java code embedded in a process definition. Chapter 5 contains a detailed discussion of BPEL.

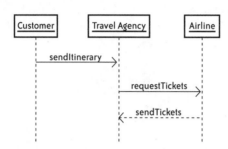

FIGURE 1-5. *BPEL travel interactions*

BPEL descends from two very different process languages: Microsoft's XLANG and IBM's Web Services Flow Language (WSFL). These languages, as well as BPEL's curious mixed-breed nature, are explored in Chapter 9.

The second standard is the Business Process Modeling Language (BPML), from the Business Process Modeling Initiative (BPMI) organization, which is an XML-based process definition language similar to BPEL. Business Process Modeling Notation (BPMN), another specification from BPMI, is a sophisticated graphical notation language for processes. Significantly, the BPMN specification includes a mapping to BPML-rival BPEL, which facilitates the execution of BPMN-designed processes on BPEL engines—a potent combination that will be explored in detail throughout this book. BPML, BPMN, and the BPEL mapping are explored in Chapter 6.

The third standard, the web services choreography, is a major topic of investigation for the World Wide Web Consortium (W3C). *Choreography* describes, from a global point of view, how web services are arranged in a control view spanning multiple participants. Choreography's global view is contrasted with the local view of process orchestration in languages such as BPEL; a BPEL process is the process of a single participant, and a choreography is the interaction model for a group of participants. Web Services Choreography Description Language (WS-CDL) is the W3C's recommended choreography standard; Chapter 8 covers the WS-CDL specification, as well as two previous approaches to choreography: Web Services Choreography Interface (WSCI) and Web Services Conversation Language (WSCL).

Fourth, the Workflow Management Coalition (WfMC) has published a BPM reference model, as well as a set of interfaces for various parts of the BPM architecture. In the reference model,* shown in Figure 1-6, a central enactment service executes processes designed in a process design tool. Though WfMC does not specify a standard graphical process notation, it does provide an exportable XML format called XML Process Definition Language (XPDL); processes built in an XPDL-compliant design tool can run on a WfMC enactment engine. The workflow API (WAPI) interface, specified by the WfMC in C code and CORBA IDL, serves three purposes: administration and monitoring of running processes; integration with external applications; and client interaction, including human activity processing. The workflow XML (WfXML) interface enables enactment services to communicate in order to split processes across one another. The WfMC model and interfaces are explored in detail in Chapter 7.

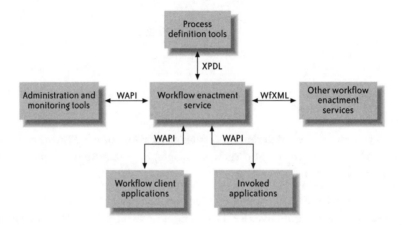

FIGURE 1-6. *WfMC reference model*

The goal of the fifth standard, a contribution of the Object Management Group (OMG) is not to build new process languages or interfaces but to build abstract BPM models conforming to its Model-Driven Architecture (MDA). The OMG's requests for proposals for Business Process Definition Meta Model (BPDM) and Business Process Runtime Interface (BPRI) specifications are discussed in Chapter 9.

The final standard in this list is a process language from OASIS called Business Process Specification System (BPSS), which is somewhat of a choreography language, but is built for business-to-business collaborations. In a typical exchange between a buyer and seller, for example, the buyer sends a request to the seller, to which the seller responds immediately with consecutive acknowledgements of receipt and acceptance. When the seller has finished processing the request, it sends an indication of this to the buyer, and the buyer in turn sends an acknowledgement of the indication to the seller. BPSS

* D. Hollingsworth, "Workflow Management Coalition: The Workflow Reference Model," January 1995, *http://www.wfmc.org*.

(discussed in Chapter 9) is designed to model this and similar collaborations precisely and succinctly.

To the casual reader, BPEL is the only standard worth considering; the others are either dead or stillborn. But this view is simplistic; each components has a role to play. For example:

- The OMG's model-driven architecture, when applied to BPM, is to BPEL what UML-based design and architecture is to Java programming. MDA will help architects conceive good BPM solutions abstractly, without having to consider the particular control structures of BPEL.

- WS-CDL, as the leading choreography language, solves a slightly different problem than BPEL. WS-CDL, in fact, complements BPEL; BPEL helps build the local view of a single participant, and WS-CDL defines the overall interparticipant exchange. BPSS can be positioned much the same way against BPEL.

- BPMN provides a graphical notation language from which BPEL code can be derived or generated. Today, many BPEL-enabled systems use proprietary design notations. BPMN can help standardize that piece.

Not long ago, WfMC and BPML were considered the leading BPM approaches. Why did they fall so quickly? What are their merits that can help us moving forward?

Vendors

Leading BPM vendors include the major application server vendors (IBM with WebSphere Business Integration, BEA with WebLogic Integration, Microsoft with BizTalk Server 2004, and Oracle with Oracle Business Integration) and several BPM specialists (including Fuego, SeeBeyond with ICAN, webMethods, FileNet, Staffware, Vitria). A full-featured BPM solution includes a process design tool, a runtime engine, administration and monitoring, and support for current integration technologies (for example, XML, web services, J2EE or .NET, and B2B).

Figure 1-7 illustrates how these components are related in BEA's WebLogic solution. The BPM engine (shaded) runs on a web services container and a J2EE application server platform; the portal layer supports BPM and non-BPM user interfaces alike. BEA's design tool, WebLogic Workshop, is used to create processes, as well as portals, web services, Enterprise JavaBeans™ (EJBs), and adapters written to the Java Connector Architecture (JCA, also known as J2C) specification. The solution also includes a set of administrative consoles to manage and monitor system activity.

Figure 1-8 shows the design view of a process in WebLogic Workshop; the rightmost menu showcases the rich set of technologies that can be integrated with a process, including EJB, file, email, HTTP, database, MQ/Series, and "application view," which represents an adapter to potentially any application, including ERP (e.g., SAP, PeopleSoft) and CRM (e.g., Siebel, Clarify).

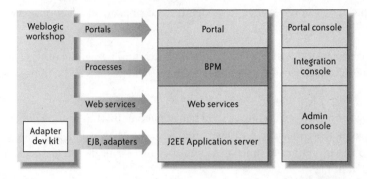

FIGURE 1-7. *BEA's Weblogic stack*

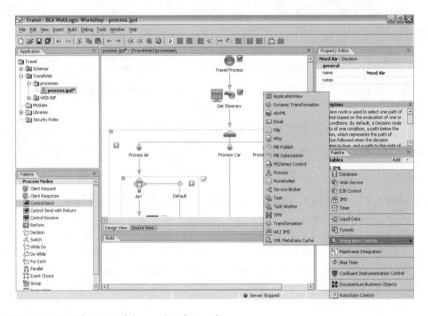

FIGURE 1-8. *BEA's WebLogic Workshop process design editor*

Some vendors, such as ITpearls and IDS Scheer, focus on the design editor piece. IDS Scheer's ARIS is a standalone editor whose processes can run on BEA's WebLogic Integration. ITpearls provides a Microsoft Visio BPMN stencil, as shown in Figure 1-9.

BPM Theory

The ideas behind BPM were not concocted by hurried developers pressured by considerations of time to market. On the contrary, process modeling is a hot topic in the community of computer scientists, and current BPM standards and products are founded on—or at least claim to be founded on—academic findings. In particular, the design of interprocess communication and choreography borrows heavily from Robin Milner's *Communicating and Mobile Systems: the Pi-Calculus* (Cambridge University Press 1999), and the process control flow semantics are modeled on the *Petri net*, a beautiful abstraction

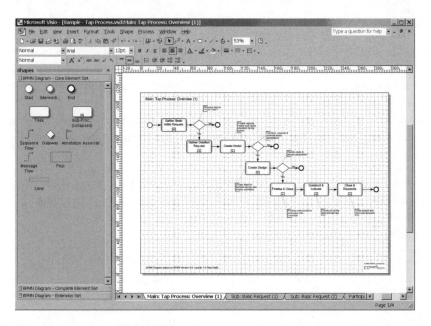

FIGURE 1-9. *ITpearls' stencils for Microsoft Visio*

fashioned by Carl Adam Petri. These theoreticians from the ivory tower are arguably the guiding lights of BPM.

Reading Milner and Petri, however, presupposes an appetite for mathematical rigor that most BPM onlookers lack. Fortunately, understanding BPM today for use in the design of actual applications does not require knowing the science of BPM; it is sufficient to understand the open specifications—such as BPEL and BPMN—that are derived from the science. Milner and Petri are required reading for those who want to understand BPM and its future deeply. Chapter 3 is a casual tour of process theory for the average reader.

Why a chapter on theory in an essentials book intended for practitioners? BPM is an emerging discipline with too many standard and vendor-specific approaches to process modeling. Looking at one process editor after another, each with a distinct set of symbols and associated semantics similar to the others but subtly different, makes one yearn for rigor and precision. Many vendors pitch their solution as being "easy" and "simpler than programming," but fail to promote the strength of the underlying process model or language. Theory helps cut through the morass not only by providing a good original model for the flow and interaction of processes, but also by helping to evaluate the quality of other approaches. Petri nets, for example, have been used not only to build new workflow languages but also to model the most complicated control flow semantics of BPEL, BPMN, WSFL, UML activity diagrams, and event-driven process chains. BPM is young and still needs to hear the voice of wisdom—theory.

Workflow

Not long ago—exactly how long is hard to estimate—everyone used the term "workflow" to refer to the subject that is now called BPM. Already confounded by hype and an excess of ideas, somewhere along the way, the process world suffered an identity crisis. But is this transition from workflow to BPM merely nomenclatural or is it tied to a genuine change in meaning? Many contemporary observers think BPM and workflow have subtly different meanings, that BPM is superior to workflow management, and, in fact, has made it obsolescent.

The landmark survey of enterprise client/server technologies, *Client/Server Survival Guide*, positions workflow as a groupware technology that complements email, imaging document management, and calendar features. Workflow is the *flow of work*, encompassing the exchange and enrichment of information:

> The classical workflow paradigm is a river that carries the flow of work from port to port and along the way value gets added. Workflow defines the operations that must be visited along the way and what needs to be done when exceptions occur.*

In the past, workflow meant passing paper from person to person. Workflow technology improved things not only by managing the flow of work but also by digitizing the information, thereby making the process as automated and paperless as possible. Figure 1-10 illustrates a typical workflow scenario.

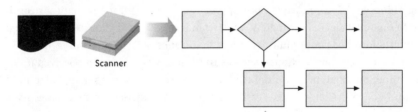

FIGURE 1-10. *Workflow process based on scanned image*

And though this approach helped speed up processes limited to a small workgroup, such as insurance claim handling, the perception of workflow by many observers, as argued by Staffware CEO Jon Pyke, is that it lacked integration capabilities. In the contemporary world of BPM, document imaging is a marginal technology; a process is expected to speak the modern dialects of XML, B2B, EAI, and web services.†

Tom Baeyens points out that in modern BPM frameworks such as BPEL, a process knows to accept a message intended for it based on message correlation (that is, based on some aspect of the message that matches the process' internal state) rather than on explicit

---

* R. Orfali, D. Harkey, and J. Edwards, *Client/Server Survival Guide*, Wiley, 1999.

† J. Pyke, "From Workflow To Business Process Management: The Subtle Evolution," *Staffware, http://is.tm.tue.nl/bpm2003/download/presentation%20Pyke.pdf.*

process ID; in other words, the process does not need to have a message sent explicitly to it. Further, the WfMC idea of the central enactment engine has been replaced by the notion of service endpoint, or communicating process; process flow has become decentralized and is now based on the idea of communicating processes.* Figure 1-11 illustrates the BPM scenario.

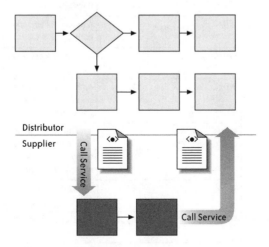

FIGURE 1-11. *BPM communicating processes*

The argument is compelling, and, in fact, grasping it is crucial to understanding what contemporary BPM is all about. But the position that workflow is the perfect expression of all the old process ideas is a straw man: workflow remains a useful word and is in fact more expressive than the term BPM, regardless of its mistaken attributions.

Roadmap

If you are new to BPM, the sheer number of terms, standards, standards bodies, and other ideas introduced in this chapter may seem overwhelming. Table 1-1 is a quick reference list of BPM standards; it also points out the chapter in which each is discussed.

TABLE 1-1. *BPM standards roadmap*

Standard	Body	Chapter	Description
Business Process Execution Language (BPEL)	OASIS	5	BPM's most popular language; represents a process as XML with web services bindings
Business Process Modeling Language (BPML)	Business Process Modeling Initiative (BPMI)	6	An XML process language similar to BPEL

---

* T. Baeyens, "The State of Workflow," *http://www.theserverside.com/articles/article.tss?l=Workflow*.

TABLE 1-1. *BPM standards roadmap (continued)*

Standard	Body	Chapter	Description
Business Process Modeling Notation (BPMN)	BPMI	6	Graphical language with a mapping to BPEL
Workflow Reference Model	Workflow Management Coalition (WfMC)	7	A basic architectural approach to workflow/BPM
Workflow API (WAPI)	WfMC	7	A functional and administrative API with definitions in C, IDL, and COM
XML Process Definition Language (XPDL)	WfMC	7	An XML process language similar to BPEL
Workflow XML (WfXML)	WfMC	7	An XML language for web service-based communication between workflow runtime engines
Web Services Choreography Interface (WSCI)	World Wide Web Consortium (W3C)	8	A mature XML language for web services choreography, or the stateful, process-oriented interactions of web services among multiple participants
Web Services Choreography Description Language (WS-CDL)	W3C	8	The W3C's official XML choreography language
Web Services Conversation Language (WSCL)	W3C	8	A basic but elegant XML choreography language
Business Process Definition Metamodel (BPDM)	Object Management Group (OMG)	9	A model for a BPM process language constructed using the Model Driven Architecture (MDA)
Business Process Runtime Interface (BPRI)	OMG	9	An MDA model for a functional and administrative BPM API
XLANG	Microsoft	9	An early XML process language ;XLANG influenced the design of BPEL
Web Services Flow Language (WSFL)	IBM	9	An early XML process language, which also influenced the design of BPEL
Business Process Specification Schema (BPSS)	OASIS	9	A process language for business-to-business collaboration

Summary

The main points of this chapter include the following:

- A business process is the step-by-step algorithm to achieve a business objective. The best visualization of a business process is a flowchart. A process can actually be executed by a process engine, provided its logic is defined precisely and unambiguously. When a process definition is input to an engine, the engine can run instances of the process. The steps of the process are called activities. Business process modeling (BPM) is the study of the design and execution of processes.

- BPM is concerned only with process-oriented applications. Not all enterprise applications qualify. The process-oriented acid test of an application is whether it is long-lived and defined at a given time by its state. The example travel agency application passes the test because of it manages itinerary state. OLTP applications, such as ATMs, fail because they lack longevity and state.

- BPM, because of various competing standards (BPEL4WS, BPML, and BPMN; WSCI, WfMC specifications), vendors (IBM, BEA, Microsoft, Staffware, See Beyond, Vitria, and others), and even computer science underpinnings (pi-calculus, Petri nets), is a maze that confounds many onlookers. This book attempts to discover, through the confusion, an elegant, process-oriented application architecture.

- Among the benefits of BPM are the formalization of current processes and the occasion for reengineering, greater efficiency, increased productivity and decreased head count, the ability to add people to a process to resolve hard problems, and the traceability of compliance processes.

- Some BPM backers dismiss workflow as an older set of ideas and technologies based on document imaging and departmental manual processing. BPM, by contrast, is about web service-powered processes that communicate with processes in other companies and are wired for EAI. The argument is unsound because it makes a straw man of workflow, but nonetheless the reasoning provides an accurate history of the field.

References

1. Y. Goland, "The Race to Create Standards: The Road To Maturity," *WebLogic Developer's Journal*, unpublished (date TBD).

2. M. Havey, "Workflow and State Machines: The Process-Oriented Application," *WebLogic Developer's Journal*, January 2004.

3. P. L. Crosman, "What's the Difference Between Workflow and BPM?" *Transform Magazine*, December 2003, *http://www.transformmag.com/showArticle. jhtml?articleID=16400140*.

4. IBM, "Business Processes: Understanding BPEL4WS," August 2002, *http://www.ibm. com*.

5. W. M. P. van der Aalst, J. Desel, and A. Oberweis (editors), *Business Process Management: Models, Techniques, and Empirical Studies*, Volume 1,806 of *Lecture Notes in Computer Science*, Springer-Verlag, Berlin, 2000.

6. W. M. P. van der Aalst and K. M. van Hee, *Workflow Management: Models, Methods, and Systems*, MIT Press, Cambridge, MA, 2002.

CHAPTER TWO

Prescription for a Good BPM Architecture

BPM STANDARDS ABOUND, EACH WITH A DISTINCT DESIGN AND FEATURE SET. This chapter scavenges these approaches in search of a general BPM application architecture that is conceptually comprehensible and meets real-world requirements. A good architecture uses the technique of divide-and-conquer to reduce a difficult problem to smaller, more manageable parts, and where possible, it solves each part not by inventing new technology but by reusing an existing approach. Applying this technique, we ask: in a BPM architecture, what is the problem to be solved, what are its parts, and which standards, if any, solve them?

The architecture presented here is intended as a reference model—with similarities to the WfMC's model (see Chapter 7) and the proposed stack of the BPMI (see Chapter 6)—targeted at product and services architects alike. The appeal for product architects is obvious: the model, though lacking the level of detail for a micro design, has the same form as a BPM product, and can help guide the overall construction. Services architects, who typically advocate buying a good vendor solution and customizing it rather than building the entire solution from scratch, need to comprehend the essential nature of the base product. Rather than treating it as a black box, these architects should have a sense of curiosity analogous to that of a driver who lifts the hood of a car and seeks to grasp the basic mechanics of all those belts and gears. There are a number of reasons why:

- BPM is an emerging subject, and in the current morass of vendors, standards, hype, and theory, having a crystal-clear notion of a good solution (whether built or bought) gives an architect a competitive advantage over the many who are still learning.

- Customers know the essential architecture of some of their IT products and technologies (e.g., database, operating system, network router), but they probably have a fuzzier notion of BPM, and they expect the services architect to help explain it to them and guide them through adoption.

- Vendor documentation seldom distinguishes clearly between standard and proprietary features. (The architecture in this chapter tries to avoid the second of these.) If the customer has been sold on BPEL, the XYZ foundation classes, BAM, and the Intel process optimizer, the services architect needs to know that BPEL and BAM are standard solution-building blocks, and to avoid the proprietary XYZ and optimizer if the customer foresees migrating to another vendor implementation someday. The customer probably does not know the difference.

- The architecture for the customer's application must use and extend the out-of-the-box features of the stack. To know how to do this, the architect needs to understand those out-of-the-box features. For example, what tools are provided to support process development and deployment? What is the strategy to patch or upgrade live production processes? What is the data model, and how can customer data entities be worked into it? How are external systems interfaces built, and how are they called from processes? How can the monitoring subsystem be customized to serve the customer's business and operational requirements?

Designing a Solution

To design a good BPM solution, you must first step back and examine the project's environment: understanding the problem, noting the local and larger-scale perspectives, and only then creating a design and testing your solution.

Understanding the Problem

To understand what a good solution looks like, you must first understand the scope of the problem to solve. The main requirement of a BPM application is the ability to design, run, and monitor and administer business processes that incorporate human and system interactions, described as follows:

Design
The design of a business process is intuitively a flowchart that outlines the steps performed over time in the resolution of a business problem. Unlike most object-oriented designs, whose audience is the technical team of a project, a process design is crafted and comprehended by both business and technical analysts. Business analysts are involved because they understand the business aspects of the process best; the design is

simply a rigorous expression of what they frequently draw on paper or on a white-board. The level of rigor, plus the anticipation of implementing a software solution to the design, draws in technical analysts. Thus, business and technical designers require a common design notation that is at once business-oriented and amenable to computer processing. They also require a graphical editor in which to sketch their design.

Run

The early workflow engines that were actually able to run designed processes, and thus to automate the execution of formerly manual procedures, must have been perceived as miraculous. Today, this miracle is a core requirement: "Run what I just drew!" But conceived more dispassionately, the executability of a process is a matter of having a runtime engine and an executable language that the engine knows how to run. More-over, a mapping is required between the design notation and the executable language, enabling the automated generation of executable code from the design. The manual coding of a process is undesirable because it slows the development cycle and ensures gaps between the design and the execution.

Monitor and administer

Monitoring, the ability to watch the progress of running processes, is crucial for pro-duction applications for two reasons: the detection of exceptions (ensuring processes are progressing as expected and not getting stuck), and real-time ad hoc querying (e.g., finding all active processes for customers in a particular account range). Administra-tion is the management of, and the ability to effect changes on, processes on the runtime engine. It includes the ability to install, shut off, or turn on process designs, and to suspend, resume, or terminate running processes. Monitoring and administra-tion require a management language and a graphical management console that can watch and modify the BPM system.

The model architecture must also smoothly accommodate both human and computer interaction:

Human interaction

A manual task is a step in a process that is meant to be executed by either a specific person, or a person in a specific role, within the company. For example, in an insur-ance claims process, the approval of a claim is a manual step that can be completed by any claims adjuster. To support manual processing, the architecture requires a role-based security model (which maps users to roles), a graphical worklist console (to show the user a list of assigned manual activities and enable completion of an activ-ity), and a corresponding worklist programming interface for the exchange of informa-tion between the console and the runtime engine.

System interaction

Other steps in a process must be able to call or be called by software components that are not built into the engine. These components can be external participants (e.g., a request for price quote from another's company's process in a buyer-seller relation-ship), internal systems (e.g., send email, query database, perform mainframe transaction), or simple inline code snippets (e.g., perform calculation, parse data). The architecture should support incoming and outgoing integration interfaces for a variety of technologies—web services, MQ/Series, JDBC, J2EE (EJB, JMS), Java, C#, and COM. The architecture should also be conversant in XML, the dominant message language of enterprise computing.

The Local Perspective Guided by the Global Contract

The job of a BPM architecture is to describe the local perspective of one company, not the global view of all partner interactions. True, the designers must be aware of the nature of partner interactions but only to ensure that the company is compliant with interprocess protocols. As Figure 2-1 illustrates, a company that is a Seller must know the rules of interaction with Buyer, Inventory, and Credit card company partners, but its main concern is the construction of its own Seller processes.

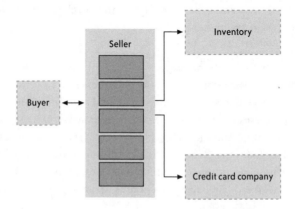

FIGURE 2-1. *Isolate the client company from its partners*

On the other hand, how can the designers be certain that their local processes interact exactly as they should with partners? Several years ago, the "global contract" governing this communication would have been documented in writing by a third-party body. As they modeled their processes, the designers would have kept a close eye on the documentation to ensure that their communications were compliant. But with the advent of web services choreography languages, notably WS-CDL, the contract can be coded in a formal language, around which a tool (considered in greater detail in the section "Local View of Choreography: WS-CDL Toolkit") can be built to generate, or to validate the compliance of, local processes.

The first cut of the Seller process, for example, can begin as code generated by a tool that interprets the choreography covering Seller, Buyer, Inventory, and Credit card company. Or, supposing the first cut had been written manually, at any subsequent stage of development, the code can be run through the tool to validate that Seller interfaces correctly with Buyer, Inventory, and Credit card company. Such a tool simplifies process design, and eliminates the eyeball approach.

Components of a Good Design

Figure 2-2 shows the main pieces of the BPM architecture and their relationships.

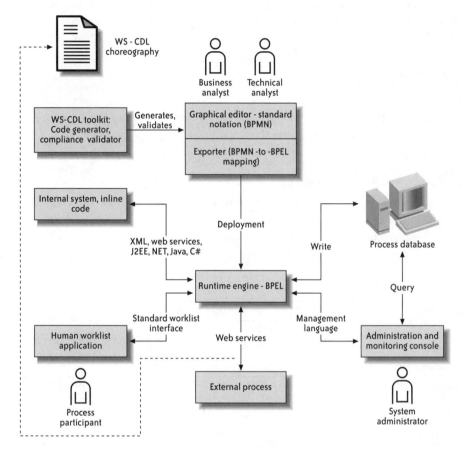

FIGURE 2-2. *A good BPM architecture*

In the center—and at the heart—of the system is the runtime engine, which executes processes written in BPEL. Business and technical analysts design the processes using a graphical editor that supports BPMN. The editor includes an exporter that generates BPEL XML code from BPMN diagrams.

Human and computer interactions drive the execution of processes in the engine. The people who participate in the process use a human workflow graphical application that connects to the engine through a programmatic worklist interface. The interface allows the user to view and execute pending manual activities. There are two types of computer interactions: internal and external. *Internal applications*, which reside on the company's network but are outside of the engine's address space, are accessed by integration technologies such as web services, J2EE, or COM, with XML as the probable message format; internal interactions can also be more lightweight inline code snippets written in programming languages such as Java or C#. *External interactions* are typically web service-based communications, governed by choreographies or business-to-business collaborations, with the processes of other companies. BPM system administrators use a graphical administration and monitoring console to maintain and track the state of the engine's processes. The console uses a management language to interface with the engine. The runtime engine maintains persistance of a process state to a database; the console hits the database directly, rather than using the management language, to perform ad hoc process queries.

For applications involving complex interactions with external participants (e.g., a B2B process), a WS-CDL choreography toolkit generates a basic BPMN model that captures the communications required of the local process; it can perform a validation, or choreography compliance check, of that model.

Run It on an Application Server

Never build a BPM application from scratch. Instead, run it on an application server, to leverage built-in application server facilities such as security, transactions, system management, and the pooling of client connections and resources. Table 2-1 summarizes a possible J2EE application server implementation of the BPM architecture.

TABLE 2-1. *BPM on J2EE*

Component	J2EE implementation
Engine	Enterprise JavaBeans
Human worklist application	Java Server Pages™ (JSP) web application
Worklist interface	EJB or web service façade to engine
Internal interactions	EJB, Java Messaging Service™ (JMS), Java Connector Architecture™ (JCA, also known as J2C), Java Database Connectivity™ (JDBC), web services via servlets
External interactions	Web services via servlets
Administration and monitoring console	JSP web application
Management interface	Java Management Extensions™ (JMX)
Process database	JDBC access
Graphical editor	Offline Windows program
Exporter	Offline utility
WS-CDL toolkit	Offline utility

This solution is a combination of out-of-the-box product functionality and custom development, as shown in Figure 2-3. The application server layer, for example, might require custom EJBs to provide functions to call from processes and custom JSPs to use in custom management consoles. The BPM layer might require extensions to the process data model and the development of reusable processes.

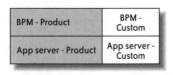

FIGURE 2-3. *BPM on an application server*

Components of the Design

Having glimpsed the BPM architecture "from 30,000 feet," we now descend to a lower altitude to get a closer look at each of its major components. This section examines the requirements and proposes designs for the notations and graphical tool, the runtime engine, the human and system interaction interfaces, the administration and monitoring facilities, and the CDL toolkit.

Notation and Graphical Tool

The need for a graphical process modeling language is often overlooked in the BPM standards race. Most BPM languages are XML-based and can be relatively difficult to compose or read. Design is best communicated with diagrams. Scan through a typical object-oriented component design document, for example, and you will discover that a single UML class diagram can convey most of the intended meaning, making many of the surrounding words redundant. If a picture is sufficiently rich, it is worth *more* than a thousand words! Standardization adds even more value. A diagram that is drawn to a standard specification is familiar to a wide audience, and its semantics are also clearly understood. Readers get the gist of a haphazardly drawn assemblage of boxes and arrows, but the lack of precision in representation makes it less intelligible.

BPM has two good graphical modeling notations—BPMN (Chapter 6) and the UML activity diagram (Chapter 3)—but BPMN is the preferred choice for our architecture because it is more expressive (it supports most of the "P4" patterns described in Chapter 4) and has a mapping to BPEL.

ITpearls' Process Modeler tool, for example, is a BPMN drawing tool with BPEL export capabilities. As Figure 2-4 shows, ITpearls provides a set of stencils that are imported into Microsoft Visio.

A BPMN diagram is drawn by dragging shapes from one of the stencils onto a canvas sheet. The ITpearls tool also embeds a Process menu in the Visio menu bar. As shown in the figure, the designer can export the diagram to a file; at the time of writing, this function was planned for BPEL and BPML formats but was not yet available.

The ability to manage the technical implementation detail is one of the greatest shortcomings of modeling languages. A BPMN drawing dragged onto a Visio canvas captures perhaps 75% of the required processing, but the remaining 25% requires

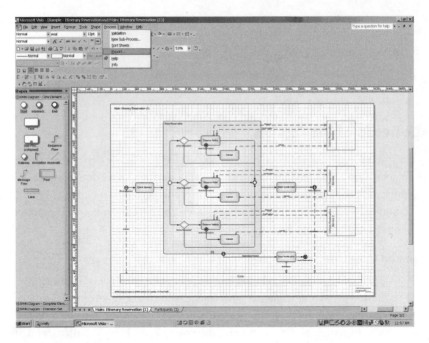

FIGURE 2-4. *ITpearls' BPMN drawing tool with Microsoft Visio*

development tool capabilities, such as a source code editor and property sheets. For example, the following are not easily modeled using drag-and-drop tools:

- A decision node that is backed by a Java code snippet that performs a complex bit of decision logic
- An activity that sends a message to an internal system, which would require a tool feature such as a property sheet that prompts for the address of the target system, the content of the message, and message header information
- An activity to invoke a web service of a partner process, which would require a tool feature such as a drop-down list of web service port types and operations.

Serving both business and technical users is challenging because business users generally want details hidden, whereas technical users require the power of a scaled-down integrated development environment. A worthwhile process modeling tool resolves these tensions by providing different views of the process: a simpler business view that controls the overall shape of the process and a technical view that has full reign over the behavior of each step.

Runtime Engine

A BPM engine, like a computer, loads programs (called *process definitions*) and runs instances of them (called *processes*). A BPM program is a series of steps, and the job of the engine is to run through the steps, much like a computer processor runs through lines of code. A BPM program is also highly event-driven, meaning that it spends much of its time waiting for a stimulus to awaken it, at which point it performs a burst of activity before returning to sleep in anticipation of the next event. A BPM program also calls other systems. The BPM engine is responsible for detecting events, injecting them into the process, and managing outbound message calls, as shown in Figure 2-5.

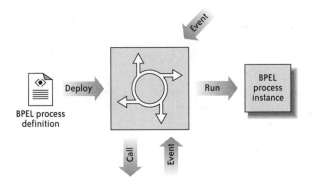

FIGURE 2-5. *BPM runtime engine*

The preferred execution language, BPEL (discussed in Chapter 5), is the most advanced and popular XML process language. Exactly how a BPEL engine works is largely irrelevant because the architecture treats is as a black box—so buy an engine from a reputable vendor, instead of building your own!

> **NOTE**
> For Java programmers keen to see a good implementation of a BPEL engine, the open source ActiveBPEL is a good bet. The web site *http:// www.activebpel.org* provides source code, binaries, and documentation, including a high-level description of the engine's architecture.

Human Interaction

The application's support for human participation in a process requires a worklist interface that allows the process to *coordinate*—that is, initiate, then wait for completion of—manual work tasks. Users view and execute pending tasks in a user-friendly graphical console designed for usability and productivity. Figure 2-6 illustrates a web-based worklist console, known as the Travel Agent Portal, for a travel agency.

The user, named Bill Smith, sees three panels. The banner at the top of the second panel welcomes him to the site and reports that he performs the roles of Agent and Supervisor. The left panel is a command menu that, among other things, presents him with links to view three lists of tasks: Resolve Error, Escalations, and Approvals. (The number in parentheses indicates the size of the list.) When one link is clicked, a summary of the task list is populated into the main panel in the bottom right. Currently, the panel shows the Resolve Error list. When the user clicks on one of its items, a separate window pops up

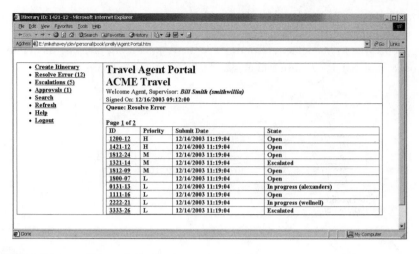

FIGURE 2-6. *Human worklist console for a travel agency*

showing information about the task and providing an editable form to complete it and send it back to the waiting process.

Behind the scenes, a web service called the Worklist offers two operations:

initiateTask

An asynchronous method called by the process to commence the task. The process passes its identity (e.g., process ID, correlated data, or service endpoint), a unique identified of the task (e.g., Resolve Error), the intended user or role (e.g., the Agent role), and any other data required by the user to work the task.

taskComplete

A callback to the process indicating completion of the process, passing back any associated data.

The state of the task is persisted to a system management database (described in detail in the later section "Administration and Monitoring"). On initiateTask, the Worklist web service writes the details of the task to a table; the worklist console pulls data from that table for display to the user and updates it as the task progresses. The normal sequence of events is shown in Figure 2-7.

The figure shows two classes: Worklist, stereotyped as a web service, and AdminDB (typically a set of stored procedures or a Java or C# data access object), representing the typical accesses to the database for task management. In the sequence diagram, when the process invokes the Worklist's initiateTask( ),Worklist persists to the database, via assign(), a record of the initial assignment (e.g., Resolve Error is assigned to role Agent). The worklist console, when the user clicks on a Worklist link, performs the query queryTasks( ) to draw a summary of tasks, and when the user selects one of the tasks, calls getTaskDetail( ) to show the full set of task data. The user then "claims" the task (more on this next) and completes it (claim( ) and complete( ), respectively), at which point the

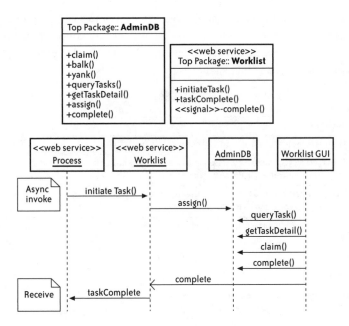

FIGURE 2-7. *Worklist interface*

console signals to the Worklist that the job is finished; the Worklist in turn invokes the taskComplete( ) callback, which awakens the BPEL process.*

> **NOTE**
>
> Several BPM products (e.g., IBM MQ Workflow) have worklist interfaces. Oracle's implementation stands out because it is designed as a web service callable from a BPEL process.

In most cases, from the perspective of the process, the identity of the person who actually performs a task is irrelevant. What is important is that person's *type* or *role*. Any travel agent, for example, can work a Resolve Error case. But in the end, a particular person does end up doing the work, and a good role-based security model is required to make it happen. Bill Smith is allowed to execute a Resolve Error task, for example, because he has the role of Agent. The security infrastructure leveraged by the BPM architecture should provide two role-based functions:

The ability to look up a user's roles

When Bill Smith logs into the console, the console should display his current roles.

Secure access control

The architecture shouldn't allow a user who isn't a travel agent to complete a Resolve Error task.

---

* The Worklist design is inspired by the TaskManager component of the Oracle BPEL Process Manager. The use of the Oracle worklist is demonstrated in Chapter 10.

During its lifetime, a task can change hands several times: from role to user, from user to role, or from user to user within a role. In the simplest case, described in the previous scenario, a task is initially assigned to a role and then claimed by a user having that role. Other possibilities are summarized in Table 2-2.

TABLE 2-2. *User-role actions*

Type	Description
Assign	The task is tagged to either a particular user or to a role.
Claim	The task is tagged to a particular user in a role. In other words, a user interested in working the task shared with other users in the role, claims it.
Yank	A claimed task is moved to a different user in the role; in other words, a user confiscates a task from its claimed user. For example, the task is escalated.
Balk	A claimed task is untagged and assigned back to the role. In other words, the user decides not to work the task.

System Interaction

No process runs in isolation. In addition to its human dependencies, a process invariably calls or is called by various types of software components. There are four possible modes of interaction as shown in Table 2-3.

TABLE 2-3. *Interaction modes*

Mode	Description
Receive	Process receives a message from another system.
Receive-Respond	Process receives a message from another system and sends back a response message.
Send	Process sends a message to another system.
Send-Receive	Process sends a message to another system and waits for the response.

Components can be divided into those that are external and internal to the company. External interactions are web service-based and follow choreography or collaboration protocols. Internal software interactions can be inline code snippets or client/server interfaces to other systems running on the corporate network.

Adapters

The BPM architecture should aim to support the widest variety of system interfaces. A naïve design would be provide individual hooks for every conceivable technology: the MQ hook, the JDBC hook, the Tuxedo hook, the Java hook, the EJB hook, the COM hook, the web service hook, the JMS hook, and so on. A cleaner, more extensible approach is to provide built-in support for the typical process technologies such as web services and XML, inline code capabilities for Java or C#, and an adapter plug-in model for anything else. The adapter plug-in model requires the following:

- The adapter must be coded to a generic interface that the runtime engine understands. On a J2EE platform, for example, a particular EJB remote interface or a Java Connector Architecture (JCA, or J2C) adapter might be required.

- The runtime engine must provide a directory into which adapters can be registered. On J2EE, this might be the Java Naming and Directory Interface (JNDI).

In Figure 2-8, adapters for SAP, MQ, mainframe and database are deployed to the engine, sitting alongside natively supported XML, web service, and Java modules.

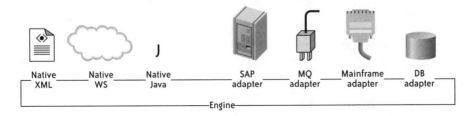

FIGURE 2-8. *System interaction: native and adapter*

The process is a web service

In many contemporary BPM approaches, including BPEL, the process not only interacts with other web services, it is *itself* a web service. Every receive node, in which the process listens for inbound messages, appears to the outside world as a web service operation. Calling that operation injects an event into the process and causes it to perform a burst of activity before either completing or waiting for the next event.

For BPM architects, this feature means that the runtime engine must include a special web services listener that knows how to accept an inbound Simple Object Access Protocol (SOAP) message, inject it into the engine, obtain the response, if any, and send it back out as a SOAP message. On a J2EE platform, because SOAP is typically transported over HTTP, this component can be an HTTP servlet that handles inbound SOAP using HTTP POST and GET methods. The design is depicted in Figure 2-9.

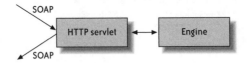

FIGURE 2-9. *Servlet as web services listener for engine*

Administration and Monitoring

The mark of a successful production application is a well-conceived and sophisticated set of administration and monitoring tools. The main tool is a graphical console that lets system administrators watch, tune, and perform management actions; in most cases, the console uses (under the covers) a standard management API to converse with the running system. A BPM console should allow operators to monitor running processes, kill hanging processes, install new process definitions, and decommission processes that are no longer required. Internally, the BPM application should support SNMP or JMX management infrastructures to facilitate these operational capabilities. With these interfaces, custom consoles can be developed to meet requirements that are not provided out of the box (e.g., sending an email to a specified group list when an error occurs while deactivating a process definition).

The first step in designing a system management interface for a particular system is to identify the managed objects and their services. Table 2-4 summarizes the BPM managed objects and required services.

TABLE 2-4. *Managed objects and required services*

Managed objects	Required services
Process definitions	• Find process definitions known to the engine. Possible filter include activated or deactivated. • Deploy: add a process definition to the list. • Remove. • Activate: switch on a process definition so that it can be instantiated. • Deactivate: switch off a process definition so that it cannot be instantiated.
Processes	• Find processes known to the engine. Possible filters include process definition, start date, completion date, process variable values, and state. • Suspend. • Resume. • Terminate.
Activities and worklist tasks	• Find activities and tasks known to the engine. Possible filters include type of role, parent process, start date, completion date, state, incoming or outgoing message values. • Suspend. • Resume. • Terminate.
Users and roles	• Add, modify or remove users from the application. • Add or remove roles from the application. • Add or remove users from roles.
Applications	• Configure connections for applications (e.g., web services, database, MQ, J2EE) that can call or be called by processes. For example, deploy a servlet to listen for inbound web service calls, and create a JAX RPC connection to invoke external web services.

Figure 2-10 illustrates a typical BPM console that provides these services.

The left panel contains a set of links representing the core managed objects. When an administrator clicks on a link, the right panel shows administrative options for the selected object. For example, clicking on Processes brings up the panel Processes—Search. The search shown in the diagram will find all processes with definition *HandleClaim.bpel* that started on or after 2002-01-01 and have a variable called claimID that starts with the text 12. The search is executed by clicking on the Search link. The list of matching processes is shown in Figure 2-11.

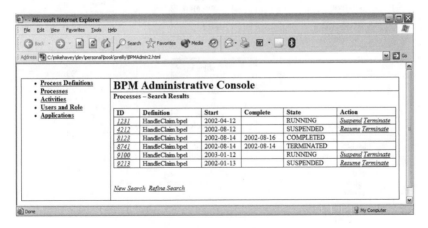

FIGURE 2-10. *Admin console: process search*

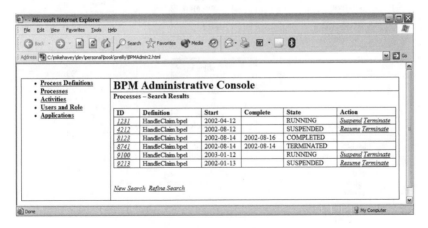

FIGURE 2-11. *Admin console: process search results*

The list provides links (the ID value) to a page that displays the full detail of the process. For convenience, the links under the Action column allow process maintenance without the need to delve into the details. The options listed in this column depend on the state. The first item (ID 1231), whose state is RUNNING, can be suspended or terminated; the second item (ID 4212), which is already SUSPENDED, can be resumed or terminated.

Persistence

Because most processes are stateful and must survive a restart of the runtime engine, the BPM implementation requires a persistent data store in which the process state is kept current in case of engine recovery. The data store is best modeled as a normalized relational database schema. Not only is this approach an accepted practice in contemporary enterprise architecture, it also benefits customers by enabling them to perform ad hoc process queries. Customers might also build reporting databases or data warehouses based on the runtime process persistence model and institute purge and replication jobs that, respectively, cleanup the runtime model and synchronize the reporting model.

Figure 2-12 shows a good BPM runtime data model.

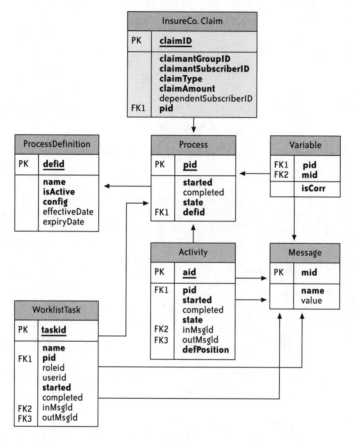

FIGURE 2-12. *Process data model*

The tables in the model include the following:

ProcessDefinition
> The process definition keeps a list of definitions deployed and known to the engine. Each definition maps a unique numeric id (defid) to a descriptive name (name), which (for simplicity) is the name of the XML process definition file (e.g., *processClaim.bpel*). The optional field effectiveDate specifies the date and time when instances can begin to be created for the definition; if it is left blank, instances can be created any time.

Similarly, expiryDate specifies the date and time after which no instances can be created; if it is left blank, the definition never expires. The isActive field is a Boolean (actually Y or N) that, when set to 'N' prevents the creation of new instances, regardless of the effective and expiry dates. The field config holds deployment settings such as the URLs of the WSDLs of the process and of each of its partners.

Process

A process, which is a running instance of a process definition, is represented by a unique numeric identifier called a pid (probably based on a database sequence), and has fields representing its state (e.g, RUNNING, SUSPENDED, COMPLETED, ABORTED), timestamps for its start and completion (started and completed, respectively), and a pointer to its process definition (defid).

Message

A message is simply a piece of data with a name and a value. The value is often an entire XML document or a piece of it. A message is identified by a unique numeric field called a mid.

Variable

A process can have zero or more variables. The table Variable, which has a many-to-one relationship to Process, holds the variable values for a given instance. Variable joins to Process on the field pid. The mid field references a record in Message, where the actual name and value are held. Finally isCorr is a Boolean (actually Y or N) that indicates whether the variable is a correlating field.

Activity

An activity is a step in a process. Its numeric database ID aid maps to defPosition, which for simplicity is the name of the activity found in the definition (e.g., adjustClaim). Activity has a many-to-one relationship to Process, joining it on its pid field. The fields started and completed represent the activity's start and completion times, respectively. The field state represents current progress (e.g., STARTED, ASSIGNED_ TO_ROLE, WAITING_MSG, RUNNING, COMPLETED, and ABORTED). An activity can have an input message and an output message, represented by isMsgId and outMsgId respectively, each of which references the Message table.

WorklistTask

A worklist task is similar in structure to an activity, having a process reference (pid), inbound and outbound messages (inMsg and outMsg, respectively), and start and completion dates. But, as mentioned earlier, the lifetime of a task spans several process activities (in BPEL, the entire sequence from invoke to receive), and a task is assigned to a particular role (roleid) or user (userid). Despite similarities to Activity, WorklistTask merits its own table.

Figure 2-12 also demonstrates how the core model can be extended with application-specific data. The shaded table InsureCo.Claim represents an insurance company's representation of a claim. The field pid links the claim to a particular record of the Process table, which represents a specific process instance. The mapping in this case is one-to-one: each claim is handled by one instance of claims business process. Table 2-5 describes some other possible scenarios; significantly, no changes are required to the core tables.

TABLE 2-5. *Modeling process-to-claim relationships*

Scenario	Implementation
One claim to one process	Claim table has pid field linking to process table.
Multiple claims are handled by one process	Same.
One claim is handled by multiple processes	Create a table called ClaimProcess with two fields: claimID, which links to the claim table, and pid, which links to the process table.
Multiple claims are handled by multiple processes	Same.

The following examples, based on an Oracle database implementation, illustrate several SQL statements that query the data model. These queries can generate reports or administer the system:

- List suspended processes based on definition purchaseOrder.bpel that were started before September 1, 2004:

```
Select p.pid from process p, processdefinition d
where p.defid=d.defid and d.name='purchaseOrder.bpel'
and p.state='SUSPENDED' and p.started<to_date('2004-09-01','YYYY-MM-DD');
```

- Find the process based on definition orderTicket.bpel whose correlation variable ticketNumber has value A12345:

```
Select p.pid from process p, processdefinition d, variable v, message m
where p.defid=d.defid and d.name='orderTicket.bpel' and
v.pid=p.pid and v.isCorr='Y' and v.mid=m.mid and m.name='ticketNumber'
and m.value is not null and m.value='A12345';
```

- List all the activities and their input and output variables of the process with ID 1012:

```
Select a.defposition, a.started, a.completed, a.state, inmsg.name, inmsg.value,
omsg.name, omsg.value
from activity a, message inmsg, message omsg
where  a.inmsgid=inmsg.mid(+) and a.outmsgid=omsg.mid(+) and a.pid=1012;
```

- List all claims in the order they were started using the custom data extension:

```
Select c.* from insureco.claim c, process p where c.pid=p.pid
order by p.started desc;
```

Process versioning basics

Over time, the definition of a process needs to change to accommodate bug fixes, enhancements, and new public interfaces. But in a production environment, applying these changes to definitions that have active and possibly long-running instances requires exquisite care. The trick is to make the change without compromising the current base.

Depending on the nature of the change, use one of the following strategies:

- If the change is minor, such as a fix or enhancement to a particular activity (e.g., fixing an XPath expression in a data transformation, or switching to a new WSDL port for a process invocation), replace the old code with the new code. To prevent access to instances while this is happening, either shut down the system or queue client requests.

- If the change is major but does not alter the public service interface (e.g., a change of control flow in the internal logic of the process), first, keep the old process definition, but deactivate it by switching its isActive flag to N. Then create a new process definition, with a unique defId, isActive set to Y, and name containing an incremental version (e.g., if the previous version was processClaim.bpel, name the new one processClaim_v2.bpel). Give the config field the same values as the previous version's. The effect is that clients do not change the way they interact with the process, but internally the system supports two versions— one for old instances, and one for new ones.

- If the change is major and represents a new public service interface (e.g., new XML format and acknowledgments now mandatory), follow the same procedure, but modify the settings in the config field of the new definition: by pointing to to a new version of the WSDL that has the updated public interface. The effect is that clients use the new interface to start new instances, and the old one only to finish old instances.

BAM and process mining

Business activity monitoring (BAM) is an exalted form of process administration and monitoring offered by vendors such as Pegasystems. BAM is targeted at the business manager who requires a sophisticated dashboard with graphical views (often in the form of graphs or charts) of process-related data updated in real time or generated as part of a report. This data can include the state of running processes and their activities, as well as aggregated statistics concerning the business subject matter of processes (e.g., if the process is for loans, view the number of approved loans so far today). Figure 2-13 illustrates a typical dashboard.[*]

BAM can also let the manager make changes in response to emerging conditions. For example, if a given process appears to be stuck waiting for the action of a particular person, the manager can reassign it to someone else. Some BAM implementations can even run on autopilot; rules can be defined to automatically perform a specific action when a particular event occurs or a particular condition takes effect (e.g., sending an email to the bank manager when a high-value customer closes an account).

In addition to providing such a rich perspective on the state of the application, BAM—by showing the most commonly traversed paths through a process and by isolating

---

[*] Pegasystems, "PegaRules Process Commander: Business Activity Monitor: Empowering BPM," Pegasystems white paper, 2003, *http://www.pega.com/downloads*.

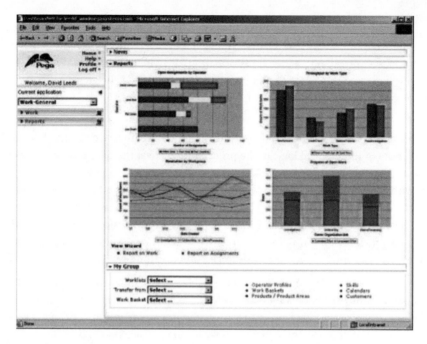

FIGURE 2-13. *Pegasystems BAM dashboard*

inefficient steps—also helps process engineers and business operations people spot continuous improvements. The dashboard might reveal, for example, that a particular process path has not been run for the past five years, suggesting a redesign in which the path is eliminated and the staff that participates in it reduced or reassigned.

The curious science of *process mining* formalizes this idea, specifying algorithms to discover the behavior of a process from the ordering of events in its logs. For example, if the logs show that, for a given process, activity A is always followed by B and then, in arbitrary order, C and D, we can guess that the process is designed such that A transitions sequentially to B, at which point it forks into two parallel paths headed by C and D, as shown in Figure 2-14.

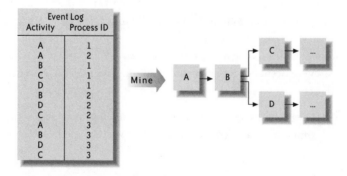

FIGURE 2-14. *Process mining: guessing process flow from the event log*

The ability to watch processes unfold "in the wild" is one of BAM's key benefits. Most processes are designed normatively, claim van der Aalst et al.* In other words, they are designed to behave as they *should* behave, but when we watch them run, we discover their *actual* behavior. In effect, by working backwards from the empirical runtime data, we can discover a process design that is potentially better than the one currently deployed.

Local View of Choreography: WS-CDL Toolkit

The most fanciful and speculative component of the architecture is the WS-CDL toolkit, which provides two tools:

The generator
Generates a process model having the required the flow of events and invocations for one participant in a multiparticipant choreography

The validator
Validates a local process model against a multiparticipant choreography

There are several problematic aspects of the architecture to consider:

- No implementation of such a toolkit is available today, though many discussions of WS-CDL highlight the value of a WS-CDL-to-BPEL generator.

- In our architecture, BPMN is a more suitable generation target language than BPEL; BPMN is our design language, and BPEL is generated from it by a separate export tool.

- BPMN is purely graphical and cannot be generated in a standard way by an automated tool. To generate BPMN code for ITpearls' Visio-based Process Modeler tool, for example, requires understanding, and coding to, the Visio object model. BPMN has no behind-the-scenes open XML representation the tool can use.

The good news is that BPMN is a sufficiently expressive language to capture the local participant view of a choreography. Further, BPMN's published mapping to BPEL adequately covers the key BPEL participant-related activity types: receive and invoke. In short, WS-CDL-to-BPMN-to-BPEL, when applied to choreography, is conceptually viable, although the first leg of that trip is potentially an uncomfortable ride.

How does the generator work? Taking as input the choreography and the identity of the required participant, the generator scans through the choreography looking for interactions involving that participant. For each interaction, the tool generates an activity in the local process. The tool is required to handle various control constructs (sequential, conditional, parallel) and to detect and encode message correlation (e.g., correlate a response and an acknowledgement with an earlier request).

---

* W. M. P. van der Aalst, B. F. van Dongen, J. Herbst, L. Maruster, G. Schimm, A. J. M. M. Weijsters, "Workflow Mining: A Survey of Issues and Approaches," *Data and Knowledge Engineering*, Volume 47, Issue 2 (Nov 2003).

Consider the following informally stated choreography:

```
A sends request to B
In parallel, B forwards request and then waits for an ack and then a response from,
respectively, C and D
B combines the two responses and sends to A
```

The local process for B resembles the following:

```
Receive request from A
Do a parallel split
    Path 1
        Send request to C
        Receive correlated ack from C
        Receive correlated response from C
    Path 2
        Send request to D
        Receive correlated ack from D
        Receive correlated response from D
Combine responses from C and D
Send combined response to A
```

As for the validator, taking as input the choreography, the identity of a participant, and the code of the participant's local process, the validator checks whether the process includes all the correct activities in the proper order. The following code for participant C is invalid because it does not include the step to send an acknowledgment:

```
Receive request from B
Send response to B
```

Standards

Table 2-6 lists the major BPM standards and where they fall within our model architecture.

TABLE 2-6. *BPM standards: where they fit*

Name	Organization	Type	Chapter
Workflow Reference Model	WfMC	Architectural model	Chapter 7
Business Process Modeling Notation (BPMN)	BPMI	Notation language	Chapter 6
UML Activity Diagram	OMG	Notation language	Chapter 3
Business Process Execution Language (BPEL)	OASIS	Execution language	Chapter 5
Business Process Modeling Language (BPML)	BPMI	Execution language	Chapter 6
XML Process Definition Language (XPDL)	WfMC	Execution language	Chapter 7
XLANG	Microsoft	Execution language	Chapter 9
Web Services Flow Language (WSFL)	IBM	Execution language	Chapter 9

TABLE 2-6. *BPM standards: where they fit (continued)*

Name	Organization	Type	Chapter
Business Process Definition Metamodel (BPDM)	OMG	Execution language and/or notation language	Chapter 9
Business Process Runtime Interface (BPRI)	OMG	• Administration and monitoring • Human interaction • System interaction	Chapter 9
Workflow API (WAPI)	WfMC	• Administration and monitoring • Human interaction • System interaction	Chapter 7
Business Process Query Language (BPQL)	BPMI	Administration and monitoring	Mentioned in Chapter 7
Web Services Choreography Interface (WSCI)	W3C	Choreography	Chapter 8
Web Services Choreography Description Language (WS-CDL)	W3C	Choreography	Chapter 8
Web Services Conversation Language (WSCL)	W3C	Choreography	Chapter 8
Workflow XML (WfXML)	WfMC	Choreography	Chapter 7
Business Process Schema Specification (BPSS)	OASIS	Choreography (and collaboration)	Chapter 9

At 17 entries, a first glance at the list is intimidating, but the number of viable candidates for our architecture is small:

- Both of the major notation languages, BPMN and UML's activity diagrams, are good, but BPMN is preferred because it is more expressive and defines a BPEL mapping.

- Of the five XML execution languages, BPEL wins by a landslide, because it is the most expressive, has a BPMN mapping, and enjoys the widest industry support.

- None of the three approaches covering administration and monitoring or human and system interaction, is suitable for our architecture. BPQL and BPRI are in infancy and need time to develop; WAPI, by contrast, is past its prime and at best has a few ideas worth harvesting.

- Choreography is used in our architecture to generate skeletal local process models having the correct logic for communication with external participants. WS-CDL is the best of the five choreography standards, and is the recommended approach of the W3C's web services choreography working group.

- The WfMC's workflow reference model in general terms is similar to, and an inspiration for, our architecture, but its details are too closely aligned with the outdated WfMC WAPI, XPDL, and WfXML.

- The OMG's BPDM process metamodel is under development. When it is released, BPDM will standardize the mapping between processes designed in BPMN but run on

BPEL. The BPMN design tool will export its processes as BPDM models, and the BPEL runtime engine will import them in that form.

From this analysis, only 3 of the 17 standards—BPMN, BPEL, and WS-CDL—currently fit into our architecture, but BPQL and BPDM look promising for a future iteration.

Summary

The main points of this chapter include the following:

- BPM is replete with competing standards, but a sound architectural approach divides a BPM application into the right parts and selects the correct standard for each.

- The requirement of a BPM application is the ability to design, run, administer, and monitor processes that incorporate system and human interactions.

- Two types of architects benefit from this discussion. Product architects learn, at a high level, a good approach to developing a BPM product. Services architects learn the essential nature of a BPM product platform, enabling them to build good solutions on it and to educate their customers about this emerging technology.

- Design, the modeling of processes by business and technical analysts, requires a graphical notation language and a graphical design tool, such as ITpearls' Process Modeler. BPMN is the best standard notation language.

- To run a process requires a runtime engine that can load designs and manage the execution of instances. However, there is no way to run a notational drawing; it is just a design artifact. A runtime engine requires an executable language, just as a computer processor requires programs that use the processor's instruction set. To bridge this gap, a mapping from notational to executable language is needed. The design tool should offer an export option that uses the mapping to generate executable code. With respect to standards, BPEL is the best and most widely adopted executable language, and our chosen notational language, BPMN, includes as part of its specification a detailed mapping to BPEL.

- Administration and monitoring is crucial for the success of a production application. An administrative console, along with a sufficient data model and a standard system management interface language, helps administrators track and change the managed objects of the runtime engine, including process definitions, processes, activities, manual tasks (worklist items), and users and roles.

- Human interactions are manual work items that are performed by particular users or users with a specific role within the organization. The process initiates this work and waits for an event for the work's completion. The users view and execute their pending tasks in a graphical worklist console. Because tasks are long-lived, their state is kept in the administration database. A special Worklist web service manages human interactions on behalf of the process.

- System interactions are connections to internal or external systems. External systems are typically web service-based partner processes. Internal systems are other applications on the corporate network with which the process needs to interface. The number of integration technologies is high, and it would be foolhardy to try to support each of them individually. The best approach is to offer the most common technologies natively (XML, web services, inline Java) and provide an adapter plug-in model for the rest (e.g., MQ, database, or mainframe).

- A process is a web service! Its event points are, in effect, service operations. For this reason, the BPM integration architecture must include a special web services listener that accepts SOAP requests and injects them into the process engine.

- The processes of this architecture are those of a particular corporation and are designed from a local perspective. The global perspective of choreography and collaboration (discussed in Chapters 8 and 9) helps build protocols with which our company must comply.

- Of the 17 major BPM standards, only 3—BPMN, BPEL, and WS-CDL—belong in our architecture. The emerging BPQL and BPDM look promising for a future iteration.

Reference

- Oracle, "BPEL Tutorial 6: Working with the TaskManager Service," *http://otn.oracle.com/bpel*.

CHAPTER THREE

The Scenic Tour of Process Theory

I n most software topics, the boundary between theory and practice in software is clearly drawn: theory is for academics who seldom descend from the ivory tower, and practice is for industry professionals who have long forgotten the concepts and application of theory. In concurrency, for example, most developers either know or have programmed semaphores, but few remember the conceptual underpinnings devised by Dijkstra.

But BPM belongs to a rarer category, in which theory informs practical design and theoretical jargon is part of the hype with customers. Somehow the abstruse terms "pi-calculus" and "Petri net"—as impressive to the ear as database management's "relational calculus" or capacity planning's "Erlang formulae"—have permeated the consciousness of the BPM community. Many BPM onlookers are familiar with and interested in pi and Petri, but have at best a vague understanding of them, and prefer an executive summary or beginner's treatment; the pedantic details are best left to graduate students.

Process theory is practically important for several reasons:

- It is mentioned frequently in connection with BPM, even in nonacademic material. Countless presentations, for example, state without explanation that BPEL is influenced by the pi-calculus and Petri nets. For the many practitioners who are intimidated by the pedantic name-dropping but are curious to uncover its meaning (asking questions such as: What is the pi-calculus? What are Petri nets? Which parts of each theory are used in BPEL? Why is BPEL based on two theories rather than one?). This chapter helps explain the nature of the connection.

- BPM is relatively immature and benefits from the ideas and rigor of theory. Control flow, for example, is often treated too casually by vendors, who are more likely to emphasize ease of programming rather than semantic precision. Regrettably, as several papers on process-design patterns have demonstrated, most vendors—and even most standards—struggle to support certain common control flow scenarios (e.g., the "multiple instances without runtime knowledge" and "interleaved parallel routing" patterns, described in Chapter 4). To build successful solutions, practitioners should insist on knowing exactly how a given process will run. To accomplish this, they should choose a good language and understand how it works. Judged on the basis of control flow, the strongest languages are those that are based on the Petri net, including BPEL and BPMN. And, arguably, understanding the nuances of these languages—e.g., dead path elimination in BPEL—requires an appreciation of the Petri net.

- Contemporary BPM and Web Services Choreography are obsessed with the construction of complex participant conversations. Choreography especially, because it is mandated to build global collaborative contracts, requires a conceptual framework that can express dynamic communicating processes precisely and concisely. The leading choreography language, WS-CDL, bases its constructions (e.g., channel passing) on the pi-calculus. BPEL is also alleged to have pi underpinnings. By learning the basics of pi, the practitioner gains insight into the use of these languages.

This chapter is a scenic guided tour of the BPM theory route. It begins by exploring which theories have influenced which standards. The pi-calculus, the Petri net, and the state machine are studied by example and with just enough detail to give a flavor for the mechanics without overdosing on algebra. This chapter also explores each theory's significance for and influence on BPM.

Family Tree

Pi-calculus and the Petri net (or some combination of the two) provide the theoretical underpinnings for most of the major BPM standards. Four of the major contemporary standards betray pi-calculus influence:

- WS-CDL
- WSCI
- BPML
- XLANG

Three other major standards derive from the Petri net:

- BPMN

- YAWL

- WSFL

Finally, BPEL is a blend, inheriting traits of pi and Petri from its parent languages XLANG and WSFL, respectively. Figure 3-1 illustrates these relationships.

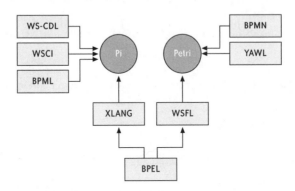

FIGURE 3-1. *Theory family tree for BPM standards*

In Figure 3-1, boxes represent standards, circles theories, and arrows dependencies. The level of dependency is extremely variable. Petri, for example, is woven into the fabric of YAWL, whereas BPMN and WSFL seem to merely draw inspiration from it. Pi's connection to each of its children is inspiration at best and mere hype at worst.

The Pi-Calculus

Developed by Scottish mathematician Robin Milner in the 1990s, the pi-calculus is a formal language for defining concurrent, communicating processes, including, but not restricted to, business processes. In its detail, the pi-calculus is a rather advanced algebraic system requiring a senior level of mathematical training. Milner's presentation of the subject is written in the mathematical idiom of definitions, theorems, and lemmas, inaccessible to most BPM onlookers.* Few business analysts or software developers could survive if required to compose their business processes as lines of pi-calculus code.

But somehow, despite its academic roots and its inherent complexity, the pi-calculus has become one of BPM's most attention-getting cocktail party terms. Popular BPM literature states boldly that major languages such as XLANG, WSCI, BPML, BPEL, and WS-CDL are

---

* R. Milner. "The Polyadic Pi-Calculus: A Tutorial," in F.L. Bauer, W. Brauer, H. Schwichtenberg (editors), *Logic and Algebra of Specification*," Berlin, Springer, 1993. (Check the "References" section for more Milner works on the subject.)

based on the pi-calculus. This stunning level of influence, charges leading BPM commentator Wil van der Aalst , is dubious, and surely nothing but hype:

> Let the people that advocate BPEL4WS, BPMN, … and WSCI show the precise relation between the language and some formal foundation. People that cannot do this but still claim strong relationships between their language and e.g., pi-calculus, only cause confusion.*

Whether or not it is hype, the pi-calculus–BPM connection merits a serious look. What, in a nutshell, is the pi-calculus, how does it apply to BPM, and what is the extent and nature of its influence on contemporary popular languages like XLANG and WS-CDL?

NOTE
Robin Milner visited Petri net creator Carl Adam Petri in Bonn in the 1980s to learn more about concurrent systems.

The Pi-Calculus in a Nutshell

As mentioned earlier, the pi-calculus is a language that defines concurrent processes that interact with one another dynamically. Each process consists of one or more *actions*, which can be arranged sequentially, in parallel or conditional paths, or recursively. An *action* is the sending or receiving of information on a channel. According the pi-calculus convention, when one process sends information to another, it includes the name of the channel to be used for the other process to respond. This name is variable and, as you will see, can change in response to changing conditions.

The process definition is a set of mathematical equations using defined symbols. Example 3-1 illustrates the interactions of a customer, a travel agent, and an airline in the booking of a travel reservation.

EXAMPLE 3-1. *Travel agency pi-calculus example*

```
1   Customer(createorder,customer)=
2       createorder<customer>.customer(result)
3   Agent(createorder,agentok,agentfail,airline)=
4       createorder(customer).airline<agentok,agentfail>.
5       Agent1(agentok,agentfail,customer)
6   Agent1(agentok,agentfail,customer)=
7       agentok(result).customer<result>+
8       agentfail(result2).customer<result2>
9   Airline(airline,agentok,agentfail)=
10      airline(agentok,agentfail).agentok<"conf no 121">
11  End2End=
12      (new corder,cust,ok,fail,air)
13      Customer(corder,cust)|Agent(corder,ok,fail,air)|Airline(air,ok,fail)
```

---

*   W. M. P. van der Aalst, "Pi calculus versus Petri nets: Let us eat 'humble pie' rather than further inflate the 'pi hype,'" *http://is.tm.tue.nl/research/patterns/download/pi-hype.pdf.*

The definition of the customer process, which sends an order to a travel agent and waits for a result, appears in lines 1 and 2. Line 1 declares that the process Customer uses channels createorder and customer. In line 2, the process first sends, on channel createorder, bound for the agency, the value customer ($\overline{\text{createorder}}$<customer>), where customer is actually the name of the channel on which it expects a reply. The notation is $\overline{p}$<q> means "send q on channel p," and although the content of q is arbitrary, in many cases it is the name of a channel. Next the customer process listens on the channel customer, which originates from the agency, for a result message (customer(result)). The notation $p(q)$ means "receive q on channel p." Separating these two actions is a period (.) representing the sequential operator. In other words, the actions are performed one after another: first the send on channel createorder, then the receive on channel customer.

The process for the travel agent spans lines 3 to 8 and is broken into two parts. The first part, entitled Agent in lines 3 to 5, receives the order request from the customer (createorder(customer)), then sends on the channel airline the values agentok and agentfail ($\overline{\text{airline}}$<agentok,agentfail>), both of which are names of channels on which to receive a response from the airline, and then transitions into the process Agent1. Agent1, in lines 6 through 8, contains two sequences separated by a plus sign (+), representing the conditional operator. Exactly one of these sequences will occur. In the first (line 7), the agent receives a message from the airline on the agentok channel (agentok(result)), signifying a successful booking, and forwards it to the customer ($\overline{\text{customer}}$<result>); the second case, on line 8, is similar, except that the agent receives a message on the agentfail channel, signifying a failed booking. Combining these definitions, the travel agency receives an order from the customer, sends it to the airline, and waits for a successful or failure event from the airline before forwarding the result to the customer.

The Airline process is defined in lines 9 and 10. (For brevity, the example is kept artificially simplistic.) The airline listens on the channel airline for the names of the channels—agentok, agentfail–to be used to respond to the agency, and then sends a confirmation "conf no=121" on the agentok channel.

The process End2End, lines 11 through 13, is the overall concurrent system of Customer, Agent, and Airline. The new statement on line 12, known as the restriction operator, creates private channels to be used among the processes. The pipe symbol in line 13 (|) is the concurrency operator. The processes Customer, Agent, and Airline run simultaneously, interacting over channels localized to the overall process End2End. The overall communication is shown in Figure 3-2.

One of the most distinctive features of the pi-calculus is mobility, in which the topology of communicating processes changes dynamically in response to changing conditions. An example of mobility is the enrollment of customers with retailers in a deregulated energy market. In scenario (1) of Figure 3-3, the customer initially buys energy directly from the supplier (a "standard supply" arrangement). In scenario (2), the customer enrolls with retailer A, and then in scenario (3) switches to competing retailer B. Finally, in scenario (4), the customer decides to drop retailer B, and return to standard supply.

FIGURE 3-2. *Pi-calculus travel agency example*

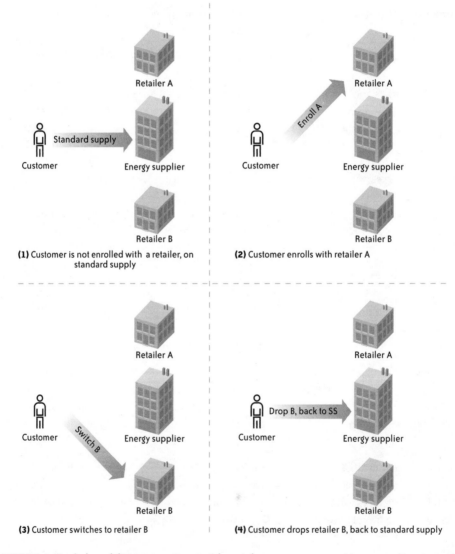

(1) Customer is not enrolled with a retailer, on standard supply

(2) Customer enrolls with retailer A

(3) Customer switches to retailer B

(4) Customer drops retailer B, back to standard supply

FIGURE 3-3. *Pi-calculus mobility: energy customer switches retailers*

As you can see in Example 3-2, the source code to model this scenario is remarkably terse:

EXAMPLE 3-2. *Energy pi-calculus example*

```
 1  CustomerSS(enroll,switch,drop,rets)=
 2     Σ(r:rets).(enroll<r,mike>.CustomerR(r,enroll,switch,drop,rets))
 3  CustomerR(r,enroll,switch,drop,rets)=
 4    Σ(r2:rets).(switch<r,r2,mike>.CustomerR(r2,enroll,switch,drop,rets)) +
 5    drop<r,mike>.CustomerSS(enroll,switch,drop,rets)
 6  Supplier(enroll,switch,drop)=
 7    (enroll(r1,c).r1<"addcust",c> +
 8    switch (r1,r2,c).r1<"dropcust",c>.r2!<"addcust",c> +
 9    drop(r1,c).r1<"dropcust",c>).Supplier(enroll,switch,drop)
10  Retailer(r)=
11    r(action,c).Retailer(r)
12  Market=
13    (new chEnroll,chSwitch,chDrop,retSet={retA,retB})
14    CustomerSS(chEnroll,chSwitch,chDrop,retSet)|
15    Supplier(chEnroll,chSwitch,chDrop) |
16    Retailer(retA)|Retailer(retB)
```

The first two processes in this sample model a customer. The first, CustomerSS in lines 1 and 2, represents a customer on standard supply who enrolls with a retailer. The obscure expression:

```
Σ(r: rets).(enroll<r,"mike">.CustomerR(r,enroll,switch,drop,rets))
```

means:

- Σ(r:rets): Choose a retailer channel r from the set of retailers rets.
- enroll<r,"mike">: Send r and the customer's name "mike" on the channel enroll.
- CustomerR(r,enroll,switch,drop,rets): Change state to that of an enrolled customer by calling the process CustomerR, passing the chosen value of r.

CustomerR, in lines 3–5, is the process for a customer enrolled with a retailer, who can either switch to a different retailer or drop the current retailer and return to standard supply. The switch option, in line 4:

```
Σ(r2 : rets).(switch <r,r2, "mike"> .CustomerR(r2,enroll,switch,drop,rets))
```

means:

- Choose a retailer channel r2 from the set of retailers rets.
- Send r2, as well as the channel of the retailer with which the customer is currently enrolled, r, and the customer's name "mike" on the channel switch.
- Keep the same state, but change the retailer of record, given by the first variable, from r to r2 by recursively calling the process (CustomerR(r2,enroll,switch,drop,rets)).

The drop option, on line 5, means send r and the customer's name "mike" on the channel drop, then change state to that of a customer on standard supply by calling the process CustomerSS.

The supplier process, in lines 6 to 9, listens on channels enroll, switch, and drop for messages from the customer. In the enrollment case, in line 7, the process receives the message from the customer on the enrollment channel (enroll(r1,c)), and then sends a message to the channel of the specified retailer (r1) to add customer c to its customer base ($\overline{r1}$<"addcust",c>). The drop case, in line 9, is similar, but the message from the customer arrives on the channel drop (i.e., drop(r1,c)) and the supplier's message to the retailer is to drop the customer ($\overline{r1}$<"dropcust",c>). The switch case, in line 8 is a combination of drop and enrollment: receive on the switch channel the channels of the new retailer (r2) and old retailer (r1), and then instruct the old retailer to drop the customer and the new retailer to add the customer. When these activities are completed, the supplier process continues recursively (Supplier(enroll,switch,drop)) on line 9), much like a daemon.

The retailer process, in lines 10 and 11, listens on its channel r for the required action and customer (r(action,c)) and then, like the supplier process, continues recursively.

The market process, in lines 12 to 16, creates a simple energy market. Line 13 creates specific instances of the enroll, switch, and drop channels (chEnroll, chSwitch, and chDrop, respectively), as well as a set, named retSet, of actual retailer channels (retA and retB). Lines 14 through16 create four concurrent process instances and pass them to the newly defined channels. The processes include a single customer on standard supply, a supplier, and two retailers using channels retA and retB, respectively. The overall system resembles a web services choreography!

> ### NOTE
> The most widely cited example of mobility is the handover protocol used in GSM cell phone networks to switch cell bases for a phone call, as a phone (normally used in a car) moves through two geographic areas.

The Pi-Calculus and BPM

BPM is fast becoming the practical study and design of solutions for elaborate, multiple-company communicating business processes. For those seeking a formal basis for BPM processing, the pi-calculus offers three key features:

Control flow
> In the pi-calculus, the sequential, parallel, conditional, and recursive behavior of a process can be declared succinctly.

Message-based communication
> The heart of the pi-calculus is its clean syntax and semantics for inbound and outbound messaging.

Mobility
> Contemporary processes cannot hardcode service endpoints but requireS the ability to pass around and change addresses dynamically. Dynamic addressing, or mobility, is the most distinctive feature of the pi-calculus.

A good BPM language has the control structures of a flow chart, and has as its most significant steps "mobile" message-based interactions. The major contemporary process languages, as it turns out, are like this anyway. XLANG, for example, has similar control structures (sequence, all, switch), explicit service-oriented message support (the operation action), and dynamic channel bindings. WS-CDL is based on interactions, message exchanges on channels, and channel passing between participants.

> ### NOTE
> WS-CDL, according to its author, is based on the Explicit Solos
> Calculus, a variant of pi-calculus, which allows a system to be modeled
> from a global viewpoint.* Robin Milner, pi-calculus creator, is an
> invited expert in the W3C Choreography Working Group.

The crux of the "hype" criticism of van der Aalst is that the use of the pi-calculus in the creation of contemporary languages is overstated; that perhaps these languages came together more casually and with less academic rigor than advertised. They might resemble the pi-calculus, but they are hardly based on it. His challenge to prove the connection, though stated in polemical language, could inspire a landmark BPM paper.

Petri Nets

The *Petri network* (or *Petri net*), a notion devised in 1962 by the mathematician Carl Adam Petri, is a formal graphical process modeling language that can design systems as diverse as train track switches and business processes. With respect to the latter, Petri nets help describe—and indeed, can be used to implement—the semantics of process control flow, including basic branch and join rules, as well as more complicated synchronization scenarios; notably, dead path elimination, a core topic in the languages WSFL and BPEL. Petri net theory saturates the literature on process patterns, a topic introduced in Chapter 4. The keen analysis of this work, undertaken by a group of pro-Petri authors referred to in this book as the P4, injects much-needed rigor into an historically ambiguous and haphazard subject. Though among BPM champions it lacks the renown of the pi-calculus, the Petri net is a valuable abstraction and merits the attention it has been paid.

Petri Nets in a Nutshell

The Petri net's characteristic appearance is that of an unusual assembly of circles, rectangles, arrows, and black dots. The beginner might at first mistake it for a state-transition diagram, reasoning that the circles and rectangles are states, the arrows transitions, and the dots some other curious artifact specific to the model. But although the Petri net shares with the state machine a preoccupation with the notion of state, to compare the two is like comparing apples and oranges.

---

* N. Kavantzas, "Aggregating Web Services: Choreography and WS-CDL" (presentation), *http://www. oracle.com/technology/tech/webservices/htdocs/spec/WS-CDL-April2004.pdf*, Oracle, April 2004

In Petri's original conception, referred to as the *classical* net, the symbols are the following:

Place
    Drawn as a circle, a place is a stopping point in a process, representing (in many cases) the attainment of a milestone.

Transition
    A transition is a rectangle that represents an event or action.

Token
    A token is a black dot residing in a place. Collectively, the set of tokens represents the current state of the process. During the execution of the process, tokens move from place to place.

Arc
    An arc is a link from a transition to a place or a place to a transition.

The Java applet design editor and simulator (at *http://is.tm.tue.nl/staff/wvdaalst/pn_applet/pn_applet.html*) shown in Figure 3-4 is a typical Petri net modeling tool, which promotes a design-and-simulate approach to building a Petri net.

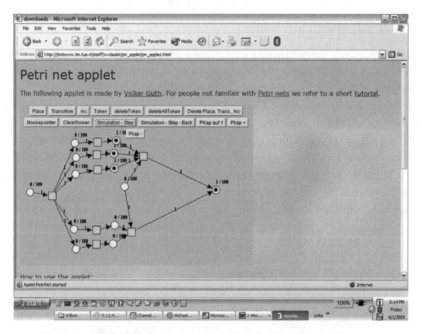

FIGURE 3-4. *Petri net simulator Java applet*

Designing a system involves dragging places and transitions onto a canvas, drawing arcs between them, and dropping an initial placement of tokens into a subset of the places. Simulating a design initiates a step-by-step run of the Petri net in which each step involves firing a transition and watching the tokens advance to new places.

Here are some elementary rules of Petri net design:

- An arc can connect a place to a transition, or a transition to a place, but never a place to a place, or a transition to a transition. Thus, the order of places and transitions alternates on a given path: place → transition → place → transition → place, and so on.

- A path should begin and end with a place.

- Place and transition are many-to-many. A place can branch into multiple transitions. Multiple places can join into a single transition. A transition can branch into multiple places. Multiple transitions can converge into a single place.

- Tokens belong in places. A transition cannot contain a token.

Here are the rules of execution:

- A transition is enabled (i.e., capable of firing) if each input place (i.e., each place that links to it) has at least one token.

- When a transition fires, it consumes a token from each input place and generates a token for each output place (i.e., each place that the place links to).

The next section illustrates these concepts in action.

Example

Consider the process by which magazine editors might vote on whether to accept an article for publication. When the article arrives, it is distributed for review and voting to a number of editors. The voting completes either when two editors accept it or when one rejects it; in the former case, the author is sent an acceptance notice, in the latter a rejection. Figure 3-5 shows the Petri net for this process.

The Petri net starts at the New place. When the Send For Vote transition fires, the net branches into three paths: two for acceptance, one for rejection. In the acceptance paths, the place Accepting links to the transition Accept, whose output place is Accepted; in effect, when Accept fires, a token is passed from Accepting to Accepted. The rejection path is similar: the transition Reject moves a token from the place Rejecting to the place Rejected. The two acceptance paths converge in the transition Send accept notice. Similarly, in the rejection path, the place Rejected links to the transition Send reject notice. Each of the send notice transitions links to the output place Done, the final step in the process. The curiously named place Mutex, an input to the send notice transitions, is discussed later in this section.

The behavior of the voting process is best understood by following the path of tokens through the net. Step (a) shows the initial placement: one token in New and one in Mutex. The shading of the transition Send for vote indicates that it is enabled; it is enabled because its one input place, New, has a token. When Send for vote fires, the token is removed from New, and tokens are populated in the Rejecting and Accepting places, thus enabling the transitions Accept and Reject, as shown in (b). Step (c) depicts the state of

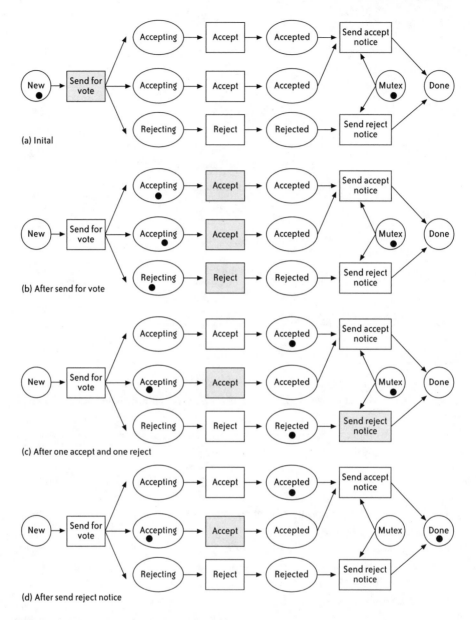

(a) Inital

(b) After send for vote

(c) After one accept and one reject

(d) After send reject notice

FIGURE 3-5. *Petri net process for vote*

the net after one acceptance and one rejection. The token from the uppermost Accepting has now moved to Accepted; likewise, Rejecting has now transitioned to Rejected. Of the two send notice transitions, only Send reject notice is enabled because both of its input places—Rejected and Mutex—have a token. When Send reject notice fires in Step (d), the tokens from Rejected and Mutex disappear, and a token is moved into Done.

Exemplifying the powerful synchronization capabilities of Petri nets is the Mutex (mutual exclusion) place, which ensures that only one notice—an acceptance or a rejection—is sent to the author. Mutex is an input place to both the Send accept notice and Send reject notice transitions, and hence neither of these transitions can fire unless Mutex has a token. However, in the initial token placement, Mutex has exactly one token. If two acceptances and one rejection occur at roughly the same time, both Send accept notice and Send reject notice will contend for that token. But when one transition fires, it will consume the token, immediately disabling the other transition, thereby preventing it from firing.

Petri Net Extensions

The high-level Petri net extends the classical conception considered previously and facilitates the construction of larger and more complex processes. It supports the following constructs:

Color

In the classical model, tokens are indistinguishable. In the color extension, each token has an associated set of attributes that distinguishes it from the others. Token identity makes possible two new Petri net features: *conditional branching* (when a transition fires, select one of several output places based on attributes of the fired token) and *guards* (when a transition is about to occur, a decision whether to allow it can be made based on the attributes of the tokens about to be passed).

The rationale for the term "color" is that in the classical model all tokens are black, but now tokens can be differentiated by color, making them distinguishable. Another way to think of it is that classically tokens had no attributes, but now they do and hence are distinguishable.

Hierarchy

Some processes are too large to be represented as a single net. The hierarchy extension permits a modular approach in which a net can initiate subnets on the firing of a transition. The idea is similar to that of child states in the state machine methodologies of the Unified Modeling Language (UML) and Real-time Object-Oriented Modeling (ROOM).

Petri Nets and BPM Patterns

The Petri net is a suitable model for control flow in business processes. Van der Aalst and his group, the P4 (mentioned previously), have published a mountain of papers on control flow and patterns, much of it applying ideas of Petri nets to demonstrate semantics. This section explores the P4 findings on basic AND, XOR, and dead path elimination patterns.*

---

* B. Kiepuszewski, A. H. M. ter Hofstede, W. M. P. van der Aalst, "Fundamentals of Control Flow in Workflows," *Acta Informatica*, 39(3):143–209, 2003

AND and XOR split and join

Every BPM modeling language permits a process to branch into parallel paths and then later join these paths back into one. In the process fragment shown in Figure 3-6, when activity A completes, activities B and C begin running in parallel; activity D begins only upon completion of both B and C.

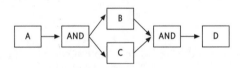

FIGURE 3-6. *Typical AND split and join in pseudocode*

Figure 3-7 shows an exclusive-OR conditional split from A to either B or C; when the split is joined back, activity D is executed.

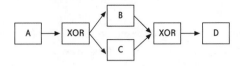

FIGURE 3-7. *Typical XOR split and join in pseudocode*

The P4 approach to modeling flow charts as Petri nets is to represent flow chart activities as transitions, where the name of the transition is the name of the activity. Some transitions—known as *lambda* (also known as *anonymous*) transitions—are left unlabeled (i.e., unnamed), as are all places. Places and lambda transitions, as we will see, combine to drive the control flow (that is, the parallel, conditional, sequential, and synchronization logic) of a process.engine. A Petri net model for the AND split and join is shown in Figure 3-8.

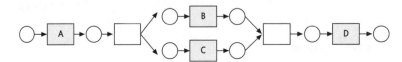

FIGURE 3-8. *Petri net AND split and join*

The Petri net model for an XOR split and an OR join is shown in Figure 3-9.

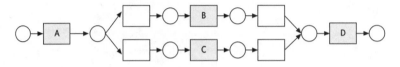

FIGURE 3-9. *Petri net XOR split and OR join*

The best way to understand the behavior of the model, in particular the unusual lambda transitions, is to trace the flow of tokens through these processes. Figure 3-10 shows the AND case.

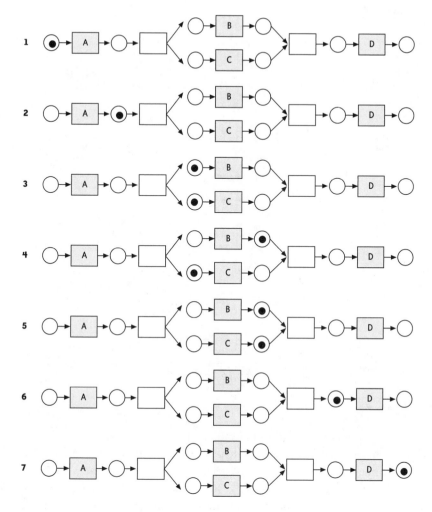

FIGURE 3-10. *Token flow in Petri AND split-join*

In Step 1, transition A is enabled because its input place has a token. When A completes, a lambda transition is enabled (Step 2) that accomplishes the split to B and C by duplicating the token from its input place to the input places of B and C. At this point, B and C are enabled (Step 3), and in unpredictable order (Steps 4 and 5), B and C complete. The lambda transition that follows B and C, by virtue of Petri net token synchronization semantics, waits for tokens from both of the branches before commencing (Step 6). Once it fires, transition D is enabled, and its completion ends the process (Step 7). The key to the split is the token duplication from a single input place to two output places; the key to the join is the synchronization of input places.

The XOR case, shown in Figure 3-11, starts the same way as the AND case.

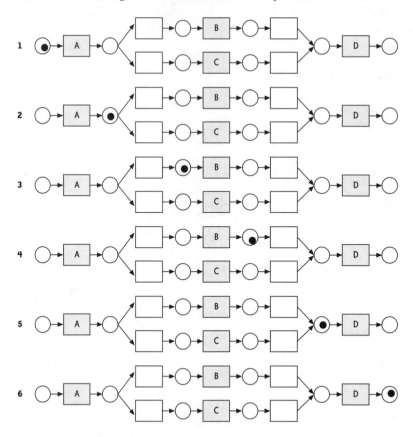

FIGURE 3-11. *Token flow in Petri XOR split-OR Join*

In Step 1, transition A, having a token in its input place, is enabled and executes. The succeeding lambda transition in Step 2 evaluates a condition based on information in the token and accordingly passes that token to exactly one of its output places. In the example, that output place is the input to B (Step 3), and when B completes (Step 4), its succeeding lambda transition passes through the token to enable D (Step 5), whose completion in Step 6 concludes the process. The key to the split is the conditional flow made possible by the color extension; the join is trivial.

Dead path elimination

Dead path elimination is a technique used in languages such as BPEL and WSFL to bypass, or "pass through," activities whose preconditions are not met. For example, in Part (a) of Figure 3-12, the activity Buy new home waits for the parallel activities Sell home and Get mortgage to complete, and it executes only if both have a true result. If at least one is false, the execution of Buy new home is skipped (i.e., can't buy a new home without financing and the sale of your old home), as is the execution of the successor activity Hire movers (i.e., don't call movers if you aren't moving).

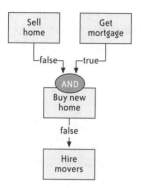

(a) Dead-path elimination scenario

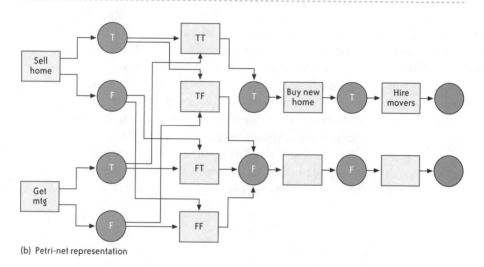

(b) Petri-net representation

FIGURE 3-12. *Dead path elimination for home move*

Part (b) shows the Petri net representation. Both the Sell home and Get mortgage transitions, representing the respective activities, branch upon completion in one of two paths: a true result leads into the place T, a false result to place F. A set of four lambda transitions waits for and aggregates the results of the two activities: TT is enabled when both activities return true, FF when both are false, TF when Sell home is true and Get mortgage false, and FT the converse of TF. The TT transition passes a token to the place T, thereby enabling the Buy home transition, and, further downstream, Hire movers. TF, FT, and FF each link to the place F, which leads into lambda transitions representing the no-op version of Buy home and Hire movers. The Petri net functions as a synchronizing truth table, allowing the purchase of the home and subsequent activities only when it receives "trues" for all inputs.

Petri Nets and the Standards

Of the major BPM standards, three—BPEL (Chapter 5), WSFL (Chapter 9), and BPMN (Chapter 6)—have roots in Petri nets. Each standard uses the notion of token passing to describe the semantics of control flow. The BPMN specification uses the token concept throughout. In WSFL and BPEL, the most striking Petri-net-inspired discussion is dead path elimination.

State Machines and Activity Diagrams

With its proud history and redoubtable theoretical credentials, the state machine (like the pi-calculus and the Petri net) is a guiding light to the practice of process design. As you will see, the representation of a process as a state diagram is markedly different from its more intuitive flow-chart implementation, and—being based on a more rigorous, more expressive system—is often clearer and more compact

State diagrams have a rich history. Alan Turing, the father of computer science, used the concept to build a model of computability. (See the sidebar "A Noble History...") State machine theorists Mealy, Moore, and Harel expanded the subject. Mealy and Moore built similar models whose essential differences—Mealy held that actions are performed in transitions, Moore that they are performed in states—were reconciled in Harel's later work on state charts. Harel allowed actions in both states and transitions, and enhanced the previously flat models with nested states and concurrent states. The UML state diagram, one of the leading contemporary approaches, is heavily influenced by Harel. The UML activity diagram (whose Version 2.0 specification, interestingly, uses Petri net token semantics), though essentially a flow charting technique, is in some respects a special case of the UML state diagram approach. Figure 3-13 depicts these historical milestones.

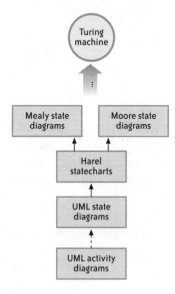

FIGURE 3-13. *State machine family tree*

A NOBLE HISTORY: THE STATE MACHINE AND THE ORIGINS OF COMPUTER SCIENCE

One of the earliest formulations of the state machine occurred in the work of Alan Turing, the father of computer science. Turing followed a line of thinkers—including Leibniz, Boole, Frege, Cantor, Hilbert, and Gödel—who sought to formalize human knowledge and make it algorithmic. (For a fascinating account, refer to Martin Davis's book *Engines of Logic: Mathematics and the Origin of the Computer*.) Writing in the 1930s, before the invention of the digital computer, Turing devised a hypothetical machine known as the Turing machine, which could run programs written as state machines. Though these programs were tedious compared to those composed in today's high-level languages, they were no less expressive; if a given problem could be solved at all, it could be solved in a Turing machine program. In a watershed finding for computer science, Turing was able to prove the existence of problems that he categorized as *undecidable*, which no Turing machine program could solve.

A modern programming languages is considered "Turing complete" if it has at least the expressive power of Turing machine programs.

_____

State Machines and Activity Diagrams in a Nutshell

The flow chart, which treats a process as a succession of activities, is one of the most natural visualization of a business process. The style is that of procedural programming; the flow chart is like a block of code run step -by step. Faced with the task of building a flow chart, most analysts simply start coding and discover their way as they go.

The state-oriented approach requires more thought up front, but can lead to a clearer and more compact implementation. Because a state diagram is a visualization of the behavior of some entity, the first step is to identify that entity and to enumerate its possible ontological conditions (that is, its set of states). Next comes the conception of the set of event-triggered transitions that moves the entity from state to state, as well as the design of the corresponding actions to be performed.

The result looks entirely different from a flow chart modeling the same behavior. To see how, consider Figure 3-14, which shows a flow chart, drawn as a UML activity diagram, for an insurance claims process.

The shapes in the diagram are activities (rounded boxes), decision points (diamonds), transitions (arrows), the start state (solid ball), stop states (solid ball with outer circle), a fork (solid horizontal line), and a signal receiver (rectangle with V-shaped tail). The process begins by forking in two directions: one that cancels the overall process on receipt of a kill signal, the other containing the mainline processing. When a new claim enters the claims department, it must first be evaluated (the Evaluate activity), at which time it

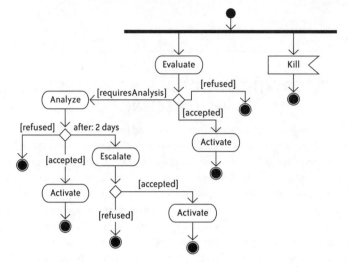

FIGURE 3-14. *Insurance claims process as flow chart*

can either be refused, accepted or passed to an adjuster (based on the conditions emanating from the decision point that follows Evaluate). Refusal immediately stops the process, whereas acceptance transitions to the Activate activity, a representation of the payment and other closing claim processing steps, which upon completion stops the flow; refusal and acceptance paths occur in other places in the process, too, and they behave identically. The requiresAnalysis path leads to the Analyze activity, having three outcomes: refusal, acceptance, or the expiration of two-day timer. On expiration, the Escalation activity, a prioritized treatment of the previous analysis step, perhaps by another adjuster or a supervisor, results in one final possible refusal/acceptance decision.

> ## NOTE
> Two common activity diagram features not used in this example are the join—a synchronization of parallel fork paths, that aren't required in this example because whichever patch completes first is meant to stop the whole flow—and swim lanes, which separate a process into streams for separate participants.

The modeling style here betrays a procedural programming approach, and leads naturally to the following representation in code:

```
On signal kill, done
Evaluate
If refused, done
Else if accepted
    Activate
    Done
Else if requiresAnalysis
    Analyze
    If refused, done
```

```
      Else if accepted
         Activate
         Done
      Else if 2 day timer expired
         Escalate
         If refused, done
         Else if accepted
            Activate
            Done
```

The UML state transition diagram shown in Figure 3-15, which represents the behavior of a claim, is markedly different.

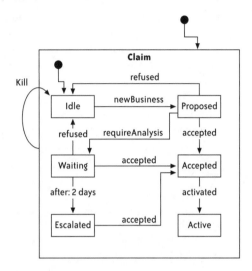

FIGURE 3-15. *Insurance claims state transition diagram*

The diagram is hierarchical, having an outer level that consists of a single state, called Claim, shown as a large rounded box, and an inner level, contained within the Claim state, with six substates: Idle, Proposed, Waiting, Accepted, Escalated, and Active (small rounded boxes). The inner level has a start state (a solid ball) that transitions to the Idle state (the transition represented by an arrow), signifying that the Idle is the initial state of the claim. The remaining inner transitions reveal that an idle claim enters the proposed state when it arrives into the claims department as new business (the newBusiness transition from Idle to Proposed). It can then be either accepted (the accept transition from Proposed to Accepted), refused (the refused transition from Proposed to Idle), or deemed worthy of further analysis (the requiresAnalysis transition from Proposed to Waiting). Refusal, regardless of the state from which it originates, always transitions to the Idle state; acceptance, from any state, transitions to the Accepted state, which leads to the Active state when the activated event occurs. A claim requiring analysis enters the Waiting state, which is subject to a two-day timer; on expiry, the claim is moved to the Escalated state.

The outer level helps model a global kill of the claim. The kill transition starts at the outer Claim state and terminates at the inner Idle state, signifying that when a kill event occurs, the claim goes Idle, regardless of its prior state. Apart from this, the outer level has no interesting behavioral features. It has just one state, which, because it is linked from the topmost start state, is the initial state of the outer level. When Claim is activated, its inner state model is initialized; the inner state is set to Idle because Idle is the initial state of the inner level.

> **NOTE**
> Other common UML state features include history and concurrent substates and transition guards.

This example uses a declarative style. Translated into code, it resembles a listing of states and transitions, rather than an algorithm:

```
Initial State: Claim, children=Idle,Proposed,Accepted,Active,Waiting,Escalated Initial
State: Idle
State: Proposed
State: Accepted; on entry, assign work item Activate
State: Active
State: Waiting; on entry, start timer T 2 days; on exit, stop timer T
State: Escalated
Transition: newBusiness from Idle to Proposed; assign work item Evaluate
Transition: refused from Proposed to Idle
Transition: refused from Waiting to Idle
Transition: refused from Escalated to Idle
Transition: requiresAnalysis from Proposed to Waiting; assign work item Analyze
Transition: accepted from Proposed to Accepted
Transition: accepted from Waiting to Accepted
Transition: accepted from Escalated to Accepted
Transition: activated from Accepted to Active
Transition: timer T expiry from Waiting to Escalated; assign work item Escalate
Transition: kill from Claim to Idle
```

Each listed state has a name, a list of child states, an indication of whether it is initial, and entry and exit actions. A transition has a name or trigger, start and end states, and an execution action. If the behavioral complexity increases, the changes are straightforward: graphically, add new states and transitions and possibly create new substates; in code, add new state and transition declarations, and modify some existing ones. By contrast, the corresponding flow chart would start to become unwieldy, the addition of new conditions or forks cluttering the diagram and making the generated code unreadable.

The Dualistic Activity Diagram: Flow Chart and State Machine

The UML activity diagram is essentially *dualistic,* to use philosophical language: it is by design both a flow chart *and* a special type of state diagram. In the previous section, you saw its flow-charting side, which, as White demonstrates,[*] is commendably expressive, with reasonable support for most of the common process patterns.

---

[*]   Stephen White, "Process Modeling Notations and Workflow Patterns," *BPTrends*, March 2004.

The other side is that of a state machine. UML backers position the activity diagram as a special kind of state diagram whose main steps are active states and whose arrows linking steps are triggerless transitions. But this approach is a bastardization of the idea of the state machine, argues Simons in a sharply critical paper: "The flowchart completely reverses the senses of state and transition."* Transitions should be legitimately event-based, and state should be determined by event reaction; if the machine is in state S1 and an event occurs that triggers transition T, which links state S1 to state S2, then the next state of the machine should be S2. But flowcharts put the logic of where to go next into the state, and the transition functions merely as a connector. Simons has a good point: how can this design claim to fit the state approach?

The activity diagram is much better off in the *monistic* form of flow chart: good as flow charts go, but lacking the clarity of the state machine.

State, Activity, and the Standards

Unlike the pi-calculus and the Petri net, the state machine approach has little direct influence on major BPM standards. Granted, all process languages have a strong notion of state, but not exactly that of Mealy, Moore, and Harel. Directed graph languages such as WSFL, XPDL, and WSCL, and BPEL's flow construct and WSCI's global model bears some resemblance to classical flat state machines, but the similarity is unremarkable.

Activity diagrams have not gained much traction in the BPM community, which, given UML's popularity in software analysis and design, is surprising. Isn't the lure of UML enough to make the activity diagram a competitive BPM model, or at least an influencer of the leading models? It seems almost no one is building activity diagram solutions, and major BPM languages bear little resemblance to activity diagrams.

Event-Driven Process Chains

A flowchart approach that has enjoyed better success among practitioners is the *event driven process chain* (EPC). As a control flow language, EPC has different syntax and semantics than the UML activity diagram but comparable expressive power; that comparison is not explored here. What is noteworthy about EPC is its multiple-view approach. As shown in Figure 3-16, an EPC's control view can link to roles in the view of organizational hierarchy (e.g., showing where a claims adjuster, required to evaluate a claim, fits into the claim department's organization), to entities in the corporate data view (e.g., pointing to Claim and Subscriber as the main entities used in the claims process), and to interfaces in the functional view (e.g., cut check for claims payment).

EPC is used in SAP R/3 workflow and ARIS, suggesting its suitability for ERP and business analysis.

---

* A. Simons, "On the Compositional Properties of UML Statechart Diagrams," *Proc. 3rd. Conf. Rigorous Object-Oriented Methods*, eds. A N Clark, A Evans and K Lano (York, 2000), 4.1-4.19

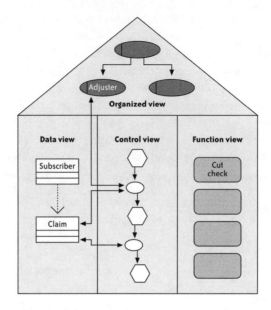

FIGURE 3-16. *Four views of an event-driven process chain*

Summary

The main points of this chapter include:

- Theory matters in BPM more than it does in most practical software fields. Theoreticians and practitioners tend to ignore each other's work, but in BPM, practitioners are keenly interested in—and indeed, actively hype—academic conceptions such as the pi-calculus, the Petri net, and, to a lesser extent, the state machine.

- The pi-calculus, developed by Scottish mathematician Robin Milner in the 1990s, is an algebraic system for building processes that communicate with each other on channels. Each process has a control flow that supports sequential, conditional, or concurrent control flow.

- Pi-calculus processes are written as sets of equations using a particular syntax. The examples developed in this chapter capture the most common elements.

- According to pi-calculus convention, when one process sends information to another, it includes the name of the channel to be used for the other process to respond. This name is variable; it can change in response to changing conditions. Channel change is referred to as mobility.

- The pi-calculus is thought to be an underpinning of process languages XLANG, BPML, WSCI, and WS-CDL, though leading BPM commentator van der Aalst thinks the connection is mostly hype.

- The classical Petri net was developed by the mathematician Carl Adam Petri in the 1960s. A Petri net is a process; its main constructs are places (stopping points in the process, but NOT states), transitions (events that drive process movement), tokens, and arcs (connecting transition to place or place to transition).

- Understanding the flow of control in a Petri net requires tracing the movement of tokens through the net. The rules of the classical net are simple: a transition can fire only if each of its input places (places that link to it) has at least one token; and when a transition fires, a token from each input place is moved to each output place (place that is linked to from the transition).

- The "state" of a Petri net is the tally of tokens in each place.

- The classical Petri net has been extended with color (guards and conditional branching) and hierarchy (subnets).

- Petri nets are good at describing control flow semantics. The group headed by van der Aalst (known as the P4) has developed theory around process pattern flow semantics and the Petri net.

- The Petri net has influenced WSFL, BPMN, and BPEL.

- The state machine has a rich history, with key contributions by Turing, Moore, Mealy, and Harel. The UML state diagram is based on Harel model, which in turn is a fusion of the classical Mealy and Moore approaches with extensions for hierarchy and concurrency.

- Compared with flow charts, the state machine is a clearer and more compact way to represent a business process. Flow charts are procedural, whereas state machines are declarative. As the complexity of a process increases, changes to the state machine are manageable, but the flow chart becomes unwieldy.

- The state machine is the behavior of an entity. It consists of a set of states and a set of transitions.

- The UML activity diagram is a both a flowcharting technique (and a good one at that, as White's analysis of its support for common process patterns shows) and a special kind of state machine whose activities are states and interactivity links triggerless transitions. Simon's paper charges that this notion is a bastardization of the idea of state machine.

- The state machine has less direct influence on BPM standards than the pi-calculus and the Petri net. The activity diagram has surprisingly little influence at all on BPM.

References

1. W. M. P. van der Aalst, A. H. M. ter Hofstede, B. Kiepuszewski, and A. P. Barros, "Workflow Patterns," *Distributed and Parallel Databases*, 14(1):5–51, 2003.

2. W. M. P. van der Aalst and A. H. M. ter Hofstede, "YAWL: Yet Another Workflow Language," *Information Systems*, 30(4):245–275, 2005.

3. P. Wohed, W. M. P. van der Aalst, M. Dumas, A. H. M. ter Hofstede, and N. Russell, "Pattern-based Analysis of UML Activity Diagrams," BETA Working Paper Series, WP 129, Eindhoven University of Technology, Eindhoven, 2004.

4. R. Milner, *A Calculus of Communicating Systems*, Secaucus, NJ, Springer, 1980.

5. R. Milner, *Communicating and Mobile Systems: The Pi-Calculus*, Cambridge University Press, Cambridge, 1999.

6. P. Gardner, "Models of Concurrent Computation" (course notes), *http://www.doc.ic.ac.uk/~pg/Concurrency/course.html*

7. L. Wischik, "Pi Calculus: Automata, State, Actions, and Interactions," *http://www.ebpml.org/pi-calculus.htm*.

8. G. T. Leavens,"Overview of the Pi-Calculus," *http://www.cs.iastate.edu/~leavens/FoCBS/henderson-node5.html*

9. W. M. P. van der Aalst and K. M. van Hee, *Workflow Management: Models, Methods, and Systems*, MIT Press, Cambridge, MA, 2004.

10. W. M. P. van der Aalst and A. H. M. ter Hofstede, "Workflow Patterns: On the Expressive Power of (Petri-net-based) Workflow Language," in K. Jensen (editor), *Proceedings of the Fourth Workshop on the Practical Use of Coloured Petri Nets and CPN Tools* (CPN 2002), volume 560 of DAIMI, pages 1–20, University of Aarhus, Denmark, August 2002.

11. B. Kiepuszewski, A. H. M. ter Hofstede, W. M. P. van der Aalst, "Fundamentals of Control Flow in Workflows," *Acta Informatica*, 39(3):143–209, 2003

12. M. Dumas, A. H. M ter Hofstede, "UML Activity Diagrams as a Workflow Specification Language," in *Proceedings of the International Conference on the Unified Modeling Language (UML)*, Toronto, Canada, October 2001.

13. M. R. Garey, *Computers and Intractability*, New York, W. H. Freeman, 1979.

14. M. Havey, "Workflow and State Machines in Weblogic Integration: The Process-Oriented Application," *Weblogic Developer's Journal*, January 2004.

15. P. Fontaine, "Insure Yourself with XML!" *http://www.infoloom.com/gcaconfs/WEB/paris2000/S25-04.HTM*.

16. M. Davis, *Engines of Logic: Mathematics and the Origin of the Computer*, New York, Norton, 2001

17. G. Booch, J. Rumbaugh, I. Jacobson, *The Unified Modeling Language User Guide*, Reading, Massachusetts, Addison Wesley, 1999.

18. S. White, "Process Modeling Notations and Workflow Patterns," *BPTrends*, March 2004.

19. Object Management Group, *OMG Unified Modeling Language Specification, Version 1.5*, *http://www.omg.org/technology/documents/formal/uml.htm*, March 2003.

20. P. Loos and P. Fettke, "Towards an Integration of Business Process Modeling and Object-Oriented Software Development," in I. Ivan, I. Rosca (eds.), Information Society-Proceeding of the Fifth International Symposium on Economic Informatics (IE 2001, Bucharest, May 9-12, 2001), pp. 835–843 , *http://archiv.tu-chemnitz.de/pub/2001/0044/data/2001_IE_Symposium.pdf*.

CHAPTER FOUR

Process Design Patterns

GOOD SOFTWARE USES, AND IN SOME CASES INVENTS, REUSABLE SOLUTIONS TO RECURRING PROBLEMS. Expert developers never begin a new project from scratch, but harvest tried-and-true ideas, selecting and morphing existing code snippets. Junior developers, in a similar position, borrow snippets from the experts, or, if they are unusually precocious, originate their own strategies. In BPM, a design pattern is a formalization of these prosaic snippets, consisting of a publishable specification of a problem-solving strategy or recipe, of sorts, for consumption and reuse by the larger development community.

Though BPM is known for its practicality (offers business benefits to its customers and an easy sell for its vendors), it cannot succeed without good, careful, deliberate design practices. Too many processes are designed too quickly, high on the hype that business requirements can be realized in executable digital form rapidly with drag-and-drop flowchart editors. Such processes are created without a strong foundation of previous experience. This chapter examines the use of design patterns in BPM as such a foundation to aid in the construction of better processes.

Design Patterns and the GoF

Few ideas in software design have been as influential as that of the design pattern. The book *Design Patterns: Elements of Reusable Object-Oriented Software* (Addison Wesley, 1995) by Gamma, Helm, Johnson, and Vlissides—a group popularly known as the "Gang of Four," or GoF—sits on numerous developers' desks and has permeated the design sense of the entire object-oriented development community.

The GoF's book is a catalog of 23 patterns related to the creation of objects (for example, the Abstract Factory Pattern), the structural relationships of objects (for example, the Façade Pattern), and the behavior of objects (for example, the Chain of Responsibility Pattern). Each pattern is documented according to a standard template, with sections such as Intent, Motivation, and Known Uses. The specification of a pattern describes the nature of the pattern, why it is important, and how it is implemented.

The Façade pattern, for example, defines a simplifying interface to a system. Its benefits include reduced complexity and weaker system coupling, and it is useful in the design of client-side interfaces. The implementation of Façade is normally an object (such as a Compiler) whose public interface is simpler than, and hides of the use of, the set of objects (such as Scanner, Parser, or CodeGenerator) belonging to the system behind the scenes.

Prior to the GoF's book, most software developers had at best a vague awareness of the concept of façade, and their ability to design a good client-side interface was a matter of good intuition. Subsequent to the book, design intuition gave way to name-dropping: developers proudly proclaimed that their interfaces were GoF façades! Good object-oriented design ideas had infiltrated the design community.

Process Patterns and the P4

The process community has taken a similar approach by identifying and codifying its own set of common problems. The article "Workflow Patterns" by van der Aalst, ter Hofstede, Kiepuszewski, and Barrios—a group referred to in this chapter as the "Process Four," or P4—lists and describes 20 patterns specific to processes.* The P4 catalog is a comprehensive account of patterns for process *control flow*. The benefit of control flow patterns is to help the process designer determine different ways to assemble activities (for example, how to implement conditional logic based on a deferred choice).

Whereas GoF patterns are documented as object models and code recipes, P4 patterns are inherently spatial and visual: a process pattern is a cluster, or constellation, of process activities arranged in just the right way to solve a difficult problem. The process patterns read like a wish list for a process notational language. Some are obvious (such as support for a sequence of activities); others are exotic (for example, multiple instances of an activity where the number of instances is not known even at runtime).

---

* W. M. P. van der Aalst, A. H. M ter Hofstede, B. Kiepuszewski, and A. P. Barrios, "Workflow Patterns," Technical report, Eindhoven University of Technology, Eindhoven, 2003, *Distributed and Parallel Databases*, 14(1):5–51, 2003.

This chapter is a reference guide to the 20 P4 patterns; it discusses each pattern's intent, alternative names, motivation, implementation details, and related patterns. The patterns are grouped into six main categories:

- Basic patterns

- Advanced branch and join patterns

- Structural patterns

- Multiple instances patterns

- State-based patterns

- Cancellation patterns

After the patterns, the chapter covers YAWL, a language proposed by the P4 to support all the patterns; provides a few patterns for areas beyond mere control flow; and concludes with a few coding recommendations.

Basic Patterns

Basic patterns cover fundamental process capabilities: running activities in a sequence; spawning, and later joining, parallel lines of execution; and branching into one of several directions based on a conditional choice. The five basic P4 patterns are: Sequence, Parallel Split, Synchronization, Exclusive Choice, and Simple Merge.

Sequence

The intent of the Sequence pattern is to run activities sequentially. For example, run activity A followed by B followed by C, and so on. This pattern is also known as Sequence Flow.

The need for activity sequencing is obvious: almost every process has at least one segment of two or more steps to be performed sequentially. In Figure 4-1, for example, the process of opening a bank account requires getting a manager to approve the account open application, updating the account database, and sending a welcome package to the customer.

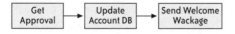

FIGURE 4-1. *The Sequence pattern in a process for opening a bank account*

Given that activity sequencing is an essential part of the notion of process, it is not surprising that all BPM vendors and specifications support the Sequence pattern. In BPEL, for example, the implementation of the bank account process uses the sequence activity:

```
<sequence>
    <invoke name="Get approval" . . . />
```

```
        <invoke name="Update account DB" . . . />
        <invoke name="Send welcome package" . . ./>
    </sequence>
```

This pattern is related to all other patterns.

Parallel Split

The intent of the Parallel Split pattern is to branch, or fork, from a single activity to multiple parallel paths. This pattern is also known as AND-split.

Parallel split is used when multiple streams of work need to execute at roughly the same time. The example of a travel agency booking is shown in Figure 4-2: when the customer's itinerary is received (Get itinerary), the process spawns separate paths to handle the bookings for air (Book airline), hotel (Book hotel), and car (Book car).

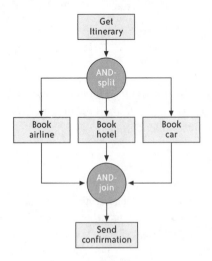

FIGURE 4-2. *Parallel Split and Synchronization in travel agency process*

The use of parallelism in this example is sensible, because the three streams are independent. Furthermore, if a delay occurs in any of the bookings (for example, if the hotel booking cannot complete until someone from the hotel calls a travel agent with a manual confirmation), the other bookings are unaffected.

Implementations of this widely supported pattern include control constructs (such as all in BPML and flow in BPEL) and explicit split elements (such as the AND gateway in BPMN, plus the split in UML activity diagrams.) The UML activity diagram implementation is shown in Figure 4-3; the upper black bar splits Get itinerary to the three booking activities.

This pattern is related to Synchronization, Exclusive Choice, Multi-Choice.

Synchronization

The intent of the Synchronization pattern is to have several parallel paths converge on a single activity, which waits for the completion of all paths before starting. The pattern is also known as AND-join.

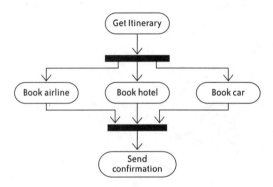

FIGURE 4-3. *A UML activity diagram of Parallel Split and Synchronization in travel reservation*

Synchronization, or the merging of parallel paths spawned by a parallel split, is a common requirement for many processes, such as the example shown in Figure 4-2, in which the activity Send Confirmation must not be started until the three preceding parallel activities Book air, Book hotel, and Book car have completed.

In languages in which parallel processing is modeled as a control structure (such as flow in BPEL and all in BPMN), the control structure itself manages the merge; for example, when the flow in BPEL completes, its child activities are guaranteed to have completed. In languages where the merge requires an explicit join element (such as the AND gateway in BPMN and the join in UML activity diagrams, shown as the lower black bar in Figure 4-3), the join element performs the merge.

The pattern is related to Parallel Split, Simple Merge, Synchronizing Merge, Multi-Merge, Discriminator.

Exclusive Choice

The intent of the Exclusive Choice pattern is to branch from a single activity to exactly one of several paths, based on the evaluation of a condition. This pattern is also known as XOR-split.

The need for exclusive choice is commonplace. Figure 4-4 shows a typical example: when a customer applies to open a bank account, if the application is approved, the customer is sent a welcome package; otherwise, the customer is sent a rejection letter.

This behavior is modeled as an XOR-split from Get approval to Send welcome package or Send rejection letter. The effect is that of an if statement in the process.

Implementations of this widely supported pattern include control constructs (such as switch in BPEL and BPML) and explicit split elements (such as the XOR gateway in BPMN and the diamond in UML activity diagrams). The UML implementation is shown in Figure 4-5; the diamond following from Get approval splits to Send welcome package or Send rejection letter.

This pattern is related to Parallel Split, Simple Merge, Synchronizing Merge, Multi-Merge, Discriminator.

Simple Merge

The intent of the Simple Merge pattern is that several exclusive conditional paths converge on a single activity, which starts executing when the one chosen path completes. The pattern is also known as XOR-join.

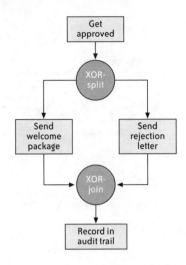

FIGURE 4-4. *Exclusive Choice and Simple Merge in a process opening a bank account*

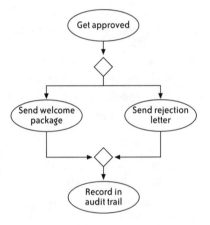

FIGURE 4-5. *UML activity diagram for Exclusive Choice and Simple Merge in a bank account opening process*

A simple merge is the endpoint—the XOR-join—of a process split started by an exclusive choice, which might be considered in programming terms as the end of an if statement. Any process that uses conditional processing requires a simple merge. The XOR-join shown in Figure 4-4 merges the paths containing activities Send welcome package and Send rejection letter into a single path in which Record in audit trail is executed.

In languages in which conditional processing is modeled as a control structure (for example, switch in BPEL and BPMN), the control structure itself manages the merge (for example, when the switch in BPEL completes, its selected case is guaranteed to have completed.) In languages in which the merge requires an explicit join element (such as the XOR gateway in BPMN and the diamond in UML activity diagrams), the join element performs the merge. In Figure 4-5, the diamond pointed to by Send welcome package and Send rejection letter is a simple merge; the subsequent Record in audit trail executes once the chosen activity completes.

This pattern is related to Synchronization, Exclusive Choice, Synchronizing Merge, Multi-Merge, Discriminator.

Advanced Branch and Join Patterns

The majority of BPM products and specifications support the basic and/or–split/join patterns described in the "Basic Patterns" section. Less well supported, but equally important, are the advanced branch and join patterns described in this section. The P4 has identified four patterns in this category: Multi-Choice, Synchronizing Merge, Multi-Merge, and the Discriminator and N-out-of-M-Join.

Multi-Choice

The intent of the Multi-Choice pattern is to choose one or more parallel branches, in which each branch is taken only if it satisfies a particular condition. The pattern is also known as Inclusive OR-split.

The Multi-Choice pattern describes the forking of a process to multiple branches where each fork is based on a condition that is known only at runtime. Multi-Choice is sometimes known as the OR-split; it differs from the Exclusive Choice pattern considered earlier, which is also known as the exclusive-OR- or XOR-split, by allowing more than one path to be spawned; exclusive choice selects exactly one direction. The P4 example, shown in Figure 4-6, describes the actions required in the aftermath of a building fire.

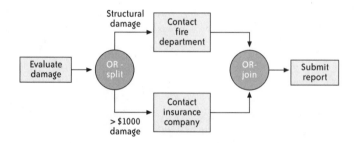

FIGURE 4-6. *The Multi-Choice and Synchronizing Merge patterns for a fire investigation process*

Either the insurance company or the fire department, or both, must be contacted. The choice is based on conditions specific to the fire; the fire department is contacted if there is structural damage to the building, and the insurance company is contacted if the estimated damaged exceeds a particular dollar value.

Multi-Choice is easy to represent in BPMN, as Figure 4-7 shows.

FIGURE 4-7. *The Multi-Choice and Synchronizing Merge patterns in BPMN for a fire investigation process*

A special inclusive OR gateway symbol (a diamond with an inner circle) with outbound conditional sequence links models the behavior compactly. More work is required in the BPEL and BPML implementations. In BPML, the only viable approach is to run multiple switch activities inside of an all (that is, multiple exclusive ORs in parallel) In BPEL, the behavior can be modeled with guarded links in a flow activity.

This pattern is related to Parallel Split, Exclusive Choice, Synchronizing Merge, Multi-Merge, Discriminator.

Synchronizing Merge

The intent of the Synchronizing Merge pattern is to join branches spawned by a Multi-Choice. In other words, it waits for all of the active paths in a parallel structure to complete. This pattern is also known as Inclusive OR-join.

Continuing the example provided in the Multi-Choice pattern, in the wake of a building fire, once all third parties have been contacted (that is, the fire department, the insurance company, or both), a report must be submitted to the company. This is depicted in Figure 4-6. The Synchronizing Merge pattern captures this scenario.

Though the idea is intuitive, many BPM products lack support for this pattern because of the thorny implementation difficulties of tracking which branch was actually executed. In the fire investigation example, the requirement is that the report be submitted exactly once; but without the right conceptual model, this requirement is hard to meet. Languages that use the Petri net conception of token passing to model control flow fare well here. In BPMN, the inclusive OR gateway handles both splits and joins, as shown in Figure 4-7; the BPMN uses tokens to explain how the gateway keeps track of the active branches.

BPEL uses the principle of dead path elimination, another Petri-net-inspired concept, to solve the problem. Though the activity Submit report requires only one of the Contact fire department and Contact insurance company activities to run, BPEL's control flow semantics prevent Submit report from executing until its knows the results of *both*. If one of these activities does not run, because its condition was not met, it passes through immediately to Submit report, as if it had run. For example, if the damage was structural but less than $1,000 in cost, Contact insurance company completes immediately, and Submit report waits for Contact fire department to execute. The mechanics of dead path elimination are examined in detail in Chapters 3 and 5.

This pattern is related to Synchronization, Simple Merge, Multi-Choice, Multi-Merge, Discriminator.

Multi-Merge

Where synchronizing merge waits for all incoming branches to complete before continuing, the Multi-Merge pattern allows each incoming branch to continue independently of the others, enabling multiple threads of execution through the remainder of the process. For example, when concurrent activities A and B are multi-merged into C, the possible combinations of execution are: ABCC, ACBC, BACC, and BCAC. This pattern is also known as Uncontrolled Join.

Ostensibly awkward and undesirable, Multi-Merge is useful (as the P4 argue) in cases where "two or more parallel branches share the same ending".* The pattern facilitates common logic for those branches upon completion. In a process that permits simultaneous auditing and processing of an

---

*   W. M. P. van der Aalst, A. H. M ter Hofstede, B. Kiepuszewski, and A. P. Barrios, "Workflow Patterns," Technical report, Eindhoven University of Technology, Eindhoven, 2003, *Distributed and Parallel Databases*, 14(1):5–51, 2003, p. 13.

application, as illustrated in Figure 4-8, each independent action should be followed by a Close case activity.

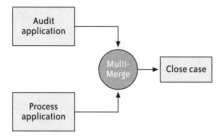

FIGURE 4-8. *The Multi-Merge pattern*

BPMN's implementation, shown in Figure 4-9, is the simplest.

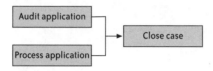

FIGURE 4-9. *The Multi-Merge pattern in BPMN*

Because there is no join of Audit application and Process application, the process allows each to transition independently to Close case.

Most other languages studied in this book, including BPEL and BPML, are stumped by this pattern, because they do not allow the same activity to be executed by separate threads. The approach shown in Figure 4-10 is a compromise: have each path run its own copy of Close case.

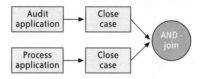

FIGURE 4-10. *An alternative Multi-Merge implementation*

This pattern is related to Synchronization, Simple Merge, Synchronizing Merge, Multi-Choice, Parallel Split, Multiple Instances Without Synchronization, Discriminator.

Discriminator and N-Out-of-M Join

In the Discriminator pattern, when multiple parallel branches converge at a given join point, exactly one of the branches is allowed to continue on in the process, based on a condition evaluated at runtime; the remaining branches are blocked. Discriminator is a special case of the N-Out-of-M Join pattern, where *M* parallel branches meet at a point of convergence and only the first *N* are let through. This pattern is also known as Complex Join.

The need for this pattern arises when only a subset of assigned work is required. In the 2-of-3-join example shown in Figure 4-11, to obtain a security clearance, an applicant must meet two of three conditions.

FIGURE 4-11. *2-of-3 join for a security clearance project*

When two of the corresponding activities complete, the activity `Grant security clearance` triggers, and the third activity is discarded.

Impressively, BPMN supports these patterns out of the box. The `complex` gateway (diamond with interior asterisk) in Figure 4-12 is configured with special routing rules for the 2-of-3 logic.

FIGURE 4-12. *BPMN 2-of-3 join for the security clearance project*

However, most other languages lack a clean solution. In BPEL, one approach would be to put the three activities in a `flow`, and, after each completes, check if another activity has already completed; if so, use the Cancel Activity pattern to cancel the third activity, thereby completing the `flow` with two completed activities.

This pattern is related to Synchronization, Simple Merge, Synchronizing Merge, Multi-Merge, Multiple Instances with Runtime Knowledge, Multiple Instances without Runtime Knowledge.

Structural Patterns

So-called "structural" patterns are actually recipes for unstructured design practices such as GOTO-style jumps and contending termination points. However, as the P4 explain, for some processes, the use of these patterns makes the design more readable and understandable. There are two structural patterns: Arbitrary Cycles and Implicit Termination.

Arbitrary Cycles

The Arbitrary Cycles pattern repeats an activity or a set of activities by cycling back to it in the process. This pattern is also known as GOTO or loop.

Most process languages and vendor implementations allow only block-structured loops such as `while-do` or `do-while`, whose entry, exit, and jump-back points are defined according to rigorous proof rules. The logic of some processes, such as the loan process shown in Figure 4-13, requires the looser approach of goto.

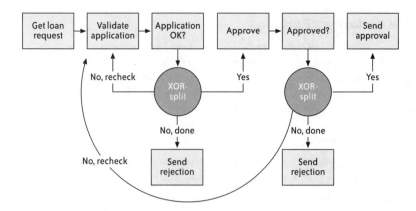

FIGURE 4-13. *The Arbitrary Cycles pattern for a loan application*

The loan process is designed to retry the Validate application activity not only when validation fails, but also downstream when something in the application prevents approval. This logic is difficult to model with a structured loop.

BPMN supports this pattern because it permits sequence flow to connect to upstream activities. BPEL does not support the pattern: its only loop is the structured while activity, and the flow activities does not permit cycles.

This pattern is related to the Multiple Instances patterns.

Implicit Termination

In most languages, a process, even if it spawns a complex tree of concurrent branches, has exactly one exit point into which all possible paths converge. The Implicit Termination pattern is a relaxation of the design rules: the process completes when the activities on each of its branches complete.

Implicit Termination helps reduce clutter and complexity in a process by relaxing the restriction for a single exit point. If a process has *N* branches, it completes only when each of the N branches completes; there is no need to join the branches prior to completion. In Figure 4-14, for example, the process spawns multiple parallel instances of the Process record activity. ("MI no sync" is one of the Multiple Instances patterns described in the next section.)

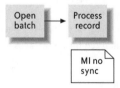

FIGURE 4-14. *The Implicit Termination pattern*

The desired behavior is to let the process continue until each instance completes. An explicit endpoint would necessitate complicated merge logic.

BPEL's flow activity supports implicit termination because it does not require its network of activities to converge on a single exit point; the flow completes when all of its activities complete.

This pattern is related to Interleaved parallel routing (but very faintly).

Multiple Instances Patterns

In the patterns discussed in this section, multiple instances of an activity run concurrently. A given language's support for these patterns requires support for the ability to spawn multiple instances, and, in three cases, the ability to perform a synchronizing merge of the branches. The four Multiple Instances (MI) patterns are: Without Synchronization, With Design-Time Knowledge, With Runtime Knowledge, and Without Runtime Knowledge.

Without Synchronization

The intent of the Without Synchronization pattern is to perform multiple concurrent instances of an activity but let each run on its own with no overall synchronization.

A batch process, for example, reads a large data file record by record and spawns a subprocess to handle each record. The implementation, as suggested by the P4, is to perform a parallel split in a loop.* Figure 4-15 illustrates this concept.

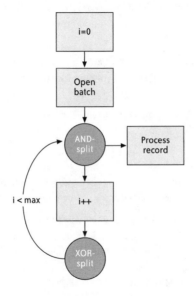

FIGURE 4-15. *The Multiple Instances Without Synchronization pattern*

BPMN supports this pattern out of the box; the activity is configured to loop in multiple parallel instances (denoted by two parallel bars marked inside the activity's box) with the flow condition set to none, as shown in Figure 4-16.

In BPEL, the behavior can be achieved by invoking an asynchronous process in multiple iterations of a while loop.

This pattern is related to other Multiple Instances patterns, Parallel Split, Multi-Merge.

---

* W. M. P. van der Aalst, A. H. M ter Hofstede, B. Kiepuszewski, and A. P. Barrios, "Workflow Patterns," Technical report, Eindhoven University of Technology, Eindhoven, 2003, *Distributed and Parallel Databases*, 14(1):5–51, 2003, p. 21.

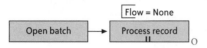

FIGURE 4-16. *The Multiple Instance Without Synchronization pattern in BPMN*

With Design-Time Knowledge

The intent of the With Design-Time Knowledge pattern is to perform N multiple concurrent instances of an activity, where N is a constant at runtime. In addition, it joins these instances before continuing with the remainder of the process.

This pattern is similar to a basic AND-split and -join, except that the activity to be performed is always the same type. In the requisition process in Figure 4-17, exactly three authorizations are required; each is performed in parallel but needs to be merged with the others before the requisition can continue.

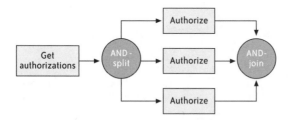

FIGURE 4-17. *The Multiple Instances With Design-Time Knowledge pattern for authorizations*

In BPMN, this requisition activity is configured to loop in multiple parallel instances with the flow condition set to `all`, as shown in Figure 4-18. In BPEL, the easiest approach is to place the three requisition activities in a `flow` activity.

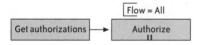

FIGURE 4-18. *BPMN implementation of the Multiple Instances With Design-Time Knowledge pattern for authorizations*

This pattern is related to other Multiple Instances patterns, Parallel Split, Synchronization.

With Runtime Knowledge

The intent of the With Runtime Knowledge pattern is to perform N multiple concurrent instances of an activity, where the value of N is known at runtime before the Multiple Instances loop is started. In addition, it joins these instances before continuing with the remainder of the process.

In terms of its observable execution behavior, this pattern is similar to the design-time pattern: N instances of an activity are run in parallel and synchronized. The motivation is the same in each case. The implementation, however, is far more challenging.

Of the approaches described by the P4, the simplest is shown in Figure 4-19.

In this example, a customer has ordered a number of books from an online store. The process must ensure the availability of each book before processing the order. Hence multiple instances of the activity Check availability are required, and the number of instances is not known until the

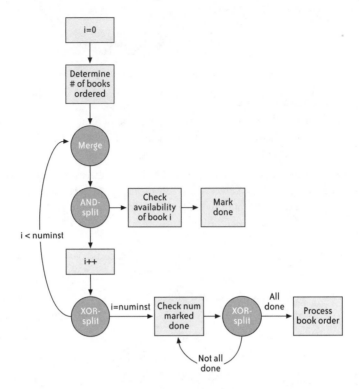

FIGURE 4-19. *The Multiple Instances With Runtime Knowledge pattern*

customer has placed the order. The process implements a loop that spawns exactly the right number of `Check availability` instances. When each instance completes, it marks itself as done (setting a flag in a table or a process variable). The activity `Check num marked done` determines whether all of the instances have completed; it repeats this check in a loop before finally transitioning to the activity `Process book order`.

None of the leading process languages has a cleaner solution than this. Implementations in BPEL, BPML, and BPMN should follow this approach.

This pattern is related to other Multiple Instances patterns, Parallel Split, Synchronization.

Without Runtime Knowledge

The intent of the Without Runtime Knowledge pattern is to perform multiple concurrent instances of an activity, where the number of instances is not known until some point during the actual processing of the instances. In addition, it joins these instances before continuing with the remainder of the process.

The motivation is the same as that of the two preceding synchronized Multiple Instances patterns. The fact that the number of instances to run is evaluated as late as possible in processing is an implementation consideration. A typical example occurs in the processing of an insurance claim: the number of eyewitness reports required to complete the claim varies all the way through; the stopping condition is evaluated in the loop.

The implementation is similar to the case in which the number of instances is known at runtime, except the governing loop is not a `for` loop that indexes over the required number of instances but a while loop that on each iteration executes a task that reevaluates the number of instances required. Figure 4-20 illustrates this pattern.

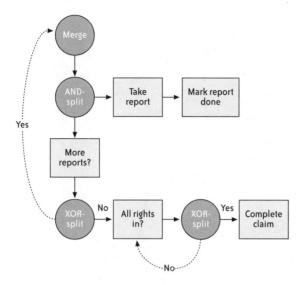

FIGURE 4-20. *The Multiple Instances Not Known At Runtime pattern*

Multiple instances of Take report are performed; the activity More reports evaluates whether to continue the loop; All reports in waits for the completion of all instances before allowing the claim to be completed.

This pattern is related to other Multiple Instance patterns, Parallel Split, Synchronization.

State-Based Patterns

State-based patterns apply to processes that are largely event-driven and spend most of the time waiting for an event to trigger the next activity. There are three state-based patterns: Deferred Choice, Interleaved Parallel Routing, and Milestone.

Deferred Choice

The intent of Deferred Choice is similar to the basic Exclusive Choice pattern, in that a decision is made to follow one of multiple paths, except the decision is not made immediately but is instead deferred until an event occurs. This pattern is also known as Event Choice and Pick.

Processes that are event-driven are likely to use this pattern. A very common scenario is to wait for either a positive or negative result to a request. The process, shown in Figure 4-21, is fairly common.

In this example, the process is waiting for either an acceptance or rejection result to an earlier request. Each event leads to a distinct execution path: acceptance means sending a welcome package; rejection means sending a rejection letter.

Though some older vendors lack support for deferred choice, as the P4 point out, most contemporary languages have explicit control structures for it. BPEL uses a pick activity to listen for exactly

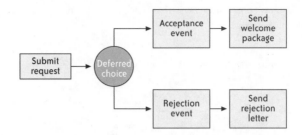

FIGURE 4-21. *The Deferred Choice pattern for acceptance or rejection*

one of several inbound service events. BPMN has a special exclusive OR gateway (the diamond with a star in the middle in Figure 4-22) for events.

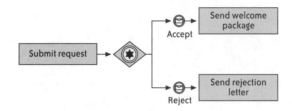

FIGURE 4-22. *The BPMN implementation of the Deferred Choice pattern for acceptance or rejection*

This pattern is related to Exclusive Choice.

Interleaved Parallel Routing

The intent of the Interleaved Parallel Routing pattern is that several activities are to be performed *in sequence* (not in parallel, as the name of the pattern suggests), but the order of execution is arbitrary and is not known at design time. This pattern is also known as Ad Hoc Process.

Though not as prevalent as other process patterns, Interleaved Parallel Routing does occur in cases where several activities must be executed but a specific ordering is impossible. A good example is given by Dumas and ter Hofstede:* an applicant to the army must take three tests—optical, medical, and dental—one after the other but in any order; when the applicant completes one test, the next one to take is determined by the availability of doctors. The desired model is depicted in Figure 4-23.

A naïve implementation of this case, as shown in Figure 4-24, would contain six execution paths— one for each permutation of the three tests.

The initial three-way split (optical, medical, or dental) creates three branches, each of which in turn bifurcates (that is, splits into two) to branches representing the remaining two choices; for example, the optical path splits into the medical and dental paths. The three-way split and the three two-way splits are *deferred choices* because they require an event—a signal that a doctor is now free—to drive the choice.

---

* M. Dumas and A. H. M. ter Hofstede, "UML Activity Diagrams as a Workflow Specification Language," in the *Proceedings of the International Conference on the Unified Modeling Language*, Springer-Verlag, Toronto, Canada, October 2001, p. 10.

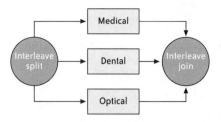

FIGURE 4-23. *The Interleave pattern*

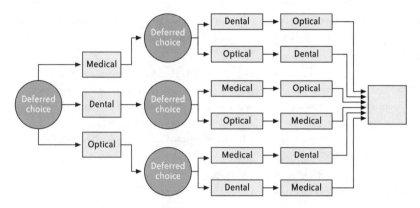

FIGURE 4-24. *Naïve implementation of Interleave*

Most BPM vendors and standards lack support for interleaved parallel routing. BPMN and BPEL, with ad hoc processes and serialized scopes, respectively, offer elegant solutions to the problem. In the BPEL solution, the process splits into parallel paths but uses a form of mutual exclusion to ensure that the paths run serially. In the following code sample, adapted from the P4's pattern analysis of BPEL,* the BPEL flow construct runs the scope activities optical, dental, and medical in parallel:

```
<flow>
    <scope name="optical" variableAccessSerializable="yes">
        <sequence>
            write to variable C
            run optical activity
            write to variable C
        </sequence>
    </scope>
    <scope name="dental" variableAccessSerializable="yes">
        <sequence>
            write to variable C
            run dental activity
            write to variable C
        </sequence>
    </scope>
    <scope name="medical" variableAccessSerializable="yes">
        <sequence>
            write to variable C
            run medical activity
            write to variable C
```

* P. Wohed, W. M. P van der Aalst, M. Dumas, and A. H. M ter Hofstede, "Pattern Based Analysis of BPEL4WS," QUT Technical Report, FIT-TR-2002-04, Queensland University of Technology, Brisbane, Australia, 2002.

```
        </sequence>
      </scope>
  </flow>
```

Mutual exclusion is enforced by having each activity flag itself as variableAccessSerializable and reference a shared process variable C. While one activity is running, the others are blocked. The order of execution is unpredictable: it can take any of the six permutations of optical, dental, and medical, but each permutation runs sequentially.

This pattern is related to Deferred Choice.

Milestone

The intent of the Milestone pattern is that an activity can be performed only when a certain milestone is reached and cannot be performed after the milestone expires. This pattern is quite distinctive and has no other names.

The most unusual and conceptually difficult of the P4 patterns, the Milestone pattern describes the scenario in which an activity can be executed only after the occurrence of an enabling event but before the occurrence of a disabling event. The activity can be performed multiple times, in fact. For example, in an auction, a bidder can place bids at any time between the start and end of bidding. A buyer can cancel an order up until the order has been shipped. Scenarios such as this are not rare; this pattern benefits designers who face them.

None of the languages considered in this book has an obvious solution. In one of the approaches described by the P4, shown in Figure 4-25, the enabling event (Open bidding) is followed by a deferred choice, with conditional paths determined by the intermediate activity (Bid) and the disabling event (Close bidding).

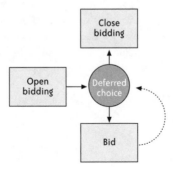

FIGURE 4-25. *Milestone pattern for an auction bid*

If the intermediate activity occurs, it loops back to the deferred choice; if the disabling event fires, it starts its own path, preventing any occurrence or recurrence of the intermediate activity. In the BPEL implementation, the deferred choice is a pick activity that resides in a while loop. If the intermediate event occurs, the loop continues with another iteration; if the disabling event occurs, the loop breaks.

This pattern is related to Deferred Choice.

Cancellation Patterns

Every process designer needs a clever strategy to cancel a process at any point during its execution. A 25-step insurance claim process, for instance, must terminate as soon as the subscriber calls to rescind the claim. The hard way to solve this problem is to add cancellation checks at each of the 25 steps; more desirable is a single check or action that covers the execution of the entire process. There are two types of cancellation patterns: Cancel Activity and Cancel Case.

Cancel Activity

The intent of the Cancel Activity pattern is to stop the execution of a particular process activity on a cancellation trigger. This pattern is also known as Kill Activity.

The Cancel Activity pattern is useful to abort a long-running or suspended activity (e.g., a manual approval that has been ignored by its owner), or to reroute a process to an escalation path. The former case is shown in Figure 4-26.

FIGURE 4-26. *The Cancel Activity pattern*

Between Step X and Step Y sits a long-running activity called Long step. To enable the cancellation of Long step during its execution, a deferred choice is established between Long step and a Cancellation event. As soon as deferred choice completes, Step Y is started, and the subsequent effects of the other activity are ignored.

Figure 4-27 shows a BPMN implementation of this pattern.

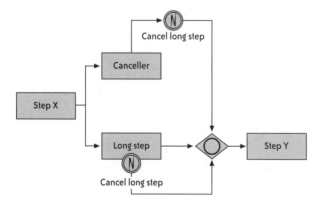

FIGURE 4-27. *A BPMN implementation of the Cancel Activity pattern*

When Step X completes, the process branches into two parallel activities: Long step and Canceller. Normally, Long step executes to completion and transitions to Step Y. But at any point during the execution of Long step, the Canceller activity can generate an exception (Cancel long step) that aborts Long step and causes it to transition immediately to Step Y. Typically the Canceller activity is event-driven: it waits, for as long as Long step is running, for a cancellation event from a user or system.

This pattern is related to Cancel Case.

Cancel Case

The intent of the Cancel Case pattern is to stop the execution of an entire process on a cancellation trigger. This pattern is also known as Kill Process.

Though most BPM vendors provide a means to cancel a process through their administration console, building the cancellation logic directly into the process code guarantees portability and enables more graceful handling. Figure 4-28 shows the basic shape of the pattern.

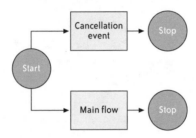

FIGURE 4-28. *The Cancel Case pattern*

When the process is started, it splits into separate paths for the main flow and receipt of a Cancellation event. If the Cancellation event arrives while the main flow is executing, it terminates the whole process.

The BPEL implementation is shown in the following code sample. At the process scope, an event handler is defined that listens for a Cancellation event; when the event arrives, the handler terminates the process:

```
<process>
   <eventHandlers>
      <eventHandler name="cancelEvent" . . .>
         <terminate/>
      </eventHandler>
   </eventHandlers>
   <sequence>
      . . . <!-- main flow -->
   </sequence>
</process>
```

The BPMN approach is shown in Figure 4-29.

The logic is similar to Cancel Activity, except that here the Canceller runs in parallel to the Main flow of the process, rather than to just a single activity. If the Canceller executes, it transitions to a stop event, which stops the entire process, regardless of the progress of the Main flow.

This pattern is related to Cancel Activity.

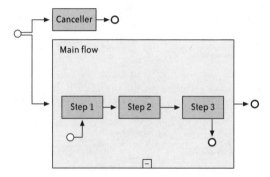

FIGURE 4-29. *A BPMN implementation of the Cancel Case pattern*

Yet Another Workflow Language (YAWL)

As part of their work on patterns, the P4 rated 15 vendor offerings (including Staffware, SAP/R3, MQ Workflow, and Lotus Domino Workflow), determining whether each vendor's product directly supports each pattern, indirectly supports each pattern with sufficient coding, or lacks support for a pattern completely. The results were disheartening: every vendor has spotty pattern coverage, most failing to support (even indirectly) half of the patterns. Even worse, among the vendors there is no conceptual consistency; every product has its own notation and execution semantics.

Motivated by dismal industry support and the absence of a universal theory of workflow, P4 authors van der Aalst and ter Hofstede created a graphical process language called Yet Another Workflow Language, or YAWL, that is rigged to support all 20 P4 patterns. A YAWL process is a Petri net extended with symbols supporting AND, OR, and XOR splits and joins, as well as multiple activity instances. The symbols are shown in Figure 4-30.*

Figure 4-31 depicts the YAWL solution to two multiple instance patterns. In this example, some number of witnesses, at least one but no more than 10, are interviewed for the processing of an insurance claim.†

In Case (a) in Figure 4-31, the number is not known until runtime; in Case (b), the number is not known even at runtime, and in certain cases, might need to be greater than 10! The notation [1,10,inf,fixed] in process_witness_statements in Case (a) means that between 1 and 10 instances of that activity are required and that the number is fixed at runtime; in Case (b), [1,10,inf,var] means between 1 and 10 instance are required and that this number is variable (var).

*   W. M. P. van der Aalst and A. H. M ter Hofstede, "Workflow Patterns: On The Expressive Power of (Petri-net-based) Workflow Languages," in K. Jensen (editor), *Proceedings of the Fourth Workshop on the Practical Use of Coloured Petri Nets and CPM Tools (CPN 2002)*, volume 560 of DAIMI, pages 1–20, University of Aarhus, Denmark, August 2002, p. 11.

†   Ibid, p. 13.

FIGURE 4-30. *YAWL symbols*

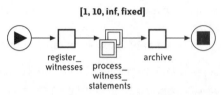

[1, 10, inf, fixed]

register_
witnesses

process_
witness_
statements

archive

(a) A workflow processing between 1 and 10 witness statements
without the possibility to add witnesses after registration.

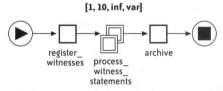

[1, 10, inf, var]

register_
witnesses

process_
witness_
statements

archive

(a) A workflow processing an arbitrary number of witnesses with
the possibility to add new batches of witnesses.

FIGURE 4-31. *YAWL examples for Multiple Instance patterns*

YAWL is interesting to read about, but it will never claim an actual production success story. First, standards to which current vendors are building, including BPMN and BPEL, are about as expressive as YAWL anyway. (White's article demonstrates the relative ease of coding the patterns in BPMN and UML activity diagrams.*) Second, there is more to a process language than support for patterns. Adopters care much more about level of difficulty, expressiveness, system integration capabilities, business analyst savvy, and

---

*   Stephen White, "Process Modeling Notations and Workflow Patterns," *BPTrends*, March 2004.

other intangibles than having an out-of-the-box solution for, say, interleaved parallel routing. Analogously, in the object-oriented world, no one has bothered to invent a language whose main purpose is to support all of the Gang of Four patterns; Java, C++, and Smalltalk dominate, even without perfect GoF pattern support.

Additional Patterns

As discussed previously, the P4 patterns are oriented towards control flow. Control flow is only one aspect of process design; the designer can also benefit from patterns describing how to communicate with external partners (communication patterns), and how to manage recurring human workflow scenarios (human workflow patterns).

Communication Patterns

Figure 4-32 illustrates a variety of common communication scenarios in a process.

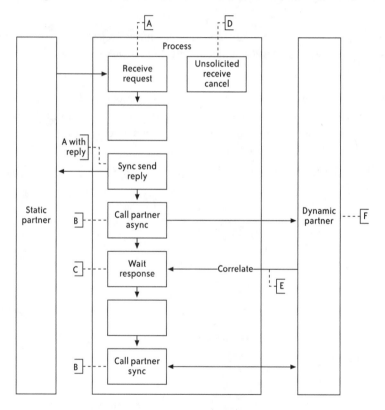

FIGURE 4-32. *Various communication patterns*

The diagram reveals a number of common patterns:

Receive Request

A process triggered by an inbound service request, as indicated by A in the figure. In BPEL, the pattern is implemented with the receive activity. If the caller expects a synchronous response, use the reply activity.

Call Partner Service

A process sends a message to the partner's service. In BPEL, the pattern is implemented in with the `invoke` activity. Synchronous and asynchronous variants are supported, as in the two steps labeled B in the diagram.

Wait for Response

A process explicitly waits for a specific event or set of events, as in the step labeled C in the diagram. In BPEL, implement using an intermediate `receive` or `pick`.

Unsolicited Event

A process responds to an unexpected event (e.g., cancellation request), as in the step labeled D of the diagram. In BPEL, implement using an `eventHandler`.

Correlate Request and Response

A process filters an inbound service request to match conversational identifiers, as indicated by E in the diagram. Implement using correlation or WS-Addressing.

Dynamic Partner

A process determines the endpoint of a partner at runtime, such as the partner indicated by F in the diagram. In BPEL, implement using `assign` to declare endpoint information at runtime.

In addition to these patterns, the Publish to Multiple Subscribers pattern (also known as Publish/Subscribe, or Pub/sub) is another common communication pattern. In this model, a process routes an event to all known subscriber services that have registered an interest. Although this pattern is not built in to any of the process languages, Figure 4-33 shows one possible implementation, in which a process queries a subscriber repository to get a list of endpoints of interested parties.

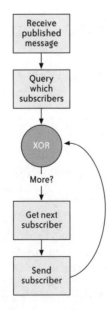

FIGURE 4-33. *The Publish/Subscribe process*

Human Workflow

Three common patterns emerge when integrating human workflow into a BPM system: Prioritization, Escalation, and Roles Compete For Task.

NOTE
A more comprehensive classification of enterprise communication patterns is provided in the book *Enterprise Application Patterns*, by Gregor Hohpe and Bobby Woolf (Addison Wesley, 2003).

In the Prioritization pattern, a manual activity is assigned an initial priority, and is reprioritized as it ages (or based on other conditions). In Escalation, a manual activity is reassigned when conditions dictate that another person or role work on it. The two patterns often occur together, as Figure 4-34 shows.

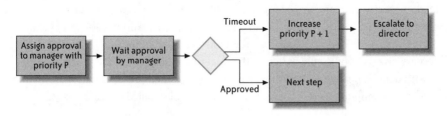

FIGURE 4-34. *Prioritization and Escalation activities*

In the example, an approval activity is assigned to the role manager with an initial priority of P. When the manager completes the activity, the process transitions to Next step. However, if after a certain duration the manager has not completed the activity, the priority is increased to P + 1, and the activity is escalated to the director role. Directors will spot the activity in the queue, notice its high priority level, and hopefully take quick action.

The second human workflow pattern, Roles Compete For Task, assigns the same task to multiple roles. The task is completed when the first role completes the task. Implementation uses the discriminator pattern, as shown in Figure 4-35. In a high-priority software support case, support, engineering, and the client account manager are assigned to the case. As soon as one resolves it, the case is closed.

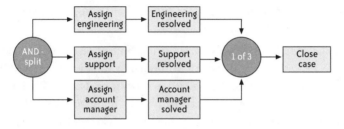

FIGURE 4-35. *Competitive task resolution*

Process Coding Standards

Process design, whether practiced by a business analyst or a developer, requires the same high standards of code quality as programming. The following guidelines can help boost quality and maintainability:

- For readability and comprehensibility, ensure that a process diagram fits on both a graphical editor screen (with no scrolling or zooming out required) and a letter-sized printed page. If it does not fit, break it into smaller subprocesses. This rule is reminiscent of the style convention in programming to keep source files to fewer than 1,000 lines, with each line restricted to 80 or fewer characters. Many development shops conduct code reviews to check for style compliance; this sense of discipline also belongs in process modeling.

- Keep the process flow coarse-grained. Process design is "programming in the large"; the boxes in a process diagram are meant to represent the major steps of the process, not detailed processing instructions (e.g., parsing messages, calculating dates, and evaluating XOR conditions). Process diagrams drawn on a whiteboard in the early stages of a BPM project are always kept simple, whereas the final production cut of the process is pregnant with detail. The key insight is to factor out fine-grained processing to subprocesses or to external components (e.g., Java code, EJBs, or DLLs) called by the process.

Summary

The main points of this chapter include the following:

- A design pattern is a solution to a common problem. The solution is published for use by the larger development community.

- The landmark book on design patterns, *Design Patterns: Elements of Reusable Object-Oriented Software*, by Gamma, Helm, Johnson, and Vlissides (the Gang of Four, or GoF) is a catalog of patterns for object-oriented design. The book has been so successful that it has permeated the thinking of almost every developer.

- To the benefit of BPM, which desperately needs well-conceived design ideas, patterns have also been published for BPM. A group consisting of van der Aalst, ter Hofstede, Kiepuszewski, and Barrios (the Process Four, or P4) has documented 20 process patterns, or arrangements of activities in a process. These patterns are divided into six categories: Basic, Advanced Split and Join, Structural, State-Based, Cancellation, and Multiple Instances.

- Disappointed that existing BPM vendors fail to implement most patterns, the P4 have invented a new process language called Yet Another Workflow Language (YAWL), which is rigged to support all patterns. YAWL is interesting, but BPMN and BPEL are almost as strong on patterns and have greater traction in the industry. Plus, pattern support is but one of many factors used to choose the right BPM solution.

- Communication and human workflow patterns are also considered, albeit in less detail than the P4 control flow patterns. Communication patterns capture basic service interactions with partners. Human workflow patterns include the escalation and prioritization of manual activities.

- Process design, whether practiced by a business analyst or a developer, requires the same high standards of code quality as programming. Two rules that boost quality and maintainability are to keep the process small enough to fit on a screen or printed page (reduce size by moving chunks of code to a subprocess) and to keep the steps of the process as coarse-grained as possible (factor out the details to external components or subprocesses).

References

1. E. Gamma, R. Helm, R. Johnson, and J. Vlissides, *Design Patterns: Elements of Reusable Object-Oriented Software*, Addison Wesley, Reading, MA, 1995.

2. M. Dumas and A. H. M. ter Hofstede, "UML Activity Diagrams as a Workflow Specification Language," in the *Proceedings of the International Conference on the Unified Modeling Language*, Springer-Verlag, Toronto, Canada, October 2001.

3. P. Wohed, W. M. P van der Aalst, M. Dumas, and A. H. M ter Hofstede, "Pattern Based Analysis of BPML (and WSCI)," QUT Technical Report, FIT-TR-2002-05, Queensland University of Technology, Brisbane, Australia, 2002.

4. P. Wohed, E. Perjons, M. Dumas, and A. H. M. ter Hofstede, "Pattern-Based Analysis of EAI Languages: The Case of the Business Modeling Language." In *Proceedings of the 5th International Conference on Enterprise Information Systems (ICEIS)*, Angers, France, April 2003.

5. G. Hohpe, B. Woolf. *Enterprise Integration Patterns: Designing, Building, and Deploying Messaging Solutions.* Addison Wesley, Reading, MA, 2003.

PART TWO STANDARDS

A detailed survey of current BPM standard models and specifications, including: BPEL; the BPMI standards (BPMN and BPEL) and the BPMI reference architecture; the WfMC standards (XPDL, WfXML, WAPI) and the WfMC reference model; web services choreography, its standards (WS-CDL, WSCI, WSCL), and the distinction between choreography and orchestration; the OMG model-driven architecture for BPM, and its RFPs for BPDM and BPRI; BPSS and collaboration; and the influence of XLANG and WSFL on BPEL.

CHAPTER FIVE

Business Process Execution Language (BPEL)

THE **BUSINESS** **PROCESS** **EXECUTION** **LANGUAGE** **FOR** **WEB** **SERVICES** (BPEL4WS, usually shortened to BPEL, which rhymes with "people") is, as its name suggests, a language for the definition and execution of business processes. Though it is not the only standard process language, BPEL is the most popular, and is beginning to saturate the process space.

There are two common ways to represent business processes: XML and notational. BPEL competes in the XML arena with BPML, XPDL, and other approaches. Notational languages include Business Process Modeling Notation (BPMN) and UML activity diagrams. Each type of representation has its merits and, as discussed in Chapter 2, a good BPM architecture requires both of them.

IBM, Microsoft, and BEA wrote the BPEL specification and subsequently handed it over to the WSBPEL technical committee of the OASIS organization (of which they are members) for standardization. The conceptual roots of BPEL coincide exactly with earlier BPM initiatives of each of the three companies: IBM's WSFL, Microsoft's XLANG and BEA's Process Definition for Java (PD4J). As discussed in Chapter 3, WSFL is based on Petri nets and XLANG uses concepts of the pi-calculus; BPEL, consequently, is a mixture of these two theories. PD4J, as discussed later in this chapter, is the basis for the Java extension to BPEL, known as BPELJ.

This chapter explores several aspects of BPEL:

- Its authors and maintainers

- How to develop a BPEL process

- Java extensions to BPEL

- BPEL's support for common BPM patterns

- A substantial example of BPEL in action

> **NOTE**
>
> OASIS, or the Organization for the Advancement of Structured Information Standards (*http://www.oasis-open.org*), is a nonprofit consortium that develops, maintains, and promotes e-business standards, including ebXML, SGML, UDDI, PKI, and BPEL. Members include Adobe, AMD, BEA, BMC, Citrix, Computer Associates, Cyclone Commerce, Dell, Documentum, EDS, Entrust, Fujitsu, FundSERV, HP, Hitachi, IBM, IDS Scheer, Intel, IONA, Microsoft, NEC, Netegrity, Nokia, Novell, Oracle, PeopleSoft, Reuters, SAP, SeeBeyond, Sun, Tibco, Verisign, Vignette, Visa, webMethods, Wells Fargo, and Xerox. The BPEL 1.1 specification is published on the corporate web sites of each of its major authors.

Anatomy of a Process

The BPEL specification* is positioned as a business process extension to existing web services standards. In the past, web services were limited to stateless interactions; BPEL and other process and choreography languages show how to build stateful, conversational business processes from web services. BPEL is a rigorous language that builds on and extends web services for interacting processes.

A BPEL process definition consists of two types of files:

- Web Services Definition Language (WSDL) files specifying the web service interfaces—partner link types, properties, port types and operations, message and part—of interest to the process, including services implemented by and called by the process. WSDL is a well-known technology with many uses besides process definition.

- BPEL files, each of which encodes in XML form the definition of a process, including its main activities, partner links, correlation sets, variables, and handlers for compensation, faults, and events.

---

* T. Andrews, M. Curbera, et al., "Business Process Execution Language for Web Services," Version 1.1. *http://www.oasis-open.org*, May 2004. Available at the following URLs: *http://dev2dev.bea.com/technologies/webservices/BPEL4WS.jsp*, *http://www-106.ibm.com/developerworks/webservices/library/ws-bpel/*, *http://msdn.microsoft.com/library/default.asp?url=/library/en-us/dnbiz2k2/html/bpel1-1.asp*, *http://ifr.sap.com/bpel4ws/*, *http://www.siebel.com/bpel*.

When combined, the WSDL and the process definition form a business control flow that can act as an interface with external parties through web services. In a sense, the main steps in a process—the ones that drive the flow—are its service touchpoints, represented by receive, pick, invoke, and reply activities. The most rigid rule of BPEL programming is that a process must begin with a receive or pick activity, implying that a process must start by being called as a service of a particular type. Thereafter, the process's logic is less constrained; it does what is requires to meet its internal business requirements and its public message interchange agreements.

Figure 5-1 depicts a BPEL travel agency process and its surroundings in a typical BPEL architecture.

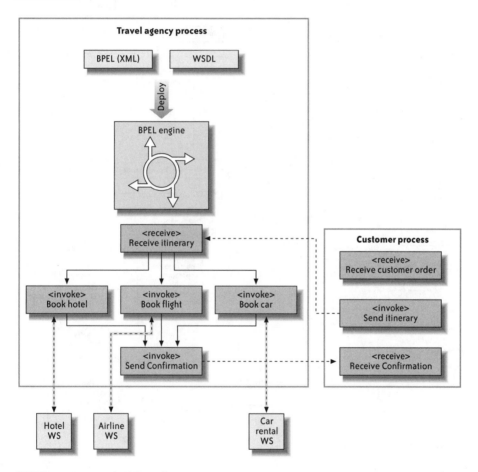

FIGURE 5-1. *Anatomy of a BPEL travel agency process*

The source code is a BPEL XML file and one or more WSDLs. The source is deployed on a BPEL execution engine, which oversees the running of the process logic. The travel agency process starts by receiving a customer's itinerary. It then attempts hotel, flight, and rental car bookings, and finally sends a confirmation to the customer. A corresponding customer process works in concert with the travel agency process; actions in one trigger the other. Interactions with the booking systems of the hotel, airline, and car rental agency are web service-driven, but, transparently to the travel agency application, the booking services are traditionally stateless, not process-oriented. (Chapter 2 develops a comprehensive architectural model featuring a BPEL runtime engine. Chapters 10 and 11 demonstrate the development, deployment, and testing of BPEL processes on the Oracle BPEL Process Manager platform.)

Figure 5-2 shows a UML class diagram of BPEL's object model, and the overall structure of a process.

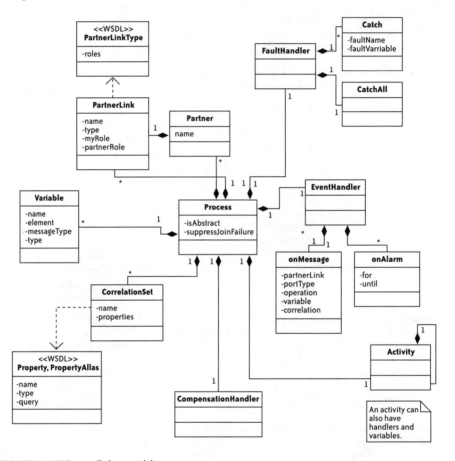

FIGURE 5-2. *BPEL overall object model*

Figure 5-3, another UML diagram, describes the types of process activities.

Table 5-1 summarizes the objects depicted in Figure 5-4.

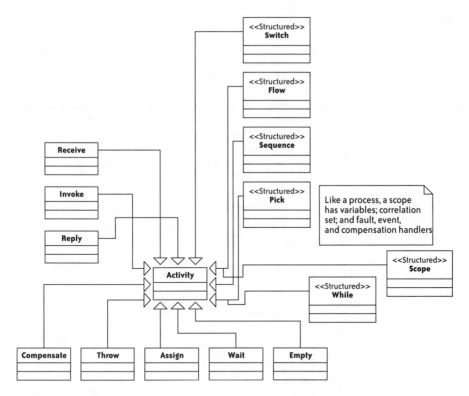

FIGURE 5-3. *BPEL activity object model*

TABLE 5-1. *BPEL objects*

Name	Description
Process	A business process containing one or more of the subsequent objects.
Variable	A variable for use in a process or a scope, with a type based on a WSDL message type, an XSD element, or an XSD basic type. A process or scope can have zero or more variables.
Property, Property Alias (from WSDL)	A property is a token of data from a WSDL message. A property alias is an XPath expression to find the value of the property.
CorrelationSet	A set of one or more properties used to correlate message data with the conversational state of the process. A process or scope can have zero or one correlation sets.
Partner Link Type (from WSDL)	A mapping of web service port types to partner roles.
Partner Link	A process' declaration of which partner links it supports and, for each, which role it performs and which role its partner is expected to perform. A process can have one or more partner links.
Partner	Not commonly used; a set of partner links. A process can have zero or more partners.

TABLE 5-1. *BPEL objects (continued)*

Name	Description
Compensation Handler	An activity, containing cancellation or rewind logic, to be executed in case a scope or process that has already completed needs to be reverted back to its initial state. A process or scope can have zero or one compensation handlers.
Fault Handler, Catch, CatchAll	A set of handlers to process exceptions, based on fault type, in a process or scope. A process or scope can have zero or one fault handlers; there is no limit on the number of catches within the handler.
EventHandler, onMessage, onAlarm	A set of handles to process unsolicited events, based on event type, in a process or scope. A process or scope can have zero or one event handlers; there is no limit on the number of event detectors within the handler.
Activity	Base type for a BPEL activity. A process or scope has exactly one activity, though that activity can be a structured activity that is broken down into smaller pieces.
Receive	An activity that receives a SOAP message on an inbound web service.
Invoke	An activity that calls a partner's web service, either synchronously or asynchronously.
Reply	An activity that returns a synchronous reply to an inbound web service call triggered by a receive.
Compensate	An activity that triggers the compensation of a given scope or process.
Throw	An activity that generates a fault, triggering the fault handler for the given process or scope.
Assign	An activity that copies data from one variable to another.
Wait	An activity that pauses the process for a specified duration, or until a specified time.
Empty	No-op. Performs no action.
Switch	An exclusive-OR structure. Executes the activity for the conditional case that evaluates to true.
Flow	A distinctive parallel activity execution structure with support for directed graph-based flow.
Sequence	Runs a set of activities sequentially.
Pick	Waits for exactly one of several events (including timeouts) to occur. Executes the activity corresponding to the first event that fires.
While	Runs an activity in a loop for as long as a given XPath-valued expression is true.
Scope	An activity with its own set of handlers, variables, and correlation sets.

BPEL Example

The best way to learn a language is to dive into it.This section provides an extended example to illustrate some of the main elements of the BPEL language. The BPEL process in Example 5-1, which is similar to that presented in Chapter 10 (and also described in the discussion of state machines in Chapter 3), manages the processing of an insurance claim.

EXECUTABLE AND ABSTRACT PROCESSES

A BPEL process can be executable or abstract. An *executable process* is built to actually run in a process engine. An *abstract process* is a protocol definition or an account of the publicly observable behavior of a given participant. Though in this book we use BPEL strictly for executable purposes, the motivation for the abstract approach is important to understand. WSDL in isolation describes only the static structure of a partner's interface: its inbound and outbound services. An abstract process, in contrast, is behavioral; it describes the control flow exhibited by the partner as its interfaces with its partners. A BPEL abstract process, in this regard, serves the same purpose as a WSCI interface (described in Chapter 8).

The BPEL code for an abstract process resembles that of an executable process, except that the abstract process contains only activities that model public interaction or drive control flow; an abstract process can use process data but only for the evaluation of conditions that affect control flow.

Abstract processes set the attribute abstractProcess="yes" in their process elements.

EXAMPLE 5-1. *BPEL example: InsuranceClaim.bpel*

```
1   <process name="InsuranceClaim"
2       targetNamespace="http://acm.org/samples"
3       suppressJoinFailure="yes"
4       xmlns:tns=http://acm.org/samples
5       xmlns=http://schemas.xmlsoap.org/ws/2003/03/business-process/
6       xmlns:xsd=http://www.w3.org/2001/XMLSchema
7       xmlns:addressing=http://schemas.xmlsoap.org/ws/2003/03/addressing
8       xmlns:bpws="http://schemas.xmlsoap.org/ws/2003/03/business-process/">
9
10      <!--
11          Partners in the process:
12            client - app that can initiate and kill
13            worklist - service that manages manual activities
14      -->
15      <partnerLinks>
16          <!--
17          <partnerLink name="client" partnerLinkType="tns:InsuranceClaim"
18              myRole="InsuranceClaimProvider"/>
19          <partnerLink name="worklist" partnerLinkType="task:TaskManager"
20              partnerRole="TaskManager" myRole="TaskManagerRequester"/>
21      </partnerLinks>
22
23      <!-- Process-level variables -->
24      <variables>
25          <variable name="status" type="xsd:string"/>
26          <variable name="initiateMsg" messageType="tns:InsuranceClaimMsg"/>
27          <variable name="killEv" messageType="tns:InsuranceClaimMsg"/>
```

EXAMPLE 5-1. *BPEL example: InsuranceClaim.bpel (continued)*

```
28              <variable name="taskResponse" messageType="task:taskMessage"/>
29          </variables>
30
31          <!-- Message correlation to be performed on the ClaimID field -->
32          <correlationSets>
33              <correlationSet name="claim" properties="tns:claimID"/>
34          </correlationSets>
35
36          <!-- Catch any errors and fix manually -->
37          <faultHandlers>
38              <catchAll>
39                  <empty name="PlaceholderForManualFix"/>
40              </catchAll>
41          </faultHandlers>
42
43          <!-- Globally receive a kill event (correlated with the claim ID from the
44              original initate) and terminate the process. -->
45          <eventHandlers>
46              <onMessage partnerLink="client" portType="tns:InsuranceClaim"
47                  operation="kill" variable="killEv">
48                  <correlations>
49                      <correlation set="claim" initiate="no"/>
50                  </correlations>
51                  <sequence>
52                      <empty/><!-- Do something, like notify internal systems of kill -->
53                      <terminate name="killClaim"/>
54                  </sequence>
55              </onMessage>
56          </eventHandlers>
57
58          <sequence>
59
60              <!-- We start with a receive activity: get the initiate message.  Will
61                  correlate on claim set defined earlier
62              -->
63              <receive partnerLink="client" portType="tns:InsuranceClaim"
64                  operation="initiate" variable="initiateMsg" createInstance="yes"
65                  name="initiateEvent">
66                  <correlations>
67                      <correlation set="claim" initiate="yes"/>
68                  </correlations>
69              </receive>
70
71              <!-- Let an agent evaluate it.  Call worklist partner to do this -->
72              <invoke name="evalClaim" partnerLink="worklist"  portType="task:TaskManager"
73                  operation="evalClaim" inputVariable="initiateMsg"/>
74
75              <!-- Get either the response or a timeout -->
76              <pick name="analyzePick">
77                  <onMessage partnerLink="worklist" portType="task:TaskManagerCallback"
78                      operation="onTaskResult" variable="taskResponse">
79                      <!-- From response extract status and set to variable 'status' -->
80                      <assign name="setStatus">
81                          <copy>
82                              <from variable="taskResponse" part="payload"
```

EXAMPLE 5-1. *BPEL example: InsuranceClaim.bpel (continued)*

```
 83                             query="/tns:taskMessage/tns:result="/>
 84                         <to variable="status"/>
 85                     </copy>
 86                 </assign>
 87             </onMessage>
 88             <!-- Timeout! 10 days have passed.  Escalate -->
 89             <onAlarm for="PT10D">
 90                 <sequence>
 91                     <!-- Call partner service to escalate -->
 92                     <invoke name="evalClaim" partnerLink="worklist"
 93                         portType="task:TaskManager" operation="escalateClaim"
 94                         inputVariable="initiateMsg"/>
 95                     <!-- Get the escalation response -->
 96                     <receive name="receiveTaskResult" partnerLink="worklist"
 97                         portType="task:TaskManagerCallback"
 98                         operation="onTaskResult" variable="taskResponse"/>
 99                   <!-- From response extract status and set to variable 'status' -->
100                     <assign name="setStatus">
101                         <copy>
102                             <from variable="taskResponse" part="payload"
103                                 query="/tns:taskMessage/tns:result="/>
104                             <to variable="status"/>
105                         </copy>
106                     </assign>
107                 </sequence>
108             </onAlarm>
109         </pick>
110
111         <!-- Look at result of claim process and act accordingly:
112             'rejected' and 'accepted' are good. Anything else, throw a fault -->
113         <switch name-"resultEval">
114             <case condition="bpws:getVariableData('status')='rejected'">
115                 <empty> <!-- perform rejection actions -->
116             </case>
117             <case condition="bpws:getVariableData('status')='accepted'">
118                 <empty> <!-- perform acceptance actions -->
119             </case>
120             <otherwise>
121                 <throw name="illegalStatus" faultName="illegalStatus"/>
122             </otherwise>
123         </switch>
124     </sequence>
125 </process>
```

The underlying business logic for this process is straightforward: when a claim arrives, an agent evaluates it and determines whether to accept or reject it. If the agent does not respond within 10 days, the activity is escalated to a manager, who then makes an accelerated accept/reject decision. At any point, the processing can be terminated with a kill event.

The code implementing this logic is an XML document with root element process; from that element, we learn that the name of the process is InsuranceClaim (line 1). The heart of the process is the sequence activity in lines 58–124, which in turn contains a set of child activities and runs them sequentially. In this example, those children are a receive activity (lines 63–69), an invoke activity (lines 72–73), a pick activity (lines 76–109), and a switch activity (lines 113–123).

The purpose of the receive activity (lines 63–69) is to listen for an inbound message containing the claims request. The process, as you will see, has a WSDL interface and implements a web service interface; the receive represents an inbound operation of that service (in this case, initate, as stated in line 64). The attribute createInstance="yes" in line 64 means that this receive activity is the trigger that starts the process.

In the invoke activity in lines 72–73, the process calls a web service operation, offered by another partner (in this example, operation evalClaim for partner worklist), to evaluate the claim. The partner service chooses an insurance agent to evaluate the claim. Several days might pass before the agent makes a decision about the claim, but the invoke call is asynchronous; it returns immediately, and the process waits for a response in the pick in lines 76–109.

The pick activity waits for one of two events to occur: the response from the worklist (handled by the onMessage element in lines 77–87) or a timeout (in onAlarm in lines 89–108). In the former case, the response arrives as another inbound message; the worklist service calls back the process by invoking its onTaskResult operation (line 78). The assign activity in lines 80–86 extracts the result field from the worklist message and copies it into a process variable called status (declared in the variables section in line 25), which is used later in the process as a decision point for acceptance or rejection processing.

CORRELATION METHOD 1: WS-ADDRESSING

How does the process correlate the response with the request made in the invoke? In other words, how can the process be sure that the response is for the right insurance claim? The answer, in this case, is the WS-Addressing standard: when the process sends a request to the worklist, it embeds a unique message ID into the SOAP header; when the worklist responds, it passes back that ID. The logic is handled at the web services container level, transparent to the BPEL code.

The BPEL specification does not require that the container support WS-Addressing. To use this method of correlation, check the capabilities of your BPEL platform. This example was test on Oracle's BPEL Process Manager, which encourages the WP-Addressing approach.

The timeout occurs after 10 days, an interval determined by the condition for="PT10D" in line 89. The timeout triggers escalation: if, after ten days, no response has arrived from the worklist on the original claim request, the process uses an invoke to call the worklist's escalateClaim service operation (lines 92–94). Like the earlier invoke, this call is asynchronous. The receive activity in lines 96–98 waits for the result, which might take several hours or days to arrive. The assign in lines 100–106 captures the result in the status variable.

Finally, the switch activity in lines 113–132 is an exclusive-OR construct that performs either acceptance or rejection logic based on the value of the status variable, which records the result returned by the worklist. The acceptance case is handled in lines 114–116; its logic (not shown in the code example for brevity) probably involves sending an acceptance letter and a check to the subscriber. The rejection handler in lines 117–119 may involve sending a rejection letter. If the result is neither an accept nor a reject (the otherwise case in lines 120–122), the activity throws a fault called illegalStatus, which triggers the faultHandler in lines 37–42. The handler in this example does very little, but it can have arbitrarily complex exception handling logic.

The requirement to kill the claim at any point is met by the eventHandlers construct in lines 45–56. The onMessage handler listens on the inbound kill web service operation (lines 46–47), using a BPEL correlation set (lines 48–50) to ensure that the kill event is for the same claim as the one under consideration in this instance of the process. The event handler explicitly terminates the process using the terminate activity in line 53.

CORRELATION METHOD 2: BPEL CORRELATION SET

Unlike WS-Addressing, which matches IDs in the message header, BPEL's correlation mechanism matches particular data fields embedded in the message body. The receive activity in lines 63–69 populates a correlation set, to be used for subsequent correlations, with data embedded in its message. In the kill event handler, the data from the kill event is compared with the data in the correlation set; if it matches, the kill event is processed; if it does not match, the kill event is rejected.

The partnerLinks element, in lines 15–21, specifies the web service interface offered by the process, as well as interfaces that are used by the process. Two partner links are listed: client represents the interface implemented by the process, which includes the inbound operations to initiate and kill a claim. The client interface is specified in a WSDL, a portion of which is displayed here:

```
<portType name="InsuranceClaim">
    <operation name="initiate">
        <input message="tns:InsuranceClaimMsg"/>
    </operation>
    <operation name="kill">
```

```
                <input message="tns:InsuranceClaimMsg"/>
            </operation>
        </portType>

        <plnk:partnerLinkType name="InsuranceClaim">
            <plnk:role name="InsuranceClaimProvider">
                <plnk:portType name="tns:InsuranceClaim"/>
            </plnk:role>
        </plnk:partnerLinkType>
```

The WSDL includes the definition of a partnerLinkType called InsuranceClaim, which defines a role called InsuranceClaimProvider, which maps to the port type InsuranceClaim, which in turn defines the initiate and kill operations. The client partner link supports the InsuranceClaimProvider role, implying that it implements the kill and initiate operation of that role's port type.

The worklist partner link is a service that this process calls to evaluate and escalate the claim; worklist calls the process back with results. The WSDL for worklist has the following port types and partner link types:

```
        <portType name="TaskManager">
            <operation name="evalClaim">
                <input message="tns:taskMessage"/>
            </operation>
            <operation name="escalateClaim">
                <input message="tns:taskMessage"/>
            </operation>
        </portType>
        <portType name="TaskManagerCallback">
            <operation name="onTaskResult">
                <input message="tns:taskMessage"/>
            </operation>
        </portType>

        <plnk:partnerLinkType name="TaskManager">
            <plnk:role name="TaskManager">
                <plnk:portType name="tns:TaskManager"/>
            </plnk:role>
            <plnk:role name="TaskManagerRequester">
                <plnk:portType name="tns:TaskManagerCallback"/>
            </plnk:role>
        </plnk:partnerLinkType>
```

The expression myRole="TaskManagerRequester" in line 20 of the process means that the process implements the TaskManagerCallback service, which defines an onTaskResult operation. The expression partnerRole="TaskManager" means that the worklist partner implements the port type TaskManager with operations evalClaim and escalateClaim.

BPEL in a Nutshell

The following sections examine the essential language constructs designers will need to understand to create a BPEL process: the basic process structure, variables and assignments, exception handling and compensation, split and join, loops, participant exchange, transactions, and extensions.

Basic Process Structure: Start, End, Activities, Sequence

A developer's first BPEL process is not easy to write. Two puzzles face the beginner:

- A BPEL process has exactly one activity (which, of course, can consist of any number of subactivities to any level of hierarchy). Which activity should that be? Which are allowed? Which are disallowed? Which are recommended?

- How is the initial inbound event handler set up? Where do you place the receive or pick in the activity described in the first problem?

The simplest approach, and the one recommended to most developers, is to use a sequence whose first activity is a receive with createInstance="yes", as in the following code example:

```
<sequence>
    <receive . . . createInstance="yes" . . .> . . . </receive>
    <!-- other activities -->
</sequence>
```

This process starts when the receive triggers, then executes the remaining steps sequentially, and exits when the last activity has completed. Error handling complicates the processing, of course; see the section "Exception Handling and Compensation" for a discussion.

Another approach is to use a receive within a flow. The receive should not have any inbound links. For example:

```
<flow>
    <receive . . . createInstance="yes" . . .> . . . </receive>
    <!-- other activities -->
</flow>
```

This process starts when the receive triggers, whereupon the remaining activities in the flow run in parallel, or, if links are used, in a directed-graph style of execution. (See the section "Split and Join" later in this chapter for more on flow.) The process finishes when the flow has merged all its activities.

In the advanced category, the BPEL specification includes an example (Section 16.3 of the BPEL 1.1 specification) with two receive nodes in a flow. The intent is not to choose one or the other events (as with a pick), but to require both in order to proceed with the remainder of the process. Both nodes compete to start the process, but because they are in a flow, when one wins, it must wait for the other to trigger and join it in the process. As the following code example shows, the flow is enclosed in a sequence, so when the flow completes, the other activities in the process run sequentially, and when they complete, the process exits normally:

```
<sequence>
    <flow>
```

```
            <receive . . . createInstance="yes" . . .>
                <correlations>. . .</correlations> <!-- corr required for multi-start -->
            </receive>
            <receive . . . createInstance="yes" . . .>
                <correlations>. . .</correlations> <!-- corr required for multi-start -->
            </receive>
        </flow>
        <!-- other activities -->
    </sequence>
```

Here are some novelties to avoid at all costs:

- Do not put basic activities (e.g., assign, empty, or wait) before the initial receive or pick.

- Do not use switch or while as the main activity of the process.

- Do not use a scope as the main activity of the process. The process has everything that a scope has—handlers, variables, correlation sets..

Variables and Assignments

Most processes need to maintain application data during the course of their execution. The data is initialized when the process begins and is subsequently read and modified. A BPEL process can define a set of variables, pass them to web service touchpoints as input or output parameters, and assign all or part of one variable to another.

Formally, a process variable has a name that is unique for its scope and a type that is either a WSDL message type or an XML Schema element or basic type. A variable is set in one of the following ways:

- Bound to the input of an inbound activity, such as a receive, pick, or eventHandler.

- Bound to the output of a synchronous invoke.

- Assigned a value with the assign activity

The assign activity is defined as a copy of data from a source to a target. The source can be a literal value, an expression, the value of the whole or part of another process variable, or part of a process variable. Table 5-2 shows an example for each type.

TABLE 5-2. *Assignment examples*

Usage	Code

From literal	`<variable name="x" type="xsd:int"/>`
	
	`<assign>`
	`    <copy>`
	`        <from>1</from>`
	`        <to variable="x"/>`
	`    </copy>`
	`</assign>`

TABLE 5-2. *Assignment examples (continued)*

Usage	Code
From expression	``` <variable name="x" type="xsd:int"/> <assign> <copy> <from expression="bpws:getVariableData('x') + 1"/> <to variable="x"/> </copy> </assign> ```
Whole copy	``` <variable name="x" type="xsd:int"/> <variable name="y" type="xsd:int"/> <assign> <copy> <from variable="y"/> <to variable="x"/> </copy> </assign> ```
Partial copy	``` In WSDL: <message name="person"> <part name="name" type="xsd:string"/> <part name="address" type="xsd:string"/> </message> In BPEL process: <variable name="person" messageType="person"/> <variable name="personAddress" type="xsd:string"/> <assign> <copy> <from variable="person" part="address"/> <to variable="personAddress"/> </copy> </assign> ```

The built-in BPEL function `bpws:getVariableData` is used to get the value of a variable. For an XSD element type, the function can use an XPath expression to extract a particular data token from the XML document. For a WSDL message type, the function can extract values from any part of the message.

In addition, see the section "The Life Event process" in Chapter 11 for an example of assigning dynamic endpoint information to a partner link.

Exception Handling and Compensation

A scope is a process code block having its own set of activities and corresponding variables; correlation sets; and handlers for fault, compensation, and events. A scope is a localized execution context: its variables are visible only within its boundaries, and its handlers apply only to its activity flow. Scopes are hierarchical; a scope can have multiple nested subscopes, each of which can in turn have additional subscopes, and so on down the chain; a process is itself a top-level scope.

Compensation handler

Compensation is a transaction that reverses the effects of a previously completed transaction. In many online transactional applications, updates to one or more systems are made within a local or distributed transaction, and are not finalized until the transaction is committed; to negate the updates, the application simply rolls back the transaction. However, business processes often run for such long periods of time that keeping open transactions for the duration is infeasible. If an earlier step needs to be negated, rather than rolling back its transaction, the process executes its compensation handler. The following code example shows a handler that invokes a rescind web service, presumably informing its partner to cancel some activity. The rescind is intended to reverse the update service invocation in the main flow of the scope block.

```
<scope name="s">
   <compensationHandler>
      <invoke operation="rescind" . . . />
   </compensationHandler>

   <invoke operation="update" . . ./>
</scope>
```

The compensation handler for a scope is invoked, using the compensate activity, from the fault handler or compensation handler of the parent scope. In the following case, the compensation handler for scope inner is called from the compensation handler of its parent scope outer. The operations update and addToStatement are compensated by rescind and removeFromStatement:

```
<scope name="outer">
   <compensationHandler>
      <sequence>
         <invoke operation="rescind" . . . />
         <compensate scope="s2"/>
      </sequence>
   </compensationHandler>

   <sequence>
      <invoke operation="update" . . ./>
      <scope name="inner">
         <compensationHandler>
            <invoke operation="removeFromStatement" . . ./>
         </compensationHandler>
         <invoke operation="addToStatement" . . ./>
         . . .
      </scope>
   </sequence>
</scope>
```

Fault handler

Compensation is the reversal of a completed scope, and *fault handling* is the processing of a break in a scope that is in-flight. When a fault is generated, either implicitly by the BPEL engine or explicitly by a throw activity, control jumps to the fault handler defined for the given fault type.* The fault handler is a set of `catch` structures, resembling the following:

```
<scope name="s1">
   <faultHandlers>
      <catch faultName="x:invalidAccount">
         . . .
      </catch>
      <catch faultName="x:closedAccount">
         . . .
      </catch>
      <catchAll">
         . . .
      </catchAll>
   </faultHandlers>
</scope>
```

BPEL faults are uniquely identified by name. Some are standard error types documented in the BPEL specification, such as `uninitializedVariable`, which is thrown by the engine when code tries to read the value of an uninitialized part of a variable. Others are application-specific, such as `x:invalidAccount` and `x:closeAccount`, which are used in the code example to represent illegitimate accesses of an account. Catch handlers are defined for both of these faults, and the `catchall` structure handles any faults not accounted for in the other catch structures. Each handler lists the activities to be performed to handle the fault. The handler can swallow the fault, leading to the resumption of processing in the scope, or it can rethrow the fault or throw a different fault, thereby propagating the fault to the parent scope.

The `throw` activity generates a fault, causing control to be passed to the fault handler defined for the given scope. In the following code example:

```
<switch name="routeRequest">
   <case name="checking". . .> . . . </case>
   <case name="savings". . .>
      <switch name="CheckAcctStatus">
         <case name="Open" . . .> . . . </case>
         <case name="Closed" . . .> <throw faultName="closedAccount"> </case>
      </switch>
   </case>
   <case name="trust". . .> . . . </case>
   <otherwise><throw faultName="invalidAccount"/></otherwise>
</switch>
```

the terminate activity is used to immediately abort the process, skipping any defined fault handling:

```
<terminate name="Unrecoverable condition met">
```

---

* If no such handler is defined, the fault is propagated to the parent scope. If the parent has no suitable handler, the fault is propagated to the parent's parent, and so on, until the topmost scope level—that is, the process level—is reached. If the fault is not handled at the process level, the process is terminated.

Event handler

An event handler enables the scope to react to events, or to the expiration of timers, at any point during the scope's execution. Two obvious uses are:

Cancellation

The scope defines a handler for a cancellation event. If it receives it, the scope can be terminated, no matter where it is in its execution.

Escalation

A timer is set on the scope. If it expires, special activities are executed to perform "business escalation."

The next code example demonstrates these uses. Cancellation is triggered by the message defined by partner link Customer, port type controller and operation cancel; the handler throws a fault to terminate the scope. Escalation occurs after two days (PT2D), at which point the handler performs logic through an invoke.

```
<scope name="s1">
   <eventHandlers>
      <onMessage partnerLink="Customer" portType="controller"
         operation="cancel" variable="cancelEvent">
         <correlations>
            <correlation set="controllerSet" initiate="no"/>
         </correlations>
         <throw faultName="x:cancelled"/>
      </onMessage>

      <onAlarm until="PT2D">
         <invoke name="escalation" . . ./>
      </onAlarm>
   </eventHandlers>
</scope>
```

Split and Join

BPEL's two activities for split and join—switch and flow—exhibit contrasting styles. switch is a traditional programmatic control structure for conditional logic. flow is an unusual graph structure with support for parallel activities connected by guarded links.

switch

switch is an exclusive-OR structured activity that consists of one or more case structures, each having a conditional expression and an associated activity. The activity performed by the switch is that of the first case whose condition evaluates to true. An optional otherwise clause can be defined with an activity but no condition; that activity is run only if none of the preceding cases have a true condition.

In the following example, a flow activity is performed if the first condition (variable i has value 1) holds; a sequence with an assign and switch is executed if the second condition (i = 2) is true. An invoke is run by default:

```
<switch>
    <case condition="bpws:getVariableData('i')=1">
        <flow> . . . </flow>
    </case>

    <case condition="bpws:getVariableData('i')=2">
        <sequence>
            <assign . . . />
            <switch> . . . </switch>
        </sequence>
    </case>

    <otherwise>
        <invoke . . ./>
    </otherwise>
</switch>
```

flow

The flow activity—BPEL's most interesting, unusual, and pedantic construct—models parallel activity execution and activity synchronization. Depending on how it is configured, flow exhibits a variety of behaviors; to understand flow, it is best to learn each case—the parallel split and join behavior, link synchronization and dependencies behaviors, and dead path elimination behavior—using an example and a diagram.

Parallel split and join. The first case for flow is perfectly suited to the P4 patterns for parallel split and join. In the following example (see Figure 5-4 and the following code), the process invokes in parallel (i.e., splits) web services for partner links A, B, and C respectively; the order of execution is unpredictable. The flow waits for each contained activity to complete (i.e., joins them) before exiting. The invocation of the service for partner link D does not occur until each of the three previous invocation finishes.

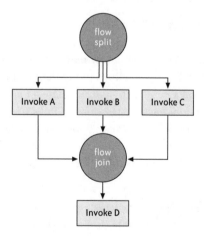

FIGURE 5-4. *BPEL flow parallel split and join*

```
<flow>
    <invoke partnerLink="A" . . ./>
    <invoke partnerLink="B" . . ./>
    <invoke partnerLink="C" . . ./>
</flow>
<invoke partnerLink="D" . . ./>
```

Links and synchronization dependencies. The BPEL flow mechanism offers several features to model the situation where one activity cannot start until one or more activities on which it depends complete. Specifically, a flow can define a set of links, each originating from a source activity in the flow and terminating at a target activity in the flow. An activity can be the source as well as the target of multiple links. In Figure 5-5, for example, A has links to B and C, X has links to B and C, B has a link to D, and C has a link to E.

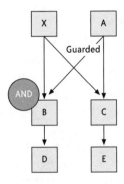

FIGURE 5-5. *BPEL synchronization*

Understanding flow in BPEL requires understanding the order in which such activities are executed, and whether a particular activity is executed at all.

In the current example, initially X and A are run in parallel. Activities B and C must wait for both X and A to complete because, according to BPEL's flow rules, an activity must wait for each of its incoming links. To complicate matters, a source activity can define a transition condition on any of its outgoing links (if not defined for a given link, the condition defaults to true), and a target activity can define a join condition evaluated based on the transition conditions each of its incoming links. The join condition is optional; if not defined, it defaults to an OR condition, which is true if any of the link transition conditions is true. The target activity executes only if its join condition evaluates to true. (The behavior when the join condition is false is examined in the next section.)

Continuing with the example, C does not define a join condition, and hence defaults to OR. That is, C executes if either X or A (or both) has a true transition condition on its link. Note that C must wait for both source activities to complete, even though it requires only one to send out a true link. Activity B defines an explicit join condition, requiring both of its incoming links, from X and A, to be true; B executes only if both X and A have a true transition condition. The link from A to B has an explicit transition condition (it is "guarded"), whereas the link from X to B is implicitly true. As for activities D and E: D waits for B to complete, and E waits for C.

The BPEL encoding of this scenario is as follows:

```
<flow>
    <links>
        <link name="AB"/>
        <link name="AC"/>
        <link name="XB"/>
        <link name="XC"/>
        <link name="BD"/>
        <link name="CE"/>
    </links>

    <invoke partnerLink="A". . .>
        <source linkName="AB" transitionCondition=". . ."/>
        <source linkName="AC"/>
    </invoke>

    <invoke partnerLink="X". . .>
        <source linkName="XB" />
        <source linkName="XC" />
    </invoke>

    <invoke partnerLink="B". . .
     joinCondition="bpws:getLinkStatus('XB') and bpws:getLinkStatus('AB')">
        <source linkName="BD" />
        <target linkName="AB" />
        <target linkName="XB" />
    </invoke>

    <invoke partnerLink="C" . . ./>
        <source linkName="CE" />
        <target linkName="AC" />
        <target linkName="XC" />
    </invoke>

    <invoke partnerLink="D" . . .>
        <target linkName="BD"/>
    </invoke>

    <invoke partnerLink="E" . . .>
        <target linkName="CE"/>
    </invoke>
</flow>
```

A link can cross activity boundaries. In Figure 5-6, activity S2 is the second activity in the sequence of S1-S2-S3, but it is also the target of a link from activity X. According to BPEL's flow rules, S2 cannot execute until both S1 and X have executed. The overall order of execution is S1-X-S2-S3 or X-S1-S2-S3.

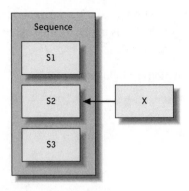

FIGURE 5-6. *BPEL cross-boundary link*

Dead path elimination. By default, if an activity's join condition evaluates to false, BPEL generates a fault called `bpws:joinFailure`; the activity is not executed, and control is diverted to a fault handler. In the first of the examples presented in the previous section, B's join condition fails if either X or A sends a false link to B.

BPEL also supports the semantics of *dead path elimination*: if the join condition of an activity is false, the activity doesn't execute but completes immediately and sends false on each of its outgoing links. For example, if B's join condition fails, and dead path elimination is enforced, B doesn't execute, and its outgoing link to D is set of false, which, because D's implicit join condition requires the link from B to be true, in turn prevents D's execution. In this case, the execution sequence is either X-A-C-E or A-X-C-E.

Deciding whether to use dead path elimination semantics is as simple as setting a flag. The attribute `suppressJoinFailure` can be set to yes or no (default is no) for any activity. If set to "yes", that activity uses dead path elimination semantics; otherwise, it uses the semantics of join fault. In the following code example, the flag is enabled for the entire flow, which means that B, a part of that flow, will use dead path elimination if its join condition is false.

```
<flow suppressJoinFailure="yes">
    <links>
        <link name="AB"/>
        <link name="AC"/>
        <link name="XB"/>
        <link name="XC"/>
        <link name="BD"/>
        <link name="CE"/>
    </links>

    <invoke partnerLink="A". . .>
        <source linkName="AB" transitionCondition=". . ."/>
        <source linkName="AC"/>
    </invoke>

    <invoke partnerLink="X". . .>
        <source linkName="XB" />
```

```
            <source linkName="XC" />
        </invoke>

        <invoke partnerLink="B". . .
          joinCondition="bpws:getLinkStatus('XB') and bpws:getLinkStatus('AB')">
            <source linkName="BD" />
            <target linkName="AB" />
            <target linkName="XB" />
        </invoke>

        <invoke partnerLink="C" . . ./>
            <source linkName="CE" />
            <target linkName="AC" />
            <target linkName="XC" />
        </invoke>

        <invoke partnerLink="D" . . .>
            <target linkName="BD"/>
        </invoke>

        <invoke partnerLink="E" . . .>
            <target linkName="CE"/>
        </invoke>
    </flow>
```

The semantics of dead path elimination are discussed further in Chapter 3.

Loops

BPEL's sole looping construct is the while activity. Unlike BPML, BPEL does not offer a foreach loop, but an example of how to iterate through a repeating XML element, a typical use of foreach, is provided in this section.

while

The while activity executes a child activity in a loop and evaluates the continuation condition before each iteration. The child activity is executed if the condition is true; otherwise, the loop exits.

In the following example, the loop iterates over a counter variable i. The integer variable is initially set to 0 and is incremented by 1 at the end of each loop iteration. The loop runs until i is 5, executing as part of a sequence an invoke activity and the assign to increment i:

```
<variable name="i" type="xsd:integer"/>
<assign>
    <copy>
        <from expression="0"/>
        <to variable="i"/>
    </copy>
</assign>

    . . .
```

```
<while condition="bpws:getVariableData(i) != 5">
  <sequence>
    <invoke . . . />
    <assign>
      <copy>
        <from expression="bpws:getVariableData(i) + 1"/>
        <to variable=";"i"/>
      </copy>
    <assign>
  </sequence>
</while>
```

Implementing foreach

Iterating over a set of XML data in BPEL is a comparatively difficult development chore, thanks to BPEL's omission of, or decision not to include, a foreach loop. The following example shows how iterate over all instances of the input element described by the following schema:

```
<element name="ForLoopRequest">
  <complexType>
    <sequence>
      <element name="input" type="string" maxOccurs="5" />
    </sequence>
  </complexType>
</element>
```

Here is an XML document based on this schema:

```
<ForLoopRequest>
  <input>Foreach</input>
  <input> is</input>
  <input> possible</input>
  <input> after all</input>
</ForEachRequest>
```

Example 5-2 is an excerpt of a BPEL process that iterates over the repeating elements of such a document.

EXAMPLE 5-2. *Iterating BPEL process*

```
1  <!-- input is a ForLoopRequest.
2      numItems is a count of the "input" elements in the input message
3      currItem is a loop counter that starts at 0 and increases by 1 to numItems
4      theItem is used in the loop to store the value in the currItem position
5      tempExpr is a string used to build XPath in the loop -->
6  <variables>
7    <variable name="input" messageType="tns:ForLoopRequestMessage"/>
8    <variable name="numItems" type="xsd:int"/>
9    <variable name="currItem" type="xsd:int"/>
10   <variable name="theItem" type="xsd:string"/>
11   <variable name="trace" type="xsd:string"/>
12   <variable name="tempExpr" type="xsd:string"/>
13 </variables>
14 . . .
```

EXAMPLE 5-2. *Iterating BPEL process (continued)*

```
15  <!-- Initialize currItem to 0 and use XPath count( ) function to get the number of
16       "input" elements. -->
17  <assign name="getNumItems">
18     <copy>
19        <from expression="bpws:getVariableData(&quot;input&quot;,&quot;payload&quot;,
20           &quot;count(/tns:ForLoopRequest/tns:input)&quot;)"></from>
21        <to variable="numItems"/>
22     </copy>
23     <copy>
24        <from expression="number(0)"></from>
25        <to variable="currItem"/>
26     </copy>
27  </assign>
28  . . .
29  <!-- the while loop, ironically named "foreach"
30       It runs until currItem = numItems -->
31  <while name="foreach"
32     condition="bpws:getVariableData('currItem') &lt;
33     bpws:getVariableData('numItems')">
34     <sequence>
35        <assign name="doForEach">
36           <!-- Increment currItem.  Need this for loop condition, as well
37                as XPath index -->
38           <copy>
39              <from expression="bpws:getVariableData(&quot;currItem&quot;)
40                 + 1"></from>
41              <to variable="currItem"/>
42           </copy>
43           <!-- The Xpath expression is of the form:
44                "/tns:ForLoopRequest/tns:input[currItem]" (index is 1-based)
45                Build it and store in tempExpr. -->
46           <copy>
47              <from expression="concat(&quot;/tns:ForLoopRequest/tns:input[&quot;,
48                 bpws:getVariableData(&quot;currItem&quot;), &quot;]&quot;)"></from>
49              <to variable="tempExpr"/>
50           </copy>
51           <!- - Evaluate the expresion and store in "theItem" -->
52           <copy>
53              <from expression="bpws:getVariableData(&quot;input&quot;,
54                 &quot;payload&quot;,bpws:getVariableData(&quot;tempExpr&quot;))">
55              </from>
56              <to variable="theItem"/>
57           </copy>
58        </assign>
59        <!-- Now, do something with "theItem" -->
60     </sequence>
61  </while>
```

Intuitively, this code performs the following logic:

```
numItems = count(/ForLoopRequest/input)
for currItem = 1 to numItems
   theItem = /ForLoopRequest/input[currItem]
```

Table 5-5 maps this intuitive code to the corresponding section in the thorny BPEL code.

TABLE 5-3. *ForEach logic*

Intended code	Actual code
numItems = count(/ForLoopRequest/input)	Assign rule, lines 19–20.
For currItem = 1 to numItems	First, currItem is assigned to 0, lines 24–25. The while condition appears in lines 32–33. currItem is incremented in lines 39–41.
theItem = /ForLoopRequest/input[currItem]	Two assign copies in lines 46–57.

Participant Exchange

One of BPEL's strongest notions is that processes communicate with each other as business partners. The partnering relationships are represented declaratively in the definition of process links, as well as in the actual communication touch points of the process flow.

Partner link types

To begin with, in the WSDL, *partner link types* map web service port types to partner roles. More formally, a partner link type has a name and one or two roles, each of which has a name and a reference by name to a port type. A partner link type with two roles represents a relationship in which partners, such as a buyer and seller, exchange service calls:

```
<partnerLinkType name="BuyerSeller">
    <role name="buyer"> <portType name="buyerPT"/> </role>
    <role name="seller"> <portType name="sellerPT"/> </role>
</partnerLinkType>
```

A partner link type with one role is suitable for interactions where the service does not need to know about its callers:

```
<partnerLinkType name="Server">
    <role name="server"> <portType name="serverPT"/> </role>
</partnerLinkType>
```

Partner links

In the BPEL process definition, *partner links* declare which partner link type roles defined in the WSDL are performed by the process and which are performed by partners. For example, a buyer process defines the link BuyerSellerLink, referencing the type BuyerSeller, with myRole set to buyer and partnerRole to seller:

```
<partnerLink name="BuyerSellerLink" partnerLinkType="BuyerSeller"
    myRole="buyer" partnerRole="seller"/>
```

If the process invokes the server service, it declares a partner link called ServerLink with partnerRole set to server:

```
<partnerLink name="ServerLink" partnerLinkType="Server" partnerRole="server"/>
```

In most BPEL examples, a partner link is mapped statically to a
particular service endpoint. See Chapter 11 (the section "The Life Event
process") for an example of a dynamic partner link, whose endpoint
information is determined at runtime.

Partners

BPEL also offers a construct known as a business partner, which has a name and a set of
partner links. For example, a given process participant that is both a seller and a shipper
can be defined as SellerShipper:

```
<partner name="SellerShipper">
   <partnerLink name="Seller"/>
   <partnerLink name-"Shipper"/>
</partner>
```

Partner interactions

BPEL process flow contains the activities receive, reply, invoke, and pick, which
implement the actual interpartner communication. receive and pick represent links
implemented by the process and called by partners (e.g., the buyer). reply and invoke
represent partner services called by this process (e.g., the seller, the server).

Table 5-4 describes the possible types of partner interactions. The pronoun my is used to
distinguish a process from its partners.

TABLE 5-4. *Partner communication patterns*

Pattern	Partner roles	Description
Async receive	MyRole = receiveWS	A partner calls my web service, which triggers logic in my process. The partner resumes control immediately.
Sync receive-reply	MyRole = receive WS PartnerRole = reply WS	A partner calls my web service, which triggers logic in my process. My process eventually sends back a response to the partner. The partner blocks for the duration; to the partner, the entire interaction is a single two-way web service invocation.
Async receive-invoke	MyRole = receive WS PartnerRole = invoke WS	A partner calls my web service, which triggers logic in my process; the partner resumes control immediately. My process eventually calls the partner's callback web service through an invoke.
Sync invoke	PartnerRole = invoke WS	My process calls the partner's web service with an invoke. The two-way web service returns a result.
Async invoke	PartnerRole = invoke WS	My process calls the partner's web service with an invoke. The "one-way" web service does not return a result.
Async invoke-receive	MyRole = receive WS PartnerRole = invoke WS	My process calls the partner's web service with an invoke. The web service later calls back by triggering my receive.

As Figure 5-7 shows, each interaction, considered from the perspective of the current
process, has a corresponding partner interaction. A partner async invoke is an async
receive for my process, whereas a partner sync invoke is a sync receive-reply for my

process. A partner async invoke-receive is asymmetrically an async receive-invoke for my process.

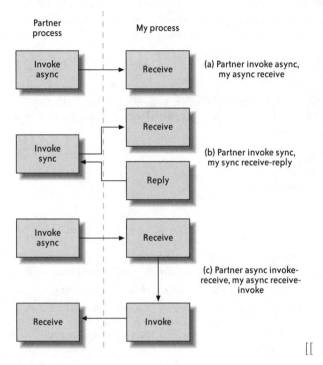

FIGURE 5-7. *Partner interactions*

The four partner interaction activities are discussed in the following sections.

invoke. The invoke activity calls a partner web service either synchronously or asynchronously. The web service is identified by partner link type and WSDL port type and operation. A synchronous web service requires both input and output variables to be passed in; an asynchronous service requires only an input variable. In case the service generates a fault, the invoke activity can define one or more fault handlers, and it can also specify a compensation handler.

The following example shows a call to a synchronous web service:

```
<invoke partnerLink="myPartner"  portType="service" operation="syncRequest"
  inputVariable="request" outputVariable="response"/>
```

receive. Whereas invoke lets a process call a partner's web service's operation, receive is a web service operation implemented by the process for use by partners. The idea, as was discussed previously, is that partners trigger the execution of a process by calling its services; for the process, the service is an event that set it in action.

Like invoke, receive uses partner link type and WSDL port type and operation to identify the service. The arguments passed in by the caller are bound to a specified variable. The following code example implements the initialRequest service, whose input is bound to the request variable. The createInstance attribute indicates that when this service is called, a new instance of the process is launched:

```
<receive partnerLink="myPartner" portType="service" operation="initialRequest"
  variable="request" createInstance="yes" />
```

The next example shows the secondRequest service, which does *not* create a new instance but listens for an event in an existing instance:

```
<receive partnerLink="myPartner" portType="service" operation="secondRequest"
  variable="request" createInstance="no" />
```

reply. The reply activity sends back a response *synchronously* to an earlier receive. The effect is that of a single web service call in which the receive accepts the input, and the reply passees back the output; the process can perform arbitrary processing logic in between. As the following code sample shows, the reply matches the partnerLink, portType, and operation attributes of the receive; the output is specified in the variable attribute

```
<reply partnerLink="client" portType="c:AccountOpenPT" operation="submitApplication"
variable="request" />

<!-- do stuff in between -->

<reply partnerLink="client" portType="c:AccountOpenPT" operation="submitApplication"
variable="confirmationNumber " />
```

pick. pick waits for one of several events to occur, then executes the activity associated with that event. Like receive, pick has a createInstance attribute that determines whether to start a new process instance when the event occurs. pick also has an optional timer (onAlarm) that executes a specified activity if none of the specified events occurs within a given duration or until a given deadline. The list of candidate events is a set of onMessage elements; the event is defined as a web service operation for a given port type and partner link, similar to the receive event definition earlier.

In the following example, the pick triggers a new process instance when it gets events ev1 or ev2. In each case, it executes some sequence of activities. The onAlarm condition fires if neither event occurs in 3 days and 10 hours. (The XPath 1.0 syntax is P3DT10H.)

```
<pick createInstance="yes">
    <onMessage partnerLink="pl" portType="pt" operation="ev1"
     variable="v">
       <sequence>. . .</sequence>
    </onMessage>

    <onMessage partnerLink="pl" portType="pt" operation="ev2"
     variable="v">
```

```
        <sequence>. . .</sequence>
    </onMessage>

    <onAlarm for="P3DT10H">
        <sequence> . . . </sequence>
    </onAlaram>
</pick>
```

Properties

A standard WSDL extension allows for the definition of *message properties,* which can be thought of as macros to access parts of WSDL messages. The definition of a message property has two parts: a `property`, which has a name and a WSDL message or XML schema type; and a `property alias`, which stipulates from which WSDL message and part the property comes. The property alias includes an XPath expression that extracts data to be represented by the property from the WSDL message. In the following code example, the property `nameProp` represents the name of a `person` message type:

```
<property name="nameProp" type="xsd:string"/>
<propertyAlias propertyName="nameProp" messageType="person" part="name"
    query="/personalData/name"/>
```

Correlation

The main use of properties in BPEL is *message correlation,* a large topic in its own right, as will be apparent shortly. The definition of a process can specify any number of correlation sets, each of which has a name and a list of message properties. In the following code sample, the correlation set `USPersonCorrSet` includes properties `nameProp` and `SSNProp`:

```
<correlationSets>
    <correlationSet name="USPersonCorrSet" properties="nameProp SSNProp"/>
</correlationSets>
```

The purpose of the correlation set is to tie together a partner conversation. A fundamental principal of BPEL is that instances of partner processes communicate with each other simply by calling each other's web services, passing application data whose structure is transparent to the BPEL engine. In BPEL, partners do not address each other by ID, but rather pass around messages containing key fields that can be correlated for the lifetime of the exchange.

The protocol governing a correlation set, from the perspective of one of the participating processes, is as follows:

1. The first step in the conversation is the `initiating` step. This step is normally a receive or an invoke. The correlation set is populated with values based on the initiating message. In the case of a receive, the values come from the inbound message. For an invoke, the values are those sent to the partner, those received back (if the invocation is synchronous), or both.

2. Each subsequent step matches the data in the set with the initialized data. A receive is triggered only if the data in the message matches the correlation set. An invoke or reply must send out data that agrees with the data in the set.

The following example illustrates the protocol. Assuming that the conversation in question is the opening of an account, the first step is a receive that, as the code shows, initiates the USPersonCorrSet set with contents of the variable request. The attribute initiate is set to Yes, indicating that this step is the first in the conversation. The createInstance attribute is also set to Yes, indicating that this step is the first in the process. If it is set to No, this activity can still begin a conversation because a process can have multiple conversations; of course, a fundamental rule of BPEL is that every process begins with the initiation of a new conversation.

```
<receive partnerLink="l" portType="pt" operation="createAccount"
    variable="request" createInstance="Yes">
    <correlations>
        <correlation set="USPersonCorrSet" initiate="Yes"/>
    </correlations>
</receive>
```

The conversation is continued with the following asynchronous invoke. The initiate attribute is set to No. BPEL requires that the data sent match the correlation set of the previous set.

```
<invoke partnerLink="l" portType="pt" operation="approveAccount"
    inputVariable="request" >
    <correlations>
        <correlation set="USPersonCorrSet" initiate="No" pattern="out"/>
    </correlations>
</invoke>
```

The final step in the conversation is a receive that retrieves the asynchronous response to the previous invoke. BPEL triggers this activity only if the data in the message matches the correlation set.

```
<receive partnerLink="l" portType="pt" operation="accountApproval"
    variable="accountApproval" >
    <correlations>
        <correlation set="USPersonCorrSet" initiate="No"/>
    </correlations>
</receive>
```

Based on this information, it is clear that any implementation of a BPEL engine requires a router component that, upon receipt of a message from a web service invocation, triggers the process instance that correlates the message. The engine is depicted in Figure 5-8. Different name/SSN combinations are routed to different process instances; process A, not yet initiated, is started by the message with name=Pete and SSN=112; subsequent messages matching those criteria are routed to process A.

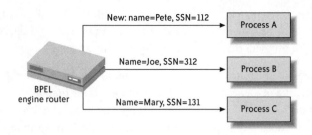

FIGURE 5-8. *BPEL correlation routing*

Transactions

Several factors make transactions hard to manage in a business process. First, a process that is long-running cannot run in a single ACID transaction; instead, it must necessarily divide its function into a number of smaller transactions. Second, the specification of standards for distributing transactions across multiple partner web services and processes is a work in progress. BPEL 1.1 anticipates, but does not support, distributed transaction coordination protocols such as WS-Transaction. Consequently, if a partner invokes a BPEL process, or a BPEL process invokes a partner, the BPEL process cannot, using a standard protocol, work together with the partner in the event of an error to reverse the effects of the interaction. The best that can be achieved is for the partners to agree on particular cancellation operations.

BPEL's strategy for the first problem is compensation (described earlier in the section "Exception Handling and Compensation"), which provides a structured and application-directed way to reverse the effects of the smaller activities that have already completed. This happens strictly locally; the second problem remains an open issue. The BPEL specification uses the term Long Running Transaction (LRT) to refer to the use of a hierarchical nesting of scoped compensation handlers to unwind previously committed work in a controlled fashion. An LRT is not a specific language feature but rather a way to describe the use of compensation to undo work performed over potentially a long period of time.

BPEL developers beware: the LRT strategy helps guide the effort, but the actual design and coding of compensation logic is still a difficult chore. The hard work is application-specific!

Extensions

Core BPEL is extended by adding attributes or elements, qualified by namespace, to BPEL elements that support extensibility. An important new BPEL extension, called BPELJ, is discussed in the next section.

BPELJ

"Pure" BPEL, examined previously, emphasizes "programming in the large," or the activity of defining the big steps of a process in a clean XML form. But a process that is

BPEL WISH LIST

As comprehensive as BPEL is, it can still be improved. The following standard enhancements would make BPEL more powerful and easier to code:

foreach
> Include an activity that can iterate over a data set. (An example of iterating over a repeating XML element using a while loop and XPath is presented in the section "Implementing foreach." earlier in this chapter.)

XML creation and update
> Enhance the assign activity to support the construction of XML elements or documents. For example, build a reply message using data from a request message.

Lightweight subprocesses or macros
> Provide a mechanism to factor out a chunk of code into a modular piece, and provide the ability to call that piece with parameters in a lightweight fashion.

More sophisticated correlation
> In addition to basic correlation set matching, allow a message listener activity (receive, pick, eventHandler) to filter on an arbitrary Boolean condition written in XPath or XQuery. In the example at the beginning of this chapter, the kill claim event handler triggers only if the kill message has the same claim ID as the original claim request. Supporting more complex queries would be desirable; for example, allowing the kill only if the claim amount is less than $1,000; the claim has been active for less than two business days; and the claim is not currently in escalation, activation, or rejection states.

Business calendars
> Provide a standard way to reference business calendars in the calculation of timeout conditions in wait and onAlarm activities (e.g., have the process wait five business days for a particular event to occur).

---

meant to actually run and be useful invariably has countless little steps, which are better implemented as lines of code than as activities in a process. Functions such as processing input, building output, interfacing with in-house systems, making decisions, and calculating dates either drive or are driven by the process but are often too complex to encode as part of the process flow.

"Programming in the small" is essential to the development of real-world processes, but is hard to accomplish with pure BPEL. The best pure BPEL can offer is web services: if a piece of logic is hard, develop it as a web service and call it from the process with an invoke activity. This approach works, but it is grossly inappropriate. First, the reason for BPEL's emphasis on web services is the goal of communicating processes; partners calls each other as services, but must a partner call pieces of itself as services? Second, the performance overhead of calling a service is obviously a showstopper; the process needs fast local access to the small logic components, as if they were an extension of the BPEL machine.

With these factors in mind, IBM and BEA have written a white paper that presents a standard Java extension of BPEL called BPEL for Java (BPELJ).* A BPELJ process, depicted in Figure 5-9, has chunks of embedded Java code, as well as invocations of separate plain old Java objects (POJOs), Enterprise Java Beans (EJBs), or other Java components. Though it still interfaces with its partner process through web services, the process internally leverages Java to perform much of the hard work.

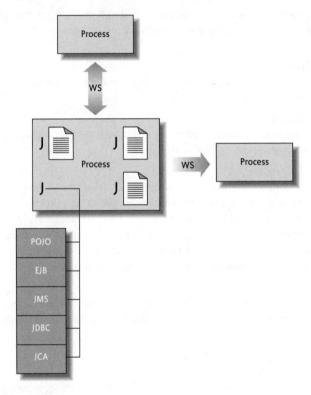

FIGURE 5-9. *The "J" in BPELJ*

BPELJ is an obvious technology choice for companies that intend to deploy their processes on J2EE platforms such as BEA Weblogic and IBM WebSphere; the platform is already Java-enabled, so it is best to use Java capabilities in the construction of the process. Luckily, BEA and IBM are building to BPELJ.

---

*   M. Blow, Y. Goland, M. Kloppman, F. Leymann, G. Phau, D. Roller, M. Rowley, "BPELj: BPEL for Java," *http://www-106.ibm.com/developerworks/webservices/library/wl-bpelj*, March 2004.

NOTE

Current BPELJ vendor implementations are difficult to find. Two BPEL toolkits—the Oracle BPEL Process Manager 2.2 and IBM's WebSphere Application Developer Integration Edition 5.1.1—have Java extensions (Oracle's is used in an example in Chapter 10), but they are proprietary. BEA is planning to develop a reference implementation of BPELJ and possibly release it as Open Source. Expect major Java application server vendors like BEA, IBM, and Oracle to be the earliest adopters and to evolve the language.

A Glimpse of BPELJ

Example 5-3 demonstrates some of the core features of BPELJ. The bold italicized parts are BPELJ-specific.

EXAMPLE 5-3. *BPELJ insurance automated claim*

```
1  <!- - Process attributes:
2       - expressionLanguage is Java by default. Can be overriden to,
3         say, XPath at the element level
4       - Java code embedded in process goes in to the Java package "com.mike.claim"
5       - The BPELJ namespace is referenced below.
6  <process name="InsuranceClaim"
7    suppressJoinFailure="yes"
8    expressionLanguage="http://jcp.org/java"
9    bpelj:package="com.mike.claim"
10   targetNamespace="http://mike.com/claim"
11   xmlns:tns="mike.com/claim"
12   xmlns="http://schemas.xmlsoap.org/ws/2003/03/business-process/"
13   xmlns:bpws="http://schemas.xmlsoap.org/ws/2003/03/business-process/"
14   xmlns:bpelj="http://schemas.xmlsoap.org/ws/2003/03/business-process/java">
15
16   <!-- Three partner links: one a web service client interface, the others
17        Java internal stuff -->
18   <partnerLinks>
19     <partnerLink name="client" partnerLinkType="tns:Claim"
20        myRole="ClaimProvider"/>
21     <partnerLink name="claimProcessor"
22        partnerLinkType="bpelj:com.mike.claim.ClaimProcessorEJB">
23     <partnerLink name="jmsPublisher"
24        partnerLinkType="bpelj:javax.jms.TopicPublisher">
25   </partnerLinks>
26
27   <!-- Two variables, one an XML, the other Java -->
28   <variables>
29     <variable name="input" messageType="tns:ClaimsMessage"/>
30     <variable name="jmsMessage" messageType="bpelj:javax.jms.TextMessage"/>
31     <variable name="claimOK" messageType="bpelj:java.lang.Boolean "/>
32   </variables>
33
```

EXAMPLE 5-3. *BPELJ insurance automated claim (continued)*

```
34      <sequence name="main">
35      <!-- process starts by receiving a claim through the client web service -->
36          <receive name="receiveClaim" partnerLink="client" portType="tns:Claim"
37             operation="initiate" createInstance="yes">
38             <output part="input" variable="input/>
39          </receive>
40
41          <!-- now invoke the Java claims processor as a partner link! -->
42          <invoke name="processClaim" partnerLink="claimProcessor" operation="execute">
43             <input part="input" variable="input"/>
44             <output variable="claimOK"/>
45          </invoke>
46
47          <!-- if claim is ok, publish the original input on a JMS topic -->
48          <switch name="pubIfOK">
49             <case>
50                <condition>claimOK</condition>
51                <bpelj:snippet name="createJMSMessage">
52                   <!-- Use partner link topic publisher to allocate a JMS message
53                       and populate it with the claim input message.
54                       Note "p_jmsPublisher" is the way to reference the partner
55                       link "jmsPublisher" in BPELJ -->
56                   <bpelj:code>
57                       jmsMessage=p_jmsPublisher.getSession().createTextMessage(input);
58                   </bpelj:code>
59                </bpelj:snippet>
60                <invoke name="PubClaim" partnerLink="jmsPublisher" operation="publish"
61                   <input part="message" variable="jmsMessage"/>
62                </invoke>
63             </case>
64             <otherwise>
65                <empty/> <!-- do nothing in this case -->
66             </otherwise>
67          </switch>
68
69      </sequence>
70  </process>
```

The process receives a claim by a web service request from a client application, then processes it using an EJB, and finally, if the claim was successful, publishes the request to a JMS topic for consumption by interested subscribers. The process extends core BPEL by defining partner links for Java components (lines 16–19), declaring Java variables (lines 25–26), using the invoke activity to call Java components (lines 37–40 and 51–53), using Java expressions to make decisions that affect flow (line 45), and embedding a snippet of Java code (lines 46–50). BPELJ features not included in this example include Java correlation, Java exception handling, and XML-Java binding.

WARNING

Some of these changes are not supported by BPEL 1.1! The Java
snippet in lines 46–50, for example, is illegal because BPEL does not
support the addition of new activity types. Similarly, the input and
output elements (lines 38–39) are not permitted in invoke and receive
activities, and the condition (line 45) in the switch activity should be an
attribute rather than a child element of case. In their joint whitepaper,
BEA and IBM admit these incompatibilities and even suggest
alternative approaches that are supported. For example, the snippet
could be overloaded in the empty activity. The alternatives are onerous
and unintuitive, which explains why the authors chose to cheat. *BPELJ
won't be ready for prime time until these issues are resolved.*

BPELJ Source Code

The source code of a pure BPEL process is a set of XML files containing WSDL and BPEL
process definitions. BPELJ source code can be either XML files with embedded Java code
or Java source files annotated with XML. The former approach is the one adopted in the
examples above; likewise, most of the samples in the BPELJ specification are XML with
embedded Java.

The latter approach, documented in the BPELJ specification as a viable alternative, makes
sense only if the number of lines of Java code is close to the number of lines of XML.
Example 5-4 shows a Java source file (*MyProcessImpl.java*) containing a comment in lines
1–15 that defines the BPEL process XML. The source file implements the class
MyProcessImpl; the source code begins on line 16. Lines 17–20 implement a method that is
called in the process on line 10.

EXAMPLE 5-4. *BPELJ sample*

```
1  /**
2   * @bpelj:process process::
3   * <process name="MyProcess">
4   *  <variables>
5   *   <variable name="x" type="bpelj:Integer"/>
6   *  </variables>
7   *   . . .
8   *  <bpelj:snippet>
9   *   <bpelj:code>
10  *    x = self.getRandomValue ( );
11  *   </bpelj:code>
12  *  </bpelj:snippet>
13  *   . . .
14  * </process>
15  **/
16  public class MyProcessImpl implements Serializable
17  {
18     Integer getRandomValue( )
19     {
```

EXAMPLE 5-4. *BPELJ sample (continued)*

```
20        return new Integer(myRand.nextInt( ));
21    }
22  }
```

A well-designed BPELJ process should be mostly pure BPEL with a smattering of Java. (Analogously, a well-designed Java Server Page is mostly markup with minimal embedded Java.) Significant Java processing can be factored out to special Java partner link types, whose source code resides in traditional Java source files, separate from the process. Consequently, XML-driven BPELJ is preferable to Java-driven BPELJ.

> ### NOTE
> BPELJ is conceptually similar to Process Definition for Java (PD4J),* a specification proposed by BEA to the Java Community Process (JSR 207) for mixing XML and Java for process definition. PD4J is the design model for BEA's WebLogic Integration 8.1. BEA, along with IBM, authored BPELJ (also submitted to JSR 207), and is building to it for its Version 9 release of WebLogic Integration. PD4J favors the Java-with-annotated-XML approach, so perhaps WebLogic Integration 9 will adopt annotated Java as its development model.

Other Language Implementations

BPELJ is the first language extension of BPEL, extending BPEL's capabilities on Java platforms. The same approach is suitable for other programming languages, notably those that figure prominently into Microsoft's .NET platform, such as C#. Expect to see such implementations soon, as BPEL increases in popularity.

BPEL and Patterns

BPEL fares exceptionally well in its support for support for P4 patterns. As rated by P4 members in its paper,† BPEL directly supports 13 of the 20 patterns, and it indirectly supports another one. The results of the paper are captured in Table 5-5.

TABLE 5-5. *BPEL support for the P4 patterns*

Pattern	Compliance (+, +–, –)	Approach	Notes
Sequence	+	sequence activity	
Parallel Split	+	flow activity	
Synchronization	+	flow activity followed by another activity, which will not execute until all parallel paths in the flow have completed.	

---

*   JSR 207, *http://www.jcp.org/en/jsr/detail?id=207.*

†   P. Wohed, W. van der Aalst, M. Dumas, A. H. M. ter Hofstede, "Pattern Based Analysis of BPEL4WS," FIT Technical Report, FIT-TR-2002-04.

TABLE 5-5. *BPEL support for the P4 patterns (continued)*

Pattern	Compliance (+, +–, –)	Approach	Notes
Exclusive Choice	+	`switch` activity.	
Simple Merge	+	`switch` activity followed by another activity, which will not execute until the one activity selected in the switch has completed.	
Multi-Choice	+	`flow` with conditional links to the activities to be chosen.	See P4 paper, p.8f.
Sync Merge	+	Use dead path elimination to join the results of the multiple choice.	
Multi Merge	-	No.	
Discriminator	-	No.	See P4 paper, p.9.
Arbitrary cycles	-	Only structured loops are allowed. No goto-like constructs.	
Implicit Termination	+	`flow` with a link out.	
Multiple Instances (MI) Without Synchronization	+	`invoke` in a `while` loop.	
MI With Design Time Knowledge	+	Run each instance as a separate activity in a `flow` activity.	
MI With Runtime Knowledge	-	Onerous.	See P4 paper, p. 11.
MI Without Runtime Knowledge	-		
Deferred Choice	+	`pick` activity	
Interleaved Parallel Routing	+-	Multiple `scopes` within a `flow` that compete for a single shared variable whose access is serialized (`variableAccessSerializable` is set to yes). The order of the scopes is arbitrary but serial.	See P4 paper, p. 12f.
Milestone	-	Poll for milestone in a `while` loop.	See P4 paper, p.14.
Cancel Activity	+	`Fault` out of the activity to be cancelled.	
Cancel Case	+	`terminate` activity	

Summary

The main points of this chapter include the following:

- BPEL is an XML-based process definition language. The XML approach has several merits, including programmability, executability, exportability, and easy web services integration capabilities.

- BPEL was originally written by IBM, Microsoft, and BEA, but has been handed over to OASIS for standardization. BPEL is based on IBM's WSFL and Microsoft's XLANG.

- The source code for a BPEL process is a set of WSDL files and a BPEL XML file. WSDL is the standard web service definition format, specifying port types, partner link types, message types, and properties. The process definition references the WSDL, creating partner links based on WSDL partner link types and variables based on WSDL-defined message types. Compensation, fault and event handlers can be defined for the process or any of its scope levels. The flow of a BPEL process includes service touchpoints (receive, invoke, reply) and control flow elements (wait, while, switch, flow, sequence, scope).

- BPELJ introduces Java extensions to "pure" BPEL, such as the ability to define Java process variable, evaluate dates and conditions with Java code, and embed code snippets. Other powerful features include Java partner links (enabling invoke calls to local Java classes in addition to pure BPEL's partner web services) and correlation based on Java classes.

- BPELJ source code can be XML with embedded Java or Java with annotated XML. The former approach is arguably better from a design perspective. The latter approach is influenced by BEA's PD4J model, used in WebLogic Integration 8.

- BPEL has built-in or easily attainable support for 14 of the 20 P4 patterns.

References

1. S. Dietzen, "Standards for Service-Oriented Architecture," *Weblogic Pro*. May/June 2004.

2. C. McDonald, "Orchestration, Choreography, and Collaboration," *http://lists.w3.org/ Archives/Public/www-archive/2003May/0009.html*

3. S. White, "Business Process Modeling Notation," Version 1.0. http://www.bpmn.org/ Documents/Introduction%20to%20BPMN.pdf, May 2004.

CHAPTER SIX

BPMI Standards: BPMN and BPML

T HE BUSINESS PROCESS MODELING INITIATIVE (BPMI, *http://www.bpmi.org*) is a nonprofit organization whose mission is to build standards and a common architecture for BPM. BPMI, started by Intalio in 2000, has grown to include a variety of organizations, including BEA, Fujitsu, IBM, IDS Scheer, Pegasystems, PeopleSoft, SAP, SeeBeyond, Tibco, Virtria, and WebMethods.

BPMI is itself a member of several key organizations, including W3C, OASIS, OMG, and the WfMC. Through these memberships, BPMI is able to contribute to discussion of essentially every current BPM standard whose specification the BPMI does not itself own: BPEL with OASIS; choreography with W3C; business process metamodels with OMG; and XPDL, WAPI, WfXML, and the workflow reference model with WfMC.

BPMI's contribution focuses on the following functional specifications:

Business Process Modeling Notation
    BPMN is a graphical flowchart language that can be used by business analysts or developers to represent a business process in an intuitive visual form. Stephen White of IBM wrote Version 1.0 of the specification in 2004.

Business Process Modeling Language

BPML is an XML language that encodes the flow of a business process in a form that can be interpreted by a process execution engine. Assaf Arkin of Intalio wrote version 1.0 of the BPML specification, which was published in November 2002.

Business Process Query Language

BPQL is a standardized administration and monitoring query language for business processes, intended as a foundation for business activity monitoring (BAM). The initial public version of BPQL has not yet been published.

Business Process Semantic Model

The OMG has proposed a BPDM, or a common model for all business process models, whose definition is based on the OMG Meta-Object Facility (MOF) foundation. BPSM, not yet published, is the BPMI's putative BPDM metamodel. (For more information on BPDM and MOF, see Chapter 9.)

Business Process Extension Layers

BPXL is a standard set of BPEL extensions for transactions, business rules, task management, and human interaction. The BPXL specification has not yet been published.

These specifications do not exist in isolation; they are pieces of BPMI's recommended BPM stack (documented in the BPMI's current material at *http://www.bpmi.org*), as shown in Figure 6-1.

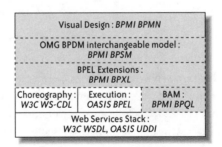

FIGURE 6-1. *BPMI's recommended BPM stack*

At the top of the stack is the visual process design layer, based on BPMN. Below it is BPSM, in which BPMN visual models are represented in a common, interchangeable metamodel form, suitable for import into the execution layer based on the OASIS group's BPEL (discussed in Chapter 5), which is extended by BPXL. BPEL, in turn, runs atop a web services messaging and transport layer, whose major standards include the W3C's WSDL and the OASIS UDDI. BPEL shares the web services base with the standard BAM query service BPQL, as well as the W3C's WS-CDL choreography (discussed in Chapter 8). BPQL enables business monitoring of BPEL processes, and WS-CDL defines the global contract governing the partner interactions of BPEL processes.

This stack is intriguing for several reasons:

- Not all pieces are based on BPMI standards. (The BPMI pieces are shaded.) BPMI embraces standards—such as BPEL, WS-CDL, and the core web services standards—of other organizations.

- Some of the BPMI pieces (dotted in the figure) are not currently published. If the stack were to be implemented today, the implementers would need to find suitable substitutes for BPSM, BPXL, and BPQL.

- BPML is nowhere to be found! Its place—the web service-based execution spot—seems to have to been stolen by BPEL. The BPMI position paper* concedes that the BPEL standard, BPML's most formidable competitor, has won the XML execution language war, and by virtue of "might makes right" is a better fit than BPML for the stack.

- The same BPMI position paper recommended Web Services Choreography Interface (WSCI) as the choreography piece, but since then BPMI has adopted WS-CDL, the W3C's official approach.

This chapter describes BPMN and BPML in detail and introduces the main aspects of each language through several feature-rich examples; each language is also rated on its support for the P4 patterns introduced in Chapter 4.†

BPMN

BPMN is a graphical flowchart-like language intended for use by business analysts and developers to build business process diagrams (BPDs). A BPD conveys in pictures what BPML and BPEL encode in XML, but it serves a different purpose: BPMN is for graphical design, whereas BPML and BPEL are for execution. The BPMN specification‡ attempts to bridge the gap by providing a mapping from BPMN to BPEL (but not, interestingly, to BPML); the mapping specifies rules to generate BPEL from a BPD, enabling the execution of a BPD. Figure 6-2 shows how a typical BPMN tool is used in the design process.

In addition to BPEL export, the tool also supports BPSM metamodel import and export, allowing the BPMN tool to exchange processes with those developed in other tools. The message broker example developed in Chapter 11 uses ITpearls' MS Visio-based BPMN tool for the design of message broker processes. ITpearls, alas, does not currently include any of these import and export features.

---

* BPMI, "BPMN and BPEL4WS: A Convergence Path Toward a Standard BPM Stack," *http://www. bpmi.org*, August 2002.

† Interestingly, the BPMN specification provides a BPEL mapping, which facilitates BPEL XML representation of BPMN diagrams; this mapping is explored at a high level later in the chapter. The BPMN specification makes no mention of BPML, though one would expect a BPMN-to-BPML mapping to resemble the BPMN-to-BPEL mapping.

‡ S. White, "Business Process Modeling Notation," Version 1.0. *http://www.bpmi.org*, May 2004.

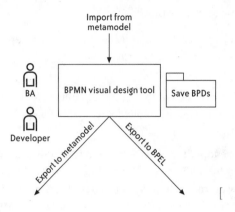

FIGURE 6-2. *Use of BPMN*

BPMN Example

The first step in learning a new language is to look at the implementation of "Hello, World!" In our case, we study "Hello, Claim!," which is an insurance claims handling process and is shown in Figure 6-3.

The process receives a claim (Get claim), examines it (Examine claim), and then splits into one of three directions, depending on whether the claim has been approved (Process approval), rejected (Process reject), or passed along for further analysis (Analysis). The analysis option has a time limit; if it is not performed quickly enough, it is aborted (Stuck), and a special escalation process (Escalate, whose steps are enclosed in the Escalate box) is run. The escalation process behaves much like its parent: it begins by examining the claim, then either approves or rejects it; no further analysis is permitted in an escalation. The parent process completes when its conditional path—approval, rejection, analysis, or escalation—completes.

Several types of symbols are used in this diagram: events, gateways, atomic activities (or tasks), compound activities (or subprocesses), sequence flow, and text annotations. Events, drawn as small circles, mark the start (e.g., Get claim) and end points of the process, as well as the intermediate timeout condition (Stuck) that occurs during analysis. Gateways (diamonds) help mark the conditional split and join portion of the process. Activities (boxes) represent actual work performed. Tasks (e.g., Examine claim) are single actions, whereas subprocesses perform arbitrarily complex logic. A subprocess can be drawn either collapsed or expanded; a collapsed process (e.g., Process reject) is drawn with a plus sign, its details hidden, but assumed to be documented in another diagram; an expanded process (e.g., Escalate) has its internal logic drawn inside of it. Sequence flow is the set of arrows connecting together the other pieces; arrows labeled with text (e.g., arrow between gateway and Process approval) are conditional, followed only if the condition is true. Text annotations (open-ended boxes) present instructional comments.

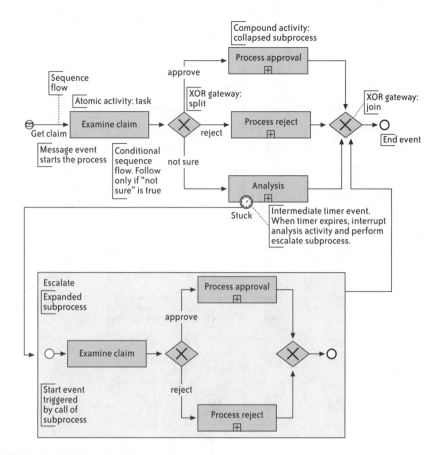

FIGURE 6-3. *BPMN insurance claims process*

BPMN in a Nutshell

This section examines the essential language constructs that designers need to understand in order to create a BPMN process: the basic process structure, variables and assignments, exception handling and compensation, split and join, loops, participant exchange, transactions, and extensions. Before delving into the details of the language, we'll first introduce the basic elements in a BPMN process—events, activities, sequence flows, and gateways—in a bit more detail.

An *event*, the first basic element of BPMN, is an occurrence that triggers a business process. Events are categorized by the stage at which they occur in a process (start, intermediate, or end) and by type (basic, message, timer, rule, exception, cancellation, compensation, link, multiple, or termination). The shape of an event is a small circle; a start event has a thin border, an end event a thick border, and an intermediate event has a double border. Figure 6-4 illustrates the complete set of events and how they are depicted.

Table 6-1 describes the role of events in more detail.

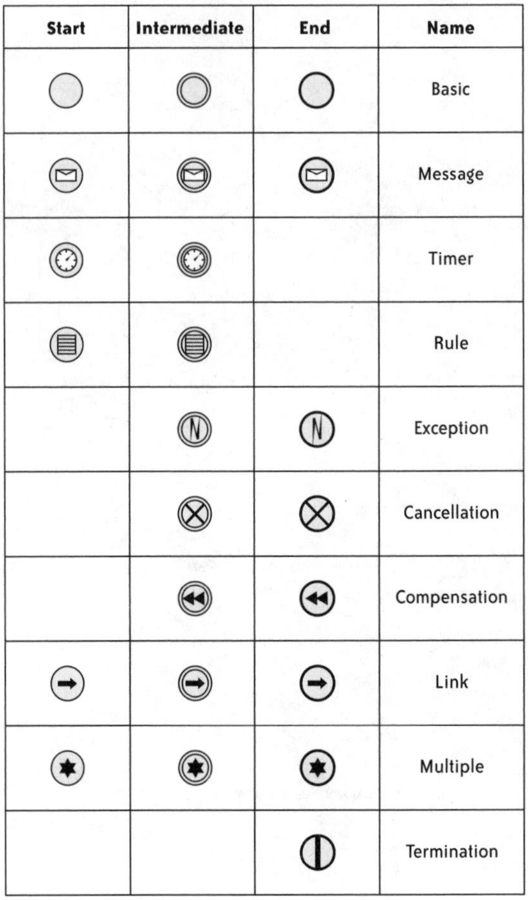

Start	Intermediate	End	Name
○	◎	○	Basic
✉	✉	✉	Message
⊙	⊙		Timer
▤	▤		Rule
	Ⓝ	Ⓝ	Exception
	⊗	⊗	Cancellation
	⊙	⊙	Compensation
→	→	→	Link
✱	✱	✱	Multiple
		ⓘ	Termination

FIGURE 6-4. *BPMN events*

TABLE 6-1. *BPMN event description*

Type	Start	Intermediate	End
Basic	Placeholder event or the start of a called subprocess.	Placeholder	Placeholder or end of a subprocess.
Message	Process is started by receipt of a message (e.g., the invocation of a web service method implemented by the process).	Process is waiting for a message (e.g., wait for response from a participant to which this process has sent a request).	A message is to be sent to a participant process (e.g., call its web service).
Timer	The start event defines a schedule for when it triggers (e.g., every Tuesday at midnight).	A point in a defined schedule has been reached.	
Rule	A condition, defined by the process, is met (e.g., process starts when a stock's price hits its 52-week high).	A condition is met. Used only for exception handling.	
Exception		Throw or catch an error.	Generate an error.
Cancellation		Perform cancellation for a given activity.	Cancel the transaction.

TABLE 6-1. *BPMN event description (continued)*

Type	Start	Intermediate	End
Compensation		Trigger and perform compensation handling.	Perform compensating action.
Link	The link start event connects to the link end event of a sibling process.	Link to or from another activity.	Connect to the link start of a sibling process.
Multiple	Two or more triggers can start the process; if any one of them occurs, the process starts. These triggers can be message, timer, rule or link types.	Two or more triggers can continue a waiting process; if any one of them occurs, the process resumes.	When the process ends, several results are required (e.g. several messages need to be sent).
Termination			Terminate all activities in the process. Perform no exception handling or compensation.

An *activity*, the second basic element of BPMN, is a step in a process that performs work. In BPMN, an activity is either atomic or compound. An atomic activity, also known as a task, performs a single action. A compound activity, also known as a process, has its own set of atomic or compound activities, as well events, gateways, and all other BPMN constructs. Processes are hierarchical: a process can have subprocesses, each of which can have subprocesses, and so on.

An activity is drawn as a box with rounded edges. When shown in a parent process, a child process is drawn as a single box bearing a plus sign (+). The plus sign represents the collapsed view of the process; the full detail is drawn in a separate diagram. Any activity—task or process—can be marked up with symbols representing compensation, multiple instances, and loops; additionally, a process can have the markup symbol tilde (~) for ad hoc processing. These possibilities are depicted in Figure 6-5.

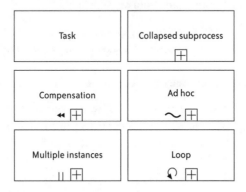

FIGURE 6-5. *BPMN activities*

A compensated activity is one that has special compensation logic to revert it (undo its effect) after completion. An ad hoc process contains a set of activities that can occur in any order; the control flow is unstructured. Loop and multiple instance activities are described in the later section "Loops." Table 6-2 summarizes the BPMN specification's suggested task types.

TABLE 6-2. *BPMN task types*

Use	Description
Service	Calls a web service
Receive	Waits for a message (an alternative to an event construct)
Send	Sends a message
User, Manual	Task is performed by a human participant (e.g., approval)
Script	Logic encoded in a programming or scripting language (e.g., run a piece of Java code)
Reference	Uses the definition of another task in the process; shares the definition rather than duplicating it

Sequence flow, the third basic element of BPMN, is the flow of control in a process, and is represented by arrows connecting source and target activities, events, or gateways. Figure 6-6 shows the three types of sequence flow arrows.

FIGURE 6-6. *BPMN sequence flow arrows*

The first arrow represents normal, unguarded flow from source to target. The second symbol is default flow, used in cases where control splits into multiple directions, each path depending on the evaluation of a condition; it fires only if none of the other guarded transitions fired. The third is a guarded transition, traversed only if its associated conditional expression evaluates to true; the diamond at the end of the arrow is not required when the transition originates from an XOR split.

A *gateway*, the final basic BPMN element, is a special controller of splits and joins. This element is discussed in more depth in the later section "Split and join."

Basic process structure: start, end, activities, sequence

A basic BPMN process has a start event, one or more activities, and an end event. The process in Figure 6-7, for example, starts with a message event that receives a partner request, and then executes activities to handle the request and send a response to the partner, before closing with a basic end event.

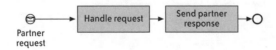

FIGURE 6-7. *BPMN sequence example*

Besides activities, intermediate events can also be key steps in the mainline sequence of a process. A typical example is the process shown in Figure 6-8, which sends a message to a partner application and then needs to waits for response before continuing. This example also shows that the end event can perform useful work; in this case, sending an acknowledgment message to the partner.

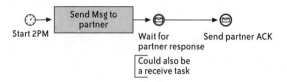

FIGURE 6-8. *BPMN sequence example with intermediate event*

Variables and assignments

In BPMN, processes and activities can have variables (known as properties), assign values to them, and make decisions based on their values. Though variables are not shown graphically in a BPD, BPMN includes them in its object model, chiefly to facilitate a mapping to BPEL.

Most BPMN editors, including ITpearls, provide an attribute editor to manipulate variables and other data associated with processes, activities, or other graphical nodes. Figure 6-9 shows how two String type properties—ClaimID and SubscriberID—are defined for the Escalate subprocess.

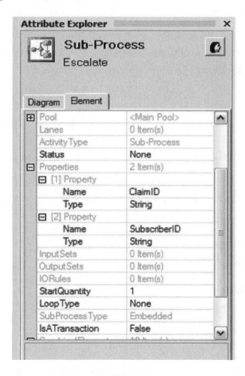

FIGURE 6-9. *BPMN process properties in ITpearls' attribute editor*

For the mechanics of variable usage, consult the BPMN specification.

Exception handling and compensation

Figure 6-10 illustrates the BPMN approach to exception handling.

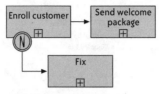

(a) Exception in Enroll customer

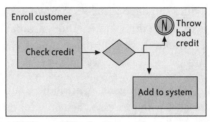

(b) Closeup of Enroll customer subprocess

FIGURE 6-10. *BPMN exception handling*

Part (a) shows the catching and handling of an exception in the subprocess Enroll customer. When Enroll customer completes normally, it transitions to Send welcome package. But if an exception occurs during its execution, the intermediate error event on the boundary of Enroll customer catches the error and passes control to the subprocess Fix, which serves as a fault handler for Enroll customer. Part (b) shows that an intermediate error event, when not on the boundary of an activity, effectively throws an exception, which triggers exception handling of the parent process. The event Throw bad credit breaks the normal flow of the parent process, Enroll customer, and precipitates the handler in Fix from part (a).

In compensation, an activity is run to reverse the effects of another activity. For example, in Figure 6-11, Cancel compensates Reserve hotel.

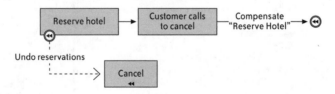

FIGURE 6-11. *BPMN compensation*

The notation is to place a compensation intermediate event (resembling a "rewind" symbol) on the boundary of the activity to be compensated, draw a dotted arrow (known as an "associated" in BPMN parlance) from the compensation event to the boundary of the compensating activity, and mark a compensation symbol inside the boundary of the compensating activity. The compensating activity must be self-contained; it cannot have any inbound or outbound sequence flow connections. The job of a compensating activity is strictly to perform the required reversal logic.

Compensation is triggered in one of two ways:

- With an explicit compensation event, as with the event `Compensate "Reserve Hotel"` shown earlier.

- If the activity to be compensated is part of transaction subprocess that is cancelled. This scenario is discussed in the later section "Transactions."

Compensation can apply to transactional and nontransactional activities alike. For transactional activities, compensation is not the same as rollback. Only a completed activity can be compensated; if that activity is transactional, because it has completed, its transaction has already committed.

Split and join

BPMN uses the *gateway* element to model split and join patterns, which represent common programming control structures such as `if-then`, `switch`, and `all`. A gateway branches and merges paths in a process. The diamond-shaped symbol is well known in flowchart languages as a decision point, but BPMN expands its use to model patterns such as AND split and join and deferred choice. Furthermore, in BPMN a gateway has two modes: it splits one incoming path into multiple outgoing paths (which we will refer to as split mode), and merges several incoming paths into one outgoing path (join mode). The BPMN gateway symbols are shown in Figure 6-12.

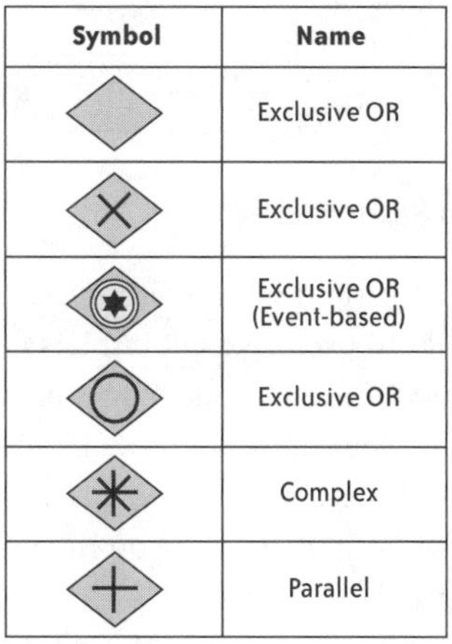

Symbol	Name
◇	Exclusive OR
⨯	Exclusive OR
⊛	Exclusive OR (Event-based)
◯	Exclusive OR
✳	Complex
✛	Parallel

FIGURE 6-12. *BPMN gateways*

The first gateway, the *exclusive OR*, uses if-then-else and switch with mutually exclusive cases as a control structure. In split mode, it evaluates a separate condition on each of its outgoing paths and lets through the first path whose condition evaluates to true; all others are ignored. Exactly one condition must be true; a default branch can be specified in case none of the other branches fire. In join mode, the exclusive OR gateway lets through the first of its multiple incoming branches and discards all others. Figure 6-13 illustrates the behavior by showing an activity (Finalize claim) that runs when either Process approval or Process rejection completes, and an activity (Evaluate claim) that splits to Process approval if the condition approved is satisfied and to Process rejection otherwise.

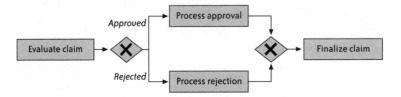

FIGURE 6-13. *BPMN exclusive OR gateway*

The second gateway, the *exclusive OR (event-based)*, uses a pick control structure. In split mode, each outgoing branch leads to an event node. The gateway lets through the branch having the first triggered event, and ignores all others. The join mode is not commonly used. For example, in the process in Figure 6-14, when the activity Request completes, the process waits for one of the two events—Receive accept or Receive reject—to occur.

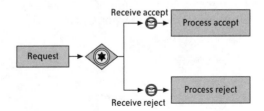

FIGURE 6-14. *BPMN exclusive OR gateway for events*

The third gateway, the *inclusive OR*, uses a switch with overlapping cases as a control structure. The split mode is similar to exclusive OR but lets through each outgoing path whose condition evaluates to true. The join mode blocks passage until each expected executing incoming path enters it. The gateway knows in advance how many active inputs to expect. Figure 6-15 illustrates both behaviors: activity Get employee change splits to Send to HR or Send to payroll or both, depending on the evaluation of conditions promotions and raise; activity Log change waits until Send to HR or Send to payroll or both of these complete, depending on which paths the splitting gateway let through.

FIGURE 6-15. *BPMN OR gateway*

The fourth gateway, *complex*, uses a control structure that is quite unique to BPMN. The split mode is not commonly used. The join mode evaluates an expression to determine which of the incoming paths to let through. As an example, in Figure 6-16 the gateway waits for two of the three parallel activities—Good credit, Natural citizen, and No criminal record—before granting security clearance.

FIGURE 6-16. *BPMN complex gateway*

The final type, the *parallel* gateway, uses all control structures in BPML and flow in BPEL. In split mode, it lets through each outgoing path. In join mode, it blocks until each incoming path completes. Figure 6-17 illustrates these two behaviors: when activity Accept claim completes, the activities Send email result and Credit subscriber bank account are run in parallel; Mark claim done, however, starts only when both Send email result and Credit subscriber bank account complete.

FIGURE 6-17. *BPMN AND gateway*

The BPMN specification is laden with references to token passing, betraying its dependency on the ideas of the Petri net. For example:

- A parallel gateway sends a token for each of its outgoing arrows. A parallel gateway waits for a token on each of its incoming arrows.
- An exclusive gateway sends a token on exactly one of its outgoing arrows, namely the one whose condition is true. An exclusive gateway waits for exactly one token from its incoming arrows.
- When multiple arrows converge on an activity without first passing through a gateway, each token that comes through will trigger the activity.
- When multiple arrows emanate from a single activity (known as "uncontrolled" flow in BPMN), a token is generated on each arrow.

Loops

BPMN's approach to looping is powerful but obscure. In most process languages, a loop is a specific type of compound activity that iterates over the set of activities inside of it. For example, the BPEL while loop in the following code sample repeats a sequence of invoke activities (A and B) for as long as its specified condition evaluates to true:

```
<while condition=". . .">
   <sequence>
      <invoke name="A" . . . />
      <invoke name="B" . . . />
   </sequence>
</while>
```

In BPMN, looping is an attribute of an activity. To make an activity loop, simply play with the attributes of the activity, and it will loop as directed. If BPEL were designed this way, its code would resemble the following, in which the sequence activity itself controls whether and how to loop:

```
<sequence looping="true" loopcondition=". . .">
   <invoke name="A" . . . />
   <invoke name="B" . . . />
</sequence>
```

In BPMN, any activity (either a task or a subprocess) can be configured either to not loop, to loop in standard mode (while or until loops), or to support multiple instances (foreach looping). The notation for standard and multiple instance (MI) loops is shown in Figure 6-18. (An activity with standard looping has a circular arrow mark in the bottom center of its box; an activity with MI has a pair of vertical parallel bars.)

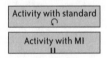

FIGURE 6-18. *BPMN notation for standard and multiple instance (MI) loops*

Figure 6-19 shows the BPMN representation of the BPEL while loop: activities A and B run sequentially in a process `AB sequence` that is configured with standard looping.

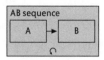

FIGURE 6-19. *BPMN while loop for a sequence of activities*

Table 6-3 summarizes the settings for a standard loop.

TABLE 6-3. *Standard loop settings*

Setting	Description
Condition	An expression that determines whether to continue looping.
Test time: before, after	When to test the condition: before the activity is run, or after it is run. In the former case, the loop will behave as a while; in the latter, as an until.
maxLoops	An upper boundary on the number of iterations.
Loop counter	Used internally. Starts at zero, is incremented by one for each iteration, and is compared with maxLoops.

If the test time is set to before, the logic of the loop is the following:

```
While (cond and loopCounter < maxLoops)
    Perform Activity
```

Otherwise, the logic of the loop is the following:

```
Do
    Perform Activity
Until (cond and loopCounter >= maxLoops)
```

In contrast to the standard loop, the MI loop is rather complicated. Table 6-4 summarizes the MI loop settings.

TABLE 6-4. *MI loop settings*

Setting	Description
MI condition	An expression that determines the number of instances to run.
Loop counter	Used internally as loop counter.
Ordering: sequential, parallel	Determines whether the instances are run sequentially or in parallel.
Flow condition: none, one, all, complex	Used only if the order is parallel. none means that as soon as each instance of the activity is executed, the next activity in the process is executed. one means that the next activity is executed only after the first instance completes; subsequent iterations execute, but do not continue onto the next activity. all means that the next activity executes only once all instances have completed. complex means that the "complex condition" expression must be evaluated to determine the rule for how to handle the next activity; complex can be used to model patterns such as N-out-of-M join.
Complex condition	A condition that determines when and how many times to execute the next activity.

Sequential processing is simple:

```
For counter = 0 to MI condition
    Perform activity
Perform next activity
```

Parallel processing with a flow condition of all resembles the following:

```
For counter = 0 to MI condition
    Spawn activity
Wait for all activities; when an activity completes, do nothing
Perform next activity
```

Parallel processing with a flow condition of one resembles the following:

```
For counter = 0 to MI condition
    Spawn activity
Wait for one activity; when it completes, perform the next activity
```

Parallel processing with a flow condition of none resembles the following:

```
For counter = 0 to MI condition
    Spawn activity
Wait for all activities; for each completed activity, perform next activity
```

Parallel processing with a flow condition of complex resembles the following:

```
For counter = 0 to MI condition
    Spawn activity
Wait for all activities
For each completed activity
    If complex condition says perform next activity, do so
```

Figure 6-20 shows scenarios in which each type of looping would be used.

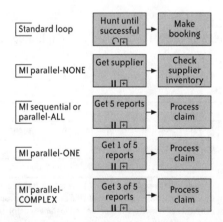

FIGURE 6-20. *BPMN loop scenarios*

Table 6-5 summarizes each of these scenarios.

TABLE 6-5. *Description of BPMN loop scenarios*

Loop type	Description
Standard	Hunt airline schedules for an available flight. When one is found, book it.
MI parallel–NONE	Loop through a list of suppliers. For each supplier, query its inventory.
MI sequential or parallel–ALL	For the investigation of an insurance claim, take reports from five witnesses (either sequentially or in parallel). When all five have completed, process the claim.
MI parallel–ONE	For the investigation of an insurance claim, take reports from five witnesses in parallel. As soon as one completes, process the claim, but in the meantime, let the others complete too.
MI parallel– COMPLEX	Similar to the previous case, but do not process the claim until three reports have completed.

Participant exchange

BPMN provides a rich framework for modeling interparticipant processing, which includes swim lanes and pools, message flow, message events, send and receive tasks, and message correlation.

A *swim lane* is a pool and each of its lanes. A *pool* represents the activities of one participant—often a company—in collaboration; a lane in a pool represents a subdivision of the participant—often a department or division of the company. Swim lanes help convey the sense that a process spans multiple participants; it depicts who does what and how the interactions are structured. For example, consider the collaboration of a supplier and a financial institution. The supplier calls the financial institution to authorize payment. The supplier, in turn, is divided into sales and distribution departments, which manage different parts of the supplier's process. Figure 6-21 illustrates this scenario.

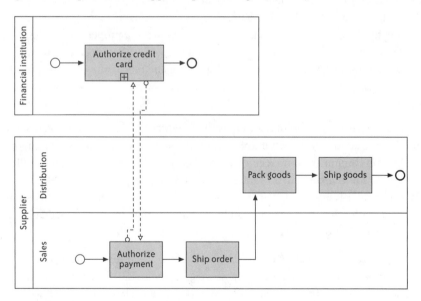

FIGURE 6-21. *BPMN swim lane, adapted from BPMN specification, V.1, p.104*

Message flow, symbolized by a dashed arrow, such as the arrow between supplier and financial institution in Figure 6-21, shows the flow of messages, or the data flow, between participants. The solid arrows of sequence flow, by contrast, capture process flow, or inter-activity control movement.

NOTE

The BPMN authors favor showing both kinds of flow in the same diagram, but this practice has drawbacks, the most obviously of which is clutter. Showing both types of flow is also common in UML activity diagrams.

Message events and send and receive tasks are also supported. Table 6-6 summarizes the five main BPMN message-exchange process elements and their BPEL mapping.

TABLE 6-6. *BPMN message exchange elements*

Type	Meaning	BPEL equivalent	From/to participant
Start message event	Inbound web service	Receive and create instance	From
Intermediate message event	Inbound web service	Receive	From
End message event	Outbound web service	Invoke or reply	To
Send task	Outbound web service	Invoke	To
Receive task	Inbound web service	Receive	From

BPMN's support for *message correlation* (which allows a process to determine whether a given inbound message, based on key data, belongs to its conversation) is something of an afterthought. Specifically, BPMN allows a process or activity property to be designated as a correlation set. Such a property can have child properties that represent members of the correlation set. Refer to the BPMN specification for the mechanics of the approach.

Transactions

BPMN also supports the notion of the *transaction*, in which a subprocess can be marked to allow it to be executed as a single unit of work. If the subprocess reaches its end point successfully, it is committed. If it receives a cancellation event, the transaction is rolled back, compensation is applied to any subactivities that require it, and a special cancellation handler is executed. A transactional subprocess is drawn with a thick border line. The cancellation handler is connected by a sequence flow to an intermediate cancel event on the border of the subprocess.

As an example, in Figure 6-22, if a cancellation occurs in the transactional subprocess Invite to conference, the updates in Add to meeting list and Add to dinner list are rolled back, the Reserve hotel activity is compensated, and the cancellation handler Manual fix is executed.

PRIVATE, ABSTRACT, AND COLLABORATIVE PROCESSES IN BPMN

BPMN supports three types of processes:

- Private (internal), representing the full orchestration logic of particular participant. Private processes can be used to model BPEL executable processes.

- Abstract (public), representing the publicly observable interparticipant exchange of a particular participant. Abstract processes can be used to model BPEL abstract processes.

- Collaborative (global), which show the overall public exchange between a set of participants. These processes are similar to the collaborations of BPSS (see Chapter 9) or WS-CDL (Chapter 8).

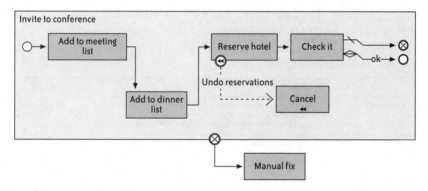

FIGURE 6-22. *BPMN exception handling*

A cancellation can be triggered either explicitly, by a cancellation end event in the subprocess, or implicitly, by a cancellation message from the transaction manager of the engine. The use of a cancellation event is shown in Figure 6-22: when the Check it activity is executed, it transitions to one of two end events: a normal end, if the variable ok evaluates to true, or a cancellation event, which cancels the subprocess.

Extensions

BPMN can be extended in two ways: by adding new symbols or by modifying existing symbols. Considering the importance of BPMN's mapping to BPEL (discussed in the next section), a key BPMN extension follows the BPELJ extension of BPEL by providing Java variables and expressions, Java-based participants, and Java-based message events and send and receive tasks. These changes would be noninvasive, affecting only the behind-the-scenes attributes of core BPMN constructs, with no impact to the visual representation.

BPEL Mapping

The BPMN specification includes a 64-page chapter on BPEL mapping, which bridges the gap between graphical design and executability. BPMN diagrams are of little consequence unless they can actually be deployed and run. The BPEL mapping allows the generation of BPEL XML from BPMN diagrams, thus making it possible to run BPMN on BPEL engines. Significantly, the BPMN specification omits, and makes no mention of, a mapping to BPML; the BPMI, as described previously, places BPEL on its stack in place of BPML.

The details of the mapping are difficult. This section is a very high-level overview; you should consult the BPMN specification for the complete picture. BPEL has fewer constructs than BPMN, which complicates the mapping. One of the weaknesses of BPMN is its excess of features (e.g., multiple instance activities and the complex gateway); this excess makes BPMN extremely expressive, but a chore to fit into the BPM stack. BPSM, described at the beginning of this chapter, might help close the gap by providing a common metamodel for these languages. Table 6-7 presents the highlights of the mapping presented in the BPMN specification.

TABLE 6-7. *BPMN mapping to BPEL*

BPMN	BPEL
Start event: all except Multiple	receive element with createInstance set to yes.
Start event: Multiple	pick element with createInstance set to yes.
End event: Message	invoke or reply element.
End event: Error	throw element.
End event: Compensation	compensate element.
End event: Terminate	terminate element.
End event: Link	invoke element.
Intermediate event: Error	Error handler if on the boundary of an activity, throw otherwise.
Activities: MI	Not a direct mapping. Use a variety of constructs.
Activities: Subprocesses	Use invoke to spawn. Embedded subprocesses implemented in scope.
Gateway: Exclusive data-based	switch element.
Gateway: Exclusive event-based	pick element.
Gateway: Inclusive	Multiple switch elements within a flow element.
Gateway: Complex	No obvious mapping.
Gateway: Parallel	flow element.
Sequence Flow	Model the flow of control from one node to another either explicitly with flow link elements or implicitly with control structures such a sequence, while, or switch.
Message Flow	No mapping.

BPMN and Patterns

BPMN is designed to implement most of the P4 patterns discussed in Chapter 4. White's paper* describes the BPMN implementation for each of the patterns. Table 6-8 summarizes White's findings.

TABLE 6-8. *BPMN support for the P4 patterns*

Pattern	Compliance (+, −, +−)	Approach
Sequence	+	Normal sequence flow
Parallel Split	+	Parallel gateway as splitter
Synchronization	+	Parallel gateway as joiner
Exclusive Choice	+	Exclusive gateway as splitter
Simple Merge	+	Exclusive gateway as joiner
Multi-Choice	+	Inclusive gateway as splitter
Sync Merge	+	Inclusive gateway as joiner
Multi-Merge	+	Uncontrolled split and join
Discriminator	+	Complex gateway as joiner to accept one out of M or N out of M incoming paths
Arbitrary cycles	+	Sequence flow allows loops
Implicit Termination	+	Multiple end events allowed; first to trigger ends process
Multiple Instances (MI) Without Synchronization	+	MI marker on activity
MI With Design Time Knowledge	+	Use MI
MI With Runtime Knowledge	+−	More advanced use of MI
MI Without Runtime Knowledge	−	Relatively difficult coding
Deferred Choice	+	Exclusive data-based gateway as splitter
Interleaved Parallel Routing	+	Yes! Ad hoc process
Milestone	+	
Cancel Activity	+	Exception handling
Cancel Case	+	Exception handling or implicit termination

BPML

BPML is an XML process definition language that, like BPEL, describes the structural representation of a process and the semantics of its execution. As with BPEL, the vision of BPML is to run XML processes on an engine element by element, according to precisely defined semantics. The code of a BPML process—laden with familiar constructs such as loops, decisions, parallel paths, variables, and structured exception handling—is readily understood by a programmer.

---

* Stephen White, "Process Modeling Notations and Workflow Patterns," *BPTrends*, March 2004.

BPML Example

Once again, the best way to start learning a new language is to dive into an example.
Example 6-1 demonstrates several features of BPML, including event-driven processes,
context, properties, schedules, exception processes, fault handlers, compensation, and
several activity types.

EXAMPLE 6-1. *BPML sample: placing an order*

```
1   <wsdl:message name="requestMessage">
2       <wsdl:part name="details" element="type:orderDetails"/>
3   </wsdl:message>
4
5   <wsdl:message name="requestAck">
6       <wsdl:part name="orderID" element="type:orderID"/>
7   <wsdl:message>
8
9   <wsdl:message name="cancelMessage">
10      <wsdl:part name="orderID" element="type:orderID"/>
11  <wsdl:message>
12
13  <wsdl:message name="requestComplete">
14      <wsdl:part name="orderID" element="type:orderID"/>
15  </wsdl:message>
16
17  <wsdl:portType name="requesterService">
18      <wsdl:operation name="onComplete">
19          <wsdl:input name="requestComplete"/>
20      </wsdl:operation>
21  </wsdl:portType>
22
23  <wsdl:portType name="serverService">
24      <wsdl:operation name="request">
25          <wsdl:input name="requestMessage"/>
26          <wsdl:output name="requestAck"/>
27      </wsdl:operation>
28      <wsdl:operation name="cancel">
29          <wsdl:input name="cancelMessage"/>
30      </wsdl:operation>
31  </wsdl:portType>
32
33  <!-- BPML main process is called orderProcess.  It is started by the action
34       "receiveOrder below. -->
35  <bpml:process name="orderProcess">
36      <bpml:event activity="receiveOrder"/>
37
38   <!-- The context element defines an exception handler and a fault handler for
39        the main process. -->
40      <bpml:context>
41          <bpml:property name="orderID"/>
42          <bpml:property name="details"/>
43          <bpml:property name="timeLimit" type="xsd:duration"/>
44
45          <!-- Set a timer.  When it expires, generate a fault to trigger the
46               fault handler -->
47          <bpml:schedule name="timeToComplete" code="tns:timeout"
```

EXAMPLE 6-1. *BPML sample: placing an order (continued)*

```
48              duration="timeLimit"/>
49
50         <!-- Handle a cancellation event here -->
51         <bpml:exception name="cancelRequest">
52            <bpml:event activity="receiveCancelRequest"/>
53
54            <bpml:action name="receiveCancelRequest" portType="serverService"
55               operation="cancel" correlate="orderID">
56               <bpml:input element="orderID" property="orderID"/>
57            </bpml:action>
58
59            <bpml:empty/> <!--placeholder for exception processing -->
60         </bpml:exception>
61
62         <!-- Handle faults here, specifically a timeout in the schedule defined
63               above -->
64         <bpml:faults>
65            <bpml:case code="tns:timeout>
66               <bpml:empty/> <!-- placeholder for exception processing -->
67            </bpml:case>
68         </bpml:faults>
69      </bpml:context>
70
71   <!-- Step 1 of process: This action starts the process, responding to the web
72     service operation request on the portType serverService, accepting as input
73          "details" and  returning "orderID". -->
74   <bpml:action name="receiveOrder" portType="serverService" operation="request">
75      <bpml:input element="details" property="details"/>
76      <bpml:output element="orderID">
77         <bpml:source property="orderID"/>
78      </bpml:output>
79      <bpml:assign property="orderID" xpath="func:newIdentifier('orderID')"/>
80   </bpml:action>
81
82   <!-- Step 2: call the subprocess "chargeCustomer" passing in "details" -->
83   <bpml:call process="chargeCustomer">
84      <bpml:output parameter="details">
85         <bpml:source property="details"/>
86      </bpml:output>
87   </bpml:call>
88
89   <!-- Step 3: call the subprocess "shipProduct" passing in "details" -->
90   <bpml:call process="shipProduct">
91      <bpml:output parameter="details">
92         <bpml:source property="details"/>
93      </bpml:output>
94   </bpml:call>
95
96   <!-- Step 4: invoke the callback web service "onComplete" of the requester,
97          sending back the orderID -->
98   <bpml:action name="notifyComplete" portType="requestService"
99      operation="onComplete">
100      <bpml:output element="orderID">
101         <bpml:source property="orderID"/>
102      </bpml:output>
```

EXAMPLE 6-1. *BPML sample: placing an order (continued)*

```
103    </bpml:action>
104
105    <!-- If we need to revert the main process after it has run, then just
106        compensate the "chargeCustomer" process -->
107    <bpml:compensation>
108      <bpml:event activity="receiveCancelRequest"/>
109      <bpml:action name="receiveCancelRequest" portType="serverService"
110        operation="cancel" correlate="orderID">
111        <bpml:input element="orderID" property="orderID"/>
112      </bpml:action>
113      <bpml:compensate process="chargeCustomer"/>
114    </bpml:compensation>
115  </bpml:process>
```

Example 6-1, adapted from two of the examples presented in the BPML 1.0 specification,[*] begins when the main process receives a receiveOrder event (lines 74–80); it immediately responds to the caller with a generated order ID (line 76, which gets its value from line 79). The mainline processing that follows consists of successive calls to subprocesses chargeCustomer (lines 83–87) and shipProduct (lines 90–94), followed by the sending of a completion event to the caller (lines 98–103).

The compensation process in lines 107–114, executed if a cancellation event is received sometime after the process has completed, triggers the compensation of the process chargeCustomer, so that the charge made earlier will be rescinded. If the cancellation event is received while the process is active, the exception handler process (lines 51–60) defined in the context is launched. Also in the context is a scheduled event (lines 47–48), that on expiry trigger the fault tns:timeout in the fault handler in lines 64–68.

The WSDL elements required by the process are defined in lines 1–31.

BPML in a Nutshell

The following sections examine the essential language constructs that designers will need to create a BPML process: the basic process structure, variables and assignments, exception handling and compensation, split and join, loops, participant exchange, transactions, and extensions.

Basic process structure: start, end, activities, sequence

BPML processes are enveloped in a package. Each process has a name, a set of activities, and optionally, a compensation handler. A process can have subprocesses, as well as a context, which in turn can contain fault handlers, exception processes, subprocesses, and properties. Context is hierarchical: if activity set B is a child of activity set A, the context

---

[*]   A. Arkin, "Business Process Modeling Language," Version 1.0. *http://www.bpmi.org*, November 2002.

of B inherits from the context of A. There are three ways to start a process: through an activity, a message, or a signal.

A process starts from an *activity* when it is called from another process using the spawn, call, or compensate activities, or the process is launched from the BPML scheduler according to a predefined timed event. In the following code sample, the process activity_start accepts two input parameters (i1 and i2, the first of which is required) and returns one output parameter (o1). When it is started, the process executes its main logic in the sequence statement.

```
<process name="activity_start">
    <parameters>
        <input name="i1" required="true"/>
        <input name="i2" required="false"/>
        <output name="o1" />
    </parameters>
    <sequence> main body here </sequence>
</process>
```

A process starts from a *message* if it receives one or more messages from a web service. The process can be configured to start when any one of the messages arrives, or only when all arrive. For a message-triggered process, the event element is populated with the list of action activities representing web service calls into the process and an exclusive flag that is true if only one event is required and false otherwise.

For example, the or_event process in the following code sample is triggered by either event ev1 or event ev2 . The event ev1 occurs when the method method1 is called on the service with port type myService; ev2 occurs when method2 is called. The and_event process is similar, except that it requires both ev1 and ev2 to occur before beginning. In each example, the main logic begins with the sequence statement.

```
<process name="or_event">
    <event activity="ev1 ev2" exclusive="true"/>
    <action name="ev1" portType="myService" operation="method1"/>
    <action name="ev2" portType="myService" operation="method2"/>
    <sequence> main body here </sequence>
</process>

<process name="and_event">
    <event activity="ev1 ev2" exclusive="false"/>
    <action name="ev1" portType="myService" operation="method1"/>
    <action name="ev2" portType="myService" operation="method2"/>
    <sequence> main body here </sequence>
</process>
```

A process starts from a *signal* if it receives one or more raised signals from within its context from another process using the raise activity. The process can be configured to trigger when any one of the signals arrives, or only when all arrive. Setting this up in the XML code is similar to setting up message-based starts, except that the event list refers to synch rather than action activities.

In the next example, the process or_signal is started when either signal s1 or signal s2 is raised by another process:

```
<process name="or_signal">
    <event activity="s1 s2" exclusive="true"/>
    <synch signal="s1"/>
    <synch signal="s2"/>
    <sequence> main body here </sequence>
</process>
```

A basic BPML process that executes A, B, and C in sequence resembles the following:

```
<process name="EZProcess">
    <event activity="A" />
    <action name="A" . . . />
    <action name="B" . . . />
    <action name="C" . . . />
</process>
```

Variables and assignments

BPML variables are called properties, which can be declared at the scope of a package or a context. A property has an XML-schema-based type and can have an initial value. In the following code sample, the variable x has initial value 1:

```
<property name="x" type="xsd:int">
    <value>1</value>
</property>
```

The assign activity sets the value of a property, as in the following case, where it increments the value of x by 1:

```
<assign property="x">
    <value>x + 1</value>
</assign>
```

The language used to read and modify property content is XPath.

Exception handling and compensation

BPML has three error handling approaches:

- An exception process is an event handler that aborts a process or a set of activities (e.g., it handles a cancellation event that reverts and aborts a process in flight). See lines 51–60 in Example 6-1.

- A fault handler catches and attempts to fix an error that occurs in an activity, much like a Java catch block. A fault can be generated either implicitly through an error, or by explicitly calling the fault activity, which functions much like the Java throw. See lines 64-68 in Example 6-1.

- A compensation process is like an exception process, except it is intended to revert a *completed*, rather than an in-flight, process; additionally, a compensation process is defined for a process, whereas an exception process is defined for a given context.

Compensation is triggered by a call to the activity compensate. See lines 107–114 in Example 6-1.

Split and join

The all activity executes a set of actions in parallel and merges its results. This activity is sometimes called the AND split and join. In the following sample, actions a, b, and c are executed in parallel; when the last of them completes the process continues with its next step:

```
<all>
    <action name="a"> ... </action>
    <action name="b"> ... </action>
    <action name="c"> ... </action>
</all>
```

The switch activity, sometimes called the XOR split and join, executes exactly one action from a set. Inside the switch activity is a sequence of case statements, each of which has a condition and associated activity. The activity to be executed is the one defined in the first case statement whose condition evaluates to true. If no case's condition is true, the activity belonging to the default case is run. The following sample illustrates this behavior:

```
<switch>
    <case>
        <condition>$tns:val>100</condition>
        <action name="a"> ... </action>
    </case>
    <case>
        <condition>$tns:val>50 and $tns:val<100</condition>
        <action name="b"> ... </action>
    </case>
    <default>
        <action name="c"> ... </action>
    </case>
</switch>
```

Loops

BPML supports three types of loops, each defined as a complex activity type: while, until, and foreach. while executes a set of activities zero or more times, checking a Boolean-valued condition at the beginning of the loop to determine whether to continue. until is similar, but it checks the condition at the end of the loop. foreach loops through a list of items, executing a set of activities for each item in the list.

The following while loop runs five times, when the value of the property myCounter is from 0 and 4 (inclusive):

```
<process name="WhileSample">
    <context>
        <property name="myCounter" type="xsd:integer">
            <value>0</value>
```

```
        </property>
    </context>
    <while>
        <condition>myCounter < 5</condition>
        <assign property="myCounter">
            <value>myCounter + 1</value>
        </assign>
        <empty> <!—placeholder for real work à
    </while>
</process>
```

The foreach loop in the next sample iterates over the list myList, gathering values 0, 2, 5, and 7 over the course of its iterations. The built-in property inst:current is set to the current position in the list in a given iteration of the loop.

```
<process name="ForEachSample">
    <context>
        <property name="myList">
            <value>0 2 5 7</value>
        </property>
    </context>
    <foreach select="myList">
        <assign property="nextItem">
            <value>$inst:current</value>
        </assign>
        <empty> <!—placeholder for real work à
    </foreach>
</process>
```

Participant exchange

A BPML process can exchange messages with external participants through web services in its action and choice activities. action can either call a web service or implement a web service that, when called, triggers an event in the process. Whereas BPEL cleanly separates these operations into invoke, receive, and reply. BPML overloads the action activity to serve all three purposes. An action is specified with a name, a WSDL port type and operation, a set of inputs and/or outputs (mapping to WSDL input and output messages types, respectively, for the given operation), and an optional correlation expression, which filters action events to trigger only for given input values. Several examples of action are provided in Example 6-1.

choice, similar to BPEL's pick, waits for exactly one of two or more events to occur, where each event is defined as an action activity, a synch activity, or a delay activity. action events in this case are asynchronous receives. Each candidate event has a set of activities defined that are executed if the event fires. Syntactically, choice consists of a set of event elements, each of which contains an activity set that begins with an action, synch, or delay. In the following code sample, the process waits for either events A or B or a timeout to occur:

```
<choice>
    <event>
        <action portType="myService" operation="A"/>
```

```
            <empty/> <!-- placeholder -->
        </event>
        <event>
            <action portType="myService" operation="B"/>
            <empty/> <!-- placeholder -->
        </event>
        <event>
            <delay duration="maxResponseTime"/>
            <empty/> <!-- placeholder -->
        </event>
    </choice>
```

Transactions

BPML is interoperable with open transaction standards such as WS-Transaction and XA. BPML defines a special fault type, `bpml:rollback`, that a process can use to trigger rollback handlers.

Extensions

BPML supports adding custom attributes or elements to most of its elements. Using the extension mechanism to add Java support (e.g., data types and invocations) would be a useful idea.

BPML and Patterns

Rated on its support for the 20 process patterns described in Chapter 4, BPML gets an average grade. According to the evaluation by members of the P4,* BPML directly supports 11 patterns, and indirectly supports 1. The remaining 8 patterns are either impossible or difficult to implement. Table 6-9 summarizes the results.

TABLE 6-9. *BPML support for the P4 pattern*

Pattern	Compliance (+, −, +−)	Approach	Notes
Sequence	+	`sequence` activity .	
Parallel Split	+	`all` activity.	
Synchronization	+	Add activity after the `all`.	
Exclusive Choice	+	`switch` activity.	
Simple Merge	+	Activity after the `switch`.	
Multi-Choice	−	*N* `switch` activities inside of an `all`. Each switch contains a single case, whose associated activity is run only if the case is true.	
Sync Merge	−	Not supported.	Rather difficult in some cases.
Multi-Merge	+−	Reasonable coding with `all` and `switch`.	See P4 paper, p. 10f.

* W. van der Aalst, M. Dumas, A. H. M. ter Hofstede, P. Wohed, "Pattern-Based Analysis of BPML (and WSCI)," FIT Technical Report, FIT-TR-2002-05.

TABLE 6-9. *BPML support for the P4 pattern (continued)*

Pattern	Compliance (+, −, +−)	Approach	Notes
Discriminator	−	Spawn, raise, and sync, but it's difficult.	See P4 paper, p. 11f.
Arbitrary cycles	−	Not supported.	Use while, until, or foreach constructs for structured looping.
Implicit Termination	+	Use spawn activity and do not synchronize.	
Multiple Instances (MI) Without Synchronization	+	spawn in a while, until, or foreach loop.	
MI With Design Time Knowledge	+	If *N* instances, place *N* call activities in an all activity.	
MI With Runtime Knowledge		Spawn in a while loop. Have subprocess raise signal on completion. Calling process synchronizes signals of the spawned processes.	
MI Without Runtime Knowledge	−	Similar to previous, with a more advanced loop conditions and synchronization.	
Deferred Choice	+	choice activity.	
Interleaved Parallel Routing	−	None.	Tricky coding. See P4 paper, p. 16f.
Milestone	−	None.	Tricky coding. See P4 paper, p. 17.
Cancel Activity	+	Use exception process to signal end of activity.	
Cancel Case	+	Use exception process to signal end of case.	

Summary

The main points of this chapter include the following:

- The BPMI organization, founded by Intalio, has published two BPM standards specifications. BPML is an XML process modeling and execution language similar to BPEL. BPMN is a graphical modeling language. A specification for BPQL—a query, administration, and monitoring language—is coming soon.

- BPMI's vision of a BPM stack consists of BPMN as the visual modeling language, BPEL with BPXL extensions as the execution language, BPQL as the query language for monitoring, WS-CDL as the choreography language, and BPSM as the process metamodel. BPMN, BPQL, BPXL, and BPSM are BPML standards, and WS-CDL is a W3C standard. The choice of BPEL (from OASIS) for execution language is surprising, given that BPMI offers competing language BPML. BPMI acknowledges BPEL's supremacy in this category.

- BPMN is a graphical flowchart language suitable for both business analysts and developers. BPMN's main constructs—processes, activities, gateways, events, pools, and swim lanes—are described in this chapter's BPMN section. BPMN's mapping to BPEL is also described at a high level; the holes in this mapping are attributable to BPMN's excess of features. BPMN was built with the P4 patterns in mind, and thus rates well on its support for patterns.

- BPML is an XML-based language that defines the flow of control and runtime semantics of a business process. BPML's notion of process, activity, context, and compensation is described in this chapter's BPML section. The section also catalogs BPML's built-in activity types (action, assign, call, and so on), and rates BPML on its support for P4 patterns.

Reference

1. Stephen White, "Introduction to BPMN, " *http://www.bpmn.org/Documents/ Introduction%20to%20BPMN.pdf.*

CHAPTER SEVEN

The Workflow Management Coalition (WfMC)

ALTHOUGH ITS INFLUENCE HAS WANED IN RECENT YEARS, the Workflow Management Coalition (WfMC, *http://www.wfmc.org*) remains a rich source of ideas about BPM. The contributions of this group include a decade-old workflow reference model and specifications for the design of its main pieces, including a client API and an exportable process definition format.

The WfMC, founded in 1993, is a nonprofit organization that writes workflow standards, including a workflow reference model and specifications for each of its core interfaces: XPDL, WAPI, and WfXML. The WfMC also produces voluminous BPM literature; notably, the annual Workflow Handbook (*http://www.wfmc.org/information/info.html*). The group is chaired by Jon Pyke and has more than 300 member organizations, including BEA, FileNet, Fujitsu, Hitachi, IBM, NEC Soft, Oracle, Sun, TIBCO (Staffware), Toshiba, Vignette, Vitria, and WebMethods.

This chapter highlights the core WfMC design ideas. The first section examines the WfMC reference model. Next, it explores XPDL, providing an extended example, a brief look at the main elements, and a summary of its support for the P4 patterns. The next section examines the major functional elements of the WAPI and provides an example. The chapter concludes with a brief look at the WfXML.

WFMC STILL MATTERS

In the fast-changing world of BPM, WfMC is an older, more established group with mature ideas. With the increasing popularity of the competing BPEL language (Chapter 5), the WfMC must somehow justify its relevance. The trick is to not compete with BPEL but complement it, as the BPMI has done (Chapter 6) by surrounding BPEL in its proposed BPM stack with BPMN (modeling notation) and soon-to-come specifications BPQL (query language for process monitoring), BPSM (common process meta-model), and BPXL (BPEL extensions). Significantly, the BPMI excludes its own execution language BPML from the stack, accepting BPEL's reign in that category. BPMI seems stronger and fresher than ever because it is building key pieces of a platform that solution providers will actually use.

WfMC's predicament is similar. Despite having a good reference stack with substantial implementations of each the major interfaces, one of those interfaces—namely, XPDL—is a competitor to BPEL. To be successful, the WfMC should drop XPDL from the stack in favor of BPEL and then demonstrate the value of the overall model and its non-XPDL interfaces. That model, whether it includes XPDL or not, is full of good, current ideas. But leaving XPDL in makes the WfMC seem as if it is working in a vacumn, with an obscure process language that no one else is using.

The Reference Model

The WfMC reference model* describes at a high level the main pieces of a workflow management system. The model's overall structure is depicted in Figure 7-1.

In Figure 7-1, the boxes represent components and the arrows interfaces. Here are its components:

Process definition tools

A process definition tool is an editor used by a business analyst or developer to compose a business process definition. Typically this tool is graphical, allowing the user to build the process by dragging and dropping boxes and arrows onto a design canvas. But the WfMC model does not require that the tool be graphical, nor does it prescribe a particular graphical representation language; there is nothing like BPMN (described in Chapter 6) in the WfMC world. The tool could just as well be a text editor. The key requirement is an ability to export the process definition in a standard form, which in turn can be executed by the workflow enactment service.

---

* D. Hollingsworth, "Workflow Management Coalition: The Workflow Reference Model," January 1995, *http://www.wfmc.org/standards/docs/tc003v11.pdf*.

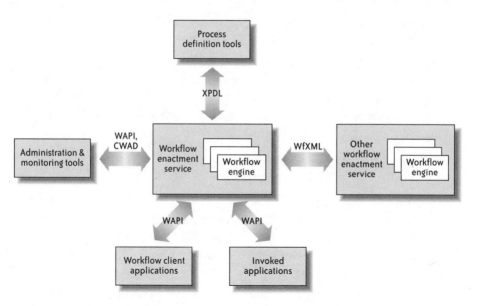

FIGURE 7-1. *WfMC reference model*

Workflow enactment services and constituent engines

An enactment service runs workflow processes. The service accepts as input process definitions imported from process definition tools. It creates and manages the overall execution of instances of these processes. A process does not run in isolation, and hence the enactment service provides open interfaces to external (client and invoked) applications and administration and monitoring tools that read the state of and participate in the execution of a process. A service can have multiple workflow engines, where each engine does the actual processing for one or more instances; the precise relationship is not adequately stated in the WfMC documentation. When the execution of a process can be distributed to multiple enactment services, an interface exists for communication between services.

Workflow client applications

Workflow client applications provide an interface for human beings in the organization to participate in the workflow process. Each activity (or step) in a process is either manual or automatic. A manual activity is assigned to a person for execution. A worklist client application finds, categorizes into work lists, and prompts for the completion of, manual activities for a specific person. For example, it shows a bank manager all pending application approvals, grouped by account type and sorted by priority; further, for each approval activity, the application allows the bank manager to either approve or reject, and the result is sent to the process instance, which then resumes its flow, the pending manual activity having completed.

Invoked applications

An invoked application is an external application called by the process in an automatic activity. A process does not run in isolation but interfaces with real systems (such as CRM, ERP, and mainframe) and infrastructure components (including email, fax, imaging, and document management) using a variety of communication mechanisms (such as J2EE, COM, web services, MOM, and JDBC).

Administration and monitoring tools

In the WfMC model, administration and monitoring covers various forms of workflow system management, including the management of users and roles (creation and maintenance of human process participants) and the monitoring of process instances (getting and setting state, and aborting stray processes).

The model's interfaces can be categorized into three groups, which are examined in greater detail in the remainder of this chapter:

XML Process Definition Language

XPDL is the XML process definition format for exchange between a process definition tool and the enactment service. An XPDL document specifies one or more process definitions, each of which is a set of activities and transitions.

Workflow Application Programming Interface

WAPI is the API, with bindings in C, CORBA IDL, and COM Automation, for interaction between the enactment service and workflow client applications, invoked applications, and administration and monitoring tools. A workflow client application uses WAPI to discover manual activities assigned to a particular user or user group; additionally, it uses WAPI to complete or reassign activities. WAPI's invoked application interface extends the enactment service with adapters (also known as *tool agents*) to perform automated activities by calling specific external systems or polling them for events. As for administration and monitoring, WAPI includes functions to query and set the state of in-flight processes, enable or disable process definitions, and abort running instances.

> **NOTE**
>
> For administration and monitoring, the WfMC has also published a specification for common workflow audit data (CWAD). According to this specification, when events in processes, activities, and manual work items occur, the workflow engine is required to capture them and persist them in a form that complies with the abstract CWAD data model. The data can then be queried for administrative, business monitoring, or business reporting purposes. (For example, what is the average duration of a particular manual activity? When is the last time a particular process was run?)
>
> CWAD event types are mapped to WAPI and WfXML services. When the WAPI function WMChangeWorkItemState is called, for instance, the engine must record the CWAD event WMChangedWorkItemState.
>
> CWAD is not a core topic in the study of the WfMC, and hence is not discussed further in this chapter.

Workflow XML

WfXML is a web-service-based communication language used between enactment services. WfXML allows enactment services to exchange information about process definitions, process instances and activities, and to cooperate in the execution of processes. The reference model adopts the notion of a heterogeneous process, whose activities span multiple enactment services. For example, in a three-step process, Steps 1 and 3 are bound for service A, and Step 2 is targeted for service B. This notion and its implementation with WfXML is described in the later section on WfXML.

The sequence diagram in Figure 7-2 illustrates the main types of interactions in the reference model. The scenario involves three activities: one manual, one automatic, and one executed on a separate enactment service.

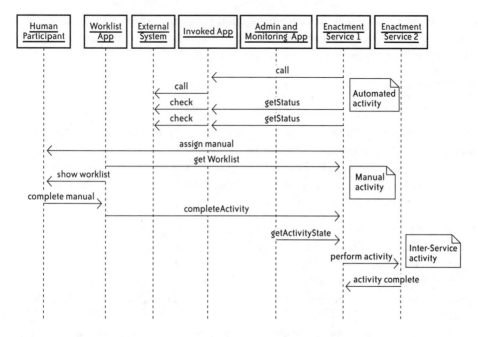

FIGURE 7-2. *Component interactions in the WfMC reference model*

In the automatic activity, the enactment service (Enactment Service 1, the main service) calls the Invoked App adapter to start the external interaction with External System. The enactment service then repeatedly calls getStatus until the invoked application has retrieved a result from the external application. In the manual activity, the service assigns an activity to a particular person. The Worklist App, which provides a user interface to the enactment service for the user, retrieves from the service all activities for that person. The Worklist App application prompts the user to complete the manual task, and notifies the enactment service of this with completeActivity. The interservice activity involves an exchange of messages (perform activity, activity complete) between the two enactment services, 1 and 2. Along the way, an administration and monitoring application watches the activities by calling into the main enactment service (e.g., getActivityState, which retrieves the state of a given activity).

XPDL

XPDL,[*] a competitor of BPEL (Chapter 5) and BPML (Chapter 6), is the WfMC's XML process definition language. In the WfMC reference architecture, XPDL is the interface between process definition tools and the enactment service. Specifically, processes designed in a tool are exported in XPDL format and loaded into the enactment service for execution, XML being a suitable external representation. Other purposes of XPDL are to move process definitions between tools. A process definition tool should have both export and import capabilities: export to XPDL, and import from XPDL.

The WfMC does not prescribe a standard graphical notation language. Exactly how a given process definition tool represents a process visually is immaterial; what is essential is its support for the import and export of XPDL.

The XPDL Model

The basic notions of XPDL and their relationships are depicted in Figure 7-3.

The topmost entity is Package, which defines an entire application or a major system. A package consists of one or more workflow process definitions and supporting entities, which include participants (a list of human or system actors that perform key process roles), applications (programmatic components called by the process), and data fields (also known as *workflow-relevant data*).

A workflow process, the central construct of XPDL, consists of one or more activities and a set of transitions. The mathematical idea of directed graph underlies this conception; each activity is a graph vertex; each transition is an arc connecting one vertex to another. The flow of a process is akin to the traversal of a graph: the process moves from one activity to another along routes specified by transitions. Additional features include conditional transitions and XOR and AND joins and splits, which give XPDL reasonable expressive power when rated on the P4 process patterns, including basic conditional and parallel branching, and still more advanced capabilities.

XPDL activities fall into three categories: route, block, and implementation. A route activity performs no work but simply forwards control to the activities targeted by its outgoing transitions; route activities are typically used to manage control flow. A block activity is a set of activities having its own execution scope, reminiscent of the BPEL scope construct.

The third type of activity, known as implementation, has three subtypes: null, tool, and subflow. A null activity is normally a manual activity, or an activity assigned to a human

---

[*]   WfMC, "Workflow Process Definition Interface—XML Process Definition Language," Version 1.0. October 2002.

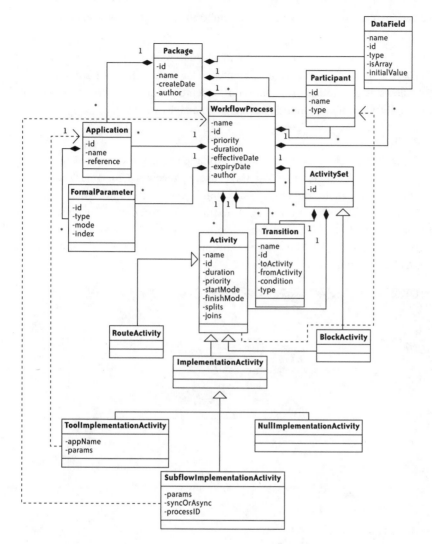

FIGURE 7-3. *The WfMC XPDL model*

participant. A tool activity calls an invoked application through a tool agent. A subflow activity invokes another workflow process, either synchronously or asynchronously, as a nested subprocess.

The key to understanding control flow in an XPDL process is to understand the organization of activities and transitions. XPDL's directed graph topology is markedly different from the structured programming style of BPEL and BPML (excepting BPEL's flow links, which mix directed graph semantics with BPEL's otherwise structured approach):

- Each activity declares its incoming transitions, and whether to merge them, using an AND or XOR join.

- Each activity declares its outgoing transitions, and whether to split them, as AND or XOR.

- Each transition has exactly one source and destination activity, and can optionally define a condition. If the condition evaluates to false, the transition is not followed. XPDL allows default (otherwise) conditions; a default condition is followed if none of the normal conditions originating from a given activity are true.

XPDL Example

The example of a travel reservation system, explored in earlier chapters, is used here to showcase several of XPDL features. The travel agency receives a customer's itinerary request, then—in parallel—attempts to book hotels, car rentals, and flights. If all the steps succeed, the process prompts a travel agent to mail a confirmation to the customer. If some bookings failed, the process assigns a work item to a travel agent to contact the customer to fix the problem. The design of this process in the Enhydra Java Workflow editor (JAWE) is shown in Figure 7-4.

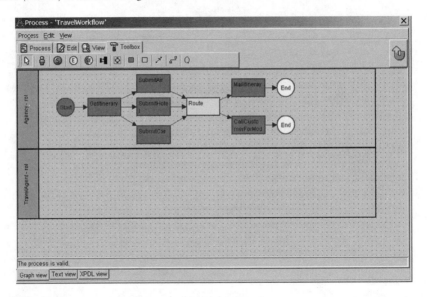

FIGURE 7-4. *The travel reservation process in Enhydra Java Workflow Editor (JAWE)*

The XPDL for this process is listed in Example 7-1.

EXAMPLE 7-1. *Travel agency XPDL sample*

```
1  <?xml version="1.0" encoding="UTF-8"?>
2  <Package Id="Travel" Name="Travel" xmlns=http://www.wfmc.org/2002/XPDL1.0
3      xmlns:xpdl=http://www.wfmc.org/2002/XPDL1.0
4      xmlns:xsi=http://www.w3.org/2001/XMLSchema-instance
5      xsi:schemaLocation="http://www.wfmc.org/2002/XPDL1.0
6      http://wfmc.org/standards/docs/TC-1025_schema_10_xpdl.xsd">
7      <PackageHeader>
8          <XPDLVersion>1.0</XPDLVersion>
```

EXAMPLE 7-1. *Travel agency XPDL sample (continued)*

```
 9            <Vendor>Together</Vendor>
10            <Created>2004-09-20 22:13:58</Created>
11        </PackageHeader>
12        <RedefinableHeader PublicationStatus="UNDER_TEST"/>
13        <ConformanceClass GraphConformance="NON_BLOCKED"/>
14
15        <!-- Three applications used by the process: one hotel, one air, one car
16              rental.  Each takes in an itinerary and returns a result. -->
17        <Applications>
18            <Application Id="HotelApp" Name="HotelApp">
19                <FormalParameters>
20                    <FormalParameter Id="itinerary" Mode="IN">
21                        <DataType>
22                            <BasicType Type="STRING"/>
23                        </DataType>
24                    </FormalParameter>
25                    <FormalParameter Id="result" Mode="OUT">
26                        <DataType>
27                            <BasicType Type="STRING"/>
28                        </DataType>
29                    </FormalParameter>
30                </FormalParameters>
31            </Application>
32            <Application Id="AirApp" Name="AirApp">
33                <FormalParameters>
34                    <FormalParameter Id="itinerary" Mode="IN">
35                        <DataType>
36                            <BasicType Type="STRING"/>
37                        </DataType>
38                    </FormalParameter>
39                    <FormalParameter Id="result" Mode="OUT">
40                        <DataType>
41                            <BasicType Type="STRING"/>
42                        </DataType>
43                    </FormalParameter>
44                </FormalParameters>
45            </Application>
46            <Application Id="CarApp" Name="CarApp">
47                <FormalParameters>
48                    <FormalParameter Id="itinerary" Mode="IN">
49                        <DataType>
50                            <BasicType Type="STRING"/>
51                        </DataType>
52                    </FormalParameter>
53                    <FormalParameter Id="result" Mode="OUT">
54                        <DataType>
55                            <BasicType Type="STRING"/>
56                        </DataType>
57                    </FormalParameter>
58                </FormalParameters>
59            </Application>
60        </Applications>
61
62        <!-- The process takes as a parameter an itinerary.
63              It uses three data fields, representing the results of
```

EXAMPLE 7-1. *Travel agency XPDL sample (continued)*

```
64              its calls to the hotel, air, and car rental applications. -->
65      <WorkflowProcesses>
66          <WorkflowProcess AccessLevel="PUBLIC" Id="TravelWorkflow"
67          Name="TravelWorkflow">
68              <ProcessHeader DurationUnit="D">
69                  <Created>2004-09-20 22:15:14</Created>
70              </ProcessHeader>
71              <RedefinableHeader PublicationStatus="UNDER_TEST"/>
72              <FormalParameters>
73                  <FormalParameter Id="itinerary" Mode="IN">
74                      <DataType>
75                          <BasicType Type="STRING"/>
76                      </DataType>
77                  </FormalParameter>
78              </FormalParameters>
79              <DataFields>
80                  <DataField Id="airResult" IsArray="FALSE">
81                      <DataType>
82                          <BasicType Type="STRING"/>
83                      </DataType>
84                  </DataField>
85                  <DataField Id="carResult" IsArray="FALSE">
86                      <DataType>
87                          <BasicType Type="STRING"/>
88                      </DataType>
89                  </DataField>
90                  <DataField Id="hotelResult" IsArray="FALSE">
91                      <DataType>
92                          <BasicType Type="STRING"/>
93                      </DataType>
94                  </DataField>
95              </DataFields>
96              <Participants>
97                  <Participant Id="TravelAgent">
98                      <ParticipantType Type="ROLE"/>
99                  </Participant>
100             </Participants>
101
102             <Activities>
103
104             <!-- The first activity is GetItinerary.  It is a manual activity
105                     performed by the travel agent role. When it completes,
106                     it does an AND split to three submit activities. -->
107                 <Activity Id="GetItinerary" Name="GetItinerary">
108                     <Implementation>
109                         <No/>
110                     </Implementation>
111                     <Performer>TravelAgent</Performer>
112                     <StartMode>
113                         <Manual/>
114                     </StartMode>
115                     <FinishMode>
116                         <Manual/>
117                     </FinishMode>
118                     <TransitionRestrictions>
```

EXAMPLE 7-1. *Travel agency XPDL sample (continued)*

```
119                         <TransitionRestriction>
120                             <Split Type="AND">
121                                 <TransitionRefs>
122                                     <TransitionRef Id="TravelWorkflow_Tra3"/>
123                                     <TransitionRef Id="TravelWorkflow_Tra4"/>
124                                     <TransitionRef Id="TravelWorkflow_Tra1"/>
125                                 </TransitionRefs>
126                             </Split>
127                         </TransitionRestriction>
128                     </TransitionRestrictions>
129                     <ExtendedAttributes>
130                         <ExtendedAttribute Name="ParticipantID" Value="Agency"/>
131                         <ExtendedAttribute Name="XOffset" Value="160"/>
132                         <ExtendedAttribute Name="YOffset" Value="60"/>
133                     </ExtendedAttributes>
134                 </Activity>
135
136                 <!-- SubmitAir calls the air application, passing the itinerary
137                      and getting back a result. -->
138                 <Activity Id="SubmitAir" Name="SubmitAir">
139                     <Implementation>
140                         <Tool Id="AirApp" Type="APPLICATION">
141                             <ActualParameters>
142                                 <ActualParameter>itinerary</ActualParameter>
143                                 <ActualParameter>airResult</ActualParameter>
144                             </ActualParameters>
145                         </Tool>
146                     </Implementation>
147                     <Performer>TravelAgent</Performer>
148                     <StartMode>
149                         <Automatic/>
150                     </StartMode>
151                     <FinishMode>
152                         <Automatic/>
153                     </FinishMode>
154                     <ExtendedAttributes>
155                         <ExtendedAttribute Name="ParticipantID" Value="Agency"/>
156                         <ExtendedAttribute Name="XOffset" Value="270"/>
157                         <ExtendedAttribute Name="YOffset" Value="10"/>
158                     </ExtendedAttributes>
159                 </Activity>
160
161                 <!-- SubmitHotel calls the hotel application, passing the itinerary
162                      and getting back a result. -->
163                 <Activity Id="SubmitHotel" Name="SubmitHotel">
164                     <Implementation>
165                         <Tool Id="HotelApp" Type="APPLICATION">
166                             <ActualParameters>
167                                 <ActualParameter>itinerary</ActualParameter>
168                                 <ActualParameter>hotelResult</ActualParameter>
169                             </ActualParameters>
170                         </Tool>
171                     </Implementation>
172                     <Performer>TravelAgent</Performer>
173                     <StartMode>
```

EXAMPLE 7-1. *Travel agency XPDL sample (continued)*

```
174                        <Automatic/>
175                    </StartMode>
176                    <FinishMode>
177                        <Automatic/>
178                    </FinishMode>
179                    <ExtendedAttributes>
180                      <ExtendedAttribute Name="ParticipantID" Value="Agency"/>
181                      <ExtendedAttribute Name="XOffset" Value="270"/>
182                      <ExtendedAttribute Name="YOffset" Value="60"/>
183                    </ExtendedAttributes>
184                </Activity>
185
186            <!-- SubmitCar calls the car rental application, passing the
187                 itinerary and getting back a result. -->
188            <Activity Id="SubmitCar" Name="SubmitCar">
189                <Implementation>
190                    <Tool Id="CarApp" Type="APPLICATION">
191                        <ActualParameters>
192                            <ActualParameter>itinerary</ActualParameter>
193                            <ActualParameter>carResult</ActualParameter>
194                        </ActualParameters>
195                    </Tool>
196                </Implementation>
197                <Performer>TravelAgent</Performer>
198                <StartMode>
199                    <Automatic/>
200                </StartMode>
201                <FinishMode>
202                    <Automatic/>
203                </FinishMode>
204                <ExtendedAttributes>
205                  <ExtendedAttribute Name="ParticipantID" Value="Agency"/>
206                  <ExtendedAttribute Name="XOffset" Value="270"/>
207                  <ExtendedAttribute Name="YOffset" Value="120"/>
208                </ExtendedAttributes>
209            </Activity>
210
211            <!-- Manual activity, performed by the travel agent, to
212                 mail the itinerary to the customer. -->
213            <Activity Id="MailItinerary" Name="MailItineray">
214                <Implementation>
215                    <No/>
216                </Implementation>
217                <Performer>TravelAgent</Performer>
218                <StartMode>
219                    <Manual/>
220                </StartMode>
221                <FinishMode>
222                    <Manual/>
223                </FinishMode>
224                <ExtendedAttributes>
225                  <ExtendedAttribute Name="ParticipantID" Value="Agency"/>
226                  <ExtendedAttribute Name="XOffset" Value="480"/
227                  <ExtendedAttribute Name="YOffset" Value="20"/>
228                </ExtendedAttributes>
```

EXAMPLE 7-1. *Travel agency XPDL sample (continued)*

```
229                     </Activity>
230
231                     <!-- Manual activity, performed by the travel agent, to
232                         call the customer to make modifications to the itinerary. -->
233                     <Activity Id="CallCustomerForMods" Name="CallCustomerForMods">
234                         <Implementation>
235                             <No/>
236                         </Implementation>
237                         <Performer>TravelAgent</Performer>
238                         <StartMode>
239                             <Manual/>
240                         </StartMode>
241                         <FinishMode>
242                             <Manual/>
243                         </FinishMode>
244                         <ExtendedAttributes>
245                             <ExtendedAttribute Name="ParticipantID" Value="Agency"/>
246                             <ExtendedAttribute Name="XOffset" Value="480"/>
247                             <ExtendedAttribute Name="YOffset" Value="100"/>
248                         </ExtendedAttributes>
249                     </Activity>
250
251                     <!-- Route activity: does a 3-way AND join from the submit
252                         activities and then does 2-way XOR split to the mail
253                         get mods manual activities. -->
254                     <Activity Id="TravelWorkflow_Act7" Name="Route">
255                         <Route/>
256                         <StartMode>
257                             <Automatic/>
258                         </StartMode>
259                         <FinishMode>
260                             <Automatic/>
261                         </FinishMode>
262                         <TransitionRestrictions>
263                             <TransitionRestriction>
264                                 <Join Type="AND"/>
265                                 <Split Type="XOR">
266                                     <TransitionRefs>
267                                         <TransitionRef Id="TravelWorkflow_Tra12"/>
268                                         <TransitionRef Id="TravelWorkflow_Tra11"/>
269                                     </TransitionRefs>
270                                 </Split>
271                             </TransitionRestriction>
272                         </TransitionRestrictions>
273                         <ExtendedAttributes>
274                             <ExtendedAttribute Name="ParticipantID" Value="Agency"/>
275                             <ExtendedAttribute Name="XOffset" Value="380"/>
276                             <ExtendedAttribute Name="YOffset" Value="60"/>
277                         </ExtendedAttributes>
278                     </Activity>
279                 </Activities>
280
281             <!-- Highlights of the transitions:
282                 1. GetItinerary routes to each of the submit activities.
283                 2. Each of the submit activities routes to the route activity.
```

EXAMPLE 7-1. *Travel agency XPDL sample (continued)*

```
284              3. The route activity routes to MailItinerary if
285                  airResult="ok" and carResult="ok" and hotelResult="ok".
286                  Otherwise, it routes to GetMods. -->
287         <Transitions>
288
289             <Transition From="GetItinerary" Id="TravelWorkflow_Tra1"
290              Name="Transition" To="SubmitAir">
291                 <ExtendedAttributes>
292                   <ExtendedAttribute Name="RoutingType" Value="NOROUTING"/>
293                 </ExtendedAttributes>
294             </Transition>
295
296             <Transition From="GetItinerary" Id="TravelWorkflow_Tra3"
297              Name="Transition" To="SubmitHotel">
298                 <ExtendedAttributes>
299                   <ExtendedAttribute Name="RoutingType" Value="NOROUTING"/>
300                 </ExtendedAttributes>
301             </Transition>
302
303             <Transition From="GetItinerary" Id="TravelWorkflow_Tra4"
304              Name="Transition" To="SubmitCar">
305                 <ExtendedAttributes>
306                   <ExtendedAttribute Name="RoutingType" Value="NOROUTING"/>
307                 </ExtendedAttributes>
308             </Transition>
309
310             <Transition From="SubmitAir" Id="TravelWorkflow_Tra8"
311              Name="Transition" To="TravelWorkflow_Act7">
312                 <ExtendedAttributes>
313                   <ExtendedAttribute Name="RoutingType" Value="NOROUTING"/>
314                 </ExtendedAttributes>
315             </Transition>
316
317             <Transition From="SubmitCar" Id="TravelWorkflow_Tra9"
318              Name="Transition" To="TravelWorkflow_Act7">
319                 <ExtendedAttributes>
320                   <ExtendedAttribute Name="RoutingType" Value="NOROUTING"/>
321                 </ExtendedAttributes>
322             </Transition>
323
324             <Transition From="SubmitHotel" Id="TravelWorkflow_Tra10"
325              Name="Transition" To="TravelWorkflow_Act7">
326                 <ExtendedAttributes>
327                   <ExtendedAttribute Name="RoutingType" Value="NOROUTING"/>
328                 </ExtendedAttributes>
329             </Transition>
330
331             <Transition From="TravelWorkflow_Act7" Id="TravelWorkflow_Tra11"
332              Name="Transition" To="MailItinerary">
333                 <Condition Type="CONDITION">
334                     airResult="ok" and carResult="ok" and hotelResult="ok"
335                 </Condition>
336                 <ExtendedAttributes>
337                   <ExtendedAttribute Name="RoutingType" Value="NOROUTING"/>
```

EXAMPLE 7-1. *Travel agency XPDL sample (continued)*

```
338                    </ExtendedAttributes>
339                </Transition>
340
341                <Transition From="TravelWorkflow_Act7" Id="TravelWorkflow_Tra12"
342                 Name="Transition" To="CallCustomerForMods">
343                    <Condition Type="OTHERWISE"/>
344                    <ExtendedAttributes>
345                      <ExtendedAttribute Name="RoutingType" Value="NOROUTING"/>
346                    </ExtendedAttributes>
347                </Transition>
348            </Transitions>
349
350            <ExtendedAttributes>
351                <ExtendedAttribute Name="StartOfWorkflow"
352                 Value="Agency;GetItinerary;90;60;NOROUTING"/>
353                <ExtendedAttribute Name="EndOfWorkflow"
354                 Value="Agency;CallCustomerForMods;580;100;NOROUTING"/>
355                <ExtendedAttribute Name="EndOfWorkflow"
356                 Value="Agency;MailItinerary;580;20;NOROUTING"/>
357                <ExtendedAttribute Name="ParticipantVisualOrder"
358                 Value="Agency;TravelAgent;"/>
359            </ExtendedAttributes>
360        </WorkflowProcess>
361    </WorkflowProcesses>
362
363    <ExtendedAttributes>
364        <ExtendedAttribute Name="MadeBy" Value="JaWE"/>
365        <ExtendedAttribute Name="Version" Value="1.2"/>
366    </ExtendedAttributes>
367 </Package>
```

The package Travel has three applications—HotelApp, CarApp, and AirApp (lines 17–60)—
and a single workflow process, called TravelWorkflow (whose definition begins at line 65).
TravelWorkflow accepts a formal parameter itinerary (lines 72–78) and has three data
fields airResult, hotelResult, and carResult (lines 79–95), as well as a participant called
TravelAgent (lines 96–100).

The first activity in the process is a manual activity called GetItinerary (lines 107–134),
assigned to the participant role TravelAgency; the purpose of GetItinerary is for an agent to
take an initial look at the itinerary and perform any initial manual processing. Upon
completion, GetItinerary performs a three-way AND split to the tool activities SubmitAir
(lines 138–159), SubmitHotel (lines 163–184) and SubmitCar (lines 188–209), which call the
applications AirApp, HotelApp, and CarApp, respectively, passing in the itinerary formal
parameter of the process and getting back a result field bound to the data field airResult,
hotelResult, or carResult. A special Route activity (defined in lines 254–278) synchronizes
with an AND join the results of the three tool activities and then branches with an XOR
split to the manual activities MailItinerary (lines 213–229) and CallCustomerForMods (lines
233–249), each assigned to the role TravelAgent. The direction of branching is determined
by the evaluation of a condition; the transition to MailItinerary (lines 331–339) is

activated only if the condition airResult="ok" and carResult="ok" and hotelResult="ok" is met; otherwise, the transition to CallCustomerForMods (lines 341–347) is followed.

XPDL Elements

The following discussion captures at a very high level the basic programming elements and techniques of XPDL.

Basic process structure

The flow of a process is defined by its activities and the transitions that connect them. An XPDL flow is a directed graph. To build a basic sequential process of the form A → B → C, use code such as the following:

```
<WorkflowProcess>
    <Activities>
        <Activity id="A"> . . . </Activity>
        <Activity id="B"> . . . </Activity>
        <Activity id="C"> . . . </Activity>
    </Activities>
    <Transitions>
        <Transition id="A2B" from="A" to="B"/>
        <Transition id="B2C" from="B" to="C"/>
    </Transitions>
    <ExtendedAttributes>
        <ExtendedAttribute Name="StartOfWorkflow" Value="A"/>
        <ExtendedAttribute Name="EndOfWorkflow" Value="C"/>
    </ExtendedAttributes>
</WorkflowProcess>
```

Notice the use of extended attributes to define the start and end activities of the process. That an extension is required for this is surprising.

Variables and assignments

XPDL variables for a process include formal parameters and data fields, shown earlier. Expressions can be built from variables, as in the condition expression in line 334 of the travel agency example. Data types can be mapped to a particular XML schema.

Exception handling and compensation

Exception transitions are supported. An exception transition fires when a particular type of exception occurs; the default exception transition is a catch-all that fires for any exception. XPDL has built-in support for timeout exceptions, but other types exceptions are engine-specific.

XPDL has no explicit compensation support.

Split and join

Three constructs can help model splits and joins:

- An activity can declare AND or XOR split and join types.
- A transition can be guarded, which helps the modeling of conditional branching.
- Route activities can help model complex flow logic.

See Example 7-1 for examples of these techniques.

Loops

An activity can transition to an upstream transition, provided the process conformance class in *nonblocked*. (A process can be configured not to allow loop-like cycles; the nonblocked setting enables cycles.) The effect is that of a GOTO. In the following code example, the sequence of activities A → B repeats until a particular condition (okToProcess) is met, in which case the control flows to activity C:

```
<Package>
    <ConformanceClass GraphConformance="NON_BLOCKED"/>   . . .
    <WorkflowProcesses>
        <WorkflowProcess>
            <Activities>
                <Activity id="A"> . . . </Activity>
                <Activity id="B"> . . . </Activity>
                <Activity id="C"> . . . </Activity>
            </Activities>
            <Transitions>
                <Transition id="A2B" from="A" to="B"/>
                <Transition id="B2C" from="B" to="C"/>
                    <Condition Type="CONDITION">okToProceed="yes"</Condition>
                </Transition>
                <Transition id="B2A" from="B" to="A"/>
                    <Condition Type="OTHERWISE"/>
                </Transition>
            </Transitions>
        </WorkflowProcess>
    </WorkflowProcesses>
</Package>
```

XPDL does not support structured loops such as while or foreach.

Participant exchange

An XPDL package can define applications, which can be defined as WSDL operations. Also, a participant type can be a system actor. The process can use these entities to communicate with external partners.

Transactions

The specification does not provide information on transactions.

Extensions

Most elements have extended attributes. For example, lines 350–359 in the travel agency example declare the start and end activities of the process. Also, in numerous places (e.g., lines 275–276), extensions are used to give activity screen positions for the graphical layout of the process.

XPDL and Patterns

In their web site *http://www.workflowpatterns.com*, members of the P4 rate the WfMC's process definition language, XPDL, on its support for the P4 patterns. The results, documented in *http://is.tm.tue.nl/research/patterns/download/ce-xpdl.pdf*,* imply that XPDL supports only 11 of the 20 P4 patterns. The P4 concludes that XPDL is relatively inexpressive, and moreover, its rules for AND and XOR splits and joins are ambiguous. The results are summarized in Table 7-1.

TABLE 7-1. *XPDL support for the P4 patterns*

Pattern	Compliance (+, +−, −)	Approach	Notes
Sequence	+	Activities A and B with a transition connection A to B.	
Parallel Split	+	AND split on activity.	
Synchronization	+	AND join on activity.	
Exclusive Choice	+	XOR split on activity.	
Simple Merge	+	XOR join on activity.	
Multi-Choice	+	AND join and split with conditions on transitions.	P4 paper, p. 12
Sync Merge	+	AND join has built-in synchronization.	Spec says yes, but van der Aalst argues that the behavior of AND is ambiguous (P4 paper, p. 18ff).
Multi Merge	−	No inclusive OR join makes this impossible.	
Discriminator	−	No.	
Arbitrary cycles	+	Transition can be defined to loop back to a prior activity.	
Implicit Termination	+	An activity can be defined without an outgoing transition, which causes the process to terminate.	
Multiple Instances (MI) Without Synchronization	+	Implementation activity can start subflow asynchronously. Do this in an arbitrary cycle, and you have this pattern.	

---

*   W. M. P. van der Aalst, "Patterns and XPDL: A Critical Evaluation of XML Process Definition Language," QUT Technical Report, FIT-TR-2003-06, Queensland, Australia, 2003.

TABLE 7-1. *XPDL support for the P4 patterns (continued)*

Pattern	Compliance (+, +−, −)	Approach	Notes
MI With Design Time Knowledge	+	Replicate activity as many times as it needs to be executed. Run in parallel.	
MI With Runtime Knowledge	−	No.	
MI Without Runtime Knowledge	−	No.	
Deferred Choice	−	No! No event choice facility exists.	
Interleaved Parallel Routing	−	No.	
Milestone	−	No.	
Cancel Activity	−	No. The only way to generate an exception is with a deadline, but deadline exception handling cannot cancel a case.	
Cancel Case	−	See previous entry.	

WAPI

WAPI* is the API offered by the enactment service for use by client applications, invoked applications, and administration and monitoring applications. WfMC's lengthy specification (171 pages), which is mostly a catalog of API functions, is devoid of examples. Specifications are provided in three languages: C, CORBA IDL, and COM Automation. The section on C emphasizes the API's functional breakdown, whereas the IDL and COM chapters provide an object-oriented view. The object-oriented view, depicted in the UML class diagram in Figure 7-5, can help you visualize the overall structure of WAPI.

The main class, `ClientConnection`, representing the main capabilities of WAPI, uses classes `ProcessDefinition`, `ProcessInstance`, `ActivityInstance`, and `WorkItem`, each of which inherits from `WorkflowObject`. A process definition has one or more process instances, which in turn has one or more activities instances, which can have a work item. The `ToolAgent` class creates an `InvokedApplication` class to perform the processing of a particular application invocation.

WAPI Functional Categories

The main functional components can be broken down into the following categories: connection, process control, activity control, worklist, administration, and application invocation.

---

* WfMC, "Workflow Management Application Programming Interface (Interface 2&3) Specification," Version 2.0. July 1998.

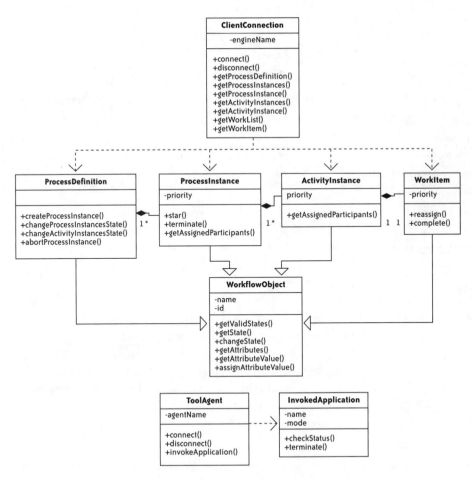

FIGURE 7-5. *WfMC WAPI class diagram*

Connection

The connection category allows an application to connect to and disconnect from a workflow engine. (That the connection is to an engine rather than to the engine's enactment service is problematic. One would think that the engine is a private worker used by the service and that client applications know only about the service.) It supports all the reference model interfaces. The major functions include:

- Connect
- Disconnect

Process control

The process control category contains a large set of functions for process definitions and their instances. Searches are based on filters (e.g., find all instances of bank account application processes for trust accounts). State functions allow the reading and modification of state (enabled and disabled for definitions; running, suspended, terminated, and completed for instances) and data (e.g., get order number from a particular shipping instance).

A process definition is instantiated with the functions CreateInstance( ) and StartProcess( )—the document admits that these two operations can be combined—and terminated with TerminateInstance( ). It supports all the reference model interfaces except invoked applications. The major functions include:

- Search process definitions and instances
- Search and modify process definition and instance states
- Search and modify process instance data
- Create, start and terminate process instances

Activity control

The activity control category consists of a set of functions to search for activity instances contained within process instances. Included is the ability to change the state of an instance; valid states are running, suspended, terminated, and completed. It supports all the reference model interfaces except invoked applications. The major functions include:

- Search and modify activity instance
- Search and modify activity data

Worklist

The worklist category provides methods to search work items in a process, as well as the states and data of work items. (A process activity can be designated as manual, meaning that its completion requires the action of a particular person or member of a group. A *work item* is an activity assigned to a user.) CompleteWorkItem( ) actions a work item, causing control of the process to resume to the next step. ReassignWorkItem( ) moves a work item from one user or group to another. It supports client interfaces from the reference model. The major functions include:

- Search work items
- Search and modify work item states
- Search and modify work item data
- Reassign and complete work item

Administration

The administration interface category consists largely of functions that allow a single change to be effected, in one fell swoop, to a set of process or activity instances. These include changing state or data, or terminating instances. It supports all the reference model interfaces except invoked applications. The major functions include:

- Mass change process instances and activity instances state
- Mass set process instance of activity instance data
- Mass process instance termination

Application invocation

In the WAPI model, special *tool agent* components provide access to invoked applications on behalf of a process. Presumably, these agents are adapters or plugins to the workflow engine that abstract the connection and communication details of the external system; the engine calls the tool agent when it encounters a process activity that is associated with an application. Before a tool agent can be accessed, it requires the establishment of a connection; the standard WAPI connection function is used for this. A particular invocation starts with the InvokeApplication( ) method; the result is obtained by polling the agent with the CheckStatus( ) method. The deficiency of the model is its lack of clarity around interactions such as synchronous and asynchronous request-response and event notification. The category supports invoked applications from the reference model. The major functions include:

- Connect to and disconnect from, a tool agent
- Invoke application
- Check application status
- Terminate application

WAPI Example: Complete All My Tasks

The example program in Example 7-2, written in a high-level pseudocode, demonstrates a simple client worklist application that uses WAPI to get and complete each work item assigned to a particular user.

EXAMPLE 7-2. *Sample WAPI code in pseudo-C*

```
1  // connect to engine at URL 10.12.131.13:9001 using credentials mike/password
2  WAPISession ses = WMConnect("mike", "password", "10.12.131.13:9001")
3
4  // open query result set
5  WMTQueryHandle queryHandle = WMOpenWorkList(ses,
6     "ACTIVITY_TYPE='Approval' and ACTIVITY_ROLE='BranchManager'")
7
8  // loop through each result
9  while(true)
10 {
11    // get next result
12    WMTWorkItem item = WMFetchWorkItem(ses, queryHandle)
13    if no more data, break
14
```

EXAMPLE 7-2. *Sample WAPI code in pseudo-C (continued)*

```
15      // Extract from item data and print such as item name and ID,
16      //   process and activity instance IDs, priority, and name of participants
17      print ("Your task is " + item.processID + " " item.workItemID)
18
19      // complete the item
20      WMCompleteWorkItem(ses, item.processID, item.workItemID)
21  }
22
23  // close query
24  WMCloseWorkList(ses, queryHandle);
25
26  // disconnect
27  WMDisconnect(ses)
28
```

The code begins on line 2 with a call to WMConnect to attach to the engine on port 9001 at the IP address 10.12.131.13 as the user mike (password password); WAPI does not specify exactly how an engine is identified, but other applications commonly listen on an IP port. The call returns a session handle held in the variable WAPISession, which is passed as an argument to each subsequent WAPI call to the engine in this session.

In line 5, the query is submitted to the engine via WMOpenWorkList. The search is for all manual activities of type Approval assigned to the role Branch Manager ("ACTIVITY_ TYPE='Approval' and ACTIVITY_ROLE='BranchManager'"). (The WAPI specification is vague on the precise formulation of a worklist filter, and examples of its use are difficult, if not impossible, to find. The specification encourages SQL-style queries, so we use a SQL-style where clause. The assumption is that workflow engine performs a select on a table having columns ACTIVITY_TYPE and ACTIVITY_ROLE.) The call returns an iterator, or cursor, held in the variable WMTQueryHandle.

The *while* loop in lines 9–21 retrieves and completes each matching activity. The call to WMFetchWorkItem in line 12 gets the next work item from the query; if no work items remain in the result set, the loop is exited in line 13. Line 17 prints out information about the work item. Line 20 calls WMCompleteWorkItem to complete the activity, passing the process ID and work item ID extracted from the work item from the result set.

When the loop is complete, successive calls to WMCloseWorkList (24) and WMDisconnect (line 27) close the result set and the engine connection respectively.

WfXML

One of the goals of the WfMC reference model is to achieve interoperability in heterogeneous processes, or processes that span multiple enactment services, possibly crossing company boundaries and workflow vendor implementations. Heterogeneous processes are common in business-to-business communication. The travel reservation system considered in the section on XPDL, for instance, requires that a travel agency process start airline, hotel and car rental agency booking processes and wait for their completion.

Conceptually, the problem to be solved is to coordinate the activities in one process with those in another, as in the example in Figure 7-6, in which the Supplier process calls the Warehouse process and also synchronizes its activities.

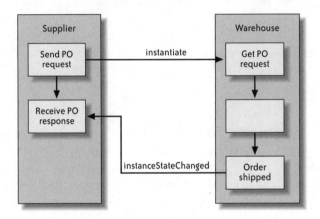

FIGURE 7-6. *A heterogeneous process spans Supplier and Warehouse*

The WfMC reference model lists several heterogeneous patterns, described in Table 7-2.

TABLE 7-2. *WfMC heterogeneous patterns*

Pattern	Description
Chained	An activity in process A triggers an activity in process B.
Nested	An activity in process A triggers process B to start. Process A waits for the completion of B before resuming.
Synchronized	Process A blocks and waits for process B to trigger it.

WfXML Specification

WfMC's interenactment protocol is a web services model called WfXML.* WfXML is built on Asynchronous Web Services Protocol (AWSP), a specification from the OASIS group (the same group that maintains BPEL) that offers a mechanism to remotely control and monitor long-running web services (*htttp://awsp.info/spec/1/0/*). WfXML extends AWSP with the ability to remotely control and monitor long-running workflows. The main components of WfXML/AWSP are shown in Figure 7-7.

In this model there are two web services: the one that implements the Observer interface and the Async Web Service (AWS) that implements the interfaces ServiceRegistry, Factory, Instance, and Activity. The AWS is the web service that can be controlled and

* WfMC, "Wf-XML 2.0: XML Based Protocol for Run-time Integration of Process Engines," Version 2.0. October 2003.

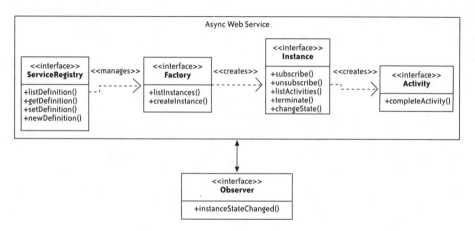

FIGURE 7-7. *WfXML components*

monitored remotely; the observer web service is the service doing the controlling and monitoring. In the WfMC reference model, an enactment service implements both services; it can control, or be controlled by, other enactment services.

Table 7-3 summarizes the he purpose and functionality of each of these interfaces.

TABLE 7-3. *WfXML components*

Interface	Purpose	API
ServiceRegistry	Management of process definitions deployed to the enactment service.	`listDefinitions()` returns a list of process definitions. `getDefinition()` returns the XPDL for a particular definition. `setDefinition()` changes an existing definition. `newDefinition()` creates a new definition on the enactment service.
Factory	Management of process instances running on the enactment service.	`listInstances()` returns a list of process instances. `createInstance()` instantiates a process definition, thereby launching a new instance on the enactment service.
Instance	Management of a particular instance.	`subscribe()` registers the observer as a listener for instance state change events; the enactment service calls the observer's `instanceStateChanged()` operation as state changes occur. `unsubscribe()` cancels the listener registration. `listActivities()` returns a list of the activities in the instance. `changeState()` forces an instance to pause, resume, or abort. `terminate()` abruptly stops the instance.
Activity	A controller for a process activity instance.	`completeActivity()` finishes a process activity instance that was pending.
Observer	Watches an AWS for events.	`instanceStateChanged()` is invoked when a process instance changes state.

WfXML Example

In the nested pattern of heterogeneous processing introduced previously, a process running on one enactment service instantiates a subprocess on a second enactment service and waits for it to complete before resuming. The sequence diagram in Figure 7-8 shows how the first enactment service can use WfXML to manage the nested remote process.

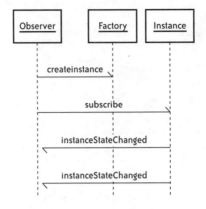

FIGURE 7-8. *WfXML example: starting and monitoring an instance*

The first enactment service implements the Observer interface so that it can subscribe to instance state events. The service begins by creating an instance of a remote process by calling the createInstance( ) operation of the Factory interface hosted on the second enactment service. Next, the first enactment service registers its instance state change subscription (subscribe( )) and over time is notified of the state change (instanceStateChanged( )). The final event should indicate that the instance has completed, at which point the first enactment service can resume its own workflow instance.

SOME THOUGHTS ON WFXML

WfXML is a good model for general remote process administration and monitoring. A process administrator's portal, for example, can be designed to use ServiceRegistry to deploy new process definitions and Instance to terminate stuck processes.

However, why do enactment services need a general protocol to communicate with each other? Why not have processes deployed on enactment services define their own, application-specific partner links? WfXML is intended as an architected solution, in the spirit of web services choreography, to the problem of multiparticipant process exchange. WfXML enables the creation of a process of processes, combining the activities of multiple participants (e.g., a supply chain process that contains the buyer, supplier, and distribution processes of entirely separate companies). The approach of WfXML is to allow the participating enactment services to control and monitor each other (e.g., supplier starts warehouse process and listens for its completion).

Summary

The main points of this chapter include:

- The WfMC was founded in 1993 and has more than 300 members. WfMC publishes BPM standards. The major standards are the reference model, XPDL, WAPI, and WfXML.

- The reference model describes the components and interfaces of a workflow/BPM architecture. Components include process definition tools, worklist client applications, invoked applications, administration and monitoring applications, and enactment services and their workflow engines. Interfaces are XPDL (XML process definition format that can be exported from a process definition tool to an enactment service), WAPI (API for client applications, invoked applications, and administration and monitoring applications), and WfXML (interenactment-service coordination).

- XPDL is the WfMC process definition language. XPDL represents a process as a directed graph of activities (manual, automatic, nested, route, and block) and transitions. The key to understanding XPDL is to grasp the flow of control brought about by guarded transitions, and AND and XOR splits and joins.

- XPDL is relatively weak on support for P4 patterns: it supports only 11 of the 20 patterns.

- WAPI is a set of C functions and equivalent IDL and COM Automation interfaces. Functional areas include connection management, process management, activity management, worklist, administration, and invoke applications.

- WfXML is the WfMC standard for communication between enactment services for the execution of heterogeneous processes, or processes that span multiple enactment services. WfXML is built on OASIS's AWSP standard for remote control and monitoring of long-running web services.

References

1. D. Hollingsworth, "The Workflow Reference Model: 10 Years On," in *Workflow Handbook 2004*. Lighthouse Point, FL, Future Strategies, 2004.

2. WfMC, "Audit Data Specification," Version 1.1. September 1998.

3. K. D. Swenson, "Connecting Systems With ASAP," WfMC/OASIS Presentation, June 2004.

4. W. M. P. van der Aalst, "Business Process Management Demystified: A Tutorial on Models, Systems, and Standards for Workflow Management," In J. Desel, W. Reisig, and G. Rozenberg (editors), *Lectures on Concurrency and Petri Nets*, volume 3,098 of *Lecture Notes in Computer Science*, pages 1–65. Springer-Verlag, Berlin, 2004.

CHAPTER EIGHT

World Wide Web Consortium (W3C): Choreography

THE TOPIC OF CHOREOGRAPHY, THE CURRENT FLAVOR OF THE MONTH IN THE WORLD OF WEB SER-VICES, refers to the attempt to build stateful, conversational, long-running, multiparticipant processes out of basic, stateless, atomic web services operations. The flurry of effort in the past few years on choreography is driven by the desire to extend the web services stack. Though choreography is not essentially a BPM technology, one of its main applications is the building of process-oriented business conversations, and hence there is an obvious link connecting choreography to BPM. Conversely, contemporary BPM languages such as BPEL are so obsessed with web services integration that many of their processes look like choreographies. The lines are blurred. This chapter explores choreography's main concepts, standard approaches, and connections to BPM.

About the W3C

Founded by Tim Berners-Lee (the father of the Web) in 1994, the World Wide Web Consortium (*http://w3c.org*) has grown into a commanding community of more than 350 organizations; it has authored many of the most important technical specifications in web and enterprise computing, including those pertaining to HTML, XML, and web services. The web services contribution alone constitutes a huge body of work, with standards for the two basic technologies—Simple Object Access Protocol (SOAP) and Web Services

Description Language (WSDL)—as well as the so-called "WS-*" family, which enhances the web services stack with support for reliability (WS-Reliability), security (WS-Security), and choreography (WS-Choreography).

What about BPM? As we have shown throughout this book, contemporary BPM has embraced the web services concept and anointed this concept as its key enabling technology. No one can write a business process without understanding and knowing how to write in WSDL. The W3C is thus relevant to BPM as the conceiver of its some of its fundamental underpinnings. But with *choreography*, the W3C actively joins the fray as a BPM thought leader. As demonstrated in greater detail later in this chapter, BPM is concerned with interacting processes; most BPM languages are built to describe the design of one of those processes, whereas a choreography language aims to capture the global process interaction model. Three W3C choreography languages are examined in this chapter:

Web Services Choreography Description Language
A work-in-progress of the Web Services Choreography Working Group, WS-CDL is a high-minded declarative language that captures from a global viewpoint the rules of message exchange for multiple web service-based participants.

Web Services Choreography Interface
Written by BEA and others in 2002, WSCI (pronounced "whiskey") is published on the W3C site as a note* and is an input to the work of the Web Services Choreography Working Group.

Web Services Conversation Language
Like WSCI, WSCL is published as a note on the W3C site. Written by Hewlett Packard in 2002, WSCL is not well-known, but its distinctive state-machine approach merits investigation.

Choreography and Orchestration

Many BPM commentators distinguish between the "orchestration" and "choreography" of web services. Both concepts imply coordination or control—the act of making individuals web services work together to form some coherent overall process. Orchestration, by convention, refers to coordination at the level of a single participant's process, whereas choreography refers to the global view, spanning multiple participants.

The distinction at first glance seems arbitrary. After all, are not the English words nearly synonymous? How is the direction of dancers fundamentally different from the arrangement of instruments? The terminology is suspect. Better terms, perhaps, are "subjective" and "objective," or "local" and "global." But regardless of the words used, the need for a distinction is crucial.

---

* In the W3C, a *note* is a document that is published for review, and is not a standard.

If modern BPM is about communicating business processes, then understanding the overall communication spanning all the processes is as important as understanding the behavior of any one process. Most BPM languages—such as BPEL, BPML, BPMN, and XPDL—focus on one process and its interactions. In purchasing, for example, the exchange of messages among buyer, seller, inventory, and credit card company is complex, but BPEL characteristically isolates one of the participants and documents its internal processes and interaction touchpoints. The BPEL approach is fundamentally subjective: if I am a seller, here is my process, and along the way, I talk to the buyer, inventory, and a credit card company. This proclivity is depicted in Figure 8-1.

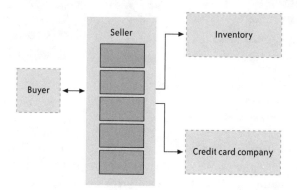

FIGURE 8-1. *Most BPM languages focus on the orchestration of one process*

The global view of choreography is different: the seller's internal logic is immaterial. What matters is the *protocol*: a buyer talks to a seller, who in turn communicates with inventory and the credit card company, as Figure 8-2 shows.

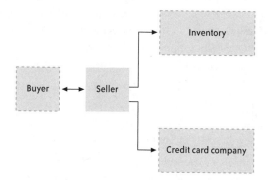

FIGURE 8-2. *Choreography describes the global picture*

One major design characteristic of choreography is that interacting participants, being distributed within or across an organization's trusted domain, cooperate by exchanging messages with no dependency on a centralized controller. A choreography definition can generate code skeletons for each participant, as the W3C's choreography documents suggest. A seller, for example, knows from a choreography which web services it is required to listen on and respond to, as well as those it needs to call. This information is enough to create a basic BPEL process, shown in Figure 8-3, with receive and invoke activities marking the web service touchpoints; the rest of the work is providing specific details.

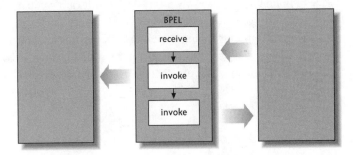

FIGURE 8-3. *BPEL skeleton from choreography*

WS-CDL

Though WSCI is more famous, the official choreography model blessed by the W3C's Choreography Working Group is WS-CDL, whose latest working draft was released by the W3C in December 2004.* WS-CDL is a brand-new XML process contract language that provides a standard way to specify technical contracts that capture (from a global viewpoint) the common observable behavior of autonomous interacting participants. The distinguishing characteristics of WS-CDL are the following:

Globally distributed participants, web service interfaces
WS-CDL choreography is seldom confined to applications on a corporate intranet. Rather, the participants are usually from different companies all over the world. Participants use web services to communicate with one anothe, and publish their service interfaces in a WSDL. (WS-CDL supports WSDL Versions 1.1 and 2.0.)

No central controller, just a formal specification
WS-CDL choreography may be global, but WS-CDL does not prescribe a global, centralized control engine to coordinate or manage participant interactions. Instead, each participant has its own engine that executes the participant's business process. The process, in turn, is required to obey the rules of interaction required by the WS-CDL choreography.

Only publicly observable participant behavior is relevant
A company's business process can have many steps, but WS-CDL is concerned only with the public face (e.g., in a BPEL process, the receive and invoke activities for relevant partner links).

---

* W3C, "Web Services Choreography Description Language," *http://www.w3.org/TR/2004/WD-ws-cdl-10-20040427/*, April 2004.

WS-CDL complements process languages

WS-CDL is not a replacement for process languages such as BPEL, BPML, or XPDL. Those languages are suited to model participant processes. WS-CDL's purpose is to model the global interaction.

Overview of WS-CDL

The object model of WS-CDL is shown in Figure 8-4.

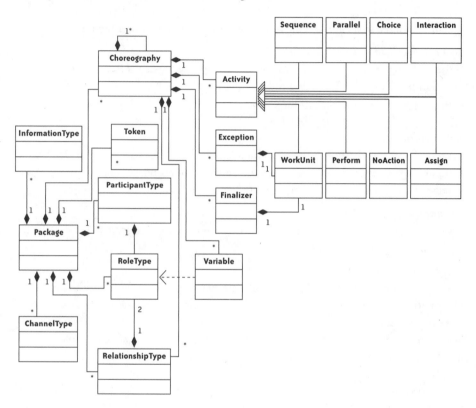

FIGURE 8-4. *WS-CDL object model*

The major objects in the model are:

Package

A grouping of choreographies, information types, channel types, relationships, roles, participants, and tokens.

InformationType

Declaration of a data type for a message or part of a message exchanged in an interaction. The following example declares the information type POShipNotice, based on an XML type identified by pons:POShipNotice:

```
<informationType name="POShipNotice" type="pons:POShipNotice"/>
```

Token

A piece of data used in a choreography. A `tokenLocator` uses an XPath expression to define how to extract a token from a message. For example, the token `POID` can be extracted from the information type `POShipNotice` as follows:

```
<token name="POID" informationType="tns:intType"/>
<tokenLocator tokenName="tns:POID" informationType="tns:POShipNotice"
    query="orderId"/>
```

Variable

A value, declared in a choreography, for a specific role. There are three types:

Information exchange capturing variables

Contain information used when sending or receiving messages (e.g., `noticeC` for the consumer role, in the following code sample):

```
<variable name="noticeC"
    informationType="tns:POShipNotice" roleTypes="tns:Consumer"/>
```

State capturing variables

Contain information about the observable changes of a role as a result of information being exchanged. For example, when a consumer sends a purchase order to a retailer, the consumer's state becomes `OrderSent` and retailer's `OrderReceived`.

Channel capturing variables

Contain information such as endpoint URL and quality of service (QoS) for a given channel.

RoleType

Enumerates the observable behaviors that a party exhibits in order to interact with other parties. In the following code snippet, for example, the `Consumer` role has behaviors `c4r`, representing its retailer activities (e.g., send PO, receive PO response) and `c4w`, its contract with warehouse (e.g., receive shipment notice). In WS-CDL, a role is mapped to a WSDL 1.1 port type or a WSDL 2.0 interface name.

```
<roleType name="Consumer">
    <behavior name="c4r" interface="cns:CRPT"/>
    <behavior name="c4w" interface="cns:CWPT"/>
</roleType>
```

RelationshipType

The affiliation of two roles (e.g., consumer and retailer), where mutual commitments between two parties are made for them to cooperate successfully:

```
<relationshipType name="CRRelationship">
    <role type="tns:Consumer" behavior="c4r"/>
    <role type="tns:Retailer" behavior="c4c"/>
</relationshipType>
```

ParticipantType

A specific entity, organization, or some other particular actor that performs one or more roles; for example, here, `ACME` is a retailer and a warehouse:

```
<participantType name="ACME">
    <role type="tns:Retailer"/>
```

```
        <role type="tns:Warehouse"/>
    </participantType>
```

ChannelType

Realizes a point of collaboration between participants by specifying where and how information is exchanged. As the example code demonstrates, a channel (RetailerChannel) is tied to a role (Retailer) and, optionally, a behavior (RC):

```
<channelType name="RetailerChannel">
    <role type="tns:Retailer" behavior="RC"/>
    <reference> <token name="tns:retailerRef"/> </reference>
    <identity> <token name="tns:POID"/> </identity>
</channelType>
```

Additionally, channel information can be passed among participants in information exchanges, as is done in the pi-calculus. The channels exchanged can be used in subsequent interaction activities. This flexibility allows the modeling of both static and dynamic message destinations when collaborating within a choreography.

Choreography

Consists of variables, activities, an exception handler (e.g., handle misaligned state), a finalizer (whose actions confirm, cancel, or otherwise modify the effects of choreography-completed actions), and other choreographies.

Sequence, parallel, choice activities

Typical control structures to support sequential, parallel, and conditional activities, respectively. In the code snippet, the interaction and perform steps are executed one after another:

```
<sequence>
    <interaction . . . />
    <perform . . . />
</sequence>
```

Interaction activity

An activity that represents an exchange between roles. The next section has numerous examples of interaction.

An interaction can have a time limit, as well as an alignment requirement that ensures the participants have a common understanding on the complementary state changes as a result of the exchange (e.g., after sending an order, a buyer should have state Order Sent, the seller Order Received). An interaction can be designated as a *choreography initiator*, indicating that it can start a choreography; as with a BPEL process, a WS-CDL choreography initiates when one of its interactions starts, but the difference is that BPEL defines initiation of a process at a single participant, whereas WS-CDL defines where initiation of a collaboration is possible in the whole distributed system, encompassing two or more participants.

WorkUnit activity

An activity that is *guarded*, meaning that it is executed only when a condition is met. The condition can be configured to wait for all its data to become available. For example, a work unit to sell an item to the highest of three bidders can be configured to wait for the three bids. It can also be set to sell the item to the highest current bidder, without waiting for more.

In the following code snippet, the work unit runs if the Boolean variable internalResponse is true:

```
<workunit name="positivePOResponse"
    guard="boolean(internalResponse)" block="false">
    . . . activities . . .
</workunit>
```

Perform activity

A compositional activity that enables reuse of choreographies. For example, a choreography Quote and Order can be created from existing building-block buyer-supplier choreographies Request for Quote and Place Order, each of which is defined separately and independently:

```
<choreography name="Quote and Order">
    <sequence>
        <perform choreographyName="Request for Quote"> . . . </perform>
        <perform choreographyName="Place Order"> . . . </perform>
    </sequence>
</choreography>
```

NoAction activity

The WS-CDL no-op activity.

Assign activity

Copies data into or extracts data from a choreography variable. Examples are provided in the following section.

WS-CDL Example

The definitive WS-CDL example is the exchange between consumer, retailer, and warehouse in the processing of a purchase order. In Example 8-1, a consumer issues a purchase order request to a retailer, who acknowledges it and then forwards it to a warehouse. If the warehouse accepts the request, the retailer indicates success to the consumer; when the warehouse ships the order, it sends a notification of shipment directly to the consumer. If the warehouse rejects the request, the retailer sends an error to the consumer.

EXAMPLE 8-1. *WS-CDL example code*

```
1   <?xml version="1.0" encoding="UTF-8"?>
2   <package name="PO" version="1.0"
3       targetNamespace="http://mike.com/cdlpo"
4       xmlns:pons="http://mike.com/cdlpo/types"
5       xmlns:cns="http://mike.com/cdlpo/Consumer"
6       xmlns:rns="http://mike.com/cdlpo/Retailer"
7       xmlns:xsd="http://www.w3.org/2001/XMLSchema"
8       xmlns:tns="http://mike.com/cdlpo/cdlpo"
9       xmlns="http://www.w3.org/2004/12/ws-chor/cdl"
10      xmlns:xsi="http://www.w3.org/2001/XMLSchema-instance"
11      xsi:schemaLocation="http://www.w3.org/2004/12/ws-chor/cdl">
12
```

EXAMPLE 8-1. *WS-CDL example code (continued)*

```
13    <!-- information types (i.e., message data)
14        1. Four PO message types (PO, POAck, POResponse, POShipNotice),
15        2. Basic types: bool, intType, uriType -->
16    <informationType name="PO" type="pons:POMsg"/>
17    <informationType name="POAck" type="pons:POAckMsg"/>
18    <informationType name="POResponse" type="pons:POResponseMsg"/>
19    <informationType name="POShipNotice" type="pons:POShipNotice"/>
20    <informationType name="bool" type="xsd:boolean"/>
21    <informationType name="intType" type="xsd:int"/>
22    <informationType name="uriType" type="xsd:anyURI"/>
23
24    <!-- tokens (i.e., data used in the choreography with locators that use
25        XPath to extract token from an information type) include POID plus
26        references to each of the channels. -->
27    <token name="POID" informationType="tns:intType"/>
28    <token name="retailerRef" informationType="tns:uriType"/>
29    <token name="consumerRef" informationType="tns:uriType"/>
30    <token name="warehouseRef" informationType="tns:uriType"/>
31    <tokenLocator tokenName="tns:POID" informationType="tns:PO" query="orderId"/>
32    <tokenLocator tokenName="tns:POID" informationType="tns:POAck" query="orderId"/>
33    <tokenLocator tokenName="tns:POID" informationType="tns:POResponse"
34       query="orderId"/>
35    <tokenLocator tokenName="tns:POID" informationType="tns:POShipNotice"
36       query="orderId"/>
37
38    <!-- Three roles: consumer, warehouse, and retailer.
39        A role consists of a set of behaviors,
40        each of which represents an web service interface/port type.
41
42        Three relationships: C to R, R to W, C to W.
43        A relationship is a set of cooperating roles.
44
45        Three channels: one for consumer, one for WH, one for retailer.
46    -->
47    <roleType name="Consumer">
48       <behavior name="c4r" interface="cns:CRPT"/>
49       <behavior name="c4w" interface="cns:CWPT"/>
50    </roleType>
51    <roleType name="Retailer">
52       <behavior name="r4c" interface="rns:RCPT"/>
53       <behavior name="r4w" interface="rns:RWPT"/>
54    </roleType>
55    <roleType name="Warehouse">
56       <behavior name="w4r" interface="wns:WPT"/>
57       <behavior name="w4c" interface="wns:WCT"/>
58    </roleType>
59    <relationshipType name="CRRelationship">
60       <role type="tns:Consumer" behavior="c4r"/>
61       <role type="tns:Retailer" behavior="r4c"/>
62    </relationshipType>
63    <relationshipType name="RWRelationship">
64       <role type="tns:Retailer" behavior="r4w"/>
65       <role type="tns:Warehouse" behavior="w4r"/>
66    </relationshipType>
67    <relationshipType name="CWRelationship">
```

EXAMPLE 8-1. *WS-CDL example code (continued)*

```
68          <role type="Consumer" behavior="c4w"/>
69          <role type="Warehouse" behavior="w4c"/>
70      </relationshipType>
71      <channelType name="RetailerChannel">
72          <role type="tns:Retailer" behavior="r4c"/>
73          <reference> <token name="tns:retailerRef"/> </reference>
74          <identity> <token name="tns:POID"/> </identity>
75      </channelType>
76      <channelType name="ConsumerChannel">
77          <role type="tns:Consumer"/>
78          <reference> <token name="tns:consumerRef"/> </reference>
79          <identity> <token name="tns:POID"/> </identity>
80      </channelType>
81      <channelType name="WarehouseChannel">
82          <role type="tns:Warehouse"/>
83          <reference> <token name="tns:warehouseRef"/> </reference>
84          <identity> <token name="tns:POID"/> </identity>
85      </channelType>
86
87      <!-- RWChoreo models the interaction between retailer and
88           warehouse. Retailer calls Warehouse handlePO operation,
89           passing a PO and getting back a Boolean (success or failure).
90           Retailer also passes consumer's channel to warehouse.
91           Sets consumerSatisfied = true/false on exit. -->
92      <choreography name="RWChoreo">
93          <relationship type="tns:RWRelationship"/>
94          <variableDefinitions>
95              <!-- this variable is the output of the choreo -->
96              <variable name="consumerSatisfied" informationType="tns:bool"
97                  roleTypes="tns:Retailer" free="true"/>
98
99              <!-- messages of WS call: poR/poW is sent from R to W
100                  okW/ok is sent back from W to R. -->
101             <variable name="poR" informationType="tns:PO"
102                 roleTypes="tns:Retailer" free="true"/>
103             <variable name="poW" informationType="tns:PO"
104                 roleTypes="tns:Warehouse" free="true"/>
105             <variable name="okW"
106                 informationType="tns:bool" roleTypes="tns:Warehouse"/>
107             <variable name="okR"
108                 informationType="tns:bool" roleTypes="tns:Retailer"/>
109
110             <!-- The two channels used in this choreo.  WChannel is the
111                  endpoint of the service.  CChannel is passed to it
112                  for a future notifcation from W to C -->
113             <variable name="WChannel" channelType="tns:WarehouseChannel"/>
114             <variable name="CChannel" channelType="tns:ConsumerChannel"/>
115         </variableDefinitions>
116         <sequence>
117             <interaction name="RWInteraction" channelVariable="tns:WChannel"
118                 operation="handlePO">
119                 <participate relationshipType="tns:RWRelationship"
120                     fromRole="tns:Retailer" toRole="tns:Warehouse"/>
121                 <exchange name="RWReq" informationType="tns:PO" action="request">
122                     <senmud variable="cdl:getVariable(poR,tns:Retailer)"/>
```

EXAMPLE 8-1. *WS-CDL example code (continued)*

```
123                <receive variable="cdl:getVariable(poW,tns:Warehouse)"/>
124            </exchange>
125            <exchange name="RWRsp" informationType="tns:bool" action="respond">
126                <send variable="cdl:getVariable(okW, tns:Warehouse)"/>
127                <receive variable="cdl:getVariable(okR, tns:Retailer)"/>
128            </exchange>
129            <record name="CChannelRecord" when="before">
130              <source variable="cdl:getVariable(poW, channel, tns:Warehouse)"/>
131              <target variable="cdl:getVariable(CChannel, tns:Warehouse)"/>
132            </record>
133        </interaction>
134        <!-- set variable consumerSatisfied with the result. -->
135        <assign roleType="tns:Retailer">
136            <copy name="popSat">
137                <source variable="boolean(cdl:getVariable(poR,
138                    Response, tns:Retailer))"/>
139                <target variable="cdl:getVariable(consumerSatisfied,
140                    tns:Retailer)"/>
141            </copy>
142        </assign>
143    </sequence>
144 </choreography>
145
146 <!-- CWChoreo models  the consumer-warehouse relationship.  Warehouse
147     sends consumer a ship notice. -->
148 <choreography name="CWChoreo">
149    <relationship type="tns:CWRelationship"/>
150    <variableDefinitions>
151        <variable name="noticeW"
152            informationType="tns:POShipNotice" roleTypes="tns:Warehouse"/>
153        <variable name="noticeC"
154            informationType="tns:POShipNotice" roleTypes="tns:Consumer"/>
155        <variable name="CChannel"
156            channelType="tns:ConsumerChannel" roleTypes="tns:Warehouse"
157            free="true"/>
158    </variableDefinitions>
159    <interaction name="POShipNoticeInteraction"
160        channelVariable="tns:CChannel" operation="handlePOShipNotice">
161        <participate relationshipType="tns:CWRelationship"
162            fromRole="tns:Warehouse" toRole="tns:Consumer"/>
163        <exchange name="CWSend"
164            informationType="tns:POShipNotice" action="request">
165            <send variable="cdl:getVariable(noticeW, tns:Warehouse)"/>
166            <receive variable="cdl:getVariable(noticeC, tns:Consumer)"/>
167        </exchange>
168    </interaction>
169 </choreography>
170
171 <!-- PO is the main choreo modeling the overall exchange.  It
172     performs the two choreos above.
173     1. The consumer-retailer interaction: consumer sends PO to retailer.
174     2. Perform the retailer-warehouse interaction.
175     3. If 2 is ok, retailer sends consumer a response, and then we
176         perform the warehouse-consumer interaction.
177     4. Else, retailer sends consumer an error. -->
```

EXAMPLE 8-1. *WS-CDL example code (continued)*

```
178    <choreography name="PO" root="true">
179       <relationship type="tns:CRRelationship"/>
180       <relationship type="tns:RWRelationship"/>
181       <relationship type="tns:CRRelationship"/>
182       <variableDefinitions>
183          <!-- message types used in the choreo -->
184          <variable name="poC" informationType="tns:PO"
185             roleTypes="tns:Consumer"/>
186          <variable name="poW" informationType="tns:PO"
187             roleTypes="tns:Warehouse"/>
188          <variable name="poR" informationType="tns:PO"
189             roleTypes="tns:Retailer"/>
190          <variable name="poAckC" informationType="tns:POAck"
191             roleTypes="tns:Consumer"/>
192          <variable name="poAckR" informationType="tns:POAck"
193             roleTypes="tns:Retailer"/>
194          <variable name="poPosRespR" informationType="tns:POResponse"
195             roleTypes="tns:Retailer"/>
196          <variable name="poNegRespR" informationType="tns:POResponse"
197             roleTypes="tns:Retailer"/>
198          <variable name="poRespC" informationType="tns:POResponse"
199             roleTypes="tns:Consumer"/>
200
201          <!-- boolean output of warehouse drives choice logic below -->
202          <variable name="internalResponse" informationType="tns:bool"
203             roleTypes="tns:Retailer"/>
204
205          <!-- retailer and consumer channels used in the choreo -->
206          <variable name="RChannel" channelType="tns:RetailerChannel"/>
207          <variable name="CChannel" channelType="tns:ConsumerChannel"/>
208       </variableDefinitions>
209
210       <sequence>
211          <!-- interaction: consumer sends retailer a PO.-->
212          <interaction name="POInteraction" channelVariable="tns:RChannel"
213             operation="handlePO" initiate="true">
214             <participate relationshipType="tns:CRRelationship"
215                fromRole="tns:Consumer" toRole="tns:Retailer"/>
216             <exchange name="POReq" informationType="tns:PO" action="request">
217                <send variable="cdl:getVariable(poC, tns:Consumer)"/>
218                <receive variable="cdl:getVariable(poR, tns:Retailer)"/>
219             </exchange>
220             <exchange name="PORsp" informationType="tns:POAck" action="respond">
221                <send variable="cdl:getVariable(poAckR, tns:Retailer)"/>
222                <receive variable="cdl:getVariable(poAckC, tns:Consumer)"/>
223             </exchange>
224             <record name="CustomerChannelRecord" when="before">
225                <source variable="cdl:getVariable(poR,
226                   PO/CustomerRef, tns:Retailer)"/>
227                <target variable="cdl:getVariable(CChannel, tns:Retailer)"/>
228             </record>
229          </interaction>
230
231          <!-- perform the RW choreo: pass in poR, save output in variables
232             poW and internalResponse -->
```

EXAMPLE 8-1. *WS-CDL example code (continued)*

```
233          <perform choreographyName="tns:RWChoreo">
234              <bind name="n1">
235                  <this variable="cdl:getVariable(poR, tns:Retailer)"
236                      role="tns:Retailer"/>
237                  <free variable="cdl:getVariable(poR, rwns:Retailer)"
238                      role="rwns:Retailer"/>
239              </bind>
240              <bind name="n2">
241                  <this variable="cdl:getVariable(poW, tns:Warehouse)"
242                      role="tns:Warehouse"/>
243                  <free variable="cdl:getVariable(poW, tns:Warehouse)"
244                      role="tns:Warehouse"/>
245              </bind>
246              <bind name="n3">
247                  <this variable="cdl:getVariable(internalResponse,tns:Retailer)"
248                      role="tns:Retailer"/>
249                  <free variable="cdl:getVariable(consumerSatisfied, tns:Retailer)"
250                      role="rwns:Retailer"/>
251              </bind>
252          </perform>
253
254          <choice>
255              <!-- if warehouse responded postively, retailer sends positive
256                   response to consumer, and performs the CW choreography
257                   so warehouse can send notice to consumer -->
258              <workunit name="positivePOResponse"
259                  guard="boolean(internalResponse)" block="false">
260                  <sequence>
261                      <interaction name="POResponseInteraction"
262                          channelVariable="tns:CChannel"operation="handlePOResponse">
263                          <participate relationshipType="tns:CRRelationship"
264                              fromRole="tns:Retailer" toRole="tns:Consumer"/>
265                          <exchange name="n1" informationType="tns:POResponse"
266                              action="request">
267                            <send variable="cdl:getVariable(poPosRespR,
268                                tns:Retailer)"/>
269                              <receive variable="cdl:getVariable(poRespC,tns:Consumer)"/>
270                          </exchange>
271                      </interaction>
272                      <perform choreographyName="tns:CWChoreo">
273                          <bind name="n1">
274                              <this variable="cdl:getVariable(CChannel, rwns:Warehouse)"
275                                  role="rwns:Warehouse"/>
276                              <free variable="cdl:getVariable(CChannel, rwns:Warehouse)"
277                                  role="rwns:Warehouse"/>
278                          </bind>
279                      </perform>
280                  </sequence>
281              </workunit>
282
283              <!-- if warehouse responded negatively, retailer sends negative
284                   response to consumer -->
285              <workunit name="negativePOResponse"
286                  guard="not(boolean(internalResponse))" block="false">
287                  <interaction name="POResponseInteraction"
```

EXAMPLE 8-1. *WS-CDL example code (continued)*

```
288                    channelVariable="tns:CChannel" operation="handlePOResponse">
289                    <participate
290                       relationshipType="tns:CRRelationship"
291                       fromRole="tns:Retailer" toRole="tns:Consumer"/>
292                    <exchange name="n1" informationType="tns:POResponse"
293                       action="request">
294                       <send variable="cdl:getVariable(poNegRespR, tns:Retailer)"/>
295                       <receive variable="cdl:getVariable(poRespC, tns:Consumer)"/>
296                    </exchange>
297                 </interaction>
298              </workunit>
299           </choice>
300        </sequence>
301     </choreography>
302 </package>
```

The example begins with the declaration of information types (lines 16–22), containing mostly message type declarations (e.g, PO, or purchase order request, in line 16). Tokens are defined in lines 27–36; for example, purchase order ID (POID) on line 27.

Lines 47–89 describe the structural composition of roles, relationships, and channels, which is depicted in Figure 8-5. Each of the three roles (represented by large boxes in the figure)—Retailer, Warehouse, and Consumer—has its own channel (shown as ovals)—RetailerChannel, WarehouseChannel, and ConsumerChannel, respectively. Each role has two web-service-based behaviors, represented by the small inner boxes; for example, the retailer's behaviors are r4c (retailer for consumer) and r4w (retailer for warehouse). The arrows show the types of message exchanges encountered in the choreography. For example, the arrow from r4w to the warehouse channel represents an exchange between the r4w behavior of the retailer and the warehouse; the arrow from the warehouse channel to w4r indicates that the warehouse uses its w4r behavior to process events on its channel. As the figure illustrates, each role has connections to the others, implying that there are three relationships: customer and retailer, consumer and warehouse, and retailer and warehouse.

Three choreographies are presented in the code. The first, in lines 92–144, describes the behavior of the retailer-warehouse relationship:

- Line 117: The interaction takes place over the warehouse channel (WChannel).

- Line 121–124: The retailer sends a purchase order to the warehouse. On the retailer's side, the purchase order is held in the variable poR; on the warehouse side, the variable is poW.

- Lines 125–128: The warehouse returns a Boolean indicating success or failure. On the warehouse side, the variable is called okW, on the retailer side okR.

- Lines 129–132: The warehouse extracts from the purchase order (poW) a reference to the consumer channel CChannel, which was sent originally by the consumer to the

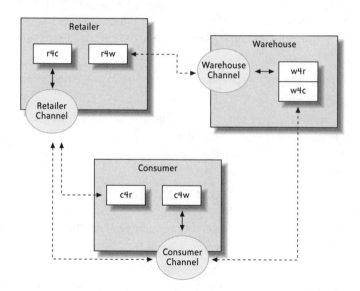

FIGURE 8-5. *Roles and channels in WS-CDL purchasing example*

retailer. The warehouse will use this channel to notify the consumer when the shipment is ready.

The second choreography, in lines 148–169, captures the warehouse-to-consumer exchange, which occurs on the consumer channel (CChannel in line 160) and involves the sending of a notification from the warehouse's noticeW variable to the consumer's noticeC variable.

The third and final choreography (lines 178–301) drives the overall exchange. In the first interaction of this choreography, in 212–229, the consumer sends the purchase order to the retailer (lines 216–219), and the retailer responds with an acknowledgment (lines 220–223). Next comes the perform activity in lines 233–252, in which the choreography invokes the retailer-warehouse choreography, passing in the purchase order the retailer received from the consumer (lines 234–239) and getting back the Boolean result (lines 246–251). The two possible outcomes of this result are treated with a choice activity. The work unit positivePOResponse (lines 258–281) is encountered if the result was true. In this case, the retailer sends a positive response to the consumer (lines 261–271) and the customer-warehouse choreography is performed (lines 272–278). In the false case (lines 285–298), the retailer sends a negative response to the consumer.

Strengths of WS-CDL

From the previous discussion, you can draw the following conclusions about the general nature of WS-CDL:

- WS-CDL is useful for building technical contracts that capture multiparticipant interactions.

- WS-CDL is declarative and based on the pi-calculus. It builds sophisticated choreographies with subtly powerful conceptions of channels, channel passing, relationships and interactions, and choreography composition.

- WS-CDL is suited to the collaborative model of intra- or interbusiness e-commerce transactions.

- WS-CDL has a complementary role with current BPM languages such as BPEL. Based on the WS-CDL standardized model, translators can generate from a choreography technical contract a BPEL process code skeleton or a Java code skeleton for a particular role, as discussed in Chapter 2.

- WS-CDL has more in common with ebXML's BPSS, discussed in Chapter 9, than with current BPM languages such as BPEL. In fact, BPSS is adding business semantics such as legal bindings above WS-CDL's technical contracts, resulting in a complete business collaboration language.

- WS-CDL is compact (it can express choreographies succinctly) and hence can scale: a reasonably small amount of WS-CDL code can describe a large set of interactions spanning a large set of participants.

The Future of WS-CDL

Whatever the merits of its model, WS-CDL faces a tough political fight. Written by Oracle, but having no support from Microsoft or IBM (an ominous sign), WS-CDL inevitably will need to justify its existence in a BPEL-dominated world. The decision for customers need not be an either/or: WS-CDL and BPEL are complementary and can coexist in a real-world BPM architecture (in fact, WS-CDL is recommended for the architecture presented in Chapter 2), but only if vendors build good WS-CDL implementations and customers buy them. WS-CDL is young; it is too soon to tell.

WSCI

Version 1.0 of WSCI* was written by BEA, Intalio, Sun, and SAP in 2002. Its syntax and semantics are strikingly similar to those of BPML, which is not surprising, given Intalio's participation in both specifications. In turn, BPML's close resemblance to BPEL seemingly implies that WSCI participates in a technology competition—XML process definition languages—that has already been won by BPEL. The temptation to dismiss WSCI outright is irresistible.

But there are subtle differences. WSCI is a web services technology, not a business process technology: it extends WSDL with a language that builds stateful, conversational processes out of stateless, atomic web services. BPM languages, by contrast, build business processes whose external interactions are web services. If web services did not exist, BPM

---

*   W3C, "Web Services Choreography Interface (WSCI) 1.0," *http://www.w3c.org/TR/wsci/*, August 2002.

languages could substitute a different integration technology, but WSCI would have no reason to exist.

Anatomy of a WSCI Application

The typical WSCI application describes a business process that spans multiple participants and has both a single global, objective view and individual subjective views for each participant. In Example 8-1, there are separate processes for Consumer, Retailer, and Warehouse, each of which controls the logic for that participant, and there is also the overall exchange of messages. If we were to model this behavior in UML, each process would be represented as an activity diagram, and the overall message exchange would be modeled as a sequence diagram, as in Figure 8-6.

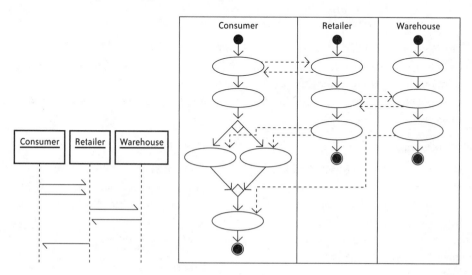

FIGURE 8-6. *Choreography in UML: global and subjective view*

The idea of WSCI, though not derived from this usage of UML, is similar in spirit: WSCI is an XML language that can model both individual participant processes as well as the global exchange. The main parts of a WSCI application are depicted in Figure 8-7.

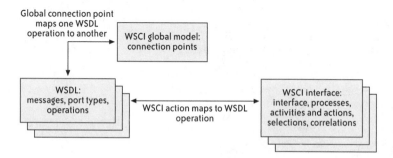

FIGURE 8-7. *Components of a WSCI application*

Here are the components:

WSDL

WSDL defines the static web service interfaces to be choreographed by WSCI.

WSCI interface

A WSCI interface specifies the process governing how the web services defined in the WSDL are used, normally from the point of view of one of the participants. The interface is intended to show only the publicly observable behavior of the participant process, and hence is not an orchestration but, is, when combined with the WSCI interfaces of the other participants, a choreography. The interface is coded using a variety of control flow patterns (sequential, parallel, conditional, iterative, and exceptional), and supports cross-service message correlation.

WSCI global model

The global model demonstrates the overall message exchange. It consists of a set of connections, each of which links the web service operation of one participant to the complementary (mirror-image) operation of another participant. For example, a retailer's operation to send a purchase order response links to a consumer's operation to receive a purchase order response.

WSCI Interface

WSCI is quite similar to BPML, and hence a detailed treatment of the WSCI interface object model or its syntax and semantics is not provided here (see the discussion of BPML in Chapter 6). The differences between WSCI and BPML are minor, the most salient of which is the treatment of the action activity, which functions as a web service integration point. In BPML, the input and output messages to a WSDL operation are explicitly mapped to process-level properties, whereas in WSCI, the input and output parameters are omitted altogether.

Instead, we focus on how a WSCI interface can be used to describe the choreography of a web service interface. In the purchasing example considered earlier, the web service interface offered by the retailer is described in Example 8-2.

EXAMPLE 8-2. *WSDL for retailer*

```
1   <?xml version = "1.0" ?>
2   <definitions name = "Retailer Purchasing"
3       targetNamespace = "http://mike.com/retailer"
4           xmlns = "http://www.w3.org/2002/07/wsci10"
5           xmlns:wsdl = "http://schemas.xmlsoap.org/wsdl/"
6           xmlns:tns = " http://mike.com/retailer"
7           xmlns:defs = " http://mike.com/purchasing/definitions">
8
9       <portType name = "Retailer">
10          <operation name = "ReceivePO">
11              <input message = "defs:poRequest"/>
12              <output message = "defs:poACK"/>
13          </operation>
14          <operation name = "SendPOToWarehouse">
```

EXAMPLE 8-2. *WSDL for retailer (continued)*

```
15              <output message = "defs:poRequest"/>
16              <input message = "defs:poACK"/>
17              <fault message = "defs:poNAK"/>
18          </operation>
19          <operation name = "SendPOResponse">
20              <output message = "defs:poResponse"/>
21          </operation>
22          <operation name = "SendPOError">
23              <output message = "defs:poError"/>
24          </operation>
25      </portType>
26  </definitions>
```

The retailer's use of the four operations listed in the WSDL, stated informally, is as follows:

1. ReceivePO triggers the retailer to begin processing the specified purchase order request, passed to it by the consumer.

2. The retailer passes the request to the warehouse by calling SendPOToWarehouse.

3. If SendPOToWarehouse returns successfully, the retailer invokes the operation SendPOResponse to notify the consumer that the purchase order request was successful. Otherwise, the retailer calls SendPOError to notify the consumer that the request failed.

Example 8-3 shows the WSCI code.

EXAMPLE 8-3. *WSCI interface for retailer*

```
1  <?xml version = "1.0" ?>
2  <wsdl:definitions name = "Retailer"
3     targetNamespace = "http://mike.com/retailer "
4     xmlns = "http://www.w3.org/2002/07/wsci10"
5     xmlns:wsdl = "http://schemas.xmlsoap.org/wsdl/"
6     xmlns:tns = "http://mike.com/retailer "
7     xmlns:defs = "http://mike.com/purchasing/definitions">
8
9     <wsdl:import  namespace = "http://mike.com/retailer "
10                  location = "http://mike.com/retailer.wsdl" />
11    <interface name = "Retailer">
12       <process name = "ProcessPO" instantiation = "message">
13          <sequence>
14             <!-- po from consumer -->
15             <action name = "ReceivePO" role = "tns:Retailer"
16                operation = "tns:Retailer/ReceivePO"/>
17             <context>
18                <!-- send po to warehouse -->
19                <action name = "SendPOToWarehouse" role = "tns:Retailer"
20                   operation = "tns:Retailer/SendPOToWarehouse"/>
21                <exception>
22                   <!-- if warehouse returns NAK, send po error to consumer -->
23                   <onFault>
24                      <action name="SendPOError" role="tns:Retailer"
```

EXAMPLE 8-3. *WSCI interface for retailer (continued)*

```
25                          operation="tns:Retailer/SendPOError"/>
26                       <!-- propagate error up -->
27                       <fault code="tns:poNAK"/>
28                    </onFault>
29                 </exception>
30              </context>
31              <!-- got out of warehouse step OK, send po response to consumer -->
32              <action name = "SendPOResponse" role = "tns:Retailer"
33                 operation = "tns:Retailer/SendPOResponse"/>
34           </sequence>
35        </process>
36     </interface>
37  </wsdl:definitions>
```

The four action elements (lines 41–42, 45–46, 50–51, and 58–59) map to the four WSDL operations, and are called in a sequence (lines 39–60). ReceivePO occurs first, followed by SendPOToWarehouse. Because SendPOToWarehouse can fault (on a negative acknowledgement), it is wrapped in a context element with an exception handler (exception) that calls SendPOError when the fault occurs. If the warehouse interaction is successful, the process calls SendPOResponse.

NOTE

Notice that the interface is enclosed in a wsdl:definitions element. Because of this, the example WSCI code could have been embedded in the WSDL document.

Notice also that in the action elements, WSCI, unlike BPML, does not explicitly show the web service input and output messages. Because of this, WSCI actions are hard to read and require constant back-and-forth cross-referencing with the WSDL.

A full implementation of the purchasing example also requires interfaces for consumer and warehouse. The WSDL and WSCI representations of these participants are omitted for brevity.

WSCI Global Model

A WSCI interface—a control flow shaped by constructs such as loops, sequences, decisions, and parallels paths—is essentially *procedural* in nature, whereas a WSCI global model, built as the declaration of a set of connections between interfaces, is *declarative*. Figure 8-8 illustrates the main pieces of a global model.

A global model references a set of WSCI interfaces and one or more connections. Interestingly, the connections are defined by WSDL port type and operation rather than WSCI interface action, which raises the question of why the WSCI interface references are required in the first place. The destination operation is a mirror image of the source, with matching message types but opposite direction, as outlined in Table 8-1.

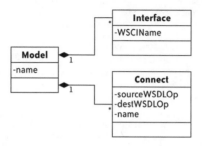

FIGURE 8-8. *WSCI global model*

TABLE 8-1. *Global model connections: destination is the mirror image of the source*

Source	Destination
Out	In
Out-In	In-Out
In	Out
In-Out	Out-In

Writing a WSCI global model

Writing a global model assumes that a WSCI interface has been created for each participant and that a WSDL exists that captures each interface action. Example 8-4 demonstrates the structure of a global model for the communication of consumer, retailer, and warehouse.

EXAMPLE 8-4. *WSCI global model sample*

```
1   <?xml version = "1.0" ?>
2   <wsdl:definitions name = "GlobalModel"
3      targetNamespace = "http://mike.com/purchasing"
4      xmlns = "http://www.w3.org/2002/07/wsci10"
5      xmlns:wsdl = "http://schemas.xmlsoap.org/wsdl/"
6      xmlns:c = "http://mike.com/purchasing/consumer"
7      xmlns:r = "http://mike.com/purchasing/retailer"
8      xmlns:w = "http://mike.com/purchasing/warehouse">
9
10     <wsdl:import  namespace = "http://mike.com/purchasing/consumer "
11        location = "http://mike.com/purchasing/consumer.wsdl" />
12     <wsdl:import  namespace = "http://mike.com/purchasing/retailer"
13        location = "http://mike.com/purchasing/retailer.wsdl" />
14     <wsdl:import  namespace = "http://mike.com/purchasing/warehouse"
15        location = "http://mike.com/purchasing/warehouse.wsdl" />
16
17     <model name = "PurchasingGV">
18
19        <interface ref = "c:Consumer" />
20        <interface ref = "r:Retailer" />
21        <interface ref = "w:Warehouse" />
22
23        <connect operations="c:Consumer/SendPO r:Retailer/ReceivePO" />
24        <connect operations="r:Retailer/SendPOToWarehouse w:Warehouse/ReceivePO" />
```

EXAMPLE 8-4. *WSCI global model sample (continued)*

```
25        <connect operations="r:Retailer/SendPOResponse
26                             c:Consumer/ReceivePOResponse"/>
27        <connect operations="r:Retailer/SendPOError c:Consumer/ReceivePOError" />
28        <connect operations="w:Warehouse/SendShipment c:Consumer/ReceiveShipment" />
29    </model>
30 </wsdl:definitions>
```

Figure 8-9 captures the global view visually. A connection is an arrow linking two operations residing in separate port types. For example, as the code states in line 23, SendPO in Consumer links to ReceivePO in Retailer. The global view does not specify the direction of the connection (which would be valuable), but that information can be found in the corresponding WSDLs. In this case, as the figure shows, SendPO is out-in and its complement ReceivePO in-out, implying that the consumer calls SendPO by passing its request and waiting for a response; the retailer's ReceivePO is triggered as an event, and the retailer sends back a response.

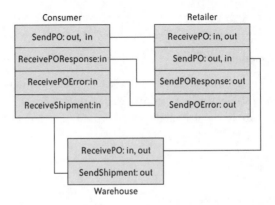

FIGURE 8-9. *WSCI global view for purchasing*

Weaknesses in WSCI

WSCI is unwieldy. Expressing complex multiparticipant choreographies in WSCI requires too many artifacts—typically one interface per participant (though WSCI's interface does support multiple roles), plus a global view. WSCI would be stronger if its global view could be enhanced to capture the behavioral elements of the interfaces; in that case only one artifact would be required to capture everything! WS-CDL, in fact, has succeeded in reconciling these two approaches.

The Future of WSCI

Despite its leadership role in the writing of the WSCI specification, BEA Systems has all but abandoned WSCI and shifted its support to BPEL, which it cowrote with IBM and Microsoft. Oracle and WSCI coauthor Sun Microsystems have supported WSCI for some time, but Oracle has been building BPEL tools recently and is the main force behind the latest choreography specification, WS-CDL.

All signs point to the demise of WSCI. Positioned as a business process language, WSCI is overwhelmed by BPEL. In the choreography layer of the emerging web services stack, WSCI is surpassed by WS-CDL.

On the other hand, to actually omit WSCI from a current discussion of choreography is premature. WSCI is still a recognizable name in the BPM community, and to not see it discussed would confuse many readers. To understand choreography, it helps to observe the contrast of WSCI to WS-CDL and to know that WSCI's effect is waning.

WSCL

WSCL, the least well-known of the choreography approaches, is easy to miss in the hunt for BPM standards. Its 24-page specification, submitted by Hewlett Packard to the W3C in the spring of 2002* (ancient history, in BPM timelines), has never caught on with vendors and has not permeated the W3C's current choreography efforts. It's too bad, because WSCL's simple, elegant approach to choreography, using the idea of the state machine, has considerable merit.

WSCL is an XML language whose main construct is a conversation, which represents a participant's web-service-based dialog with the other participants in the attainment of a business goal. The steps of the conversation are called interactions, in which the participant either calls or is called by other participants. WSCL supports four types of interactions, which are summarized in Table 8-2.

TABLE 8-2. *WSCL interactions*

WSCL type	WSDL type	Content	Description
Receive	One-way	Input message	Participant reacts to an inbound request message.
Send	Notification	Output message	Participant sends a message outbound.
Receive-send	Request-response	Input message, output message, multiple output fault messages	Participant reacts to an inbound request message and sends back a response message.
Send-receive	Solicit-response	Output message, input message, multiple input fault messages	Participant sends a message outbound and waits for the response to come back.

The link from one interaction (the source) to another (the destination) is called a transition. In the case where a source interaction has more than one outcome (e.g., success or one of several types of faults), the transition must specify which outcome—the source interaction condition—to follow to traverse to the destination.

Two special interactions, called Start and End, determine the beginning and end, respectively, of the conversation.

---

* W3C, "Web Services Conversation Language (WSCL) 1.0," *http://www.w3.org/TR/2002/NOTE-wscl10-20020314/*, March 2002.

Figure 8-10 shows the UML activity diagram representation of a WSCL conversation, from the retailer's view, of the purchasing scenario considered earlier. In the diagram, interactions are drawn as activities (rounded boxes)—except the start and end interactions, drawn as solid ball and solid ball with outer circle, respectively—and transitions as arrows. Each interaction has a name and a stereotype. The POToWarehouse interaction has two possible outcomes (POWarehouseACK and POWarehouseNAK), which transition to two separate destinations (POResponseToConsumer and POErrorToConsumer, respectively), shown in the diagram as an XOR split using the diamond symbol.

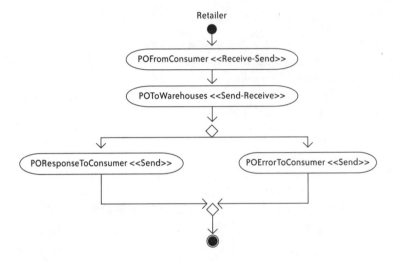

FIGURE 8-10. *WSCL purchasing example*

In the XML code in Example 8-5, the interactions are defined in lines 5–29, the transitions in lines 33–58. The first major step occurs when the retailer receives a purchase order request from the consumer in the interaction with ID POFromConsumer in lines 6–11. The retailer immediately sends back an acknowledgement (the outbound message in line 9), and the transition in lines 37–40 moves the conversation to the interaction POToWarehouse, defined in lines 12–19. In that interaction, the retailer sends the purchase order request to the warehouse (the outbound XML in line 13), and gets back either an acknowledgement (line 15) or a negative acknowledgement (line 17). The transition for the acknowledgement in lines 41–45 links to the interaction POResponseToConsumer, which, according to the definition in lines 20–23, sends a response message to the consumer. The transition for the negative acknowledgement (lines 46–50) moves control to the interaction POErrorToConsumer (lines 24–27), which sends an error to the consumer.

EXAMPLE 8-5. *WSCL sample*

```
1  <?xml version="1.0" encoding="UTF-8"?>
2  <Conversation name="POConversation"
3          xmlns="http://www.w3.org/2002/02/wscl10"
4          initialInteraction="Start"  finalInteraction="End"  >
```

EXAMPLE 8-5. *WSCL sample (continued)*

```
5    <ConversationInteractions>
6      <Interaction interactionType="ReceiveSend" id="POFromConsumer">
7        <InboundXMLDocument hrefSchema="http://mike.com/PurchaseOrderReq.xsd"
8                id="POReq"/>
9        <OutboundXMLDocument hrefSchema="http://mike.com/PurchaseOrderAck.xsd"
10               id="POAck"/>
11     </Interaction>
12     <Interaction interactionType="SendReceive" id="POToWarehouse">
13       <OutboundXMLDocument hrefSchema="http://mike.com/PurchaseOrderReq.xsd "
14               id="POWarehouseReq"/>
15       <InboundXMLDocument hrefSchema="http://mike.com/PurchaseOrderAck.xsd"
16               id="POWarehouseACK"/>
17       <InboundXMLDocument hrefSchema="http://mike.com/PurchaseOrderNak.xsd"
18               id="POWarehouseNAK" />
19     </Interaction>
20     <Interaction interactionType="Send" id="POResponseToConsumer" >
21       <OutboundXMLDocument hrefSchema="http://mike.com/PurchaseOrderRsp.xsd"
22               id="POResponse"/>
23     </Interaction>
24     <Interaction interactionType="Send" id="POErrorToConsumer" >
25       <OutboundXMLDocument hrefSchema="http://mike.com/PurchaseOrderError.xsd"
26               id="POError"/>
27     </Interaction>
28     <Interaction interactionType="Empty" id="Start" />
29     <Interaction interactionType="Empty" id="End" />
30   </ConversationInteractions>
31
32   <ConversationTransitions>
33     <Transition>
34       <SourceInteraction href="Start"/>
35       <DestinationInteraction href="POFromConsumer"/>
36     </Transition>
37     <Transition>
38       <SourceInteraction href="POFromConsumer"/>
39       <DestinationInteraction href="POToWarehouse"/>
40     </Transition>
41     <Transition>
42       <SourceInteraction href="POToWarehouse"/>
43       <DestinationInteraction href="POResponseToConsumer"/>
44       <SourceInteractionCondition href="POWarehouseACK "/>
45     </Transition>
46     <Transition>
47       <SourceInteraction href="POToWarehouse"/>
48       <DestinationInteraction href="POErrorToConsumer"/>
49       <SourceInteractionCondition href="POWarehouseNAK "/>
50     </Transition>
51     <Transition>
52       <SourceInteraction href="POResponseToConsumer"/>
53       <DestinationInteraction href="End"/>
54     </Transition>
55     <Transition>
```

EXAMPLE 8-5. *WSCL sample (continued)*

```
56          <SourceInteraction href="POErrorToConsumer"/>
57          <DestinationInteraction href="End"/>
58      </Transition>
59  </ConversationTransitions>
60  </Conversation>
```

Writing a WSCL Application

A WSCL application is written as an XML file that references the WSCL schema, as well as application message schemas representing the interaction input and output messages. Imagining a graphical WSCL editor is easy:

1. Drag start and end interactions onto the canvas.

2. Import a number of WSDL definitions into the editor. Drag their operations on the canvas as interactions.

3. Draw transitions by connecting arrows between interactions.

4. Select the menu option Save as XML.

Weaknesses in WSCL

Here are the three main deficiencies of WSCL:

- A conversation is the subjective view of a single participant, not a global view encompassing all participants. All WSCL interactions in a given conversation are for one role (e.g., retailer), although the identity of that role is not specified in the XML code. A send interaction, for example, represents a participant of that role sending a message (e.g., PO response) to another participant (e.g., consumer), whose role is not explicitly specified either. WS-CDL interactions, by contrast, are always tied to a specific *relationship* of roles, and a choreography can support multiple relationships. One implication of WSCL's subjectivity is that important interactions that do not directly involve the conversation's role (e.g., warehouse sends shipping notice to the consumer) are not captured at all in the conversation code. WS-CDL avoids this problem because of its ability to describe multiple roles and relationships.

> ### NOTE
> WSCL is *not* an orchestration language. Although a conversation captures the view of a single participant, it is the *publicly observable* view (i.e., just the interactions, not any other internal logic), and hence is essentially a choreography.

- WSCL's state machine is too simplistic, lacking (for example) adequate exception handling and hierarchical state.

- The relationship to WSDL is too weak. Why not reference port type and operation, rather than individual schema links, in the declaration of an interaction?

The Future of WSCL

Do not expect to see any WSCL implementations in the coming years. WSCL is far too obscure; its elegant approach cannot help it, and its weaknesses cannot hurt it. Nonetheless, those two factors make WSCL a prime case study for choreography; specifically, the importance of a global view.

Summary

The major points of this chapter are:

- Choreography is the attempt to build stateful, conversational, long-running, multiparticipant processes out of basic stateless, atomic web services operations.

- Orchestration is the coordination of web services within a single process. Choreography is coordination at the global level. Orchestration is subjective; choreography is subjective.

- The standards body behind the choreography effort is the W3C's Choreography Working Group. The W3C's other work on web services includes WSDL and SOAP, as well as the WS-* stack. WS-Choreography is one of its more recent contributions, and WS-CDL is its current— albeit unfinished—standard. Previous approaches, published on the W3C site but of diminishing importance, are WSCI and WSCL.

- WS-CDL is the officially endorsed W3C choreography language. A taut declarative language based on XML, WS-CDL presents a global view of a multiparty process and is especially suitable for B2B collaborations. The main concepts of WS-CDL are choreography, interaction, and channel. WS-CDL allows participants to pass around channels (web service-based communication links) in the spirit of the pi-calculus. A powerful feature of WS-CDL is that of guarded interactions, which initiate only if preconditions are met and can be configured to wait for all required data to become available before evaluating the precondition.

- WS-CDL is in its infancy. The specification is incomplete and is devoid of examples. WS-CDL's future is hard to predict, but it will likely face competition from BPEL. WS-CDL lacks strong industry backing. Oracle is the principal author, but Microsoft and IBM are in the BPEL camp.

- WSCI is an XML language that extends WSDL to model the orchestration of each participant in a process as well as the global model of interaction The former model, called interface, resembles BPML and supports the same set of P4 process patterns. The latter, the global model, is a declarative enumeration of links connecting interface actions.

- WSCI, though not exactly a BPM process language like BPEL, is often positioned against it. In the face of BPEL's enormous popularity and its powerful backing by IBM, Microsoft, and BEA, WSCI, supported by Sun and Oracle but not by its principal author BEA, has effectively died.

- WSCL, submitted by HP to the W3C in 2002, is the most obscure of the choreography languages. Its lack of popularity is regrettable, for its state-machine approach is compelling.

- A WSCL conversation, which represents one participant's view of a choreography, is a state machine consisting of interactions and transitions. An interaction, which can be conceived as a state, represents a web service operation. Special dummy start and end interactions, with no web services meaning, also exist to control the start and end of the conversation. The direction of a WSCL interaction, following the WSDL model, can be one-way receive or send or bidirectional send-receive or receive-send. A transition connects one interaction to another. Because a bidirectional interaction can have multiple outcomes (one success and multiple faults), a transition that connects such an interaction to another must identify which outcome to consider.

- WSCL's main weaknesses are its omission of a global model and the simplicity of its state model (e.g., no exception handling, no state hierarchy, and the weakness of the WSDL relationship).

References

1. W3C, "Web Services Choreography Requirements," *http://www.w3c.org/TR/2004/WD-ws-chor-reqs-20040311/*, March 2004.

2. W3C, "Web Services Choreography Model Overview," *http://www.w3c.org/TR/2004/WD-ws-chor-model-20040324/*, March 2004.

3. W. van der Aalst, M. Dumas, A. H. M. ter Hofstede, P. Wohed, "Pattern-Based Analysis of BPML (and WSCI)," FIT Technical Report, FIT-TR-2002-05.

4. T. Olavsrud, "Will BPEL and WSCI Come Together?" in *InternetNews*, May 2003, *http://www.internetnews.com/dev-news/print.php/2211121*.

5. C. McDonald. "Orchestration, Choreography, and Collaboration," *http://java.sun.com/developer/onlineTraining/webcasts/pdf/35plus/cmcdonald2.pdf*.

6. *http://www.ebpml.org/ws_-_cdl.htm*.

CHAPTER NINE

Other BPM Models

THE DOMINANT **BPM** STANDARDS—**BPMI'S BPML** AND **BPMN** SPECS, the works of the WfMC, W3C's choreography, and the mighty BPEL—were examined in detail in previous chapters. This chapter presents four additional models that are important but peripheral. Each elucidates an important idea that merits attention, but none is a major contemporary core BPM approach. Consequently, they require a briefer treatment than that of the major standards. The four models are:

Object Management Group process definition and process runtime interface models
The OMG is soliciting proposals for abstract models for business process definitions and process runtime interfaces. The nature of these models and their significance is examined later in this chapter.

Microsoft XLANG
Microsoft, as one of the key BPEL authors, made sure the best ideas of its earlier XLANG language were woven into the fabric of BPEL. BPEL fans should know a little about the nature of XLANG and its influence on BPEL.

IBM Web Services Flow Language
WSFL is another XML process language that, like XLANG, is dead but, thanks to IBM's BPEL authors, lives on in BPEL. WSFL's directed graph approach is examined as an influencer of BPEL.

Chapter 8 introduced the concepts of orchestration and choreography. BPSS is the leading collaboration standard, and is examined from the collaborative perspective.

OMG: Model-Driven BPM

Established in 1989, the Object Management Group (OMG, *http://www.omg.org*), is a consortium of more than 500 companies, and is best known for its standards-based work on the Common Object Request Broker Architecture (CORBA), UML, and MDA. Though CORBA's popularity has been declining ever since its boom in the mid-1990s, UML continues to thrive after more than a decade, and the newborn MDA is enjoying burgeoning press coverage and vendor interest.

The OMG recently has taken an interest in BPM, publishing Requests for Proposals (RFPs) for the specification of abstract models for business process diagrams and business process runtime interfaces.* The RFP process—to be managed by the OMG's Business Enterprise Integration Domain Task Force (BEIDTF), headed by EDS and Hendryx Associates—is in its early stages, but its intriguing feature is not the competition of bids, but the type of solution being sought. The OMG wants an MDA for BPM—a mutually beneficial arrangement, because not only is BPM a compelling example of an MDA, MDA promises to be a boon to BPM.

Members of the OMG include AT&T, BEA, Borland, Boeing, CA, Citigroup, Compaq, Compuware, Ericsson, Ford, Fujitsu, Glaxo Smith Kline, HP, Hitachi, Hyperion, IBM, IONA, Microsoft, NASA, NEC, Oracle, Pfizer, Rational, SAP, SAS, Siemens, Sprint, Sun, and Unisys.

Model-Driven Architecture

MDA is, in a sense, a means of unifying disparate approaches to a given software problem. Software has seemingly countless types of models: relational data models, object-oriented models, business process models, and others. MDA accepts the diversity but provides a mechanism to map one model to another. The key idea is to base all models on a common foundation. Two approaches are recommended:

Meta-Object Facility

MOF is an abstract modeling language, based on a subset of UML 2.0, for the definition of *metamodels*, or models of models. Any MOF-based metamodel can be mapped to any other MOF-based metamodel. Current metamodels standardized by the OMG include Common Warehouse Metamodel (CWM)—for data warehousing models—and UML itself. CWM can generate more specific data models, such as entity-relationship models for particular domains. Object-oriented designs for particular applications can be built in UML.

---

* OMG Business Enterprise Integration DTF: *http://bei.omg.org/bei_info.htm.*

UML profile

A UML profile is an extension to UML that supports a particular technology. For example, the EAI UML profile defines how to use UML to model application integration architecture. From the EAI profile, you can derive particular platform implementations, such as J2EE or MQ/Series.

Another key feature is the ability to move models between MDA-based tools. XML Metadata Interchange (XMI) enables a MOF-based model to be represented as an XML document, structured according to an XML schema specific to the type of model. In Figure 9-1, for example, an object-relational (OR) mapping tool can be built to accept, from an entity-relationship (ER) tool, relational data models as CWM XMI documents. The OR tool can then generate an object-oriented representation of the data model and output it as a UML XMI document, which can then be fed into an object-oriented (OO) tool.

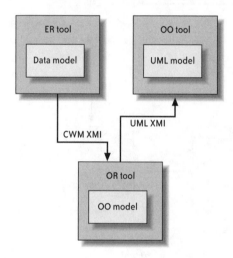

FIGURE 9-1. *XMI for OR mapping*

BPM and MDA

The OMG's primary interest in BPM is in two areas: process definitions and runtime interfaces. The OMG has published RFPs seeking MDA models for the BPDM* and BPRI† standards.

BPDM

The commonality of process definition languages is remarkable. BPEL, BPML, BPMN, XPDL, XLANG, WSFL, and UML activity diagrams are variations on a theme. The RFP for

---

* OMG, *Business Process Definition Metamodel Request for Proposal*, OMG, *http://www.omg.org/cgi-bin/doc?bei/2003-01-06*, January 2003.

† OMG, *"Business Process Runtime Interfaces Platform Independent Model Request for Proposal"* OMG, *http://www.omg.org/docs/bei/02-06-08.pdf*, June 2002.

BPDM seeks the authoritative MOF metamodel, or UML profile, for a process definition that isolates what is common and elemental. The model that is eventually ratified by the OMG will sit alongside UML and CWM in the MOF hierarchy and will be interchangeable with them through XMI. In addition, the model makes it easier to map between existing process languages. In Figure 9-2, a BPEL tool exchanges processes with a BPMN tool as BPDM XMI documents. Each tool can both export and import its processes as BPDM XMI, and can also import UML XMI originating from a UML modeling tool. (See the later sidebar "UML To BPEL: IBM's Emerging Technologies Toolkit" for more on the UML dimension.)

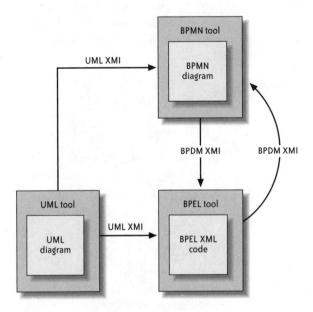

FIGURE 9-2. *Tools exchange process models, thanks to MDA*

The requirements for BPDM are obvious: a notion of process, activity, and choreography; support for basic patterns such as AND, OR, and loops; role assignment and access control; auditing; and event publication and subscription. An initial submission prepared by EDS, Data Access Technologies, Borland, and 88 Solutions* posits a model, shown in Figure 9-3, based on Enterprise Distributed Object Computing (EDOC), an emerging process-oriented application framework. The particulars are too immature to warrant discussion in the book at this time. What is significant is the attempt to devise a unified theory of process definition.

---

* EDS, Data Access Technologies, Borland, 88 Solution, *Initial Submission to Business Process Metamodel RFP*, OMG, bei/2003-08-01, August 2003.

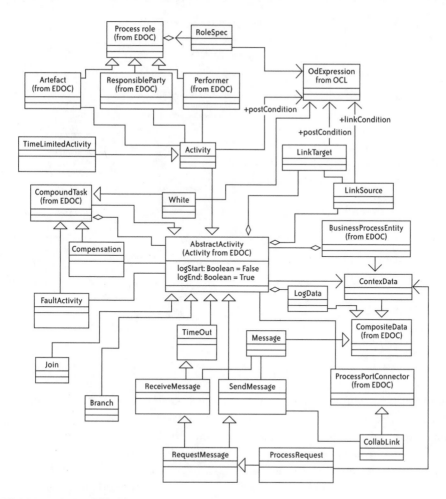

FIGURE 9-3. *BPDM model from EDS response to OMG RFP*

NOTE

The OMG is collaborating with BPMI (the group that owns the BPML and BPMN specifications) on BPDM. The BPMI is building a BPDM metamodel known as Business Process Semantic Model (BPSM). The OMG is also pursuing the BPEL group of OASIS; BPEL support is considered essential for BPDM.

BPRI

BPRI is an interface describing instances of processes and their activities, including current state, current variable values, and history. Like the WfMC's WAPI interface (examined in Chapter 7), BPRI offers administration and monitoring services, as well as human and application participant coordination. The main entities and their relationships are depicted in Figure 9-4.

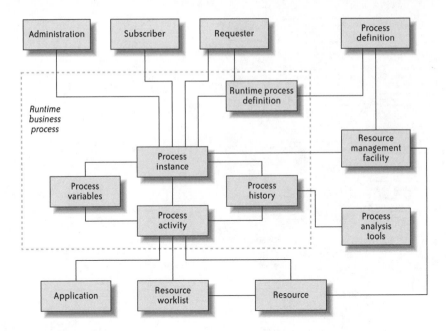

FIGURE 9-4. *OMG BPRI model from OMG BPRI RFP*

At the center of the diagram, surrounded by a dotted box, are the primary runtime elements, including process instance, its activities and variables, and its historical information store, which special process analysis tools tap into for reporting purposes. An instance, which instantiates a process definition, is initiated by a requester, is administered (e.g., get and set state, find active instances) by an administrator, and is monitored (e.g., tracking when an instance terminates) by a subscriber. Activities are generally performed either by human beings (Resource) or systems (Application). Activities assigned to human beings are organized into worklists, and human beings are grouped into work roles through the resource management facility.

The OMG recommends a runtime model similar to Example 9-5. The model should be platform-independent, from which platform-specific models based on CORBA or J2EE, for instance, can be derived. As with BPDM, the possibility of a unified theory for a BPM API is intriguing. Standardization in this area is far less active than with process definition; with the exception of WAPI, most APIs are proprietary vendor interfaces.

UML to BPEL: IBM's emerging technologies toolkit

IBM, an ardent supporter of UML, BPEL, and MDA, has built a tool to generate BPEL code from UML diagrams. The tool, known as the Emerging Technologies Toolkit (ETTK),* is a plug-in to the open-source Java development studio Eclipse. The plug-in

---

* K. Mantell, "From UML to BPEL: Model-Driven Architecture in a Web Services World," IBM, *http://www-128.ibm.com/developerworks/webservices/library/ws-uml2bpel/index.html,* Sept. 2003.

inputs a file in the form of UML XMI and outputs WSDL and BPEL files. The UML model can be created in IBM's Rational Rose or Rational XDE products, each of which supports the design of UML models and their export to XMI.

The ETTK requires that the UML model have the following diagrams:

- A class diagram with the stereotype <<process>>. The class represents the BPEL process; its class-level attributes represent BPEL variables.

- An activity graph, whose activities represent the activities of the BPEL process.

The end-to-end view is shown in Figure 9-5.

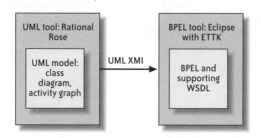

FIGURE 9-5. *IBM ETTK generates BPEL from UML*

Other OMG BPM RFPs

Newer and probably less crucial are the OMG-solicited models described in Table 9-1. These are works in progress.

TABLE 9-1. *OMG business rule RFPs*

Model	Description
Business Rules Management (BRM)	A MOF model capturing the overall management of business rules, including creation, comparison, analysis and reporting.
Business Semantics of Business Rules (BSBR)	A MOF model for documenting the structure and meaning of business rules.
Organization Structure Meta-model (OSM)	A MOF model for an organizational directory schema. Presumably, OSM is important to BPM because the assignment of manual activities in a process requires a notion of "role" that relates to groupings in an organizational directory.
Production Rule Representation (PRR)	A MOF model for the representation of production rules (i.e., rules used by an inference engine).

ebXML BPSS: Collaboration

The concepts of choreography and orchestration, discussed in previous chapters, pertain to the management of inter- and intraprocess flow, respectively. The pervasive business-to-business (B2B) ecommerce concept of collaboration, whose name, like those of choreography and orchestration, conveys a sense of coordinating individual entities, has a subtly different meaning. The leading model for collaboration is found in the OASIS group's specification of the Business Process Specification Schema (BPSS),* an XML language that is part of the larger electronic business XML (ebXML) B2B system.

The key elements of BPSS are the following:

Business transaction
A business transaction is an exchange of data between two partners that is treated as an atomic unit of work; if it fails at any point, both partners agree that exchange is null and void. A business transaction has a requesting and a responding activity and optional signals (acknowledgment messages).

Binary collaboration
A binary collaboration is an exchange between two authorized partners, each of which performs a role (e.g., buyer and seller): one is the initiating role; the other is the responding role. The collaboration consists of a set of activities, each of which can be either a business transaction or another binary collaboration.

Multiparty collaboration
A multiparty collaboration is an exchange between more than two partners, though it is defined in terms of a set of binary collaborations. For example, in the exchange between customer, retailer, and vendor, there are two binary collaborations: one in which the customer is the buyer and the retailer the seller, the other in which the retailer is the buyer and the vendor is the seller.

Choreography
Choreography is the explicit control of flow among activities of a binary collaboration; specifically, control of the start and completion states, forks, synchronization, and transitions.

The structure of a business transaction is depicted in Figure 9-6. One partner sends a request to a second, to which the second partner eventually responds; in between are acknowledgments of receipt and acceptance. In some cases, response or acknowledgement messages are not required. A time limit can be placed on a message (e.g., the response must arrive within five business days from receipt of the request), as well as the legal requirement for nonrepudiation (that is, acknowledgment of receipt).

A binary collaboration, shown in Figure 9-7, is a set of business transactions (e.g., create order and notify shipment) performed by two partner roles (e.g., buyer and seller). The dotted arrows show the direction of message interaction (e.g., buyer initiates a create order; seller initiates a notify shipment).

The choreography of that collaboration is shown in Figure 9-8. The create order business transaction is the first transaction, and it is followed by notify shipment, which is the last transaction.

---

* UN/CEFACT, *ebXML Business Process Specification Schema, Version 1.09,* August 2003, *http://xml. coverpages.org/UN-CEFACT-BPSS-V1pt09-DRAFT.pdf.*

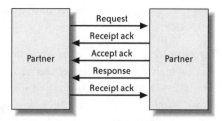

FIGURE 9-6. *A BPSS business transaction*

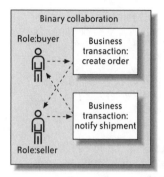

FIGURE 9-7. *A BPSS binary collaboration*

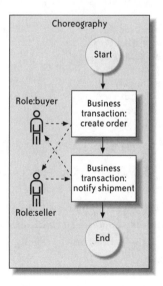

FIGURE 9-8. *A BPSS choreography of a binary collaboration*

The difference between choreography and collaboration is this: collaboration is a set of precise, transactional message exchanges with legal and business trade ramifications, whereas choreography is higher-level control flow over the set of transactions. As for orchestration, it does not naturally fit the BPSS approach because that approach emphasizes the inter-partner view rather than a given partner's internal process. BPSS has more in common with WS-CDL, discussed in Chapter 8, than with current BPM languages such as BPEL and BPML.

Example 9-1 contains an excerpt of BPSS XML that represents the example choreographed collaboration, in which the declaration of the binary collaboration (starting at line 1) includes roles buyer and seller (lines 2–3) and the business transactions Create Order and Notify Shipment (lines 4–12), as well as the start state (line 13) and the two end states (lines 17–20: one for success, one for failure). The Transition element (lines 14–16) connects Create Order to Notify Shipment.

EXAMPLE 9-1. *BPSS collaboration for order*

```
 1  <BinaryCollaboration name="Product Fulfillment" timeToPerform="P5D">
 2      <InitiatingRole name="buyer"/>
 3      <RespondingRole name="seller"/>
 4      <BusinessTransactionActivity name="Create Order"
 5          businessTransaction="Create Order"
 6          fromAuthorizedRole="buyer"
 7          toAuthorizedRole="seller"/>
 8      <BusinessTransactionActivity
 9          name="Notify shipment"
10          businessTransaction="Notify of advance shipment"
11          fromAuthorizedRole="seller"
12          toAuthorizedRole="buyer"/>
13      <Start toBusinessState="Create Order"/>
14      <Transition
15          fromBusinessState="Create Order"
16          toBusinessState="Notify shipment"/>
17      <Success fromBusinessState="Notify shipment"
18          conditionGuard="Success"/>
19      <Failure fromBusinessState="Notify shipment"
20          conditionGuard="BusinessFailure"/>
21  </BinaryCollaboration>
```

Microsoft XLANG: BPEL Forerunner

Microsoft published XLANG* in 2001 as the business process language for its BizTalk ecommerce suite. Compared with the offerings of more recent BPM standards, XLANG is a relatively simple language, but its ideas, along with those of WSFL, form the basis for the design of BPEL. As an author and supporter of BPEL, Microsoft has turned away from XLANG and effectively shelved it. (BPM time moves rapidly!) Nonetheless, understanding XLANG is valuable for two reasons:

- Its influence on BPEL
- Its basis in the pi-calculus

---

* S. Thatte, "XLANG: Web Services for Business Process Design," Microsoft, *http://www.gotdotnet.com/team/xml_wsspecs/xlang-c/default.htm*, 2001.

The pi-calculus connection is examined in Chapter 3. This chapter focuses on the first point.

XLANG is an early XML-based, web services-aware process definition language. An XLANG process is defined in a WSDL as part of the definition of a WSDL service. The XLANG process defines the behavior of the service.

> **NOTE**
> Basic WSDL knowledge is essential to understanding XLANG. In previous chapters we have seen that a WSDL port type is a set of operations with message input and output types. A WSDL port binds a port type to a specific transport endpoint. A service is a set of ports. Calling a web service means connecting to one of its ports and interfacing with one of the port's operations by exchanging messages with it.

In the code sample in Example 9-2, the service AcctService (lines 31–49), which has ports AcctPort (lines 32–34) and AcctCallbackPort (lines 35–37) corresponding to port types AcctPT (lines 8–12) and AcctCallbackPT (lines 12–21) respectively, is augmented with an XLANG behavior (lines 39–48) that consists of three action activities. The first activity (lines 42–43) launches the XLANG process when the operation UpdateAcct is invoked on the AcctPort port of the enclosing service. The second and third activities (line 44–45) invoke the operations ACK and UpdateResponse, respectively, on port AcctCallbackPort. The activities are executed in order. The process is stateful: the first activity, whose activation attribute is set to true, launches the process, and the second and third continue it; because there are no further activities, the process stops after completion of the third activity.

EXAMPLE 9-2. *Update account WSDL and XLANG process*

```
1   <?xml version="1.0"?>
2   <definitions name="UpdateAccount"
3       targetNamespace="http://mike.com/xlang/acct"
4       xmlns:tns=" http://mike.com/xlang/acct"
5       xmlns:xlang="http://schemas.microsoft.com/biztalk/xlang/
6       xmlns="http://schemas.xmlsoap.org/wsdl/">
7
8   <portType name="AcctPT">
9       <operation name="UpdateAcct">
10          <input message="..."/>
11      </operation>
12  </portType>
13
14  <portType name="AcctCallbackPT">
15      <operation name="ACK">
16          <output message="..."/>
17      </operation>
18      <operation name="UpdateResponse">
19          <output message="..."/>
```

EXAMPLE 9-2. *Update account WSDL and XLANG process (continued)*

```
20        </operation>
21     </portType>
22
23     <binding name="AcctBinding" type="tns:AcctPT">
24        <!-- details omitted -->
25     </binding>
26
27     <binding name="AcctCallbackBinding" type="tns:AcctCallbackPT">
28        <!-- details omitted -->
29     </binding>
30
31     <service name="AcctService">
32        <port name="AcctPort" binding="tns:AcctBinding">
33           <soap:address location="http://a.com/ws/acct.jws"/>
34        </port>
35        <port name="AcctCallbackPort" binding="tns:AcctCallbackBinding">
36           <soap:address location="http://x.com/ws/acct.jws"/>
37        </port>
38
39        <xlang:behavior>
40           <xlang:body>
41              <xlang:sequence>
42                 <xlang:action operation="UpdateAcct" port="AcctPort"
43                    activation="true"/>
44                 <xlang:action operation="ACK" port="AcctCallbackPort"/>
45                 <xlang:action operation="UpdateResponse" port="AcctCallbackPort"/>
46              </xlang:sequence>
47           </xlang:body>
48        </xlang:behavior>
49     </service>
50  </definitions>
```

The use of the action activity to invoke or receive a web service operation is reminiscent of BPML, as are XLANG's control flow activities (sequence, switch, all, and while) compensation and exception handling, context scoping, and message correlation. XLANG's influence on BPEL is considerable (as will be discussed further later), but so is its influence on BPML.

XLANG, like WSCI and other choreography languages, also provides for the definition of a global view of service interactions. Referred to as the business process contract the global view is a like a sequence diagram, capturing participants and their exchange of messages. In Example 9-3, the two participants have services AcctService and AcctUserService, representing the provider and caller, respectively, of account update. The contract in lines 16–26 requires that AcctPort in service AcctService interfaces with port AcctRequestPort in service AcctUserService (the connect in lines 19–21) and that AcctCallbackPort in AcctService connects with AcctResponse port in AcctUserService (lines 22–24). The direction of message exchange is not captured in the contract; direction is given in the WSDL definitions imported in lines 11–14.

EXAMPLE 9-3. *Update account XLANG business process contract*

```
1   <?xml version="1.0"?>
2   <definitions name="AcctContract"
3      targetNamespace="http://mike.com/xlang/acct/contract"
4      xmlns:tns=" http://mike.com/xlang/acct/contract"
5      xmlns:xlang="http://schemas.microsoft.com/biztalk/xlang/"
6      xmlns:acct="http://mike.com/xlang/acct"
7      xmlns:user="http://mike.com/xlang/user "
8      xmlns="http://schemas.xmlsoap.org/wsdl/">
9
10     <!-- import the acct and user namespaces -->
11     <import namespace="http://mike.com/xlang/acct"
12        location=http://mike.com/xlang/acct.wsdl/
13     <import namespace="http://mike.com/xlang/user"
14        location="http://mike.com/xlang/user.wsdl"/>
15
16     <xlang:contract>
17        <xlang:services refs="acct:AcctService user:AcctUserService"/>
18        <xlang:portMap>
19           <xlang:connect
20              port="acct:AcctService/AcctPort"
21              port="user:AcctUserService/AcctRequestPort"/>
22           <xlang:connect
23              port="acct:AcctService/AcctCallbackPort "
24              port="user:AcctUserService/AcctResponsePort"/>
25        </xlang:portMap>
26     </xlang:contract>
27  </definitions>
```

IBM WSFL: BPEL Forerunner

IBM published Web Services Flow Language[*] in 2001 with the familiar purpose of standardizing the design of web-service-oriented business processes spanning multiple participants. WSFL has so much in common with BPML, WSCI, XLANG, BPEL, and other XML-based process languages that given also its complete lack of industry support, it is tempting to discount it entirely. Indeed, even IBM has given up on it, but only because IBM decided to join forces with Microsoft and BEA on BPEL. As it turns out, IBM's involvement in the design of BPEL resulted in core WSFL ideas (e.g., flow, dead path elimination) infiltrating BPEL. WSFL's influence on BPEL makes it worthy of investigation.

WSFL supports the definition of two types of process models:

Flow model
    The orchestration of web service operations for a single participant.

---

[*]   F. Leymann, *"Web Services Flow Language (WSFL 1.0)"*, IBM, *http://www-306.ibm.com/software/ solutions/webservices/pdf/WSFL.pdf*, 2001.

Global model

The exchange, or choreography, of messages by web service invocation across a set of participants.

The ubiquitous purchasing example (used in countless BPM discussions) demonstrates a WSFL implementation of both models. Figure 9-9 shows the exchange of messages between three participants: Consumer, Retailer, and Warehouse. Each participant has its own flow model, shown as the arrangement of circles (representing *activities*) and solid arrows (*control links*) running from top to bottom starting immediately below the participant name. The dotted arrows, which connect activities across different flows, are called *plug links*; the global model captures the complete set of these external interactions.

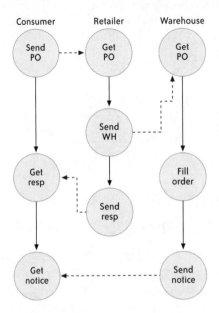

FIGURE 9-9. *WSFL purchasing example*

The consumer flow model begins by sending a purchase order to the retailer, then waiting for a response from the retailer and a shipping notice from the warehouse. The retailer flow model starts by receiving the purchase order from the consumer; the retailer then sends the purchase order to the warehouse, and, subsequently, sends a response to the consumer. The warehouse flow model, triggered by receipt of the purchase order from the retailer, sends a shipping notice back to the consumer once the warehouse has filled the order.

As with every other XML-based process language, WSFL source code is a combination of standard WDSL and process definition XML. In the case of WSFL, the process XML normally resides a separate file that references the WSDL port types and message definitions. Most of the activities in the process definition map to port type operations. Activities that are triggered by the receipt of a message terminate a plug link (e.g., Get PO), whereas those that send a message originate a plug link (e.g., Send Notice). The remaining activities (e.g., Fill Order) have no web services interaction but perform internal logic, such as calling Java code, an operating system program, or a CICS transaction.

The code sample Example 9-4 lists the WSDL for the retailer. Its port type, RetailerPT, is listed in lines 9–21.

EXAMPLE 9-4. *Retailer WSDL*

```
 1  <?xml version = "1.0" ?>
 2  <definitions name = "Retailer Purchasing"
 3      targetNamespace = "http://mike.com/retailer"
 4          xmlns = "http://www.w3.org/2002/07/wsci10"
 5          xmlns:wsdl = "http://schemas.xmlsoap.org/wsdl/"
 6          xmlns:tns = " http://mike.com/retailer"
 7          xmlns:defs = " http://mike.com/purchasing/definitions">
 8
 9      <portType name = "RetailerPT">
10          <operation name = "ReceivePO">
11              <input message = "defs:poRequest"/>
12              <output message = "defs:poACK"/>
13          </operation>
14          <operation name = "SendPOToWarehouse">
15              <output message = "defs:poRequest"/>
16              <input message = "defs:poACK"/>
17          </operation>
18          <operation name = "SendPOResponse">
19              <output message = "defs:poResponse"/>
20          </operation>
21      </portType>
22  </definitions>
```

The retailer flow model is shown in Example 9-5.

EXAMPLE 9-5. *Retailer WSFL flow model*

```
 1  <definitions name="retailer "
 2      targetNamespace="http://mike.com/retailer "
 3      xmlns:r="http://mike.com/retailer"
 4      xmlns:w="http://mike.com/warehouse"
 5      xmlns:c="http://mike.com/consumer"
 6      xmlns:defs = " http://mike.com/purchasing/definitions">
 7      xmlns="">
 8
 9  <!--  A service provider flow for each participant: retailer, wh, consumer -->
10      <serviceProviderType name="warehouseFlow">
11          <portType name="w:WarehousePT"/>
12      </serviceProviderType>
13      <serviceProviderType name="retailerFlow">
14          <portType name="r:RetailerPT"/>
15      </serviceProviderType>
16      <serviceProviderType name="consumerFlow">
17          <portType name="c:ConsumerPT"/>
18      </serviceProviderType>
19
20      <!-- Flow model for retailer to handle PO -->
21      <flowModel name="processPO" serviceProviderType="retailerFlow">
```

EXAMPLE 9-5. *Retailer WSFL flow model (continued)*

```
22          <flowSource name="retailerFlowSource">
23              <output name="processInstanceData" message="defs:poRequest"/>
24          </flowSource>
25
26          <!-- warehouse and consumer will be the other service providers -->
27          <serviceProvider name="warehouse" type="warehouseFlow"/>
28          <serviceProvider name="consumer" type="consumerFlow"/>
29
30          <export lifecycleAction="spawn">
31              <target portType="r:RetailerPT" operation="receivePO">
32                  <map . . . . . /> <!-- data mapping skipped -->
33              </target>
34          </export>
35
36          <activity name="sendPOToWarehouse">
37              <input name="poRequest" message="defs:poRequest"/>
38              <output name="poResponse" message="defs:poResponse"/>
39              <performedBy serviceProvider="warehouse"/>
40              <implement>
41                  <export portType="r:RetailerPT"
42                     operation="sendPOToWarehouse">
43                      <map . . . . . /> <!-- data mapping skipped -->
44                  </export>
45              </implement>
46          </activity>
47
48          <activity name="sendResponse">
49              <input name="poResponse" message="defs:poResponse"/>
50              <performedBy serviceProvider="consumer"/>
51              <implement>
52                  <export portType="r:RetailerPT" operation="sendPOResponse">
53                      <map . . . . . /> <!-- data mapping skipped -->
54                  </export>
55              </implement>
56          </activity>
57
58          <dataLink name="initialDataLink" source="retailerFlowSource"
59              target="sendPOToWarehouse"/>
60          <!-- other data links not shown -->
61
62          <controlLink name="sendWH-sendResp" source="sendPOToWarehouse"
63              target="sendPOResponse"/>
64      </flowModel>
65  </definitions>
```

Lines 10–18 define service provider types for the three participants; the names and WSDL port types are stipulated for each. The retailer's flow model begins on line 21; the model, named processPO, is an orchestration of the retailerFlow service provider type. Lines 22–27 declare that the retailer flow will reference—that is, will interact with—the other two service providers.

Determining how this process starts requires some digging. First, the flowSource element, defined in lines 22–24, specifies the input source of the process; the flow source is named retailerFlowSource and accepts as its input a defs:poRequest WSDL message. Next, line 58 specifies a data link that connects the flow source to the activity sendPOToWarehouse. Finally, according to the export in lines 30–34, this process is spawned when the operation receivePO on port type r:RetailerPT is called. Bringing it all together, when that WSDL operation is called, this process commences and control is passed to the sendPOToWarehouse activity.

Each activity has a name, an input and an output, a stipulation of which of the declared service provider performs the activity, and a statement of the implementation of the activity: web-service based (export) or internal. Lines 36–56 list the activities. The list matches the list of nodes in the retailer flow depicted in Figure 9-9, with one exception: ReceivePO is missing from the XML sample because it represents the initialization step of the spawn; it is not strictly an activity.

The flow of control from one activity to another is dictated by control links. This flow has only one control link, listed in lines 62–63, which connects sendPOToWarehouse to sendPOResponse—the last step in the process. A WSFL flow, like XPDL described in Chapter 7, is modeled as a directed graph whose nodes are activities and arcs are control links are arcs. Each control link connects a source activity to a target activity.

The three web service-based activities in the retailer flow represent interactions with external participants. The specific web service is given by the port type and operation; for example, sendPOToWarehouse, in lines 36–46, references port type r:Retailer and operation sendPOToWarehouse. You may not see that the direction of interaction for a given action (i.e., whether it is a send or a receive) is immediately obvious. You may also need to look at the WSDL: the activity is a send if the corresponding WSDL operation begins with an output message and a receive if the operation begins with an input. Table 9-2 describes the details for the three web-service-based agent activities.

TABLE 9-2. *Direction of interaction for retailer activities*

Activity	Operation	Send/receive	Service provider
Receive PO (the initiating activity)	receivePO	Receive (and send back a result synchronously)	Consumer
Send PO to Warehouse	sendPOToWarehouse	Send (with a result returned synchronously)	Warehouse
Send response to Consumer	sendPOResponse	Send	Consumer

NOTE

The retailer flow is sequential, but WSFL's flow model also supports conditional transitions, splits and joins, loops, and dead path elimination. The semantics are similar to that of the BPEL flow activity. The influence on BPEL is noted in the next section.

The global model captures the overall choreography across service providers. A web service interaction between one provider and another is represented as a plug link. It maps the sender's port type and operation to those of the receiver. An excerpt from this example's global model is shown in Example 9-6; some code is removed for sake of brevity.

EXAMPLE 9-6. *Purchasing WSFL global model*

```
1   <definitions name="Purchasing"
2       targetNamespace="http://mike.com/purchasing "
3       xmlns:tio="http://mike.com/purchasing"
4       xmlns="">
5
6       <globalModel . . .>
7       . . .
8       <!-- the four plug links from the diagram -->
9       <plugLink>
10         <source serviceProvider="consumer" portType="c:ConsumerPT"
11             operation="sendPO"/>
12         <target serviceProvider="retailer" portType="r:RetailerPT"
13             operation="receivePO"/>
14      </plugLink>
15      <plugLink>
16         <source serviceProvider="retailer" portType="r:RetailerPT"
17             operation="sendPOToWarehouse"/>
18         <target serviceProvider="warehouse" portType="w:WarehousePT"
19             operation="receivePO"/>
20      </plugLink>
21      <plugLink>
22         <source serviceProvider="retailer" portType="r:RetailerPT"
23             operation="sendPOResponse"/>
24         <target serviceProvider="consumer" portType="r:ConsumerPT"
25             operation="receivePOResponse"/>
26      </plugLink>
27      <plugLink>
28         <source serviceProvider="warehouse" portType="r:WarehousePT"
29             operation="sendShipNotification"/>
30         <target serviceProvider="consumer" portType="r:ConsumerPT"
31             operation="receiveShipNotification"/>
32      </plugLink>
33      . . .
34    </globalModel>
35 </definitions>
```

The four plug links are listed in lines 9–32. In the first (lines 9–14), the consumer—via the sendPO operation of the ConsumerPT port type—sends a purchase order to the retailer (receivePO operation in RetailerPT). In the second (lines 15–20), the retailer (sendPO in RetailerPT) sends the purchase order to the warehouse (receivePO in WarehousePT). The third and fourth cases follow the same pattern: the source web service operation sends to that of the target. As with the flow model, the global model uses a directed graph representation; the nodes of the graph are web service operations, the arcs invocations between them.

BPEL, XLANG, and WSFL

The design of BPEL borrows elements from both XLANG and WSFL. Table 9-3 lists the major BPEL features and their corresponding features in XLANG and WSFL.

TABLE 9-3. *XLANG and WSFL influences on BPEL*

BPEL feature	XLANG	WSFL
Partner, partner links	Business party contracts	Global model, service providers, plug links
Process variables	No, implicit only	No, implicit only
Correlation	Correlation sets, correlation attributes of `operation` actions	
Exception handling	Per-context exception handler	Weak, use control links to custom exception activities
Compensation	Per-context compensation handler	
Scope	`context` element	
Invoke	`operation` action	Activity
Receive	`operation` action	Activity
Reply	`operation` action	Activity
Wait	`delay` action	
No op	`empty` action	Internal activity
Sequence	`sequence` action	Yes, as graph
Switch	`switch` action	Yes, as graph
While	`while` action	Yes, as graph, supports loops
Pick	`pick` action	
Flow	`All` action provides parallelism but not with `flow` links	Flow model, control links
Assign		
Global event handler		
Dead path elimination		Inherent support, crucially important concept
Subprocess		
Process initiation	An `operation` action with `activation` set to `true`	Lifecycle service has `spawn` operation

Two conclusions can be drawn from this survey:

- XLANG and WSFL are very different approaches, and, depending on your point of view, coexist either peacefully or tenuously in BPEL. XLANG is programmatic, where programming language-like elements such as while, sequence, and switch structure the control flow. WSFL prefers a directed graph approach, which control flow is the traversal of activities over links. The majority of BPEL resembles XLANG, but its flow activity, and its related concept of dead path elimination, is obviously derived from WSFL.

- BPEL is much more advanced than either of its ancestors, with support for process variables and global event handlers. In addition, in BPEL the direction of web service interaction (receive, invoke, and reply activities) is clearer than in WSFL and XLANG, which require you to refer back to the WSDL for the ordering of input and output message types on an operation.

Summary

The main points of this chapter include the following:

- This chapter covers four important but peripheral BPM approaches: the OMG BPM metamodels, XLANG and WSFL, and BPSS.

- The OMG, best known for its CORBA standards, is an emerging BPM player, having recently published RFPs for the specification of abstract BPM models of process definition (BPDM) and process runtime interface (BPRI). More important than the RFP process and its current bids is the OMG's idea that BPM can have a model-driven architecture. In a nutshell, MDA, when applied to BPM, helps bridge the gap between disparate process languages by specifying a common foundation—either a MOF metamodel or a UML profile—allowing BPDM-aware BPM tools to exchange particular process definitions more easily. For example, a BPMN tool can export a diagram as a BPMN XMI document, which can then be imported into a BPEL tool and transformed into a BPEL process definition.

- Microsoft's XLANG is an XML process definition language that is interesting for two reasons: its use of the pi-calculus (examined in Chapter 3) and its influence on BPEL. BPEL began as a synthesis of XLANG and IBM's WSFL. The XLANG contribution is its programmatic style of web services orchestration—using familiar control structures such as all, while, and sequence, surrounding action steps that model web service interactions—and its global model, which resembles BPEL's partner link interface. XLANG is dead; Microsoft, as one of the principal BPEL authors, is now building to BPEL rather than to XLANG.

- IBM's WSFL, an XML process definition language that uses directed graphs rather than programmatic constructs to describe a process, is the other main influence on BPEL. The influence of the directed graph approach, as well as the concept of dead path elimination, is clearly seen in BPEL's flow construct. WSFL has both process-level orchestration, in which control links connect web services, as well as global orchestration, and plug links connect activities across the processes of multiple participants. WSFL is also interesting for its application of the Petri net, which is explored in Chapter 3.

- The precise communication of business partners in B2B ecommerce requires a stronger notion than choreography. In the ebXML BPSS, a collaboration is a set of precise, transactional message exchanges with legal and business trade ramifications. Each exchange is referred to as a business transaction, which begins when one party (e.g., a buyer) sends a request to another (e.g., a seller); the second party then acknowledges receipt and acceptance of the request and sends a response, for which the first party then acknowledges receipt. Choreography helps structure the flow of control from one transaction to another. For example, a buyer-seller relationship can be specified to be the sequence of `Create Order` and `Notify Shipment` transactions.

References

1. D. S. Frankel, "BPM and MDA: The Rise of Model-Driven Enterprise Systems," *BPTrends,* June 2003.

2. P. Harmon, "The OMG's Model Driven Architecture and BPM," *BPTrends,* May 2004.

3. P. Harmon, "The OMG Continues Its Work on Business Process Standards," *BPTrends Advisor,* September 2004.

PART THREE EXAMPLES

Two substantial examples of business processes in action: human workflow in the processing of an insurance claim, and a BPM-centric enterprise message broker. The reader can build and test these examples using Oracle's BPEL Process Manager and other free tools.

CHAPTER TEN

Example: Human Workflow in Insurance Claims Processing

IN THIS CHAPTER (AND THE NEXT), WE WILL BUILD FEATURE-RICH, working examples that demonstrate some of the key concepts of process modeling. This chapter shows the design of a BPEL insurance claims process that is driven by human workflow, or by human participants performing manual activities. (See the section "Human Interaction" in Chapter 2 for a discussion of human workflow architecture.)

The process is implemented in Oracle BPEL Process Manager, a BPEL 1.1–compliant runtime engine that includes a design editor, an administrative console, and a human task manager subsystem; this chapter provides everything you need to know to download, install, and configure a working environment for the example.*

The UML activity diagram in Figure 10-1 provides a high-level overview of the behavior of the insurance process.

When the process begins, the Evaluate activity is started, which represents manual work in which an insurance agent examines the details of the claim and decides whether to accept or reject it outright, or to pass it to an adjuster for further analysis, as part of the

---

* Oracle, "BPEL Quick Start Guide," *http://www.oracle.com/technology/products/ias/bpel/pdf/orabpel-QuickStart.pdf.*

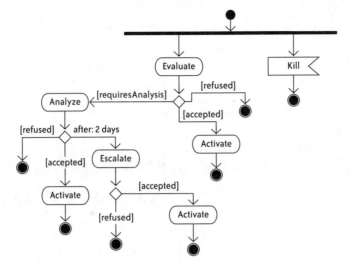

FIGURE 10-1. *UML activity diagram of insurance process*

Analyze activity. That activity can also result in an acceptance or refusal, and it can also time out if not completed in two days. The time-out triggers a transition to the Escalate activity, a manual task performed by a manager, who decides once and for all whether to accept or reject the claim. The processing of rejection and acceptance is the same throughout; rejection stops the process, and acceptance triggers the Activate activity, where the claim is finalized in the insurance company's systems and payment is sent to the subscriber. The process can be cancelled at any point during its execution; in parallel with its mainline processing, the process listens for a kill signal and terminates upon receipt.

Figure 10-2 illustrates a BPEL structure for this example.

The process begins with a receive activity that inputs the initial claim. The rest of the main logic is modeled as a flow activity with conditional links. The first activity is Eval sequence, which manages the execution of the Evaluate manual task asynchronously as an invoke-receive sequence; that is, it calls a service to start the task and waits for its completion. From the Eval sequence originate three conditional links: rejected, accepted, or requiresAnalysis, transitioning to Rejection logic, Activation logic, or Analyze sequence, respectively. Like Eval sequence, Analyze sequence starts its task with an invoke, but the remainder of its processing is more complex: it uses a pick to wait either for completion of the task (onMessage) or timeout (onAlarm). Completion means rejection or acceptance, leading, as before, into Rejection logic or Activation logic, respectively. A timeout links to the Escalate sequence, whose invoke-receive structure is isomorphic to that of Eval sequence. Escalate sequence is the penultimate step, preceding either Rejection logic or Activation logic depending on its decision of rejection or acceptance. In the background, an onMessage listener in a process-scoped EventHandler listens for a kill message and terminates the process on receipt.

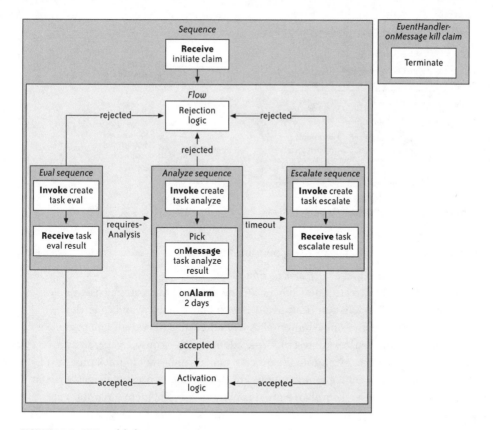

FIGURE 10-2. *BPEL model of insurance process*

Oracle BPEL Process Manager

In 2004, Oracle joined the BPEL fray by acquiring Process Manager from Collaxa. The main pieces of Process Manager are a graphical design tool that plugs into the popular Open Source Java IDEs Eclipse (and also to Oracle's own JDeveloper), as well as an execution engine that runs on most major J2EE application servers, including JBoss, BEA's Weblogic, IBM's Websphere, and Oracle's own Oracle Application Server (Oracle AS); a standalone lightweight version is also available. The solution also includes a web-based administration console (and a Java management API for custom management development) and a database to which process state is persisted (or *dehydrated*). Figure 10-3 illustrates the Process Manager stack.

Process Manager is a compelling choice for developing the example:

It is free, easy to download, and easy to assemble
> You can download a free evaluation copy of BPEL Process Manager from Oracle's site to get a feel for the product. In this chapter's example, we will use the standalone server, eliminating the need to set up a full-fledged application server. The only missing pieces are a recent Java Development Kit and Eclipse, both free and easy to download.

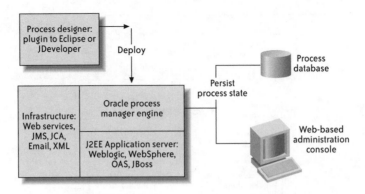

FIGURE 10-3. *Oracle BPEL Process Manager architecture*

It is BPEL-compliant

BPEL Process Manager appears to support most of BPEL 1.1.

It facilitates rapid development, testing, and administration

The time required to create a new process (a one-step wizard creates a basic application), develop its first iteration (intuitive IDE with both graphical and code view), deploy it to the server (a single button-click from the IDE suffices, and the compile is very fast), and run a successful test of it (the administrative console generates an HTML form to inject an event into the process, and an audit trail to track progress) is admirably small, and subsequent iterations are equally fast. Process Manager is a complete solution, and it works well as a rapid application development environment.

It uses a Task Manager Service

Oracle includes a reasonably functional human worklist subsystem, shown in Figure 10-4, whose design is similar to the ideal worklist component described in Chapter 2. In Oracle's usage, a BPEL process assigns a manual task by asynchronously calling the Oracle Task Manager service. A custom worklist application discovers the task by calling the Oracle Java Worklist API. The same API allows the worklist application to complete the task, and the service subsequently calls back the process with the result.*

In the OAS 10*g*R2 release of BPEL Process Manager, Oracle introduced several enhancements to its human workflow capabilities:

- Out-of-the-box support for common human workflow patterns, such as simple approval, sequential and parallel approval, ad hoc processing, and automatic escalation

- Task assignment by role, user, or group; role-based task access control; integration with LDAP directory servers

- Task auditing, expiration, and delegation

---

* Oracle, "BPEL Tutorial: Tutorial 6: Working with the Task Manager Service," *http://www.oracle.com/technology/products/ias/bpel/pdf/orabpel-Tutorial6-TaskManagerServiceTutorial.pdf.*

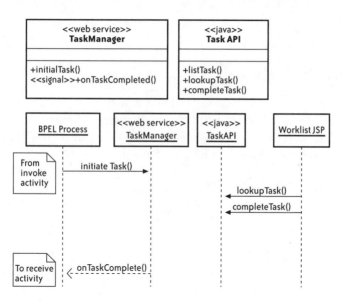

FIGURE 10-4. *Oracle task manager*

- A customizable worklist web application that provides users with the ability to see tasks and action them

- A notification service that delivers task information to users by email, phone, fax, and SMS. Users can perform actions on tasks by email

Setting Up the Environment

To run the example, you need a machine with 1 GB of free disk space and 512-MB RAM, running either Windows XP or Windows 2000 operating systems; no other operating systems are supported. In addition, you need to install the following software and components on your machine.* Installation is straightforward if done in the order listed:

1. Internet Explorer (IE) 6. No other browsers are certified.

2. Sun JDK 1.4.2.05, which is available from *http://java.sun.com/j2se/1.4.2/download.html*.

3. Eclipse 3.0, which is available from *http://www.eclipse.org/downloads/index.php*. Make sure the JDK's bin directory is on the path when starting Eclipse.

4. Oracle BPEL Process Manager 2.1.1 Standalone Edition, which is available from *http://download.oracle.com/otn/nt/bpel/orabpel_2.1.1_win32.exe*.

5. Oracle BPEL Process Designer 0.9.10 for Eclipse, which is available from *http://download.oracle.com/otn/nt/bpel/bpelz_0.9.10_win32.exe*. The installer registers an Eclipse plug-in on your behalf.

---

*   Some of these sites require registration before you can download the software.

For official requirements and setup instructions, refer to Oracle's documentation at *http:// otn.oracle.com/bpel*.

Developing the Example

Because the insurance process is not trivial and uses new and possibly unfamiliar tools, its implementation (the topic of this section) is divided into several iterations. The discussion covers not only the proper BPEL implementation of the insurance process but also how to use Process Manager to build it. At a high level, the steps are:

1. Create the project and define its WSDL.

2. Create the variables, partner links, correlation, and receive node.

3. Add flow and a manual task.

4. Complete the additional coding.

These steps all assume the default configuration for all required software.

Create the Project and Define its WSDL

The first step is to create a new project in BPEL designer and to establish its WSDL interface. The steps in this process are:

1. Start the BPEL server and the BPEL designer; click on the links Start BPEL PM Server and BPEL PM Designer in the folder *Oracle BPEL Process Manager* in the Windows Start Menu. (*Note:* the latter link starts Eclipse, for which Designer is a plug-in.)

2. Create a new BPEL application in Designer by choosing File → New → Project. In the dialog box, select Oracle BPEL Project and click Next. On the next page, in the Name edit field, enter InsuranceClaim and click the Finish button.

3. Create a file called *messages.wsdl* in the Insurance Claim project. Right-click Insurance Claim in the left Navigator Menu. In the context menu, select New → Other, and in the dialog box, select File, under Simple. Name the file *messages.wsdl*, and give it the content shown in Example 10-1.

EXAMPLE 10-1. *messages.wsdl*

```
1   <?xml version="1.0"?>
2   <definitions name="IMSG"
3     targetNamespace="http://acm.org/samples"
4     xmlns:tns="http://acm.org/samples"
5     xmlns:bpws="http://schemas.xmlsoap.org/ws/2003/03/business-process/"
6     xmlns:xsd="http://www.w3.org/2001/XMLSchema"
7     xmlns="http://schemas.xmlsoap.org/wsdl/">
8
9     <types>
10      <schema attributeFormDefault="qualified"
11        elementFormDefault="qualified"
12        targetNamespace="http://acm.org/samples"
13        xmlns="http://www.w3.org/2001/XMLSchema">
14
```

EXAMPLE 10-1. *messages.wsdl (continued)*

```
15              <!-- Our XML message type, InsuranceClaimMsg consists of
16                  an id and a data
17              -->
18          <element name="InsuranceClaimMsg">
19              <complexType>
20                  <sequence>
21                      <element name="id" type="string" />
22                      <element name="data" type="string" />
23                  </sequence>
24              </complexType>
25          </element>
26      </schema>
27  </types>
28
29  <!-- The WSDL message is just the InsuranceClaimMsg described earlier -->
30  <message name="InsuranceClaimMsg">
31      <part name="payload" element="tns:InsuranceClaimMsg"/>
32  </message>
33
34  <!-- Define  a BPEL property alias for the ID field -->
35  <bpws:property name="claimID" type="xsd:string"/>
36  <bpws:propertyAlias propertyName="tns:claimID"
37      messageType="tns:InsuranceClaimMsg" part="payload"
38      query="/tns:InsuranceClaimMsg/tns:id"/>
39  </definitions>
```

4. Edit the file *InsuranceClaim.wsdl*. Double-click on that file, found in the Navigator Menu under Insurance Claim. Replace its current contents with the code in Example 10-2.

EXAMPLE 10-2. *InsuranceClaim.wsdl*

```
1   <?xml version="1.0"?>
2
3   <definitions name="InsuranceClaim"
4       targetNamespace="http://acm.org/samples"
5       xmlns:tns="http://acm.org/samples"
6       xmlns:plnk="http://schemas.xmlsoap.org/ws/2003/05/partner-link/"
7       xmlns="http://schemas.xmlsoap.org/wsdl/"
8       xmlns:bpws="http://schemas.xmlsoap.org/ws/2003/03/business-process/"
9       xmlns:xsd="http://www.w3.org/2001/XMLSchema">
10
11  <!-- Import messages.wsdl for access to InsuranceClaimMsg type -->
12  <import namespace="http://acm.org/samples" location="messages.wsdl"/>
13
14  <!-- port type, InsuranceClaim, has operations initiate and kill -->
15  <portType name="InsuranceClaim">
16      <operation name="initiate">
17          <input message="tns:InsuranceClaimMsg"/>
18      </operation>
19      <operation name="kill">
20          <input message="tns:InsuranceClaimMsg"/>
21      </operation>
22  </portType>
23
```

EXAMPLE 10-2. *InsuranceClaim.wsdl (continued)*

```
24      <!-- Define a partner link type with role "InsuranceClaimProvider".
25           This role implements the InsuranceClaim port type.
26      -->
27      <plnk:partnerLinkType name="InsuranceClaim">
28         <plnk:role name="InsuranceClaimProvider">
29             <plnk:portType name="tns:InsuranceClaim"/>
30         </plnk:role>
31      </plnk:partnerLinkType>
32  </definitions>
```

The file *InsuranceClaim.wsdl* in Example 10-2 defines the service interface for client applications of the InsuranceClaim process. This interface has one port type, called InsuranceClaim, with two operations, initiate and kill (lines 15–22). A partner link type is defined in lines 27–31 that maps the port type to a role called InsuranceClaimProvider. As will be seen later, the process adopts this role; it acts as InsuranceClaimProvider to clients. The message type passed into the operations is called InsuranceClaimMsg, which is defined in *messages.wsdl*; the *InsuranceClaim.wsdl* file uses the import statement in line 12 to reference it.

The WSDL message type InsuranceClaimMsg is defined in lines 30-32 of *messages.wsdl* (Example 10-1), and has only one message part, payload, of a type whose schema is listed in lines 18–25. The type consists of two fields: id and data. A BPEL property and alias for the id field, required for message correlation, as we will discover later, is stipulated in lines 35–38.

WARNING

Oracle BPEL PM sometimes gets confused when the WSDL interface of a process that has already been deployed is changed in Designer. If the change makes the new version incompatible with the old, Designer generates errors during the process build. To work around this, try the following:

1. Delete the temporary directory that holds the version of the process used by the runtime engine. The directory is of the form *<BPEL_DIR>\ domains\default\tmp\.bpel_<PROCESSNAME>_1.0.jar*, where *<BPEL_DIR>* is the directory in which you installed PM, and *<PROCESSNAME>* matches the name of the Designer project. For example: *C:\orabpel211\ domains\default\tmp\.bpel_InsuranceClaim_1.0.jar*.

2. If the problem remains, open the administrative console and undeploy the process by selecting the Processes tab → process name → Undeploy button.

3. No luck? Restart the BPEL server.

Create Variables, Partner Links, and Correlation

Once the initial setup work is done, we can start developing the process to the point where it has at least the initial receive activity and can build properly. We also add the required process variables, partner links, and correlations. The following steps illustrate how:

1. Double click on *InsuranceClaim.bpel* (created in the previous section) in the Navigator panel. Your screen should resemble Figure 10-5.

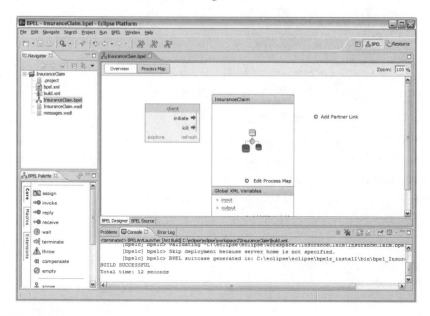

FIGURE 10-5. *Initial process screen*

2. Click on the client in the leftmost box and fill in the edits on the dialog box with the values shown in Figure 10-6. Click Done.

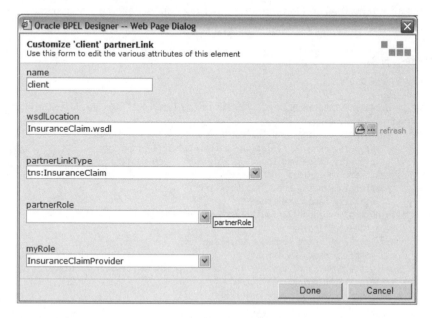

FIGURE 10-6. *Client configuration*

3. Click Add Partner Link and fill in the dialog box with the data in Figure 10-7, using the name evalWorklist. Repeat twice more with exactly the same data, except the names are anaWorklist and esWorklist.

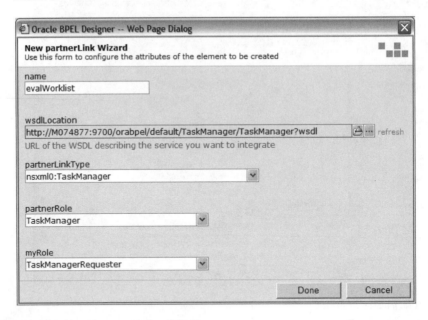

FIGURE 10-7. *Task Manager partnerLink configuration*

4. Open *bpel.xml* by right-clicking on it from the Navigator and selecting Open With → Text Editor from the context menu. Add to it the italicized pieces shown in Example 10-3 to enable correlation in the process.

EXAMPLE 10-3. *bpel.xml*

```
1   <?xml version="1.0"?>
2   <BPELSuitcase>
3      <BPELProcess id="InsuranceClaim" src="InsuranceClaim.bpel" useCorrelationSet="yes">
4         <partnerLinkBindings>
5            <partnerLinkBinding name="client">
6               <property name="correlation">correlationSet</property>
7               <property name="wsdlLocation">InsuranceClaim.wsdl</property>
8            </partnerLinkBinding>
9            <partnerLinkBinding name="evalWorklist">
10              <property name="wsdlLocation">
11   http://localhost:9700/orabpel/default/TaskManager/TaskManager?wsdl</property>
12           </partnerLinkBinding>
13           <partnerLinkBinding name="anaWorklist">
14              <property name="wsdlLocation">
15   http://localhost:9700/orabpel/default/TaskManager/TaskManager?wsdl</property>
16           </partnerLinkBinding>
17           <partnerLinkBinding name="esWorklist">
18              <property name="wsdlLocation">
19   http://localhost:9700/orabpel/default/TaskManager/TaskManager?wsdl</property>
20           </partnerLinkBinding>
```

EXAMPLE 10-3. *bpel.xml (continued)*

```
21          </partnerLinkBindings>
22      </BPELProcess>
23  </BPELSuitcase>
```

5. Back in *InsuranceClaim.bpel*, right-click on the global variable output and select Delete Element from the context menu. Next, right click on the variable input and select Edit XML Variable from the context menu. In the dialog box, change the name to initiateMsg and the message type to tns:InsuranceClaimMsg. Click Done to commit. Create two additional variables, in each case by clicking Add XML Variable. Name the first variable status and set its Simple XML Type to xsd:string. Name the second variable killEv, and set its Message Type to tns:InsuranceClaimMsg.

6. Click Edit Process Map, which opens the screen shown in Figure 10-8. Right-click on the invoke activity, and select Delete Element from the context menu.

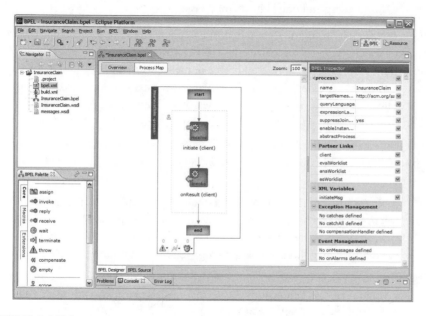

FIGURE 10-8. *Initial process map*

7. Click on the BPEL Source tab to switch to the source code view of the process. To the existing code, add the following definition of a correlation set between the variables section and the sequence section:

```
<correlationSets>
    <correlationSet name="claim" properties="tns:claimID"/>
</correlationSets>
```

8. Add correlation to the current receive activity; replace the current receive element with the following code:

```
<receive xmlns=http://schemas.xmlsoap.org/ws/2003/03/business-process/
    partnerLink="client" portType="tns:InsuranceClaim"  operation="initiate"
    variable="initiateMsg" createInstance="yes" name="initiateEvent">
```

```
<correlations>
    <correlation set="claim" initiate="yes"/>
</correlations>
</receive>
```

9. Build the process by selecting the menu item BPEL → Build and Deploy BPEL Project. Track the build output in the Console tab at the bottom of the screen; look for the text "BUILD SUCCESSFUL."

Add Flow and a Manual Task

Although the basic elements are now defined, the process currently does very little. It is started with the receive activity that maps to the WSDL operation initiate and then immediately finishes. Expanding the process involves dragging shapes from the BPEL Palette into the Process Map or by editing the code directly. We will use a combination of these approaches to complete the coding effort. In this section, we will use drag and drop to create the flow activity and one of its manual tasks.

1. Drag a flow activity from the Core tab of BPEL Palette to the Process Map just below the receive activity. In the property editor (BPEL Inspector) on the right side, set the name of the flow to MainFlow, and add three branches using the menu item Add Branch, accessible when clicking on the down arrow next to <flow>. We now have a skeletal flow containing five parallel activities; a portion of this element is shown in Figure 10-9.

2. Change the names of the five sequences to EvalSeq, AnalyzeSeq, EscalateSeq, RejectSeq, and ActivateSeq. To do this, click on each sequence and edit the Name field in the property editor.

3. Drag a User Task Macro from the Macros tab of BPEL Palette into the EvalSeq sequence. In the dialog box entitled User Task, enter the name EvaluateClaim, and click Done. Notice that the activity created is a scope activity. Click on it and in the property editor, change the name of the scope to EvaluateClaim.

4. Expand the scope activity and select the assign activity configureTask. Edit the copy rule for assignee; in the Expression edit, replace assignee@acm.org with agent and click Done. Next, edit the copy rule for attachment-type bpws:getVariableData("initiateMsg","payload","/tns:InsuranceClaimMsg") in the Expression edit, and click Done. Delete the copy rule for duration.

5. The scope EvaluateClaim has an inner scope named EvaluateClaimUserInteraction. Expand it and select the activity initiateTask; in the property editor change the partner link to evalWorklist. Do the same thing with the activity onTaskResult. Finally, select the activity readPayload, change its name to setStatus, and edit its copy rule; enter $taskResponse/payload/task:task/task:conclusion for the "From Variable, Part and Query" and $status for the" To Variable, Part and Query." Click done. Figure 10-10 shows a fully expanded view of the task.

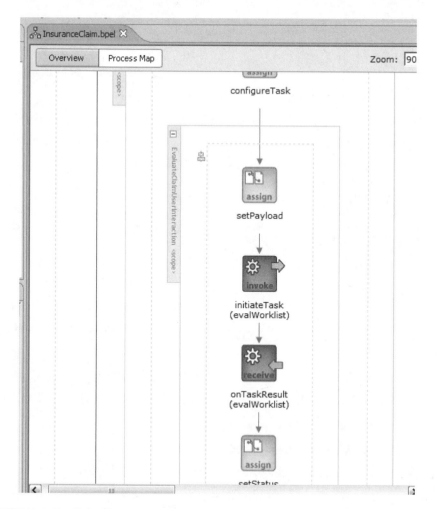

FIGURE 10-9. *Main flow in BPEL Designer*

The complex logic for a manual task created by the macro from the palette works as follows:

- The `configurationTask` assign activity sets the input value, a complex datatype that includes name, assignee, priority, and an arbitrary attachment. The person who works the task uses this data to determine the nature of the work required.

- The inner scope's job is to initiate the task by invoking the Task Manager service (with an `invoke` activity), and then to wait for its completion (with a receive). Behind the scenes, the invoke causes the task to be published to a task list, accessible to the assignee through a custom user interface. In that interface, the assignee completes the task, passing back relevant data; the Task Manager, in turn, invokes the callback that triggers the receive, passing the response data from the assignee.

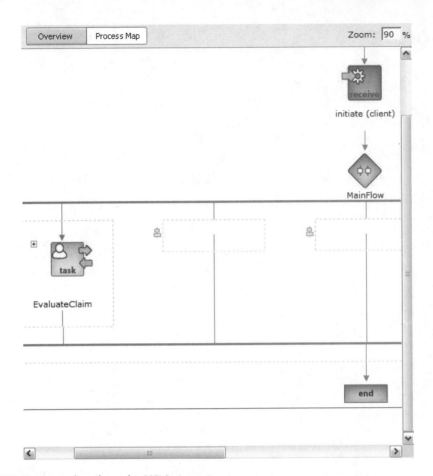

FIGURE 10-10. *EvaluateClaim task in BPEL Designer*

The setStatus assign activity is not part of the macro but a custom step in our implementation. It extracts the Conclusion field from the response data and sets it as the value of the global variable status. As will be seen later, the value of that variable determines the conditional linking of the flow.

The section "Testing the Example" later in this chapter describes how to view and complete tasks in the BPEL administrative console.

Complete the Coding

Many additional drags and drops are still required, but for brevity, we will complete the coding by editing the source view directly, replacing the current contents with the listing in Example 10-4. The highlights of the code—ignoring, for the time being, the italicized lines—are the following:

- Lines 79–85 show the receive activity designed previously. The receive responds to the initiate operation and creates the correlation set claim.

- Lines 87–93: The assign activity sets the global variable status to indicate that the process has initiated.

- The flow links, representing the transitions within the flow activity, are declared in lines 97–106. This section must be coded by hand; BPEL Designer does not support the graphical manipulation of flow links.

- EvalSeq, from lines 109–196, which we composed graphically in the previous section, are expanded here with the introduction of source flow links in lines 114–119. Notice that the links are conditional, guarded by a check on the value of the variable status. The link evalAnalysis, for example, is followed only if status is set to requiresAnalysis.

- AnalyzeSeq, in lines 197–292, is similar to EvalSeq, except in addition to being the source of links, it is also a target (line 198). Next, after invoking the Task Manager, rather than waiting merely for task completion, AnalyzeSeq uses a pick activity (lines 256–287) to wait either for completion or for a timeout, and sets the status variable to different values depending on the outcome.

- EscalateSeq, in lines 293–365 is very similar to EvalSeq.

- Lines 366–384: RejectSeq is the target of any link that evaluates a status of rejected. Notice the use of the proprietary Java extension bpelx:exec in lines 378–382 to print the message CLAIM REJECTED to the standard output of the BPEL server.

NOTE
The Oracle Java extension does not follow the BPELJ recommendation, and hence cannot be ported to other Java-enabled BPEL containers. (The Oracle exec tag appears to roughly match the BPELJ snippet.)

- Lines 385–403: ActivateSeq is similar to RejectSeq, except that it is the target of accepted links

EXAMPLE 10-4. *Final BPEL code*

```
1   <process name="InsuranceClaim"
2       targetNamespace="http://acm.org/samples"
3       suppressJoinFailure="yes"
4       xmlns:tns=http://acm.org/samples
5       xmlns=http://schemas.xmlsoap.org/ws/2003/03/business-process/
6       xmlns:bpelx=http://schemas.oracle.com/bpel/extension
7       xmlns:ora=http://schemas.oracle.com/xpath/extension
8       xmlns:xsd=http://www.w3.org/2001/XMLSchema
9       xmlns:services=http://services.otn.com
10      xmlns:task=http://services.oracle.com/bpel/task
11      xmlns:addressing=http://schemas.xmlsoap.org/ws/2003/03/addressing
12      xmlns:bpws="http://schemas.xmlsoap.org/ws/2003/03/business-process/">
13
14      <!--
15          Partners in the process:
16              client      - app that can initiate and kill
17              evalWorklist - service that this process calls to initiate
18                             a human workflow task to evaluate a claim
```

EXAMPLE 10-4. *Final BPEL code (continued)*

```
19          anaWorklist - similar to evalWorklist, but for analysis of a claim
20          esWorklist  - similar, but for escalation of a claim
21      -->
22      <partnerLinks>
23        <!--
24        <partnerLink name="client" partnerLinkType="tns:InsuranceClaim"
25            myRole="InsuranceClaimProvider"/>
26        <partnerLink name="evalWorklist" partnerLinkType="task:TaskManager"
27            partnerRole="TaskManager" myRole="TaskManagerRequester"/>
28        <partnerLink name="anaWorklist" partnerLinkType="task:TaskManager"
29            partnerRole="TaskManager" myRole="TaskManagerRequester"/>
30        <partnerLink name="esWorklist" partnerLinkType="task:TaskManager"
31            partnerRole="TaskManager" myRole="TaskManagerRequester"/>
32      </partnerLinks>
33      <variables>
34        <variable name="status" type="xsd:string"/>
35        <variable messageType="tns:InsuranceClaimMsg" name="initiateMsg"/>
36        <variable messageType="tns:InsuranceClaimMsg" name="killEv"/>
37      </variables>
38
39      <!-- Message correlation to be performed on the ClaimID field -->
40      <correlationSets>
41        <correlationSet name="claim" properties="tns:claimID"/>
42      </correlationSets>
43
44      <!--This code is commented out because it does not work.  See note below.
45          Its purpose is to globally receive a kill event (correlated with the claim ID from the
46          original initate) and terminate the process.
47      <eventHandlers>
48        <onMessage xmlns=http://schemas.xmlsoap.org/ws/2003/03/business-process/
49            partnerLink="client" portType="tns:InsuranceClaim" operation="kill"
50            variable="killEv">
51            <correlations>
52              <correlation set="claim" initiate="no"/>
53            </correlations>
54            <sequence>
55              <assign name="setStatusKilled">
56                <copy>
57                  <from expression="string('killed')">
58                  </from>
59                  <to variable="status"/>
60                </copy>
61              </assign>
62              <bpelx:exec xmlns:bpelx=http://schemas.oracle.com/bpel/extension
63                  language="java" version="1.4" name="jkill">
64                  <![CDATA[
65            System.out.println("**** CLAIM KILLED ****");
66        ]]>
67              </bpelx:exec>
68              <terminate name="killClaim"/>
69            </sequence>
70        </onMessage>
71      </eventHandlers>
72      -->
73
```

EXAMPLE 10-4. *Final BPEL code (continued)*

```
74      <sequence>
75
76         <!-- We start with a receive activity: get the initiate message.  Will
77            correlate on claim set defined earlier
78         -->
79         <receive xmlns=http://schemas.xmlsoap.org/ws/2003/03/business-process/
80            partnerLink="client" portType="tns:InsuranceClaim" operation="initiate"
81            variable="initiateMsg" createInstance="yes" name="initiateEvent">
82            <correlations>
83               <correlation set="claim" initiate="yes"/>
84            </correlations>
85         </receive>
86         <!-- keep track of where we are: set variable 'status' to 'initiated' -->
87         <assign name="setStatus">
88            <copy>
89               <from expression="string('initiated')">
90               </from>
91               <to variable="status"/>
92            </copy>
93         </assign>
94
95         <!-- The flow, described in detail earlier in this chapter -->
96         <flow name="MainFlow">
97            <links>
98               <link name="evalReject"/>
99               <link name="evalAccept"/>
100              <link name="evalAnalysis"/>
101              <link name="anaReject"/>
102              <link name="anaAccept"/>
103              <link name="anaTO"/>
104              <link name="esReject"/>
105              <link name="esAccept"/>
106           </links>
107
108           <!-- This sequence has the logic for evaluation of a claim. -->
109           <sequence name="EvalSeq">
110              <!--
111                 The three outcomes, based on the value of the variable 'status'.
112                 Each link is a "target" in a sequence later.
113              -->
114              <source linkName="evalReject"
115                transitionCondition="bpws:getVariableData('status')='rejected'"/>
116              <source linkName="evalAccept"
117                transitionCondition="bpws:getVariableData('status')='accepted'"/>
118              <source linkName="evalAnalysis"
119             transitionCondition="bpws:getVariableData('status')='requiresAnalysis'"/>
120              <scope name="EvaluateClaim" variableAccessSerializable="no">
121                 <variables>
122                    <variable name="EvaluateClaimTask" element="task:task"/>
123                 </variables>
124                 <sequence>
125                 <!-- Set the variable EvaluateClaimTask with data specific to the
126                      analysis task: e.g., title, assignee, priority, attachment
127                 -->
128                    <assign name="configureTask">
```

EXAMPLE 10-4. *Final BPEL code (continued)*

```
129                         <copy>
130                             <from expression="string( 'EvaluateClaim' )"/>
131                             <to variable="EvaluateClaimTask"
132                                 query="/task:task/task:title"/>
133                         </copy>
134                         <copy>
135                             <from expression="string( 'InsuranceClaim' )"/>
136                             <to variable="EvaluateClaimTask"
137                                 query="/task:task/task:creator"/>
138                         </copy>
139                         <copy>
140                             <from expression="string( 'agent' )"/>
141                             <to variable="EvaluateClaimTask"
142                                 query="/task:task/task:assignee"/>
143                         </copy>
144                         <copy>
145                             <from expression="3"/>
146                             <to variable="EvaluateClaimTask"
147                                 query="/task:task/task:priority"/>
148                         </copy>
149                         <copy>
150                             <from variable="initiateMsg" part="payload"
151                                 query="/tns:InsuranceClaimMsg/tns:data"/>
152                             <to variable="EvaluateClaimTask"
153                                 query="/task:task/task:attachment"/>
154                         </copy>
155                     </assign>
156                     <scope name="EvaluateClaimUserInteraction"
157                         variableAccessSerializable="no">
158                         <variables>
159                             <variable name="taskRequest"
160                                 messageType="task:taskMessage"/>
161                             <variable name="taskResponse"
162                                 messageType="task:taskMessage"/>
163                         </variables>
164                         <sequence>
165                             <assign name="setPayload">
166                                 <copy>
167                                     <from variable="EvaluateClaimTask"/>
168                                     <to variable="taskRequest" part="payload"/>
169                                 </copy>
170                             </assign>
171
172                     <!--call evalWorklist partner to initiate the task, passing
173                             the data defined above.
174                     -->
175                             <invoke name="initiateTask" partnerLink="evalWorklist"
176                                 portType="task:TaskManager" operation="initiateTask"
177                                 inputVariable="taskRequest"/>
178                     <!-- get back the result, possibly a long time later -->
179                             <receive name="receiveTaskResult"
180                                 partnerLink="evalWorklist"
181                                 portType="task:TaskManagerCallback"
182                                 operation="onTaskResult" variable="taskResponse"/>
183                     <!-- set variable 'status' with result.Use for routing -->
```

EXAMPLE 10-4. *Final BPEL code (continued)*

```
184                        <assign name="setStatus">
185                           <copy>
186                              <from variable="taskResponse" part="payload"
187                                 query="/task:task/task:conclusion">
188                              </from>
189                              <to variable="status"/>
190                           </copy>
191                        </assign>
192                     </sequence>
193                  </scope>
194               </sequence>
195            </scope>
196         </sequence>
197         <sequence name="AnalyzeSeq">
198            <target linkName="evalAnalysis"/>
199            <source linkName="anaReject"
200              transitionCondition="bpws:getVariableData('status')='rejected'"/>
201            <source linkName="anaAccept"
202              transitionCondition="bpws:getVariableData('status')='accepted'"/>
203            <source linkName="anaTO"
204              transitionCondition="bpws:getVariableData('status')='timeout'"/>
205            <scope name="AnalyzeClaim" variableAccessSerializable="no">
206               <variables>
207                  <variable name="AnalyzeClaimTask" element="task:task"/>
208               </variables>
209               <sequence>
210                  <assign name="configureTask">
211                     <copy>
212                        <from expression="string( 'AnalyzeClaim' )"/>
213                        <to variable="AnalyzeClaimTask"
214                           query="/task:task/task:title"/>
215                     </copy>
216                     <copy>
217                        <from expression="string( 'InsuranceClaim' )"/>
218                        <to variable="AnalyzeClaimTask"
219                           query="/task:task/task:creator"/>
220                     </copy>
221                     <copy>
222                        <from expression="string( 'adjuster' )"/>
223                        <to variable="AnalyzeClaimTask"
224                           query="/task:task/task:assignee"/>
225                     </copy>
226                     <copy>
227                        <from expression="3"/>
228                        <to variable="AnalyzeClaimTask"
229                           query="/task:task/task:priority"/>
230                     </copy>
231                     <copy>
232                        <from variable="initiateMsg" part="payload"
233                           query="/tns:InsuranceClaimMsg/tns:data"/>
234                        <to variable="AnalyzeClaimTask"
235                           query="/task:task/task:attachment"/>
236                     </copy>
237                  </assign>
238                  <scope name="AnalyzeClaimUserInteraction"
```

EXAMPLE 10-4. *Final BPEL code (continued)*

```
239                          variableAccessSerializable="no">
240                      <variables>
241                        <variable name="taskRequest"
242                          messageType="task:taskMessage"/>
243                        <variable name="taskResponse"
244                          messageType="task:taskMessage"/>
245                      </variables>
246                      <sequence>
247                        <assign name="setPayload">
248                          <copy>
249                            <from variable="AnalyzeClaimTask"/>
250                            <to variable="taskRequest" part="payload"/>
251                          </copy>
252                        </assign>
253                        <invoke name="initiateTask" partnerLink="anaWorklist"
254                          portType="task:TaskManager" operation="initiateTask"
255                          inputVariable="taskRequest"/>
256                        <pick name="analyzePick">
257                          <onMessage partnerLink="anaWorklist"
258                            portType="task:TaskManagerCallback"
259                            operation="onTaskResult" variable="taskResponse">
260                            <sequence>
261                              <assign name="setStatusEvaluated">
262                                <copy>
263                                  <from variable="taskResponse" part="payload"
264                                    query="/task:task/task:conclusion">
265                                  </from>
266                                  <to variable="status"/>
267                                </copy>
268                              </assign>
269                            </sequence>
270                          </onMessage>
271                          <onAlarm for="PT1M">
272                            <sequence>
273                              <invoke name="stopEvalTask"
274                                partnerLink="anaWorklist"
275                                portType="task:TaskManager"
276                                operation="completeTask"
277                                inputVariable="taskRequest"/>
278                              <assign name="setStatusAnalyzeTimeout">
279                                <copy>
280                                  <from expression="string('timeout')">
281                                  </from>
282                                  <to variable="status"/>
283                                </copy>
284                              </assign>
285                            </sequence>
286                          </onAlarm>
287                        </pick>
288                      </sequence>
289                    </scope>
290                  </sequence>
291                </scope>
292              </sequence>
293            <sequence name="EscalateSeq">
```

EXAMPLE 10-4. *Final BPEL code (continued)*

```
294                <target linkName="anaTO"/>
295                <source linkName="esReject"
296                  transitionCondition="bpws:getVariableData('status')='rejected'"/>
297                <source linkName="esAccept"
298                  transitionCondition="bpws:getVariableData('status')='accepted'"/>
299                <scope name="EscalateClaim" variableAccessSerializable="no">
300                  <variables>
301                     <variable name="EscalateClaimTask" element="task:task"/>
302                  </variables>
303                  <sequence>
304                     <assign name="configureTask">
305                        <copy>
306                           <from expression="string( 'EvaluateClaim' )"/>
307                           <to variable="EscalateClaimTask"
308                              query="/task:task/task:title"/>
309                        </copy>
310                        <copy>
311                           <from expression="string( 'InsuranceClaim' )"/>
312                           <to variable="EscalateClaimTask"
313                              query="/task:task/task:creator"/>
314                        </copy>
315                        <copy>
316                           <from expression="string( 'manager' )"/>
317                           <to variable="EscalateClaimTask"
318                              query="/task:task/task:assignee"/>
319                        </copy>
320                        <copy>
321                           <from expression="1"/>
322                           <to variable="EscalateClaimTask"
323                              query="/task:task/task:priority"/>
324                        </copy>
325                        <copy>
326                           <from variable="initiateMsg" part="payload"
327                              query="/tns:InsuranceClaimMsg/tns:data"/>
328                           <to variable="EscalateClaimTask"
329                              query="/task:task/task:attachment"/>
330                        </copy>
331                     </assign>
332                     <scope name="EscalateClaimUserInteraction"
333                        variableAccessSerializable="no">
334                        <variables>
335                           <variable name="taskRequest"
336                              messageType="task:taskMessage"/>
337                           <variable name="taskResponse"
338                              messageType="task:taskMessage"/>
339                        </variables>
340                        <sequence>
341                           <assign name="setPayload">
342                              <copy>
343                                 <from variable="EscalateClaimTask"/>
344                                 <to variable="taskRequest" part="payload"/>
345                              </copy>
346                           </assign>
347                           <invoke name="initiateTask" partnerLink="esWorklist"
348                              portType="task:TaskManager" operation="initiateTask"
```

EXAMPLE 10-4. *Final BPEL code (continued)*

```
349                             inputVariable="taskRequest"/>
350                         <receive name="receiveTaskResult" partnerLink="esWorklist"
351                             portType="task:TaskManagerCallback"
352                             operation="onTaskResult" variable="taskResponse"/>
353                         <assign name="setStatus">
354                             <copy>
355                                 <from variable="taskResponse" part="payload"
356                                     query="/task:task/task:conclusion">
357                                 </from>
358                                 <to variable="status"/>
359                             </copy>
360                         </assign>
361                     </sequence>
362                 </scope>
363             </sequence>
364         </scope>
365     </sequence>
366     <sequence name="RejectSeq">
367         <target linkName="evalReject"/>
368         <target linkName="anaReject"/>
369         <target linkName="esReject"/>
370         <assign xmlns=http://schemas.xmlsoap.org/ws/2003/03/business-process/
371             name="setStatusRejectComplete">
372             <copy>
373                 <from expression="string('Reject Letter Sent')">
374                 </from>
375                 <to variable="status"/>
376             </copy>
377         </assign>
378         <bpelx:exec xmlns:bpelx=http://schemas.oracle.com/bpel/extension
379             language="java" version="1.4" name="jreject">
380             <![CDATA[
381     System.out.println("**** CLAIM REJECTED ****");          ]]>
382         </bpelx:exec>
383         <!-- terminate the process, see following note -->    <terminate/>
384     </sequence>
385     <sequence name="ActivateSeq">
386         <target linkName="evalAccept"/>
387         <target linkName="anaAccept"/>
388         <target linkName="esAccept"/>
389         <assign xmlns=http://schemas.xmlsoap.org/ws/2003/03/business-process/
390             name="setStatusAcceptComplete">
391             <copy>
392                 <from expression="string('Letter and Reimbursement Sent')">
393                 </from>
394                 <to variable="status"/>
395             </copy>
396         </assign>
397         <bpelx:exec xmlns:bpelx=http://schemas.oracle.com/bpel/extension
398             language="java" version="1.4" name="jactivate">
399             <![CDATA[
400     System.out.println("**** CLAIM ACCEPTED AND ACTIVATED ****");          ]]>
401         </bpelx:exec>
402         <!-- terminate the process, see following note --> <terminate/>
403     </sequence>
```

EXAMPLE 10-4. *Final BPEL code (continued)*

```
      <!-- at any time in the flow, respond to the kill event by terminating the
          process.  See note below -->
404      <sequence name="CancelSeq">
405        <receive
406          xmlns="http://schemas.xmlsoap.org/ws/2003/03/business-process/"
407          partnerLink="client" portType="tns:InsuranceClaim"
408          operation="initiate" variable="initiateMsg" createInstance="no"
409          name="initiateEvent">
410          <correlations>
411            <correlation set="claim" initiate="no"/>
412          </correlations>
413        </receive>
414        <assign name="setStatus">
415          <copy>
416            <from expression="string('killed')">
417            </from>
418            <to variable="status"/>
419          </copy>
420        </assign>
421        <bpelx:exec xmlns:bpelx=http://schemas.oracle.com/bpel/extension
422          language="java" version="1.4" name="jkill">
423          <![CDATA[
424      System.out.println("**** CLAIM KILLED ****");
425      ]]>
426        </bpelx:exec>
427        <terminate/>
428      </sequence>
429    </flow>
430  </sequence>
431 </process>
```

If you read that code in Example 10-4 carefully, you will notice that it does not conform to the design prescribed in Figure 10-2. earlier; specifically, it does not use an eventHandlers block to process cancellation. (The eventHandlers code is commented out in lines 44–72.) During unit testing, it was discovered that the BPEL engine did not properly route kill messages to the eventHandler. The changes required to work around the problem are italicized in Example 10-4:

• A new block called CancelSeq (lines 405-429) is added to the flow statement. The logic of CancelSeq is nearly identical to the onMessage handler for the kill operation in the preferred implementation, except it is not globally scoped but works only while the flow activity is running, which, thankfully, covers most of the duration of the process anyway.

• To handle cases where no kill event arrives, and the claim is either rejected or activated successfully, terminate activities are added to RejectSeq (line 383) and ActivateSeq (line 402), respectively. Without explicit termination, the event wait in CancelSeq would block interminably, preventing the process from completing. The process would hang forever, despite having successfully handled the claim.

WS-ADDRESSING AND CORRELATION

Notice that in the code generated by the task macro, there is no explicit correlation tying together the invoke-receive sequence of activities (e.g., lines 112–119 in Example 10-4). When the Task Manager service invokes the callback onTaskResult implemented by the InsuranceClaim process, how does the BPEL engine know which instance of the process to trigger? The absence of an explicit correlation makes it impossible for the BPEL engine to compare data in the message with data held in a process correlation set.

The answer is WS-Addressing, a web services standard under construction by Microsoft, IBM, and other companies. Under the covers, when the InsuranceClaim process invokes the Task Manager, the BPEL engine, using syntax specified in the WS-Addressing specification, embeds information into the SOAP header such as a universally unique identifier (UUID) and a reply address. When Task Manager responds, the engine uses the original reply address and UUID to route the message to the correct instance of InsuranceClaims process.

Though Oracle PM supports both WS-Addressing and BPEL correlation, Oracle's samples and tutorials emphasize the former approach.

For more on WS-Addressing, see D. Box, et al., "Web Services Addressing," *http://msdn.microsoft.com/webservices/default.aspx?pull=/library/en-us/dnglobspec/html/ws-addressing.asp.*

A Killer App

As you will see later in the section "Testing the Example," of the two operations in the client interface of the InsuranceClaim process, only initiate can be exercised out of the box with the Oracle BPEL administrative console. The console provides a test HTML form to start a process, but no equivalent form to inject into the process an arbitrary intermediate event. Thus, in order to test the InsuranceClaim's kill operation, we need to write a simple client application that calls it. This application can be written in Java or .NET, but that requires additional tools, not to mention additional skills. Instead, we will write a process called InsuranceClaimKiller that acts as a simple pass through to InsuranceClaim, calling its kill method with an invoke activity immediately after starting. Admittedly a heavyweight, contrived solution, our killer process can be developed and deployed rapidly, and when it is started using the console's process initiation test form, a kill message is sent directly to an in-flight InsuranceClaim process, achieving our original objective. The source code of the InsuranceClaimKiller process is provided in three listings:

In the first listing, *InsuranceClaimKiller.wsdl*, the process supports a single operation, called kill (lines 13–15), whose input is the same WSDL type that is input by the kill operation of the InsuranceClaim process. Example 10-5 shows the listing.

EXAMPLE 10-5. *InsuranceClaimKiller.wsdl*

```
1  <?xml version="1.0"?>
2  <definitions name="InsuranceClaimKillTester"
3    targetNamespace="http://acm.org/samples"
4    xmlns:tns="http://acm.org/samples"
5    xmlns:plnk="http://schemas.xmlsoap.org/ws/2003/05/partner-link/"
6    xmlns="http://schemas.xmlsoap.org/wsdl/">
7
8    <!-- Import to get definition of InsuranceClaimMsg -->
9    <import namespace="http://acm.org/samples" location="messages.wsdl"/>
10
11   <!-- the tester has a kill operation in its port type -->
12   <portType name="InsuranceClaimKillTester">
13      <operation name="kill">
14         <input message="tns:InsuranceClaimMsg"/>
15      </operation>
16   </portType>
17
18   <!-- Partner link type for the killer -->
19   <plnk:partnerLinkType name="InsuranceClaimKillTester">
20      <plnk:role name="InsuranceClaimKillTesterProvider">
21         <plnk:portType name="tns:InsuranceClaimKillTester"/>
22      </plnk:role>
23   </plnk:partnerLinkType>
24  </definitions>
```

The second listing, *bpel.xml*, specifies the partner link bindings for the process. In lines 10–14, the partner link Claims Process is mapped to the InsuranceClaim process. Example 10-6 shows the listing.

EXAMPLE 10-6. *bpel.xml for InsuranceClaimKiller*

```
1  <?xml version="1.0"?>
2  <!-- Two partners: client is the killer, ClaimProcess the process to be killed -->
3  <BPELSuitcase>
4    <BPELProcess useCorrelationSet="yes" id="InsuranceClaimKiller"
5       src="InsuranceClaimKiller.bpel">
6       <partnerLinkBindings>
7          <partnerLinkBinding name="client">
8             <property name="wsdlLocation">InsuranceClaimKiller.wsdl</property>
9          </partnerLinkBinding>
10         <partnerLinkBinding name="ClaimProcess">
11            <property name="wsdlLocation">
12 http://localhost:9700/orabpel/default/InsuranceClaim/InsuranceClaim?wsdl
13            </property>
14         </partnerLinkBinding>
15      </partnerLinkBindings>
16   </BPELProcess>
17  </BPELSuitcase>
```

The third listing, *InsuranceClaimKiller.bpel*, is the heart of the killer process and is simplicity itself, having but two atomic activities. It begins with a receive activity (lines 21–24) that responds to the killer's kill operation. Next, and last, is an invoke (lines 26–28) that calls the kill operation of InsuranceClaim, passing as input the same value received in the previous step. Example 10-7 contains the listing.

EXAMPLE 10-7. *InsuranceClaimKiller.bpel*

```
1  <process name="InsuranceClaimKiller" targetNamespace=http://acm.org/samples
2     suppressJoinFailure="yes"
3     xmlns:tns=http://acm.org/samples
4     xmlns="http://schemas.xmlsoap.org/ws/2003/03/business-process/"
5     xmlns:bpelx="http://schemas.oracle.com/bpel/extension"
6     xmlns:ora="http://schemas.oracle.com/xpath/extension"
7     xmlns:bpws="http://schemas.xmlsoap.org/ws/2003/03/business-process/">
8
9     <!--Two partners: This process is the killer. -->
10    <partnerLinks>
11       <partnerLink name="client" partnerLinkType="tns:InsuranceClaimKillTester"
12          myRole="InsuranceClaimKillTesterProvider"/>
13       <partnerLink name="ClaimProcess" partnerLinkType="tns:InsuranceClaim"
14          partnerRole="InsuranceClaimProvider"/>
15    </partnerLinks>
16    <variables>
17       <variable name="input" messageType="tns:InsuranceClaimMsg"/>
18    </variables>
19    <sequence name="main">
20       <!-- Process starts when a kill message comes into the process -->
21       <receive name="receiveInput" partnerLink="client" operation="kill"
22          variable="input" createInstance="yes"
23          portType="tns:InsuranceClaimKillTester">
24       </receive>
25       <!-- When that happens, send kill event to claims process -->
26       <invoke partnerLink="ClaimProcess" portType="tns:InsuranceClaim"
27          operation="kill" name="callKill" inputVariable="input">
28       </invoke>
29    </sequence>
30 </process>
```

Testing the Example

This section presents two test scenarios:

- Test case 1: InsuranceClaim is started, the EvaluateClaim task is completed with an outcome of requiresAnalysis, the AnalyzeClaim task times out, and the EscalateClaim task is completed with an acceptance.

- Test Case 2: InsuranceClaim is started and, after a short time, is killed.

Test Case 1: Accepted on Escalation

To start, open the BPEL administrative console in a browser. The URL for the default, out-of-the-box domain is *http://localhost:9700/BPELConsole/login.jsp*. Log in using the password bpel. The first page to come up after login is the Dashboard, shown in Figure 10-11, which lists the currently deployed processes. If you do not see the InsuranceClaim and InsuranceClaimKiller processes, open BPEL Designer and build and deploy each of them by selecting BPEL → Build and Deploy BPEL Project.

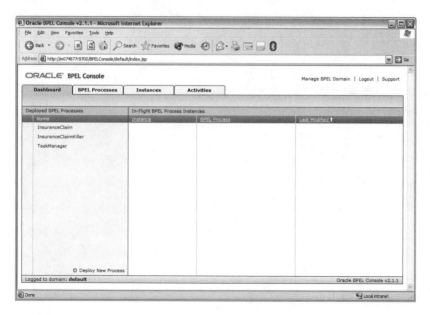

FIGURE 10-11. *Oracle BPEL Console Dashboard*

Clicking on InsuranceClaim brings up the initiation test form, as shown in Figure 10-12.

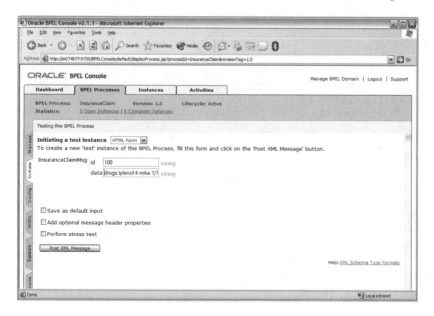

FIGURE 10-12. *Process Initiate for InsuranceClaim*

Enter the data shown for id and data, and click Post XML Message to start the process. Within a moment of initiation, the EvaluateClaim task is assigned to an agent. To see the task, navigate to the task list page at *http://localhost:9700/BPELConsole/default/tasks.jsp*, shown in Figure 10-13.

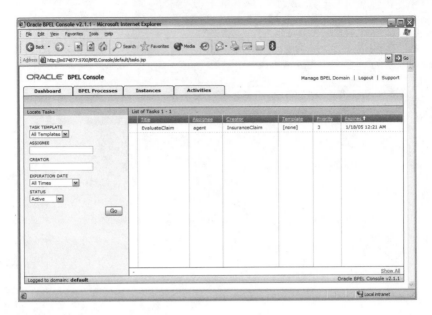

FIGURE 10-13. *BPEL Console Task List page*

Click on the task to bring up the page shown in Figure 10-14.

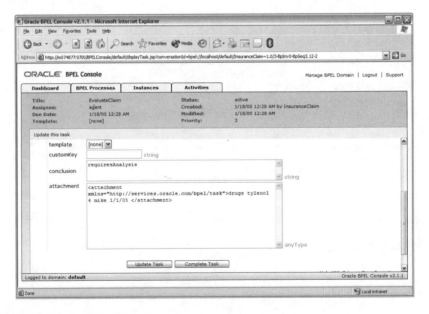

FIGURE 10-14. *EvaluateClaim Task page*

In the EvaluateClaim task page, enter in the Conclusion edit field the value requiresAnalysis, and click the Complete Task button. Check the task list page to confirm that the AnalyzeClaim is currently assigned to an adjuster, but leave that task alone. After a minute, the timer on AnalyzeClaim expires and a new escalation task, called EvaluateClaim and assigned to a manager, is created. Click on the escalation task, and on its task page, complete the task with the conclusion accepted.

The InsuranceClaim process is complete. To see an audit trail or visual trace of the instance, select the instance from the Instances tab, and then select the Audit or Flow tabs from the instance page.

Test Case 2: Kill

The kill test is simpler, requiring only two actions: the initiation of the InsuranceClaim process and, shortly thereafter, the initiation of the InsuranceClaimKiller process. Because both processes accept the same message type as input, the initiation test forms (reached from the Dashboard by clicking on the process link) are identical. The kill succeeds only if the id field used matches the id used to start the target InsuranceClaim instance. To confirm the kill, check the Dashboard's list of recently completed processes, as in Figure 10-15, which suggests, given the proximity of the Last Modified times, that instance 9 of InsuranceClaimKiller killed instance 7 of InsuranceClaim.

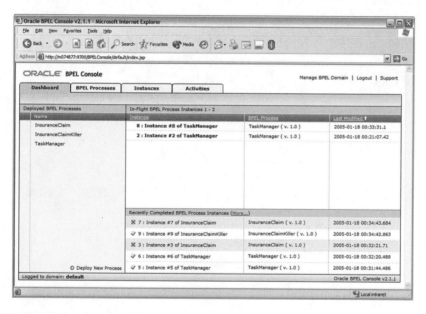

FIGURE 10-15. *Kill confirmation: 9 killed 7*

Summary

The main points in this chapter include the following:

- A BPEL implementation of a human workflow-oriented insurance claims process is demonstrated using Oracle BPEL Process Manager. The example was introduced in the discussion in Chapter 3 of state machines. The nature of architecture of human workflow is discussed in Chapter 2.

- Oracle BPEL Process Manager includes a graphical design tool that runs on Eclipse, a runtime engine that can run standalone or on most of the leading J2EE application servers, and a web-based administrative console.

- Oracle BPEL Process Manager is recommended for this example for the following reasons: it's free and easy to download and assemble, it's BPEL 1.1–compliant, it's designed to facilitate rapid development, and it offers a good task manager implementation.

- Our to-be Insurance Claims process uses a flow activity with conditional links to model the complex mainline logic, and a globally scoped event handler to process cancellations. But during unit testing it was discovered, possibly revealing a product bug, that messages bound for the event handler were not reaching it. To work around the problem, the event handler was removed and the cancellation logic moved to a receive activity in the flow activity. The workaround was successful.

References

1. M. Havey, "Workflow and State Machines in Weblogic Integration: The Process-Oriented Application," *Weblogic Developer's Journal*, January 2004.

2. P. Fontaine, "Insure Yourself with XML!" *http://www.infoloom.com/gcaconfs/WEB/paris2000/S25-04.HTM*

CHAPTER ELEVEN

Example: Enterprise Message Broker

EXCEPT FOR THE "Hello, World!" program, no program has been written as many times by as many people as the Message Broker. Seemingly every vendor and every consultant in the integration space has posited Message Broker as that central enterprise hub through which the message-oriented communications of all systems ought to pass. Without it, every enterprise is a mess of heterogeneous point-to-point cross-talk. But if the individual systems can be programmed to talk to the broker, the broker—a smarter communicator than other system out there—guarantees to relay the message to the right parties. Every company knows how messy application integration can be, and is naturally attracted to the idea of a broker.

This chapter begins by exploring the nature of a BPM-powered Message Broker that, running on message-oriented or service-oriented middleware, uses processes to drive routing logic. The bulk of the chapter is an example of a set of brokering processes, designed using BPMN notation (using ITpearls' Process Modeler plug-in for MS Visio) and implemented in BPEL (using Oracle BPEL Process Manager, as described in Chapter 10).

What Is a Message Broker?

A Message Broker is a centralized hub that simplifies communication among heterogeneous systems. A Message Broker is not a technological breakthrough, but a sensible solution to a common problem: a dramatic increase in number of point-to-point connections between applications in the enterprise.

If there are *N* applications, and every application links to every other application, the total number of point-to-point connections required is $N * (N - 1)/2$. If applications instead connect through a central Message Broker, this number is reduced to just *N*, as in Figure 11-1, where a tangled web of 36 connections is replaced with a tidy 9.

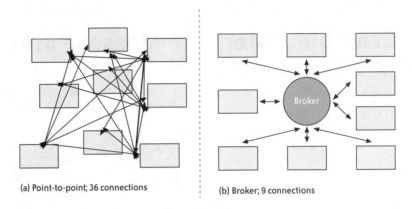

(a) Point-to-point; 36 connections

(b) Broker; 9 connections

FIGURE 11-1. *Point-to-point connections versus connections through a Message Broker*

The argument is a straw man because no company ever requires anywhere near the mathematical maximum number of links. Worse than the quantity of connections is the quality: each connection potentially has its own transport mechanism and message format, and in many cases is poorly documented, hard to integrate, or hard to maintain. Some systems are new, some are legacy, some speak XML, some fixed-position text, and some obscure binary.

A Message Broker's solution is, first, to be a central integration point with a well-documented and clearly understood interface. New applications requiring enterprise integration simply plug into this open architecture. A good broker supports a variety of transports, such as MQ/Series, web services, FTP, and others, though many companies prefer to standardize on just one. As for message format, many Message Broker implementations mandate the use of a canonical format,* which abstracts many common types of entities referred to in interapplication communication.

Though canonical format can apply across an industry (and especially in B2B entities), achieving the required abstraction even within a single company is a challenge. In company X, for example, some divisions identify a customer by social security number (SSN), whereas others use a proprietary 11-digit format. The canonical XML form of

---

* A canonical format is a common format for exchanging information, and can apply across an industry (for example, the OAGIS standard from the Open Applications Group) or an enterprise.

customer for company X supports both, as well as common forms of name, addresses, and phones:

```
<Customer>
   <Name/>
   <Addresses/>
   <Phones/>
   <SSN/>
   <OurWeird11DigitID/>
</Customer>
```

In addition to its open interface, a Message Broker helps existing applications participate by providing adapter-based integration. If system Y's inbound interface is binary over named pipe, for example, but the Message Broker expects it to offer a web service that accepts canonical XML, then system Y requires an adapter that exposes itself as a web service that accepts canonical XML, but internally transforms the XML to binary and sends the binary on the named pipe. Message Broker interfaces with the adapter as it would with any other participant, unaware of the internal adaptation.

> ### NOTE
> An *adapter* is a component that helps plug an external system (e.g., SAP, Siebel, or a mainframe application) into a particular infrastructure. An adapter always has two parts: the part that knows how to converse with the external system and the part that fits into the infrastructure. In a BPM message broker, that infrastructure is web services; the adapter delivers messages from the external system to the process by calling the process's web service; the process calls the adapter's service to deliver messages to the system.

BPM and Message Broker

Having *N* systems connect to a central broker over common transports and with canonical messaging is worthless unless the central broker performs useful work. The precise work required by the broker is company-specific, but it generally involves listening for inbound messages, sending outbound messages, and performing rule-based logic in between.

BPM is the perfect candidate for implementing this functionality. As Figure 11-2 illustrates, the flow logic of a BPM process can be coded to listen for inbound canonical messages from one application, and to send a canonical message (after some decision making) to an application through its adapter, and to then wait for its response.

Although BPM is a good fit here, several considerations are worth noting:

- Processes used in the broker are for enterprise *infrastructure*, and are not intended to serve the needs of a particular line of business. They are for routing across lines of business, and thus are not *business* processes per se.

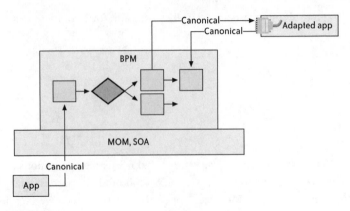

FIGURE 11-2. *Message Broker architecture*

- Routing is not a single, universal process, but, for a given company, a specific set of processes. Significant custom development is always required. Never buy a message broker product that positions itself as the HAL of the enterprise.

- A broker process is more like a choreography than an orchestration because its purpose is the management of participants—even if they are intraenterprise applications and not external parties, rather than logic of particular scenario.

The final point suggests that choreography standards such as WS-CDL are more suitable broker-process technologies than are pure BPM models such as BPEL. Perhaps, but BPEL also fits, and its immense lead in vendor support makes it the clear winner. A BPEL broker process, as we will discuss later, has a distinctive message communication look: numerous partner links and receive, reply, and invoke activities.

The architecture supporting a BPM message broker should resemble the one presented in Chapter 2: a graphical modeling tool that can export BPEL code to execute on a runtime processor; an adapter-based systems interface; and administration and monitoring capabilities with an extensible data model. The elements used in this chapter's example are a BPMN modeling tool from ITPearls (with no export capability) and a BPEL engine with administration, monitoring, and adapters from Oracle; adapter capabilities are not demonstrated here.

Example: Employee Benefits Message Broker

This example illustrates how a hypothetical company might use BPM to implement a message broker. Company X is building a new messaging infrastructure for its various employee benefits systems. As illustrated in Figure 11-3, at the center of this infrastructure is a BPM-based message broker for medical and life insurance that manages interactions between the Human Resources department (HR), the Payroll department, and HR Portal applications and systems (see following explanation).

ENTERPRISE SERVICE BUS

A message broker is a central hub for application communication in a single enterprise. The grander notion of Enterprise Service Bus (ESB), being promised currently by seemingly every integration vendor and solution provider, describes a decentralized, distributed, extended-enterprise messaging router. Applications scattered across several distinct companies can plug into a common ESB bus and communicate with one another. This model, if and when it becomes real, is a marked improvement over today's state of affairs, in which most companies do not even have an intraenterprise broker, and even for those that do, communicating with other enterprises is a comparatively complicated solution.

A good presentation of ESB, including the use of BPEL for orchestration, is found in O'Reilly's *Enterprise Service Bus* by Dave Chappell.

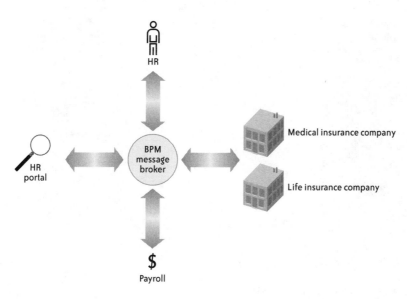

FIGURE 11-3. *Employee benefits broker architecture*

The main source of messages is HR Portal, a new web application that allows the company's employees to manage some of their own HR needs. A few of the tasks that HR Portal allows include:

- Recording various life events that affect coverage, such as births or marriages

- Modifying pension contributions

- Adjusting medical insurance coverage; for instance, increasing dental coverage or decreasing vision care

The changes are sent to the broker, which applies rules in its processes to route them to HR, Payroll, and insurance companies. Communications with the broker are through web services. Messages are represented in a canonical XML form.

BPMN Process Models

In this example, the broker has three main processes: a Life Event process to handle life events, a Pension process to handle pension changes, and a Medical process to handle insurance changes. Although we will code the processes in BPEL, we begin by modeling them in the leading graphical notation standard, BPMN; design should always precede implementation! The BPMN modeling tool that we will use is ITpearls' Process Modeler 2. 0, which is nothing more than a stencil for Microsoft Visio 2000. To draw a BPMN diagram, create a new Visio drawing and drag symbols from the BPMN stencil onto the page. The software, and a free evaluation license, can be downloaded from *http://www.itp-commerce.com/processmodeler/*. The tool is shown in Figure 11-4.

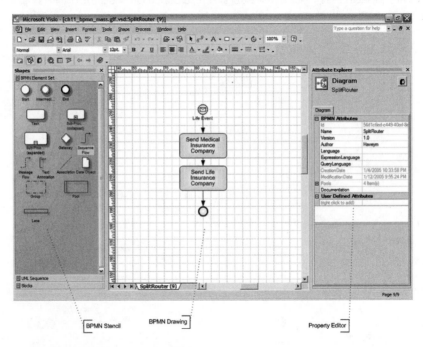

FIGURE 11-4. *BPMN Modeler using ITpearls' in MS Visio*

NOTE

Alas! ITpearls' product does not currently support BPEL export, so it cannot generate BPEL code directly from our BPMN diagrams. We will use BPMN strictly for visual design, and code the BPEL processes from scratch, guided by the BPMN blueprints.

The Life Event process

Figure 11-5 shows the BPMN diagram for the Life Event process. The process is started on receipt of a Life Event message, which is then sent in successive steps to the medical and life insurance companies. Although exceedingly simple, the process performs an important publish-subscribe function; if it did not exist, some other, less elegant, ad hoc mechanism would be required to deliver life events to the insurance companies.

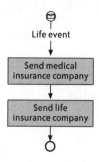

FIGURE 11-5. *BPMN diagram for the Life Event process*

The Pension process

The Pension process, shown in Figure 11-6, is more complicated and exhibits several workflow and EAI patterns. The process begins by receiving an event requesting a change in pension contribution amount. The process then branches into two conditional paths using an inclusive-OR gateway (the topmost diamond with a circle inside). If the contribution to be changed is the company's contribution, the path beginning with the Send HR activity is followed. If the change is to the employee's contribution, the Send payroll activity is run. If both conditions hold, both paths are followed. The bottommost inclusive-OR gateway joins the paths, waiting for both to complete before allowing the process to complete. The split and join patterns used here are, respectively, the Multiple Choice and Synchronizing Merge patterns (documented in Chapter 4).

The process also exhibits the Content-Based Routing EAI patterns described in Gregor Hohpe's catalog at *http://www.eaipatterns.com*.* The process examines its initial pension event for information that determines whether the change is for the company, the employee, or both. Based on that decision, the process proceeds to send the message to HR (for company contribution), Payroll (for employee contribution), or both; in other words, the process routes the message based on content.

On the HR path, after sending the message to the HR system, the process waits for a confirmation event. The Payroll path is simpler, having a send to Payroll but no confirmation.

---

*   See also G. Hohpe, B. Woolf, *Enterprise Integration Patterns: Designing, Building, and Deploying Messaging Solutions*, Addison-Wesley, 2003 (*http://ww.eaipatterns.com*).

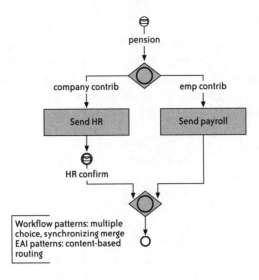

FIGURE 11-6. *BPMN diagram for the Pension process*

The Medical process

The process handling medical coverage changes is the hardest and most interesting of our examples. The HR portal gathers information from the employee on five separate web pages—each gathering information on employees, spouses, dependents, coordination of benefits (COB), and beneficiaries, respectively—and sends a message for each page to the broker. But the HR back-end system requires a single, consolidated message. The responsibility of the broker process is to gather each of the portal messages, combine them, and submit to HR.

The BPMN diagram is shown in Figure 11-7. Because of the complexity (contrived complexity, rigged to make the process more interesting), the logic is divided into two processes, Main and Helper, drawn as swim lanes in the pool Medical Benefits Application. The Main process simply listens for one of the five message types, adds to it a special Session ID field, and sends the modified message to the Helper process. The Session ID has the same value for each message in a five-message sequence but is unique to that sequence. The field is calculated based on the field MsgID, a unique number found in each HR portal message; related messages are indexed off this base value. As we've defined it in this example, the MsgID for an Employee message is always a multiple of five (e.g., 30); the Spousal message is that number plus 1 (e.g., 31); the Dependent message that number plus 2 (e.g., 32); the COB message that number plus 3 (e.g., 33); and the Beneficiaries message that number plus 4 (e.g., 34). The Session ID is calculated as MsgID div 5, which means the value of the MsgID field divided by 5, truncated to an integer (e.g., 6 for any MsgId value in the range 30 to 34).

Table 11-1 demonstrates the math for two sequences.

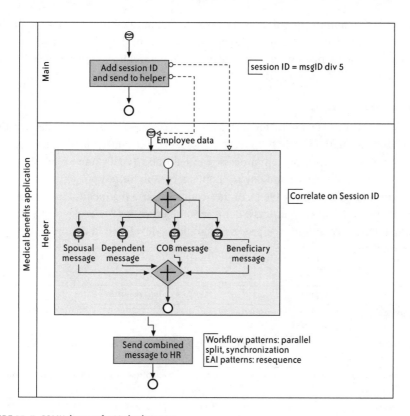

FIGURE 11-7. *BPMN diagram for Medical process*

TABLE 11-1. *Message ID and Session ID for medical sequences*

Message ID	Message type	Session ID
30	Employee	6
31	Spousal	6
32	Dependents	6
33	COB	6
34	Beneficiaries	6
35	Employee	7
36	Spousal	7
37	Dependents	7
38	COB	7
39	Beneficiaries	7

The Helper process begins by receiving the first message in the session, Employee data, and then waits in parallel for each of the remaining four messages, correlating on the Session ID. When each of the messages has been gathered, the process combines them and sends to HR. Among the BPMN constructs used in this example are message links (dotted arrows depicting the flow of messages from Main to Helper), an expanded subprocess (Get remaining messages), and the use of the AND gateway (a diamond with a plus sign) to model the workflow patterns Parallel Split and Synchronization. On the subject of patterns, the combining of messages into a single message is essentially the EAI pattern Resequencer, also described in the EAI patterns catalog.

BPEL Processes

Now that we have a BPMN model for each major process, we're ready to implement the Message Broker using the Oracle BPEL Process Manager (introduced in Chapter 10). The full implementation consists of eight processes: one for Life Events; one for Pension; two for Medical (main and helper); and one to simulate, or stub for test purposes, each of the target systems—HR, Payroll, the life insurance company, and the medical insurance company. Table 11-2 lists each process. Because some processes under development require the interfaces of others, the processes should be developed in the order they appear in the table.

TABLE 11-2. *BPEL process summary*

Process	Purpose	Design notes
Pension service	Simulates service interface of company's pension system.	
HR service	Simulates service interface of company's HR system.	When called, automatically sends back confirmation.
Life insurance company	Simulates life insurance company Life Event service.	Implements standard WSDL interface for Life Event subscription.
Medical insurance company	Simulates medical insurance company Life Event service.	Implements standard WSDL interface for Life Event subscription.
MB Life Event publisher	Publishes life event messages to life and medical insurance companies.	Uses dynamic addressing.
MB Pension	Routes pension adjustment messages to HR and/or Payroll systems.	
MB Med Helper	Aggregates a five-message medical adjustment sequence and sends it to the HR system.	
MB Med Main	Listens for medical adjustment messages and routes them to MB Med Helper, adding a correlating Session ID to each.	

This chapter walks you through the step-by-step mechanics of developing processes in Oracle BPEL Process Designer. You can also refer to Chapter 10 for a click-by-click account of how to create, code, and build processes in this tool.

Canonical XML

The first step in the implementation is to define a canonical XML message structure called CanonicalBenefits that describes how information is exchanged between broker processes and systems. This type, defined in lines 9–32 in the code sample Example 11-1 (the complete listing of *canon.wsdl*), captures information about the employee (empid, empname,

empdivision) and the type of message (msgtype, msgsubtype), and contains numeric message
identifiers (msgid, sesid), and a free-text field (data) whose meaning is application-specific.
The listing also defines a WSDL message type, BenefitsMessage (lines 35–37), intended as
the input or output type of every web service operation used in this example. Lines 41–48
define BPEL properties for use in correlation of the msgid or sesid fields of the canonical
message.

EXAMPLE 11-1. *canon.wsdl*

```
1   <?xml version="1.0"?>
2   <definitions name="canon"
3       targetNamespace="http://acm.org/samples"
4       xmlns:tns="http://acm.org/samples"
5       xmlns:bpws="http://schemas.xmlsoap.org/ws/2003/03/business-process/"
6       xmlns:xsd="http://www.w3.org/2001/XMLSchema"
7       xmlns="http://schemas.xmlsoap.org/wsdl/">
8
9   <types>
10      <schema attributeFormDefault="qualified"
11          elementFormDefault="qualified"
12          targetNamespace="http://acm.org/samples"
13          xmlns="http://www.w3.org/2001/XMLSchema">
14
15          <!-- The schema definition for the CanonicalBenefits message, to be
16              used by all participants.  -->
17          <element name="CanonicalBenefits">
18              <complexType>
19                  <sequence>
20                      <element name="msgid" type="string" />
21                      <element name="sesid" type="string" />
22                      <element name="empid" type="string" />
23                      <element name="empname" type="string" />
24                      <element name="empdivision" type="string" />
25                      <element name="msgtype" type="string" />
26                      <element name="msgsubtype" type="string" />
27                      <element name="data" type="string"/>
28                  </sequence>
29              </complexType>
30          </element>
31      </schema>
32  </types>
33
34  <!-- The WSDL message type for the XML CanonicalBenefits message -->
35  <message name="BenefitsMessage">
36      <part name="payload" element="tns:CanonicalBenefits"/>
37  </message>
38
39  <!-- BPEL property aliases defined for both sesid and msgid.  Correlation
40      to be performed on each. -->
41  <bpws:property name="msgid" type="xsd:string"/>
42  <bpws:property name="sesid" type="xsd:string"/>
43  <bpws:propertyAlias propertyName="tns:msgid"
44      messageType="tns:BenefitsMessage" part="payload"
45      query="/tns:CanonicalBenefits/tns:msgid"/>
46  <bpws:propertyAlias propertyName="tns:sesid"
```

EXAMPLE 11-1. *canon.wsdl (continued)*

```
47        messageType="tns:BenefitsMessage" part="payload"
48        query="/tns:CanonicalBenefits/tns:sesid"/>
49  </definitions>
```

The greatest challenge in the construction of canonical XML is satisfying the data requirements of all participants. In this example, stakeholders from the HR Portal, the HR and Payroll systems, and the life and medical insurance companies would have met numerous times to agree upon the correct set of fields. Sometimes the diversity of these disparate applications makes complete consensus impossible, necessitating compromises such as the data field, which can be used in place of a more formal hierarchical structure because not everyone could agree on that structure.

The Life Event process

Once the canonical form is established, we can implement the processes themselves. The WSDL for Life Events is shown in Example 11-2. In its port type, declared in lines 26–30, the WSDL refers to the canonical message type BenefitsMessage, defined in *canon.wsdl*; the import in line 10 makes the artifacts of *canon.wsdl* available to this WSDL. The port type contains a single operation, called initiate.

The types declaration in lines 12–23 includes a second import, this time of the standard WS-Addressing schema. The relevance of this will be examined shortly.

EXAMPLE 11-2. *MBLifeEventPublisher.wsdl*

```
 1  <?xml version="1.0"?>
 2  <definitions name="MBLifeEventPublisher"
 3     targetNamespace="http://acm.org/samples"
 4     xmlns:tns="http://acm.org/samples"
 5     xmlns:plnk="http://schemas.xmlsoap.org/ws/2003/05/partner-link/"
 6     xmlns="http://schemas.xmlsoap.org/wsdl/"
 7     xmlns:wsa="http://schemas.xmlsoap.org/ws/2003/03/addressing">
 8
 9     <!-- Import canon.wsdl, because we need to reference its artifacts. -->
10     <import namespace="http://acm.org/samples" location="canon.wsdl"/>
11
12     <types>
13        <schema attributeFormDefault="qualified"
14           elementFormDefault="qualified"
15           targetNamespace="http://samples.otn.com"
16           xmlns="http://www.w3.org/2001/XMLSchema">
17
18           <!-- Need accesss to WS-addressing stuff too. -->
19           <import namespace=http://schemas.xmlsoap.org/ws/2003/03/addressing
20             schemaLocation="http://localhost:9700/orabpel/xmllib/ws-addressing.xsd"/>
21
22        </schema>
23     </types>
24
25     <!-- Supports a single operation "initiate" -->
26     <portType name="MBLifeEventPublisher">
```

EXAMPLE 11-2. *MBLifeEventPublisher.wsdl (continued)*

```
27        <operation name="initiate">
28            <input message="tns:BenefitsMessage"/>
29        </operation>
30    </portType>
31
32    <!-- Define partner link type for the port type  -->
33    <plnk:partnerLinkType name="MBLifeEventPublisher">
34        <plnk:role name="LifeEventPublisher">
35            <plnk:portType name="tns:MBLifeEventPublisher"/>
36        </plnk:role>
37    </plnk:partnerLinkType>
38 </definitions>
```

The process itself (Example 11-3) is a modest 78 lines, and the implementation logic starts with a receive activity on line 27, which corresponds to the WSDL-defined `initiate` operation. The canonical message passed to the process here originates in HR Portal and is routed to the medical and life insurance companies, in lines 33–54 and lines 56–76, respectively. The partner links for these companies are defined dynamically rather than statically, as is commonplace. The dynamic definition is achieved by building a WS-Addressing `EndpointReference` structure (lines 34–45 and 57–68), stipulating an explicit service address and name, and setting that structure as the value of the partner link (lines 46–49 and 69–72).

EXAMPLE 11-3. *MBLifeEventPublisher.bpel*

```
1  <process name="MBLifeEventPublisher"
2     targetNamespace="http://acm.org/samples"
3     suppressJoinFailure="yes" xmlns:tns=http://acm.org/samples
4     xmlns=http://schemas.xmlsoap.org/ws/2003/03/business-process/
5     xmlns:bpelx=http://schemas.oracle.com/bpel/extension
6     xmlns:ora=http://schemas.oracle.com/xpath/extension
7     xmlns:wsa=http://schemas.xmlsoap.org/ws/2003/03/addressing
8     xmlns:xsd=http://www.w3.org/2001/XMLSchema
9     xmlns:bpws="http://schemas.xmlsoap.org/ws/2003/03/business-process/">
10
11    <!-- Two partner links: one for the client that initates the process, the other
12         ("dynamicSubscriber") a placeholder for each registered subcriber -->
13    <partnerLinks>
14        <partnerLink name="client" partnerLinkType="tns:MBLifeEventPublisher"
15            myRole="LifeEventPublisher"/>
16        <partnerLink name="dynamicSubscriber"
17            partnerLinkType="tns:MBLifeEventSubscriber"
18            partnerRole="LifeEventSubscriber"/>
19    </partnerLinks>
20    <variables>
21        <variable name="input" messageType="tns:BenefitsMessage"/>
22        <!-- partnerRef is a pointer to a dynamic subscriber -->
23        <variable name="partnerRef" element="wsa:EndpointReference"/>
24    </variables>
25    <sequence name="main">
26        <!-- Step 1: Start by getting message from client via initiate method -->
27        <receive name="receiveInput" partnerLink="client" operation="initiate"
```

EXAMPLE 11-3. *MBLifeEventPublisher.bpel (continued)*

```
28              variable="input" createInstance="yes"
29              portType="tns:MBLifeEventPublisher"/>
30         <!-- Step 2: Set partnerRef with the value of the first subscriber:
31              the medical company.  Two data: (a) URL,
32              (b) must conform LifeEventSubscriber role -->
33         <assign name="assignPartner">
34           <copy>
35             <from>
36               <wsa:EndpointReference
37                 xmlns="http://schemas.xmlsoap.org/ws/2003/03/addressing">
38 <wsa:Address>http://localhost:9700/orabpel/default/MedicalInsuranceCompany
39 </wsa:Address>
40 <wsa:ServiceName xmlns:ns1="http://services.otn.com">ns1:MedicalInsuranceCompany
41 </wsa:ServiceName>
42               </wsa:EndpointReference>
43             </from>
44             <to variable="partnerRef"/>
45           </copy>
46           <copy>
47             <from variable="partnerRef"/>
48             <to partnerLink="dynamicSubscriber"/>
49           </copy>
50         </assign>
51         <!-- Step 3: Call the dynamic subscriber's serrvice -->
52         <invoke name="callPartner" partnerLink="dynamicSubscriber"
53           portType="tns:MBLifeEventSubscriber" operation="initiate"
54           inputVariable="input"/>
55         <!-- Step 4: repeat of Step 2, but URL is that of life insurance company -->
56         <assign name="assignPartner2">
57           <copy>
58             <from>
59               <wsa:EndpointReference
60                 xmlns="http://schemas.xmlsoap.org/ws/2003/03/addressing">
61 <wsa:Address>http://localhost:9700/orabpel/default/LifeInsuranceCompany
62 </wsa:Address>
63 <wsa:ServiceName xmlns:ns1="http://services.otn.com">ns1:LifeInsuranceCompany
64 </wsa:ServiceName>
65               </wsa:EndpointReference>
66             </from>
67             <to variable="partnerRef"/>
68           </copy>
69           <copy>
70             <from variable="partnerRef"/>
71             <to partnerLink="dynamicSubscriber"/>
72           </copy>
73         </assign>
74         <!-- Step 5: repeat of step 3 -->
75         <invoke partnerLink="dynamicSubscriber" portType="tns:MBLifeEventSubscriber"
76           operation="initiate" inputVariable="input" name="callPartner2"/>
77     </sequence>
78 </process>
```

The curious use of dynamic addressing in this example has the following advantage: the list of subscribers can be expanded without the need to create new partner links. One partner link suffices, and as the process iterates through its list of subscribers, it sets the link's endpoint, invokes the service, and continues. Each subscriber, of course, must implement a service of the type expected by the process. Although the endpoint is dynamic, the service definition is not. Each subscriber must build to the same WSDL, using the partner link type (in this case, MBLifeEventSubscriber) and the role (LifeEventSubscriber) specified in lines 16–18. In the subscriber WSDL, listed in Example 11-4, the operation initate takes as input the canonical BenefitsMessage payload.

EXAMPLE 11-4. *MBLifeEventSubscriber.wsdl*

```
1   <?xml version="1.0"?>
2   <definitions name="MBLifeEventSubscriber"
3      targetNamespace="http://acm.org/samples"
4      xmlns:tns="http://acm.org/samples"
5      xmlns:plnk="http://schemas.xmlsoap.org/ws/2003/05/partner-link/"
6      xmlns="http://schemas.xmlsoap.org/wsdl/"
7      xmlns:wsa="http://schemas.xmlsoap.org/ws/2003/03/addressing">
8
9      <import namespace="http://acm.org/samples" location="canon.wsdl"/>
10
11     <portType name="MBLifeEventSubscriber">
12        <operation name="initiate">
13           <input message="tns:BenefitsMessage"/>  <!-- canonical type -->
14        </operation>
15     </portType>
16
17     <!-- dynamic partner link referenced in BPEL above. -->
18     <plnk:partnerLinkType name="MBLifeEventSubscriber">
19        <plnk:role name="LifeEventSubscriber">
20           <plnk:portType name="tns:MBLifeEventSubscriber"/>
21        </plnk:role>
22     </plnk:partnerLinkType>
23   </definitions>
```

For test purposes, simple processes simulating services of the life and medical insurance companies are provided. Example 11-5 shows the life insurance process; the process simply swallows the Life Event process (received in lines 19–21) and exits. The code for the medical insurance company (not shown, but left as an exercise for the reader) is nearly identical.

EXAMPLE 11-5. *LifeInsuranceCompany.bpel*

```
1   <process
2      name="LifeInsuranceCompany" targetNamespace=http://acm.org/samples
3      suppressJoinFailure="yes"
4      xmlns:tns=http://acm.org/samples
5      xmlns=http://schemas.xmlsoap.org/ws/2003/03/business-process/
6      xmlns:bpelx=http://schemas.oracle.com/bpel/extension
7      xmlns:ora="http://schemas.oracle.com/xpath/extension">
8
9      <!-- supports MBLifeEventSubscriber partner link type -->
10     <partnerLinks>
11        <partnerLink name="client" myRole="LifeEventSubscriber"
```

EXAMPLE 11-5. *LifeInsuranceCompany.bpel (continued)*

```
12              partnerLinkType="tns:MBLifeEventSubscriber"/>
13      </partnerLinks>
14      <variables>
15        <variable name="input" messageType="tns:BenefitsMessage"/>
16      </variables>
17      <sequence name="main">
18        <!-- the simplest process possible: receive the message, and that's it -->
19        <receive name="receiveInput" partnerLink="client"
20          portType="tns:MBLifeEventSubscriber" operation="initiate" variable="input"
21          createInstance="yes"/>
22      </sequence>
23    </process>
```

The Pension process

The service interface of the Pension process, specified in the WSDL listing in
Example 11-6, consists of a single operation, called initiate, that accepts a canonical
benefits message.

EXAMPLE 11-6. *MBPension.wsdl*

```
1   <?xml version="1.0"?>
2   <definitions name="MBPension"
3       targetNamespace="http://acm.org/samples"
4       xmlns:tns="http://acm.org/samples"
5       xmlns:plnk="http://schemas.xmlsoap.org/ws/2003/05/partner-link/"
6       xmlns="http://schemas.xmlsoap.org/wsdl/">
7
8       <import namespace="http://acm.org/samples" location="canon.wsdl"/>
9
10      <portType name="MBPension">
11        <operation name="initiate">
12            <input message="tns:BenefitsMessage"/>
13        </operation>
14      </portType>
15
16      <plnk:partnerLinkType name="MBPension">
17        <plnk:role name="PensionProvider">
18            <plnk:portType name="tns:MBPension"/>
19        </plnk:role>
20      </plnk:partnerLinkType>
21    </definitions>
```

In the BPEL code for the process (Example 11-7), the receive activity in lines 27–28 starts
the process when the initiate operation is invoked. The remainder of the process (lines
29–60) implements an inclusive OR split and join with two switch statements inside a
flow, or two conditional sets of logic running in parallel. The first switch (lines 30–45)
searches the msgsubtype element of the initiating benefits message for the text "company";
if the pattern matches, the notify operation of the HR service is called (lines 35–36), and
the process waits for a confirmation (lines 37–39). The second switch (lines 46–57) calls
the pensionUpdate operation of the Pension service if the original benefits message
contains "employee."

EXAMPLE 11-7. *MBPension.bpel*

```
1  <process name="MBPension"
2    targetNamespace="http://acm.org/samples"
3    suppressJoinFailure="yes"
4    xmlns:tns=http://acm.org/samples
5    xmlns=http://schemas.xmlsoap.org/ws/2003/03/business-process/
6    xmlns:bpelx=http://schemas.oracle.com/bpel/extension
7    xmlns:ora=http://schemas.oracle.com/xpath/extension
8    xmlns:bpws="http://schemas.xmlsoap.org/ws/2003/03/business-process/">
9
10   <!-- three partner links: one for client that starts this process,
11        one for payroll and one for HR, each of which is conditionally
12        called by this process. -->
13   <partnerLinks>
14     <partnerLink name="client" partnerLinkType="tns:MBPension"
15       myRole="PensionProvider"/>
16     <partnerLink name="payroll" partnerLinkType="tns:PayrollService"
17       partnerRole="PayrollService"/>
18     <partnerLink name="hr" partnerLinkType="tns:HRPartnerLink"
19       partnerRole="HR" myRole="HRListener"/>
20   </partnerLinks>
21   <variables>
22     <variable name="input" messageType="tns:BenefitsMessage"/>
23     <variable name="hrConfirmation" messageType="tns:BenefitsMessage"/>
24   </variables>
25   <sequence name="main">
26     <!-- Step 1: the process is started by a client initate -->
27     <receive name="receiveInput" partnerLink="client" portType="tns:MBPension"
28       operation="initiate" variable="input" createInstance="yes"/>
29     <flow name="InclOR">
30       <switch name="companyContrib">
31         <!-- Step 2a: if "company" appears in the "msgsubtype" field, execute
32              the sequence that invokes HR and waits for its confirmation -->
33         <case condition="contains(bpws:getVariableData(&quot;input&quot;, &quot;payload&quot;,
&quot;/tns:CanonicalBenefits/tns:msgsubtype&quot;), string(&quot;company&quot;))">
34           <sequence>
35             <invoke name="sendHR" partnerLink="hr" operation="notify"
36               portType="tns:HRService" inputVariable="input"/>
37             <receive createInstance="no" name="confirm" partnerLink="hr"
38               portType="tns:HRCallback" operation="confirm"
39               variable="hrConfirmation"/>
40           </sequence>
41         </case>
42         <otherwise>
43           <empty name="nop"/>
44         </otherwise>
45       </switch>
46       <switch name="empContrib">
47         <!-- Step 2b: if "employee" appears in the "msgsubtype" field, execute
48              the sequence that invokes pension -->
49         <case condition="contains(bpws:getVariableData(&quot;input&quot;, &quot;payload&quot;,
&quot;/tns:CanonicalBenefits/tns:msgsubtype&quot;), string(&quot;employee&quot;))">
50           <invoke name="sendPayroll" partnerLink="payroll"
51             portType="tns:PayrollService" operation="pensionUpdate"
52             inputVariable="input"/>
53         </case>
```

EXAMPLE 11-7. *MBPension.bpel (continued)*

```
54                <otherwise>
55                    <empty name="nop"/>
56                </otherwise>
57            </switch>
58        </flow>
59    </sequence>
60 </process>
```

Stubbed implementations of the Payroll and HR services are shown in the next listings. The Payroll service is exceedingly simple, listening on its pensionUpdate endpoint (defined in lines 12–14 the WSDL in Example 11-8, and implemented as a receive activity in lines 18–20 of the BPEL in Example 11-9), and exiting immediately thereafter.

EXAMPLE 11-8. *PayrollService.wsdl*

```
1  <?xml version="1.0"?>
2  <definitions name="PayrollService"
3     targetNamespace="http://acm.org/samples"
4     xmlns:tns="http://acm.org/samples"
5     xmlns:plnk="http://schemas.xmlsoap.org/ws/2003/05/partner-link/"
6     xmlns="http://schemas.xmlsoap.org/wsdl/">
7
8     <import namespace="http://acm.org/samples" location="canon.wsdl"/>
9
10    <!-- Payroll port type supports pensionUpdate operation -->
11    <portType name="PayrollService">
12       <operation name="pensionUpdate">
13          <input message="tns:BenefitsMessage"/>
14       </operation>
15    </portType>
16
17    <!-- And here is its partner link type -->
18    <plnk:partnerLinkType name="PayrollService">
19       <plnk:role name="PayrollService">
20          <plnk:portType name="tns:PayrollService"/>
21       </plnk:role>
22    </plnk:partnerLinkType>
23 </definitions>
```

The next code listing is for Example 11-9.

EXAMPLE 11-9. *PayrollService.bpel*

```
1  <process name="PayrollService"
2     targetNamespace="http://acm.org/samples"
3     suppressJoinFailure="yes"
4     xmlns:tns=http://acm.org/samples
5     xmlns=http://schemas.xmlsoap.org/ws/2003/03/business-process/
6     xmlns:bpelx=http://schemas.oracle.com/bpel/extension
7     xmlns:ora="http://schemas.oracle.com/xpath/extension">
8     <!-- PayrollService partner link type is the one defined in the WSDL. -->
9     <partnerLinks>
10       <partnerLink name="client" partnerLinkType="tns:PayrollService"
11          myRole="PayrollService"/>
```

EXAMPLE 11-9. *PayrollService.bpel (continued)*

```
12        </partnerLinks>
13        <variables>
14          <variable name="input" messageType="tns:BenefitsMessage"/>
15        </variables>
16        <sequence name="main">
17          <!-- A simple process: get the message and then exit -->
18          <receive name="receiveInput" partnerLink="client"
19            portType="tns:PayrollService" variable="input" createInstance="yes"
20            operation="pensionUpdate"/>
21        </sequence>
22      </process>
```

The HR service is similar, except upon the trigger of its notify service (declared in lines 12–14 of the WSDL in Example 11-10 and implemented in the BPEL in lines 17–19 of Example 11-11), it immediately sends back a confirmation on its callback port type (the invoke activity is shown in lines 21–23 of Example 11-11. The next listing, Example 11-10, is for *HRService.wsdl*.

EXAMPLE 11-10. *HRService.wsdl*

```
1   <?xml version="1.0"?>
2   <definitions name="MBPension"
3     targetNamespace="http://acm.org/samples"
4     xmlns:tns="http://acm.org/samples"
5     xmlns:plnk="http://schemas.xmlsoap.org/ws/2003/05/partner-link/"
6     xmlns="http://schemas.xmlsoap.org/wsdl/">
7
8     <import namespace="http://acm.org/samples" location="canon.wsdl"/>
9
10    <!-- Two port types: the service and its callback -->
11    <portType name="HRService">
12      <operation name="notify">
13        <input message="tns:BenefitsMessage"/>
14      </operation>
15    </portType>
16    <portType name="HRCallback">
17      <operation name="confirm">
18        <input message="tns:BenefitsMessage"/>
19      </operation>
20    </portType>
21
22    <!-- A partner link type for each port type -->
23    <plnk:partnerLinkType name="HRPartnerLink">
24      <plnk:role name="HR">
25        <plnk:portType name="tns:HRService"/>
26      </plnk:role>
27      <plnk:role name="HRListener">
28        <plnk:portType name="tns:HRCallback"/>
29      </plnk:role>
30    </plnk:partnerLinkType>
31  </definitions>
```

The next listing, Example 11-11, is for *HRService.bpel*.

EXAMPLE 11-11. *HRService.bpel*

```
1   <process name="HRService"
2     targetNamespace="http://acm.org/samples"
3     suppressJoinFailure="yes"
4     xmlns:tns="http://acm.org/samples"
5     xmlns="http://schemas.xmlsoap.org/ws/2003/03/business-process/"
6     xmlns:bpelx="http://schemas.oracle.com/bpel/extension"
7     xmlns:ora="http://schemas.oracle.com/xpath/extension">
8     <partnerLinks>
9       <partnerLink name="client" partnerLinkType="tns:HRPartnerLink"
10          partnerRole="HRListener" myRole="HR"/>
11    </partnerLinks>
12    <variables>
13      <variable name="input" messageType="tns:BenefitsMessage"/>
14    </variables>
15    <sequence name="main">
16      <!-- Step 1: client interface receiveInput is called -->
17      <receive name="receiveInput" partnerLink="client"
18          portType="tns:HRService" variable="input"
19          createInstance="yes" operation="notify"/>
20    <!-- Step 2: immediately invoke callback confirm, passing back same msg -->
21      <invoke name="confirm" partnerLink="client"
22          portType="tns:HRCallback" operation="confirm"
23          inputVariable="input"/>
24    </sequence>
25  </process>
```

The Medical process

As described at the beginning of this chapter, the Medical process is divided into two sections, Main and Helper (discussed in the next two sections), to simplify the implementation.

Main. The Main medical process, when it receives a benefits message, adds to the message a session ID, and sends that message to the Helper process. The WSDL for the main process (Example 11-12) is simple, having but one port type operation, called initiate, declared in line 11.

EXAMPLE 11-12. *MBMedMain.wsdl*

```
1   <?xml version="1.0"?>
2   <definitions name="MBMedMain"
3     targetNamespace="http://acm.org/samples"
4     xmlns:tns="http://acm.org/samples"
5     xmlns:plnk="http://schemas.xmlsoap.org/ws/2003/05/partner-link/"
6     xmlns="http://schemas.xmlsoap.org/wsdl/">
7
8     <import namespace="http://acm.org/samples" location="canon.wsdl"/>
9
10    <portType name="MBMedMain">
11      <operation name="initiate">
12        <input message="tns:BenefitsMessage"/>
13      </operation>
14    </portType>
15
```

EXAMPLE 11-12. *MBMedMain.wsdl (continued)*

```
16      <plnk:partnerLinkType name="MBMedMain">
17        <plnk:role name="MedMainProvider">
18          <plnk:portType name="tns:MBMedMain"/>
19        </plnk:role>
20      </plnk:partnerLinkType>
21    </definitions>
```

In the BPEL implementation (Example 11-13), the receive activity in lines 23–24 is the entry point mapping to the initiate operation. The long assign activity that follows it, spanning lines 25–45, calculates the value of MsgID div 5 (lines 27–31), then sets the SesID field with that value (lines 39–44). It also calculates MsgId mod 5 (lines 33–37), a value representing the remainder when dividing the message ID by 5. This value is zero for the first message in the five-message medical sequence, and nonzero for subsequent messages. The switch statement in lines 46–59 tests this number to determine how to call the helper process; if the value is zero, it calls the Helper's first operation (lines 49–51); otherwise, it calls the Helper's next operation (lines 55–57).

EXAMPLE 11-13. *MBMedMain.bpel*

```
1    <process name="MBMedMain"
2      targetNamespace="http://acm.org/samples"
3      suppressJoinFailure="yes"
4      xmlns:tns=http://acm.org/samples
5      xmlns=http://schemas.xmlsoap.org/ws/2003/03/business-process/
6      xmlns:bpelx=http://schemas.oracle.com/bpel/extension
7      xmlns:ora=http://schemas.oracle.com/xpath/extension
8      xmlns:bpws=http://schemas.xmlsoap.org/ws/2003/03/business-process/
9      xmlns:xsd="http://www.w3.org/2001/XMLSchema">
10     <partnerLinks>
11       <partnerLink name="client" partnerLinkType="tns:MBMedMain"
12         myRole="MedMainProvider"/>
13       <partnerLink name="helper" partnerLinkType="tns:MBMedHelper"
14         partnerRole="MedHelperProvider"/>
15     </partnerLinks>
16     <variables>
17       <variable name="input" messageType="tns:BenefitsMessage"/>
18       <variable name="msgDiv" type="xsd:int"/>
19       <variable name="msgMod" type="xsd:int"/>
20     </variables>
21     <sequence name="main">
22       <!-- Step 1: get the message from the HR portal -->
23       <receive name="receiveInput" partnerLink="client" portType="tns:MBMedMain"
24         operation="initiate" variable="input" createInstance="yes"/>
25       <assign name="assignVars">
26         <!-- Step 2a: set variable msgDiv to MsgId div 5 -->
27         <copy>
28           <from expression="floor(bpws:
getVariableData(&quot;input&quot;,&quot;payload&quot;,&quot;/tns:CanonicalBenefits/tns:msgid&quot;)
div 5)">
29           </from>
30           <to variable="msgDiv"/>
31         </copy>
```

EXAMPLE 11-13. *MBMedMain.bpel (continued)*

```
32            <!-- Step 2b: set variable msgMod to MsgId mod 5 -->
33            <copy>
34               <from expression="bpws:getVariableData(&quot;input&quot;,&quot;payload&quot;,&quot;
tns:CanonicalBenefits/tns:msgid&quot;) mod 5">
35               </from>
36               <to variable="msgMod"/>
37            </copy>
38            <!-- Step 2c: populate SesId field with msgDiv -->
39            <copy>
40               <from expression="bpws:getVariableData(&quot;msgDiv&quot;)">
41               </from>
42               <to variable="input" part="payload"
43                  query="/tns:CanonicalBenefits/tns:sesid"/>
44            </copy>
45         </assign>
46         <switch name="switch-1">
47            <!-- If MsgMod = 0, call helper's "first" operation -->
48            <case condition="bpws:getVariableData(&quot;msgMod&quot;)='0'">
49               <invoke name="invoke-1" partnerLink="helper"
50                  portType="tns:MBMedHelper" operation="first"
51                  inputVariable="input"/>
52            </case>
53            <!-- If MsgMod != 0, call helper's "next" operation -->
54            <otherwise>
55               <invoke name="invoke-1" partnerLink="helper"
56                  portType="tns:MBMedHelper" operation="next"
57                  inputVariable="input"/>
58            </otherwise>
59         </switch>
60      </sequence>
61 </process>
```

Helper. The Helper's first and next operations are declared in lines 11 and 14, respectively, of its WSDL in Example 11-14.

EXAMPLE 11-14. *MBMedHelper.wsdl*

```
1  <?xml version="1.0"?>
2  <definitions name="MBMedHelper"
3     targetNamespace="http://acm.org/samples"
4     xmlns:tns="http://acm.org/samples"
5     xmlns:plnk="http://schemas.xmlsoap.org/ws/2003/05/partner-link/"
6     xmlns="http://schemas.xmlsoap.org/wsdl/">
7
8     <import namespace="http://acm.org/samples" location="canon.wsdl"/>
9
10    <portType name="MBMedHelper">
11       <operation name="first">
12          <input message="tns:BenefitsMessage"/>
13       </operation>
14       <operation name="next">
15          <input message="tns:BenefitsMessage"/>
16       </operation>
17    </portType>
18
```

EXAMPLE 11-14. *MBMedHelper.wsdl (continued)*

```
19      <plnk:partnerLinkType name="MBMedHelper">
20        <plnk:role name="MedHelperProvider">
21          <plnk:portType name="tns:MBMedHelper"/>
22        </plnk:role>
23      </plnk:partnerLinkType>
24   </definitions>
```

Example 11-15, is initiated in the receive activity in lines 30–36; the receive is mapped to the first operation and initializes a correlation set on the session ID field. The flow activity in lines 39–68 has four receive operations, running in parallel, each mapped to the next operation and correlating on session ID. The flow activity waits for each receive to complete, whereupon the process has gathered all five of the original messages, stored in process variables msg1, msg2, msg3, msg4, and msg5. The assign activity in lines 71–101 combines them into a single message, stored in the variable combinedMsg; it first copies msg1 to combinedMsg (lines 73–76), then appends the element called data of each other message to the data element of combinedMsg. In lines 103–104, combinedMsg is sent to the notify operation of the HR Service.

EXAMPLE 11-15. *MBMedHelper.bpel*

```
1   <process name="MBMedHelper"
2      targetNamespace="http://acm.org/samples"
3      suppressJoinFailure="yes"
4      xmlns:tns=http://acm.org/samples
5      xmlns=http://schemas.xmlsoap.org/ws/2003/03/business-process/
6      xmlns:bpelx=http://schemas.oracle.com/bpel/extension
7      xmlns:ora=http://schemas.oracle.com/xpath/extension
8      xmlns:bpws="http://schemas.xmlsoap.org/ws/2003/03/business-process/">
9
10     <partnerLinks>
11       <partnerLink name="client" partnerLinkType="tns:MBMedHelper"
12         myRole="MedHelperProvider"/>
13       <partnerLink name="hr" partnerLinkType="tns:HRPartnerLink" partnerRole="HR"/>
14     </partnerLinks>
15     <variables>
16       <variable name="msg1" messageType="tns:BenefitsMessage"/>
17       <variable name="msg2" messageType="tns:BenefitsMessage"/>
18       <variable name="msg3" messageType="tns:BenefitsMessage"/>
19       <variable name="msg4" messageType="tns:BenefitsMessage"/>
20       <variable name="msg5" messageType="tns:BenefitsMessage"/>
21       <variable name="combinedMsg" messageType="tns:BenefitsMessage"/>
22     </variables>
23     <correlationSets>
24       <correlationSet name="ses" properties="tns:sesid"/>
25     </correlationSets>
26     <sequence>
27       <sequence name="main">
28         <!-- Step 1: the "first" operation called.  Store the message in "msg1".
29              Correlate on SesId -->
30         <receive name="receiveInput" partnerLink="client"
31            portType="tns:MBMedHelper" variable="msg1" createInstance="yes"
32            operation="first">
```

EXAMPLE 11-15. *MBMedHelper.bpel (continued)*

```
33                <correlations>
34                    <correlation set="ses" initiate="yes"/>
35                </correlations>
36            </receive>
37            <!-- Step 2: wait for 4 calls of next, where each correlates on sesId.
38                Store results in msg2, msg3, msg4, msg5 -->
39            <flow>
40                <receive name="receiveInput" partnerLink="client"
41                    portType="tns:MBMedHelper" operation="next" variable="msg2"
42                    createInstance="no">
43                    <correlations>
44                        <correlation set="ses" initiate="no"/>
45                    </correlations>
46                </receive>
47                <receive name="receiveInput" partnerLink="client"
48                    portType="tns:MBMedHelper" operation="next" variable="msg3"
49                    createInstance="no">
50                    <correlations>
51                        <correlation set="ses" initiate="no"/>
52                    </correlations>
53                </receive>
54                <receive name="receiveInput" partnerLink="client"
55                    portType="tns:MBMedHelper" operation="next" variable="msg4"
56                    createInstance="no">
57                    <correlations>
58                        <correlation set="ses" initiate="no"/>
59                    </correlations>
60                </receive>
61                <receive name="receiveInput" partnerLink="client"
62                    portType="tns:MBMedHelper" operation="next" variable="msg5"
63                    createInstance="no">
64                    <correlations>
65                        <correlation set="ses" initiate="no"/>
66                    </correlations>
67                </receive>
68            </flow>
69        </sequence>
70        <!-- Step 3: Build "combinedMsg" out of msg1 . . msg 5 -->
71        <assign xmlns="http://schemas.xmlsoap.org/ws/2003/03/business-process/"
72            name="buildMsg">
73            <copy>
74                <from variable="msg1"></from>
75                <to variable="combinedMsg"/>
76            </copy>
77            <copy>
78                <from expression="concat(bpws:getVariableData(&quot;combinedMsg&quot;,
&quot;payload&quot;, &quot;/tns:CanonicalBenefits/tns:data&quot;), bpws:
getVariableData(&quot;msg2&quot;, &quot;payload&quot;, &quot;/tns:CanonicalBenefits/tns:data&quot;
79                </from>
80                <to variable="combinedMsg" part="payload"
81                    query="/tns:CanonicalBenefits/tns:data"/>
82            </copy>
83            <copy>
```

EXAMPLE 11-15. *MBMedHelper.bpel (continued)*

```
84              <from expression="concat(bpws:getVariableData(&quot;combinedMsg&quot;,
&quot;payload&quot;, &quot;/tns:CanonicalBenefits/tns:data&quot;), bpws:
getVariableData(&quot;msg3&quot;, &quot;payload&quot;, &quot;/tns:CanonicalBenefits/tns:data&quot;))">
85              </from>
86              <to variable="combinedMsg" part="payload"
87                  query="/tns:CanonicalBenefits/tns:data"/>
88          </copy>
89          <copy>
90              <from expression="concat(bpws:getVariableData(&quot;combinedMsg&quot;,
&quot;payload&quot;, &quot;/tns:CanonicalBenefits/tns:data&quot;), bpws:
getVariableData(&quot;msg4&quot;, &quot;payload&quot;, &quot;/tns:CanonicalBenefits/tns:data&quot;))">
91              </from>
92              <to variable="combinedMsg" part="payload"
93                  query="/tns:CanonicalBenefits/tns:data"/>
94          </copy>
95          <copy>
96              <from expression="concat(bpws:getVariableData(&quot;combinedMsg&quot;,
&quot;payload&quot;, &quot;/tns:CanonicalBenefits/tns:data&quot;), bpws:
getVariableData(&quot;msg5&quot;, &quot;payload&quot;, &quot;/tns:CanonicalBenefits/tns:data&quot;))">
97              </from>
98              <to variable="combinedMsg" part="payload"
99                  query="/tns:CanonicalBenefits/tns:data"/>
100         </copy>
101     </assign>
102     <!-- Step 4: call HR service, passing "combinedMsg" -->
103     <invoke name="sendHR" partnerLink="hr" portType="tns:HRService"
104         operation="notify" inputVariable="combinedMsg"/>
105   </sequence>
106 </process>
```

Testing the Broker

The Initiate Process page in the Oracle BPEL administrative console can be the source of
events driving broker interactions to simulate the HR Portal. Figure 11-8 shows the page
to test the Life Events process. The text edit fields (msgid, sesid) are the elements of the
canonical XML structure, the message type used by all broker processes. To trigger Life
Events, enter data in some or all of the fields, and click Post XML Message. The process
does not validate the data, so any input will suffice.

If successful, the Life Events process will start the processes Life Insurance Company and
Medical Insurance Company. To confirm this, navigate to the Dashboard tab and check
for these processes under Recently Completed BPEL Process Instances. In Figure 11-9,
Life Event (instance 703) is immediately followed by Medical Insurance Company (704)
and Life Insurance Company (705), implying that Life Event functioned properly.

The procedure to test the Pension process is similar. Pension checks the value of the field
msgsubtype. If the field contains the text "company," Pension starts the HR Service process;
if it contains "employee," Pension triggers Payroll Service; if it contains both (e.g.,
"company and employee"), Pension launches both. As with Life Events, the Dashboard is

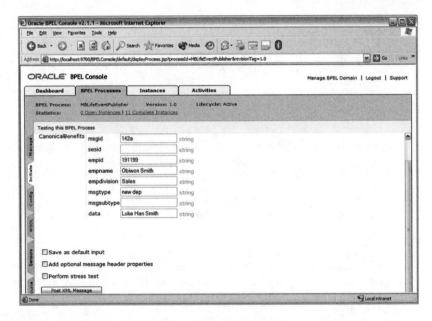

FIGURE 11-8. *Oracle BPEL Console test utility*

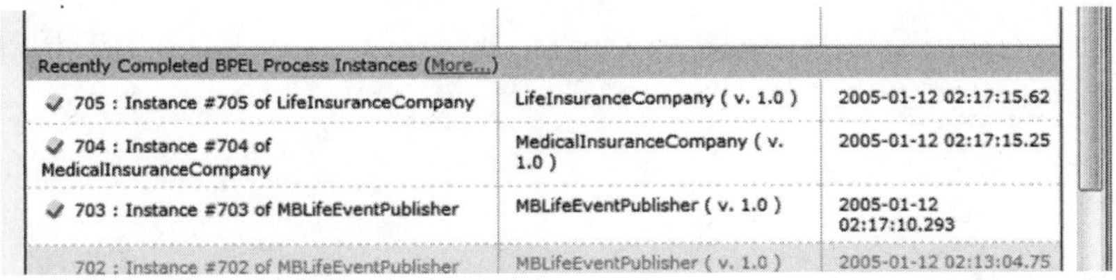

Recently Completed BPEL Process Instances (More...)		
✓ 705 : Instance #705 of LifeInsuranceCompany	LifeInsuranceCompany (v. 1.0)	2005-01-12 02:17:15.62
✓ 704 : Instance #704 of MedicalInsuranceCompany	MedicalInsuranceCompany (v. 1.0)	2005-01-12 02:17:15.25
✓ 703 : Instance #703 of MBLifeEventPublisher	MBLifeEventPublisher (v. 1.0)	2005-01-12 02:17:10.293
702 : Instance #702 of MBLifeEventPublisher	MBLifeEventPublisher (v. 1.0)	2005-01-12 02:13:04.75

FIGURE 11-9. *Dashboard confirmation of Life Event process*

the quickest indicator of success: check for target processes immediately following the initiation of Pension.

To exercise Medical, run five initiations of Medical Main using values of msgid that follow the rules described in the earlier section "BPMN Process Models"; the values should follow an ascending sequence at a multiple of five (e.g., 30, 31, 32, 33, 34). Check the Dashboard for five instances of Medical Main, one Medical Helper, and one HR Service, as in instances 801 to 807 in Figure 11-10.

Summary

The main points in this chapter include the following:

- Hyped by vendors and consultants, the Message Broker is not a technological break-through but a sensible solution to the common problem of intersystem interactions in the enterprise.

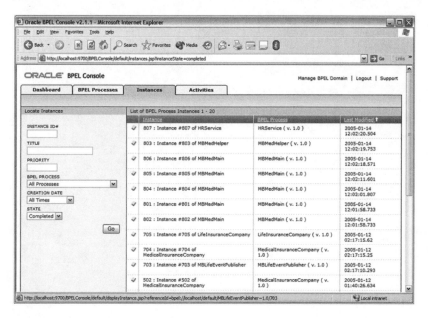

FIGURE 11-10. *Dashboard confirmation of medical process*

- One manifestation of that problem is the proliferation of point-to-point interfaces. In the worst case, if there are N systems and each connects to each other, the number of required interfaces is $N * (N - 1)/2$. But if each system connects solely to the central hub of Message Broker, only N connections are needed.

- The quantity of connections is one concern, but even more troublesome is the quality. The diversity of interface transport mechanisms and messaging formats in a large enterprise is unmanageable. To introduce Message Broker into a corporate architecture requires standardization of these layers, including the adoption of technologies such as ESB and canonical XML. Systems that cannot be reworked to fit this model require adapters.

- BPM is a good technology fit for Message Broker; BPM processes are good representations of complex message routing logic.

- A lengthy example of an Employee Benefits Message Broker is provided. The broker is a set of business processes that routes messages from an HR Portal web application to two internal systems—HR and Payroll—and two insurance companies—life and medical. The three processes are Life Events Publisher, Pension, and Medical. BPMN diagrams and BPEL implementations are developed.

Key BPM Acronymns

BPM is rife with three-letter acronyms (or TLAs). The following list decodes some of the most important terms.

ACID   Atomic, Consistent, Isolated, Durable; the properties of a transaction

AWSP   Asynchronous Web Services Protocol

B2B   Business-to-Business

BAM   Business Activity Monitoring

BEIDTF   Business Enterprise Integration Domain Task Force

BPD   Business Process Diagram

BPDM   Business Process Definition Metamodel

BPEL4WS   Business Process Execution Language for Web Services; from the OASIS group

BPELJ   BPEL for Java

BPM   Business Process Modeling, sometimes called Business Process Management

BPDM   Business Process Definition Metamodel

BPML   Business Process Modeling Language

BPMN   Business Process Modeling Notation; another specification from BPMI

BPMI   Business Process Modeling Initiative; an organization, not a specification

BPRI   Business Process Runtime Interface

BPQL Business Process Query Language

BPSM Business Process Semantic Model

BPSS Business Process Specification System

BPXL Business Process Extension Layers

BRM Business Rules Management

BSBR Business Semantics of Business Rules

CORBA Common Object Request Broker Architecture

CWM Common Warehouse Metamodel

CWAD Common workflow audit data

EAI Enterprise Application Integration

ebXML Electronic business XML

EDOC Enterprise Distributed Object Computing

EJBs Enterprise JavaBeans

ER Entity-relationship

ESB Enterprise Service Bus

ETTK Emerging Technologies Toolkit; from IBM

J2EE Java 2 Enterprise Edition

JAWE Java Workflow editor; from Enhydra

JCA Java Connector Architecture

JDBC Java Database Connectivity

JMS Java Messaging Service

JMX Java Management Extensions

JSP Java Server Pages

LRT Long-running transaction

MDA Model-Driven Architecture

MOF Meta-Object Facility

OASIS Organization for the Advancement of Structured Information Standards

OMG Object Management Group

OO Object-Oriented

OR Object-Relational

OSM Organization Structure Metamodel

POJOs Plain Old Java Objects

PD4J Process Definition for Java

PKI Public Key Infrastructure

PRR Production Rule Representation

RFPs Requests for Proposals

SOA Service-oriented Architecture

SOAP Simple Object Access Protocol

UDDI Universal Description, Discovery, and Integration

UML Unified Modeling Language

UUID Universally unique identifier

WAPI Workflow API

WfMC Workflow Management Coalition

WfXML Workflow XML

WSBPEL Web Services Business Process Execution Language

WSCI Web Services Choreography Interface

WSCL Web Services Conversation Language

WS-CDL Web Services Choreography Description Language

WSDL Web Services Definition
Language

WSFL IBM's Web Services Flow
Language

W3C World Wide Web Consortium

XLANG XML Language

XMI XML Metadata Interchange

XPDL XML Process Definition Language

INDEX

A

abstract processes, 109, 161
abstractProcess attribute, 109
action activity, 167, 170
actions, pi-calculus and, 50
activities
    automated, 5, 7
    BPDM and, 234
    BPEL and, 108, 115, 162
    BPML processes and, 166, 167
    BPMN and, 146, 150, 151
    BPRI and, 236
    branching, 76, 77
    canceling, 91
    compensation and, 152
    dead path elimination, 62
    defined, 4, 5, 149
    forking, 76
    insurance claims processing
        example, 255–256
    looping and, 156
    merging conditional paths, 77
    milestones and, 90
    multiple instances of, 84–87
    processes and, 180
    queues and, 6
    repeating, 82
    sequencing, 75
    shapes, 65
    split and join and, 191
    subflow, 180
    synchronizing, 76
    transactions and, 238
    WS-CDL and, 209
    WSFL, 244, 247
    XLANG and, 242
    XPDL and, 189, 190
activity control category (WAPI), 193, 195
activity diagrams, 64–69, 226, 233
    (see also UML activity diagrams)
Activity interface (WfXML), 198, 199
ActivityInstance class (WAPI), 193
Ad Hoc Process pattern, 88

ad hoc processes, 149
adapters
    defined, 287
    enactment services and, 179
    message brokers and, 288
    system interaction and, 32, 33
    WAPI and, 178, 196
administration
    BPM standards and, 43
    BPRI and, 235
    business process, 23
    enactment services and, 179
    external interactions, 26
    J2EE implementation, 26
    message brokers and, 288
    model architecture and, 33–41, 43
    Oracle BPEL Process Manager and, 258
    WAPI and, 193
    WfMC and, 178
administration category (WAPI), 193, 195
all activity, 153, 169, 242
AND split and join
    BPML processes and, 169
    BPMN processes and, 153
    Petri nets and, 60–62
    XPDL and, 180, 181, 191
    YAWL support, 93
AND-join pattern, 76
AND-split pattern, 76
application category (WAPI), 193, 196
application servers, 26
applications
    invoked, 177
    packages and, 191
    process-oriented, 8, 9
    WAPI and, 193, 194
    XPDL and, 180, 189
Arbitrary Cycles pattern
    BPEL support, 141
    BPML support, 172
    BPMN support, 163
    functionality, 82, 83
    XPDL support, 192

architecture
    BPM standards, 42–44
    design components, 27–42
    designing solutions, 22–26
arcs, Petri nets and, 56, 57
ARIS (IDS Scheer), 14
Arkin, Assaf, 144
assign activity
    BPEL, 249
    BPML processes and, 168
    description, 108
    example, 125
    guidelines, 116
    split and join, 120
    WS-CDL and, 210
assignments
    BPDM support, 234
    BPEL and, 116–117
    BPML processes and, 168
    BPMN processes and, 151, 152
    XPDL and, 190
Async Invoke pattern, 129
Async Invoke-Receive pattern, 129
Async Receive pattern, 129
Async Receive-Invoke pattern, 129
Async Web Service (AWS), 198
Asynchronous Web Services Protocol
    (AWSP), 198
atomic activities, 149
attributes, extended, 190, 192
auditing, 234, 258
automated activities, 5, 7
automated tasks, 5
AWS (Async Web Service), 198
AWSP (Asynchronous Web Services
    Protocol), 198

B

B2B (business-to-business) ecommerce, 237,
    286
Baeyens, Tom, 16
BAM (business activity monitoring), 39–41,
    144
Basel Accord, 8
Basic event (BPMN), 148
basic patterns
    Exclusive Choice pattern, 77, 141, 163,
        171, 192
    Parallel Split pattern, 76, 163, 171, 192,
        294
    Sequence pattern, 75, 140, 163, 171, 192
    Simple Merge pattern, 77, 141, 163, 171,
        192
    Synchronization pattern, 76, 140, 163,
        171, 192, 294

BEA
    BPEL specification, 103
    BPELJ and, 136
    BPM vendor, 13
    WebLogic Integration, 14
    WSCI and, 218, 224
BEIDTF (Business Enterprise Integration
    Domain Task Force), 232
Berners-Lee, Tim, 203
binary collaboration, 238, 240
BizTalk (Microsoft), 13, 240
block activity, 180
BPDM (Business Process Definition
    Metamodel)
    description, 18
    model architecture, 43
    OMG and, 144, 233
    overview, 12, 233–237
BPDs (business process diagrams), 145
BPEL (Business Process Execution Language)
    background, 10, 11
    basic process structure, 115–116
    BPDM and, 237
    BPM stack, 144, 145
    BPML and, 218
    BPMN and, 145
    BPSS and, 239
    business processes and, 104–108
    choreography and, 203
    dead path elimination, 55, 62, 80
    description, 17
    ETTK and, 236
    example, 108–114
    exception handling and
        compensation, 117–120
    extensions, 134
    IBM and, 236
    ITpearls support, 291
    language constructs, 114–134
    loops, 125–128
    mapping, 162
    message brokers, 288, 294–310
    model architecture and, 42, 43
    OASIS group, 10
    OMG architecture and, 13
    participant exchange, 128–133
    Petri net and, 48, 49, 64
    pi-calculus and, 48, 49
    process definition and, 233
    process design and, 25
    runtime engine, 255
    split and join, 120–125
    state machines and, 69
    transactions, 134
    variables and assignments, 116–117
    WfMC and, 176

wish list for, 135
WS-CDL and, 218
WSCI and, 225
WSFL and, 243–248, 249, 250
XLANG and, 231, 240–243, 249, 250
XML support, 103
XPDL and, 180
(see also insurance claims processing)
BPEL for Java (see BPELJ)
BPEL Process Manager (Oracle), 255, 257–259, 294
BPEL4WS (see BPEL)
BPELJ (BPEL for Java)
overview, 134–140
patterns and, 140, 141
PD4J and, 103
BPM (business process modeling)
benefits of, 7, 8
BPEL and, 249, 250
BPSS and, 237–240
defined, 3
design components), 27–42
designing solutions, 22–26
MDA and, 233
message brokers and, 287–288
OMG and, 231, 232–237
overview, 3–7, 9, 10
pi-calculus and, 49, 54, 55
process-oriented applications and, 8, 9
standards, 10, 10–13, 17, 18, 42–44
theory, 14, 47, 48
vendors, 13, 14
web services and, 204
workflow, 16, 17
WSFL and, 243–248, 249, 250
XLANG standard, 240–243, 249, 250
BPMI (Business Process Modeling Initiative)
background, 143
BPEL and, 176
BPEL mapping and, 162
BPM stack, 145
BPML standard, 10, 11, 17, 42
BPMN standard, 11, 18, 42
BPQL standard, 43
OMG collaboration, 237
BPML (Business Process Modeling Language)
BPEL and, 13, 162
BPM stack, 145
BPMI and, 144
BPMN and, 145
BPSS and, 239
description, 17
example, 164–166
language constructs, 166–171
model architecture, 42

overview, 11, 163
patterns, 171–172
pi-calculus, 48
process definition and, 233
WSCI and, 218, 220
WSFL and, 243
XLANG and, 242
XML support, 103
XPDL and, 180
bpml:rollback fault type (BPML), 171
BPMN (Business Process Modeling Notation)
BPEL and, 13, 162, 176
BPM stack, 144
BPMI and, 143
description, 18
example, 146
language constructs, 147–162
message brokers, 290–294
model architecture and, 42, 43
notational representation and, 103
overview, 11, 145
patterns, 27, 163
Petri nets and, 48, 49, 64
process definition and, 233
process design and, 25
WS-CDL and, 26
BPQL (Business Process Query Language)
BPEL and, 176
BPM stack, 145
BPMI and, 144
model architecture and, 43
BPRI (Business Process Runtime Interface)
description, 18
model architecture and, 43
OMG and, 233
overview, 12, 235–236
BPSM (Business Process Semantic Model)
BPDM metamodel, 237
BPEL and, 176
BPM stack, 144, 145
BPMI and, 144
BPMN and, 145
BPSS (Business Process Specification Schema)
collaboration, 232, 237–240
description, 18
model architecture, 43
overview, 10, 12
WS-CDL and, 218
bpws:getVariableData function (BPEL), 117
bpws:joinFailure fault (BPEL), 124
BPXL (Business Process Extension Layers), 144, 145, 176
branch and join patterns
Discriminator pattern, 81, 82, 141, 163, 172, 192

branch and join patterns (*continued*)
  Multi-Choice pattern, 79, 141, 163, 171, 192
  Multi-Merge pattern, 80, 81, 163, 171, 192
  N-out-of-M Join pattern, 81, 82
  Sync Merge pattern, 163, 171, 192
  Synchronizing Merge pattern, 80
branches
  activities and, 76, 77
  blocking, 81
  conditional, 191
  continuing independently, 80
  joining, 80
  split and join, 154
  termination points, 83
BRM (Business Rules Management) OMG RFP, 237
BSBR (Business Semantics of Business Rules) OMG RFP, 237
business activity monitoring (BAM), 39–41, 144
business analysts, 22, 25, 98
business architects, 7
business calendars, 135
Business Enterprise Integration Domain Task Force (BEIDTF), 232
business process
  BPEL and, 104–108
  common representations, 103
  control flow in, 59
  defined, 3
  design of, 22
  running, 23
  state diagrams for, 9
  terms defined, 5
  (see also pi-calculus)
Business Process Definition Metamodel (see BPDM)
business process diagrams (BPDs), 145
Business Process Extension Layers (see BPXL)
business process management (see BPM)
business process modeling (see BPM)
Business Process Modeling Initiative (see BPMI)
Business Process Modeling Language (see BPML)
Business Process Modeling Notation (see BPMN)
Business Process Runtime Interface (see BPRI)
Business Process Semantic Model (see BPSM)
Business Process Specification Schema (see BPSS)

Business Rules Management (BRM) OMG RFP, 237
Business Semantics of Business Rules (BSBR) OMG RFP, 237
business-to-business (B2B) ecommerce, 237, 286

C

C language, 193
C# language, 23
call activity, 167
Call Partner Service pattern, 96
Cancel Activity pattern
  BPEL support, 141
  BPML support, 172
  BPMN support, 163
  functionality, 91
  XPDL support, 193
Cancel Case pattern
  BPEL support, 141
  BPML support, 172
  BPMN support, 163
  functionality, 92
  XPDL support, 193
cancellation event
  BPML processes and, 166, 168
  BPMN processes and, 148, 160, 161
cancellation patterns
  Cancel Activity pattern, 91, 141, 163, 172, 193
  Cancel Case pattern, 92, 141, 163, 172, 193
canonical format, 286, 294–296
catch (BPEL object), 107, 118
catchall (BPEL object), 107, 119
Chain of Responsibility Pattern, 74
Chained pattern, 198
changeState( ) API (WfXML), 199
channels
  dynamic bindings, 55
  pi-calculus and, 50, 51, 54
  variables and, 208
  WS-CDL and, 209
ChannelType object (WS-CDL), 209
CheckStatus( ) method, 196
choice activity, 170
choreography
  BPDM and, 234
  BPM standards and, 43
  BPSS and, 237, 238
  collaboration and, 239
  defined, 11
  message brokers and, 288
  model architecture and, 43
  orchestration and, 204–206
  pi-calculus and, 48

web services, 10, 11
web services and, 203
WS-CDL and, 41, 42, 206–218
WSCI and, 218–225
WSCL and, 225–229
WSFL and, 244, 248
ClientConnection class (WAPI), 193
collaboration
    B2B and, 237
    binary, 238, 240
    BPMI and OMG, 237
    BPMN support, 161
    BPSS and, 232, 237–240
    choreography and, 239
    multiparty, 238
Collaxa, 257
color extension (Petri net), 59
COM Automation language, 193
Common Object Request Broker Architecture
    (see CORBA)
Common Warehouse Metamodel
    (CWM), 232, 233
common workflow audit data (CWAD), 178
communication patterns
    Call Partner Service pattern, 96
    Correlate Request and Response
        pattern, 96
    Dynamic Partner pattern, 96
    overview, 95–96
    partner interactions, 129–131
    Receive Initiating Request pattern, 95
    Unsolicited Event pattern, 96
    Wait for Response pattern, 96
compensate activity, 108, 167, 168
compensated activity, 149
compensation
    BPEL and, 117–120, 249
    BPML processes and, 166, 168
    BPMN processes and, 149, 152, 153
    defined, 118
    guidelines, 134
    XLANG and, 242, 249
    XPDL and, 190
compensation handlers
    description, 107
    invoke activity and, 130
    overview, 118
completeActivity( ) API (WfXML), 199
CompleteWorkItem( ) function (WAPI), 195
completion state, 238
Complex Join pattern, 81
compound activities, 149
computer interaction (see system interaction)
concurrency operator, 51
conditional branching, 59
conditional paths, 77
connection category (WAPI), 193, 194, 196

control flow
    ad hoc processes, 149
    choreography and, 239
    insurance claims processing, 266–268
    Petri net and, 14, 55, 59
    pi-calculus and, 54
    process definition and, 105
    process patterns for, 74, 95
    vendors and, 48
    WSCI and, 222
    WSFL and, 247
    XLANG and, 242
    XPDL and, 181
conversation, WSCL and, 225, 228
CORBA (Common Object Request Broker
    Architecture), 12, 193, 232
Correlate Request and Response pattern, 96
correlation
    BPEL wish list, 135
    insurance claims processing, 262–266
    message, 132, 160
    WS-Addressing standard and, 278
correlation sets, 113, 132
CorrelationSet (BPEL object), 107
createInstance attribute, 112, 115, 131, 133
createInstance( ) API (WfXML), 199, 200
CreateInstance( ) function (WAPI), 195
CRM, 177
CWAD (common workflow audit data), 178
CWM (Common Warehouse
    Metamodel), 232, 233

D

data fields, 180, 189, 190
data warehousing, 232
Davis, Martin, 65
dead path elimination
    BPEL, 249
    overview, 62–63
    Petri nets and, 55
    split and join, 124, 125
    Synchronizing Merge pattern and, 80
Deferred Choice pattern
    BPEL support, 141
    BPML support, 172
    BPMN support, 163
    functionality, 87
    XPDL support, 193
deferred choices, 88
delay activity, 170
design
    business analysts and, 98
    of business processes, 22
    components of, 25–26, 27–42
    Petri nets and, 56, 57
    for solutions, 22–26

design patterns, 73, 74, 98
destination activity, 182
Discriminator pattern
    BPML support, 172
    BPMN support, 163
    functionality, 81, 82, 141
    XPDL support, 192
dualist activity diagrams, 68, 69
Dynamic Partner pattern, 96

E

EAI (enterprise application integration), 7,
    10, 294
ebXML, 237–240
Eclipse, 257, 259, 284
ecommerce, 237, 286
EDOC (Enterprise Distributed Object
    Computing), 234
EJB (Enterprise JavaBean), 13, 23, 26
Emerging Technologies Toolkit (ETTK), 236
employee benefits message broker
    BPEL processes, 294–310
    BPMN process models, 290–294
    canonical XML, 294–296
    Life Event process, 291, 296–299
    Medical process, 292–294, 304–309
    Pension process, 291, 300–303
    testing, 309, 310
Empty object (BPEL), 108, 138
enactment services
    defined, 177
    WAPI and, 178, 193
    WfXML and, 179, 198, 199, 200
    XPDL and, 180
end event
    BPEL mapping, 162
    BPMN processes and, 150, 151
End interaction, 225
end state, 240
enterprise application integration (see EAI)
Enterprise Distributed Object Computing
    (EDOC), 234
Enterprise JavaBean (see EJB)
enterprise message broker (see message
    brokers)
Enterprise Service Bus (ESB), 289
entity-relationship (ER) tool, 233
EPC (Event Driven Process Chain), 69
ER (entity-relationship) tool, 233
ERP, 69, 177
ESB (Enterprise Service Bus), 289
Escalation pattern, 97
ETTK (Emerging Technologies Toolkit), 236
Event Choice, Pick pattern, 87
Event Driven Process Chain (EPC), 69
event handlers, 115, 120, 249

eventHandler handle, 108, 113, 116
events
    BPDM support, 234
    BPML processes and, 166, 170
    BPMN example, 146
    defined, 147
    exclusive OR gateway for, 154
exception event (BPMN), 148
exception handling
    BPEL and, 117–120, 249
    BPM benefits, 7
    BPML processes and, 166, 168
    BPMN processes and, 152, 153
    as manual activity, 5
    WS-CDL and, 209
    WSCL, 228
    WSFL and, 249
    XLANG and, 242, 249
    XPDL and, 190
Exclusive Choice pattern
    BPEL support, 141
    BPML support, 171
    BPMN support, 163
    functionality, 77
    XPDL support, 192
exclusive OR-split pattern, 79
exclusive XOR-split pattern, 79
executable process, 109
Explicit Solos Calculus, 55
exporting
    BPDM and, 233
    BPMN and, 145
expressions, 117, 190
extended attributes, 190, 192
extensions
    BPEL, 134
    BPELJ, 140
    BPML processes and, 171
    BPMN processes and, 161
    XPDL and, 192
external interactions, 25, 26

F

Façade pattern, 74
Factory interface (WfXML), 198, 199, 200
fault activity, 168
fault handlers, 107, 118, 168
filters, WAPI and, 194, 197
flow object (BPEL)
    description, 108
    example, 115
    influences on, 249
    split and join, 121–125
flowcharts
    depicted, 4
    process design and, 22

state machines and, 68, 69
visualization with, 65
foreach loops
    BPEL wish list, 135
    BPML processes and, 169, 170
    BPMN processes and, 156
    implementing, 126–128
    XPDL and, 191
forks
    activities and, 76
    choreography of, 238
    processes, 79
    shapes, 65

G

Gang of Four (GoF), 73, 74
gateways
    BPEL mapping, 162
    BPMN and, 146, 153–155
    defined, 150
getDefinition( ) API (WfXML), 199
global contracts, 24
GoF (Gang of Four), 73, 74
GOTO pattern, 82
graphical editors, 22, 25, 26
guards, 59, 68

H

heterogeneous patterns, 198
heterogeneous processes, 197, 199
Hewlett Packard, 225
hierarchy, 67, 149, 228
hierarchy extension (Petri net), 59
Hohpe, Gregor, 291
human interaction
    BPM standards and, 43
    model architecture and, 23, 29–32, 43
    process design and, 25
human workflow, 97, 258
    (see also insurance claims processing)

I

IBM
    BPEL specification, 103
    BPELJ and, 136
    BPM vendor, 13
    UML and, 236
    WS-CDL and, 218
    WSCI and, 224
    (see also WSFL)
IDS Scheer, 14
if-then structure, 153
implementation activity, 180

Implicit Termination pattern
    BPEL support, 141
    BPML support, 172
    BPMN support, 163
    functionality, 83
    XPDL support, 192
importing
    BPDM and, 233
    BPMN and, 145
inclusive OR-join pattern, 80
inclusive OR-split pattern, 79
initiate attribute, 133
initiate operation (WSDL), 266
Instance interface (WfXML), 198, 199, 200
instances
    changing states, 195
    process, 4, 5
instanceStateChanged( ) API (WfXML), 199,
    200
insurance claims processing
    description, 255–256
    developing example, 260–280
    Oracle BPEL Process Manager, 257–259
    setting up environment, 259
    testing example, 280–283
Intalio, 218
integration
    EAI, 7, 10, 294
    message brokers and, 287
    model architecture and, 23
interaction activity, 209
interactions
    defined, 225
    external, 25, 26
    transitions and, 225
interfaces
    BPRI and, 235–236
    Façade pattern, 74
    message brokers and, 286, 287, 288
    model architecture and, 23
    OMG and, 233
    proprietary, 236
    WAPI activity control and, 195
    WS-CDL and, 206
    WSCI and, 220–224
    WSDL and, 113
    XPDL and, 180
Interleaved Parallel Routing pattern
    BPEL support, 141
    BPML support, 172
    BPMN support, 163
    functionality, 88–90
    XPDL support, 193
internal interactions, 25, 26

invoke activity
    BPEL and, 105, 135, 249
    BPELJ and, 138
    BPMN processes and, 156
    choreography and, 205
    correlation sets and, 132, 133
    description, 108, 130
    example, 111, 112, 125
    guidelines, 116
    message brokers and, 288, 303
    partner interactions, 129
InvokeApplication( ) method, 196
invoked applications, 177
IP addresses, 197
ITpearls
    BPEL support, 291
    BPM design and, 14
    BPMN tool, 145, 151, 288, 290

J

J2C specification, 13
J2EE
    BPELJ and, 136
    BPM implementation, 26
    Oracle BPEL Process Manager and, 257
    system interaction, 23
Java Connector Architecture (JCA), 13, 26
Java Database Connectivity (JDBC), 23, 26
Java language
    BPELJ and, 139, 140
    BPMN extensions, 161
    system interaction, 23
Java Management Extensions (JMX), 26
Java Messaging Service (JMS), 23, 26
Java Server Pages (JSP), 26
JCA (Java Connector Architecture), 13, 26
JCP, 137
JDBC (Java Database Connectivity), 23, 26
JDeveloper, 257
JDK, 259
JMS (Java Messaging Service), 23, 26
JMX (Java Management Extensions), 26
join element, 77, 78
JSP (Java Server Pages), 26

K

Kill Activity pattern, 91
Kill Process pattern, 92

L

Life Event process (message broker), 291,
    296–299
link event (BPMN), 149
links, split and join, 122–123
listDefinitions( ) API (WfXML), 199

listInstances( ) API (WfXML), 199
local perspective, 24
Long Running Transaction (LRT), 134
loop pattern, 82
loops
    BPDM support, 234
    BPEL and, 125–128
    BPMN processes and, 156–159
    scenarios for, 159
    settings for, 157
    XPDL and, 191
LRT (Long Running Transaction), 134

M

Manual task type (BPMN), 150
manual tasks, 5, 266–268
MDA (Model-Driven Architecture)
    BPEL and, 13
    BPM and, 233
    IBM and, 236
    OMG and, 10, 232
    OMG specifications, 12
    overview, 232, 233
Medical process (message broker), 292–294,
    304–309
message brokers
    BPM and, 287–288
    canonical XML, 294–296
    employee benefits example, 288–310
    Life Event process, 291, 296–299
    Medical process, 292–294, 304–309
    overview, 285–287
    Pension process, 291, 300–303
    testing, 309, 310
message correlation, 132, 160
message events, 148, 160
message flow, 160, 162
message properties, 132
messaging
    BPM support, 55
    BPML processes and, 167
    BPSS and, 238
    Petri nets and, 57
    pi-calculus and, 54
    (see also message brokers)
metamodels, 232, 233
Meta-Object Facility (MOF), 144, 232, 233
Microsoft
    BizTalk, 240
    BPEL specification, 103
    BPELJ and, 140
    BPM vendor, 13
    Visio 2000, 290
    WS-CDL and, 218
    WSCI and, 224
    (see also XLANG standard)

Milestone pattern
    BPEL support, 141
    BPML support, 172
    BPMN support, 163
    functionality, 90
    XPDL support, 193
Milner, Robin, 14, 49, 55
mobility, 51, 54
model architecture (see architecture)
Model-Driven Architecture (see MDA)
MOF (Meta-Object Facility), 144, 232, 233
MOM interface, 7
monitoring
    BPM standards and, 43
    BPRI and, 235
    business process, 23
    enactment services and, 179
    external interactions, 26
    J2EE implementation, 26
    message brokers and, 288
    model architecture and, 33–41, 43
    WAPI and, 193
    WfMC and, 178
MQ/Series, 23
Multi-Choice pattern
    BPEL support, 141
    BPML support, 171
    BPMN support, 163
    functionality, 79
    message brokers, 291
    XPDL support, 192
Multi-Merge pattern
    BPEL support, 141
    BPML support, 171
    BPMN support, 163
    functionality, 80, 81
    XPDL support, 192
multiple event (BPMN), 149
multiple instances, 156, 157, 159
multiple instances patterns
    With Design-Time Knowledge
        pattern, 85, 141, 163, 172, 193
    With Runtime Knowledge pattern, 85,
        86, 141, 163, 172, 193
    Without Runtime Knowledge pattern, 86,
        141, 163, 172, 193
    Without Synchronization pattern, 84,
        141, 163, 172, 192

N

Nested pattern, 198
.NET interface, 7
newDefinition( ) API (WfXML), 199
noAction activity, 210
notation and graphical tool, 27–28

notational representation, 103
N-out-of-M Join pattern, 81, 82
null activity, 180

O

OASIS group
    AWSP and, 198
    BPEL standard, 10, 11, 17, 42, 144
    BPMI and, 143
    BPSS standard, 10, 12, 18, 43, 232
    WSBPEL technical committee, 103
Object Management Group (see OMG)
object-oriented (OO) tool, 233
object-relational (OR) tools, 233
Observer interface (WfXML), 199
Ockham's Razor, 10
OMG (Object Management Group)
    BPDM standard, 12, 18, 43, 144
    BPM models, 231, 232–237
    BPMI and, 143
    BPRI standard, 12, 18, 43
    business rule RFPs, 237
    MDA and, 10, 12
    UML activity diagrams, 42
onAlarm element
    business calendars and, 135
    description, 108
    example, 112
    pick activity and, 131
onMessage element, 108, 112, 131
OO (object-oriented) tool, 233
operation action (XLANG), 249
OR (object-relational) tools, 233
OR split and joins, 93
Oracle
    BPEL Process Manager, 255, 257–259,
        294
    BPM vendor, 13
    Task Manager service, 258
    WS-CDL and, 218
    WSCI and, 224
Oracle Business Integration, 13
orchestration
    BPSS and, 237, 239
    choreography and, 204–206
    message brokers and, 288
    WSCL and, 228
    WSFL and, 243
Organization Structure Metamodel (OSM)
    OMG RFP, 237
OR-split pattern, 79
OSM (Organization Structure Metamodel)
    OMG RFP, 237

P

P4 (Process Four)
  BPEL and, 140
  BPMN and, 27
  Petri nets and, 55, 59, 71
  process patterns and, 74–92
packages
  applications and, 191
  defined, 180
  WS-CDL and, 207
  XPDL and, 189
parallel processing, 155, 158, 159
Parallel Split pattern
  BPEL support, 140
  BPML support, 171
  BPMN support, 163
  functionality, 76
  message brokers, 294
  XPDL support, 192
participant exchange
  BPEL and, 128–133
  BPML processes and, 170
  BPMN and, 159–160
  XPDL and, 191
participants
  choreography and, 205
  defined, 180
  message brokers and, 288
  orchestration and, 204
  WS-CDL and, 206, 208
  WSCL and, 228
  WSFL and, 247
  XLANG and, 242
  XPDL and, 189
ParticipantType object (WS-CDL), 208
partner link types
  BPELJ and, 140
  defined, 128
  description, 107
  example, 114
  receive activity and, 131
partner links
  defined, 128
  description, 107
  example, 114
  insurance claims processing, 262–266
  message brokers and, 288
partners
  binary collaboration, 238
  BPEL and, 249
  BPMN processes and, 150
  communication patterns, 129–131
  correlation and, 132
  defined, 129
  description, 107

  multiparty collaboration, 238
  receive activity and, 130
  transactions and, 134, 238
Patriot Act, 8
patterns
  BPDM support, 234
  BPELJ and, 140, 141
  BPML and, 171–172
  BPMN and, 163
  communication, 95–96, 129–131
  design, 73, 74, 98
  human workflow, 97
  XPDL and, 192–193
  (see also process patterns)
PD4J (Process Definition for Java), 103
Pension process (message broker), 291, 300–303
perform activity, 210
persistence, 35–38
Petri nets
  BPEL and, 103
  control flow and, 14
  family tree, 48, 49
  language strength and, 48
  overview, 55–64
  tokens and, 156
  YAWL as, 93
Petri, Carl Adam, 14, 55
pi-calculus
  channel information and, 209
  choreography and, 48
  family tree, 48, 49
  overview, 49–55
  WS-CDL and, 218
  XLANG standard and, 103, 240
pick activity
  BPEL and, 105, 249
  BPMN processes and, 154
  description, 108, 131
  example, 112
  guidelines, 116
  partner interactions, 129
  process structure, 115
  variables and, 116
pipe symbol (|), 51
place
  Petri nets and, 56, 57, 58, 63
  split and join example, 61, 62
plain old Java objects (POJOs), 136
plug links, 244
POJOs (plain old Java objects), 136
pool, 159
port types
  connections and, 222, 224
  invoke activity and, 130
  mapping to, 128, 244

message broker example, 303
    participant exchange and, 170
    pick activity and, 131
    receive activity and, 131
    reply activity and, 131
    roles and, 114, 208
    WSDL and, 104, 114, 141, 241
PPR (Production Rule Representation) OMG
    RFP, 237
Prioritization pattern, 97
private processes, 161
problems, understanding, 22, 23
procedural programming, 65, 66
process control category (WAPI), 193, 194,
    195
process control flow (see control flow)
process definition
    BPELJ and, 139
    control flows and, 105
    defined, 5
    instances and, 4
    language support, 233
    OMG and, 233
    packages and, 180
    unified theory of, 234
    WAPI and, 194, 195
    WfMC and, 176
    WfXML and, 179
    XPDL and, 178, 180
Process Definition for Java (PD4J), 103
process design
    design patterns, 73–74
    process patterns, 74–92
    YAWL and, 93–95
process mining, 39–41
process patterns
    basic, 75–78
    branch and join, 75, 79–82
    cancellation, 75, 91–92
    control flow and, 74, 95
    multiple instances, 75, 84–87
    P4 and, 74–92
    state-based, 75, 87–90
    structural, 75, 82–83
<<process>> stereotype, 237
process theory
    overview, 14, 47, 48
    Petri net, 55–64
    pi-calculus, 49–55
    state machines, 64–69
ProcessDefinition class (WAPI), 193
processes
    abstract, 109, 161
    ad hoc, 149
    BPDM and, 234
    BPEL and, 107, 115–116

    BPMN supported, 161
    canceling, 92
    coding standards, 98
    communication patterns, 95, 96
    compound activities as, 149
    defined, 3
    enactment services and, 177
    executable, 109
    forking, 79
    global, 161
    heterogeneous, 199
    insurance claims, 255–256
    invoked applications and, 177
    loops and, 191
    swim lanes for, 159
    WAPI worklists and, 195
    WfXML and, 197
    WS-CDL and, 207
    WSFL, 246
    XLANG, 241
    XPDL and, 180, 189
    (see also business process)
processing modeling (see BPM)
ProcessInstance class (WAPI), 193
product architects, 21
Production Rule Representation (PRR) OMG
    RFP, 237
profiles, UML, 233
properties
    BPML processes and, 168
    BPMN processes and, 151
    description, 107, 132
property alias, 107, 132
Publish to Multiple Subscribers pattern, 96
Publish/Subscribe pattern, 96
Pyke, Jon, 16, 175

Q

queues, 6

R

raise activity, 167
Real-time Object-Oriented Modeling
    (ROOM), 59
ReassignWorkItem( ) function (WAPI), 195
receive activity
    BPEL and, 105, 249
    BPELJ and, 138
    choreography and, 205
    correlation sets and, 113, 132, 133
    description, 108, 130
    example, 111, 112, 115
    guidelines, 116
    message brokers and, 288
    partner interactions, 129

receive activity (*continued*)
    process structure, 115
    variables and, 116
Receive Initiating Request pattern, 95
Receive interaction (WSCL), 225
receive task, 160
Receive task type (BPMN), 150
Receive-send interaction (WSCL), 225
Reference task type (BPMN), 150
RelationshipType object (WS-CDL), 208
reply activity
    BPEL and, 105, 249
    correlation sets and, 133
    description, 108, 131
    message brokers and, 288
    partner interactions, 129
Resequencer pattern, 294
Roles Compete For Task pattern, 97
RoleType object (WS-CDL), 208
rollback handlers, 171
ROOM (Real-time Object-Oriented
    Modeling), 59
route activity, 180, 191
rule event (BPMN), 148
runtime engine
    BPEL, 255
    external interactions, 26
    good design and, 25
    J2EE implementation, 26
    model architecture and, 28, 29

S

SAP, 218
scope (BPEL object)
    compensation handlers and, 118
    defined, 117
    description, 108
    event handlers and, 120
    guidelines, 116
Script task type (BPMN), 150
security model, role-based, 23
Send interaction (WSCL), 225
send task (BPMN), 150, 160
Send-receive interaction (WSCL), 225
sequence activity, 242, 249
sequence flow
    BPEL mapping, 162
    BPMN processes and, 150, 151, 153
    defined, 150, 160
Sequence Flow pattern, 75
sequence object (BPEL), 108, 111, 115
Sequence pattern
    BPEL support, 140
    BPML support, 171
    BPMN support, 163

    functionality, 75
    XPDL support, 192
sequential operator, 51
service architects, 21, 22
Service task type (BPMN), 150
ServiceRegistry interface (WfXML), 198,
    199, 200
setDefinition( ) API (WfXML), 199
signals, BPML processes and, 167
Simple Merge pattern
    BPEL support, 141
    BPML support, 171
    BPMN support, 163
    functionality, 77
    XPDL support, 192
Simple Object Access Protocol (SOAP), 203
SOAP (Simple Object Access Protocol), 203
solutions, designing, 22–26
source activity, 182
source interaction condition, 225
spawn activity, 167
split and join
    BPEL and, 120–125
    BPML processes and, 169
    BPMN processes and, 153–155
    Petri nets and, 60–62
    With Design-Time Knowledge
        pattern, 85
    XPDL and, 191
split and join patterns, 291
standards
    BPM, 10, 10–13, 17, 18, 42–44
    BPRI and, 236
    coding guidelines, 98
    organizations involved in, 103
    Petri nets and, 49, 64
    pi-calculus, 48
    process coding, 98
start event, 150, 151, 162
Start interaction, 225
start state
    activity diagrams, 67
    BPSS and, 240
    choreography of, 238
    shapes, 65
StartProcess( ) function (WAPI), 195
state machines
    activity diagrams and, 67, 68
    flowcharts and, 68, 69
    hierarchy extension and, 59
    overview, 64–69
    Petri nets and, 55
    WSCL, 228
state-based patterns
    Deferred Choice pattern, 87, 141, 163,
        172, 193

Interleaved Parallel Routing pattern, 88–
    90, 141, 163, 172, 193
    Milestone pattern, 90, 141, 163, 172, 193
stop state, 65
structural patterns
    Arbitrary Cycles pattern, 82, 83, 141, 163,
        172, 192
    Implicit Termination pattern, 83, 141,
        163, 172, 192
subflow activity, 180
subscribe( ) API (WfXML), 199, 200
Sun Microsystems, 218, 224, 259
swim lanes, 66, 159
switch activity
    BPEL, 111, 113, 249
    BPELJ and, 138
    BPML processes and, 169
    BPMN processes and, 153, 154
    description, 108
    Exclusive Choice pattern and, 77
    guidelines, 116
    Multi-Choice pattern and, 79
    Simple Merge pattern and, 78
    split and join, 120
    XLANG and, 242
Sync Invoke pattern, 129
Sync Merge pattern
    BPEL support, 141
    BPML support, 171
    BPMN support, 163
    XPDL support, 192
Sync Receive-Reply pattern, 129
synch activity, 167, 170
synchronization, 122–123, 238
Synchronization pattern
    BPEL support, 140
    BPML support, 171
    BPMN support, 163
    functionality, 76
    message brokers, 294
    XPDL support, 192
Synchronized pattern, 198
Synchronizing Merge pattern, 80, 291
system interaction
    BPM standards and, 43
    model architecture and, 23, 32–33, 43
    process design and, 25

T

Task Manager service (Oracle), 258
tasks
    BPMN example, 146
    defined, 4, 5
    insurance claims processing, 266–268
    manual, 5, 266–268
technical analysts, 22, 25

terminate activity, 113, 119
terminate( ) API (WfXML), 199
TerminateInstance( ) function (WAPI), 195
termination event (BPMN), 149
testing
    insurance claims processing, 278, 280–
        283
    message brokers example, 309, 310
    Oracle PPEL Process Manager and, 258
throw activity, 108, 119
timeouts, 112, 146, 190
timer event (BPMN), 148
tokens
    BPMN and, 156
    Petri nets and, 56, 57, 58, 59, 63
    properties as, 107
    split and join example, 61, 62
    WS-CDL and, 208
tool activity, 180
tool agents (see adapters)
ToolAgent class (WAPI), 193
transactions
    BPEL and, 134
    BPML processes and, 171
    BPMN processes and, 160
    BPSS and, 238
    compensation and, 118, 153
    XPDL and, 191
transitions
    activity diagrams and, 67, 68
    choreography of, 238
    defined, 225
    exception handling, 190
    guarded, 191
    Petri nets and, 56, 57, 58, 59, 63
    processes and, 180
    shapes, 65
    split and join example, 61, 62
    state machines and, 65, 69
    XPDL and, 181, 189, 190
truth tables, 63
Turing, Alan, 64, 65
Tuxedo, 32

U

UDDI, 104, 144
UML (Unified Modeling Language)
    ETTK and, 237
    IBM and, 236
    MOF and, 232
    OMG and, 232
    process definition and, 233
    profiles, 233
    state machines and, 59

UML activity diagrams
    insurance process, 255
    model architecture, 42, 43
    notational representation, 103
    Petri nets and, 64
    process definition and, 233
    usage of, 69
    WSCL conversation, 226
UML class diagrams, 106, 193, 237
UML profiles, 233
Unified Modeling Language (see UML)
Unsolicited Event pattern, 96
unsubscribe( ) API (WfXML), 199
until loops, 156, 169
User task type (BPMN), 150

V

van der Aalst, Wil, 49, 55, 59
variables
    BPEL and, 107, 116–117, 249
    BPML processes and, 168
    BPMN processes and, 151, 152
    insurance claims processing, 262–266
    WS-CDL and, 208, 209
    XPDL and, 190
vendors, 13, 14, 93, 94
Visio (Microsoft), 290

W

W3C (World Wide Web Consortium)
    background, 203, 204
    BPMI and, 143
    choreography, 11, 204–206
    Choreography Working Group, 55
    standards, 10
    WS-CDL standard, 11, 13, 18, 43, 206–
        218
    WSCI standard, 11, 18, 43, 218–225
    WSCL standard, 11, 18, 43, 225–229
wait activity, 108, 135, 249
Wait for Response pattern, 96
WAPI (workflow API) interface
    BPRI and, 235
    description, 18
    model architecture and, 43
    overview, 12, 178, 193–197
    WfMC and, 175
web services
    BPM and, 204
    choreography, 10, 11, 203
    J2EE implementation, 26
    system interaction, 23
    WfXML and, 198
    WS-CDL and, 206

WSCI and, 218
WSCL and, 225
Web Services Choreography Description
    Language (see WS-CDL)
Web Services Choreography Interface (see
    WSCI)
Web Services Conversation Language (see
    WSCL)
Web Services Flow Language (see WSFL)
WebLogic Integration (BEA), 13, 14, 136
WebLogic Workshop (BEA), 13
WebSphere Business Integration (IBM), 13,
    136
WfMC (Workflow Management Coalition)
    background, 175
    BPEL and, 13, 176
    BPMI and, 143
    WAPI interface, 12, 18, 43, 193–197, 235
    WfXML interface, 12, 18, 43, 197–200
    on workflow, 16
    Workflow Reference Model, 10, 12, 18,
        42, 43, 176–180
    XPDL standard, 12, 18, 42, 43, 180–193
WfXML (Workflow XML)
    description, 18
    model architecture, 43
    overview, 12, 179, 197–200
    WfMC and, 175
while loops
    BPEL, 125–128, 249
    BPML processes and, 169
    BPMN and, 156
    description, 108
    guidelines, 116
    WAPI and, 197
    XLANG and, 242
    XPDL and, 191
White, Stephen, 68, 94, 143
With Design-Time Knowledge pattern
    BPEL support, 141, 172
    BPMN support, 163
    functionality, 85
    XPDL support, 193
With Runtime Knowledge pattern
    BPEL support, 141, 172
    BPMN support, 163
    functionality, 85, 86
    XPDL support, 193
Without Runtime Knowledge pattern
    BPEL support, 141, 172
    BPMN support, 163
    functionality, 86
    XPDL support, 193
Without Synchronization pattern
    BPEL support, 141, 172
    BPMN support, 163

functionality, 84
XPDL support, 192
work items, 195
workflow
  BPM, 16, 17
  client applications, 177, 178
  CWAD and, 178
  WAPI and, 196, 197
  WfMC and, 177
  (see also BPM)
workflow API interface (see WAPI interface)
Workflow Management Coalition (see
  WfMC)
Workflow Reference Model
  description, 18
  model architecture and, 42, 43
  overview, 10, 12, 176–180
  WfMC and, 175
Workflow XML (see WfXML)
WorkItem class (WAPI), 193
worklist category (WAPI), 193, 195
workUnit activity, 209
World Wide Web Consortium (see W3C)
WS-Addressing standard, 112, 278, 296
WS-CDL (Web Services Choreography
  Description Language)
  BPEL and, 13
  BPM stack, 144, 145
  BPSS and, 239
  broker processes and, 288
  channels and, 55
  choreography overview, 41, 42
  description, 18
  example, 210–217
  external interactions and, 26
  future of, 218
  global contracts and, 24
  J2EE implementation, 26
  model architecture and, 43
  object model, 207–210
  Oracle and, 224
  overview, 11, 204
  pi-calculus and, 48
  strengths, 217
WS-Choreography standard, 204
WSCI (Web Services Choreography
  Interface)
  BPMI and, 145
  description, 18
  future of, 224, 225
  global model, 222–224
  interface, 220–224
  model architecture, 43
  overview, 11, 204
  pi-calculus, 48
  state machines and, 69

typical application, 219, 220
weaknesses, 224
WSFL and, 243
WSCL (Web Services Conversation
  Language)
  description, 18
  model architecture, 43
  overview, 11, 204, 225–229
  state machines and, 69
WSDL (Web Services Description Language)
  BPEL and, 104
  BPM stack, 144
  BPML processes and, 166
  ETTK and, 236
  insurance claims processing, 260–262
  interfaces and, 113
  message brokers example, 296–309
  message properties, 132
  W3C and, 203
  WS-CDL and, 206
  WSCI and, 218, 220
  XLANG and, 241
wsdl:definitions element, 222
WSFL (Web Services Flow Language)
  BPEL and, 49, 103, 249, 250
  dead path elimination, 55, 62
  description, 18
  model architecture, 42
  overview, 11, 231, 243–248
  Petri nets and, 49, 64
  process definition and, 233
WS-Reliability standard, 204
WS-Security standard, 204
WS-Transaction protocol, 134, 171

X

XA standard, 171
XLANG standard (Microsoft)
  BPEL and, 49, 103, 249, 250
  control structures, 55
  description, 18, 231
  model architecture, 42
  overview, 11, 240–243
  pi-calculus, 48
  process definition and, 233
  WSFL and, 243
XMI (XML Metadata Interchange), 233
XML
  BPEL and, 104, 135, 162
  BPELJ and, 139
  BPML and, 163
  business processes and, 103
  canonical, 294–296
  system interaction, 23
  WS-CDL and, 206
  WSCI and, 219

XML (*continued*)
 WSCL and, 225, 228
 WSFL and, 243, 244
 XLANG and, 241
 XPDL and, 180
XML Metadata Interchange (XMI), 233
XML Process Definition Language (see
 XPDL)
XOR split and join
 BPML processes and, 169
 Petri nets and, 60–62
 XPDL and, 180, 181, 191
 YAWL and, 93
XOR-join pattern, 77
XOR-split pattern, 77
XPath language, 168

XPDL (XML Process Definition Language)
 description, 18
 elements, 190–192
 example, 182–190
 model for, 42, 43, 180–182
 overview, 12, 178, 180–193
 patterns, 192–193
 process definition and, 233
 WfMC and, 175, 176
 XML support, 103

Y

YAWL (Yet Another Workflow
 Language), 49, 93–95

ABOUT THE AUTHOR

MICHAEL HAVEY, an architect in IBM's Global Services division, has worked in the software industry for 10 years, specializing in enterprise integration and BPM. Michael has two degrees, both from the University of Toronto: a B.A. in mathematics and philosophy and a B.S. in computer science. Away from work, Michael enjoys spending time with his family and writing about software. Michael lives near Ottawa, Canada.

COLOPHON

OUR LOOK IS THE RESULT of reader comments, our own experimentation, and feedback from distribution channels. Distinctive covers complement our distinctive approach to technical topics, breathing personality and life into potentially dry subjects.

Mary Anne Weeks Mayo was the production editor and Nancy Kotary was the copyeditor for *Essential Business Process Modeling*. Colleen Gorman and Claire Cloutier provided quality control. Lucie Haskins wrote the index.

Michele Wetherbee is the creative director for the *Theory in Practice* book series. MendeDesign designed the cover and created the cover artwork of this book. Karen Montgomery produced the cover layout in Adobe InDesign CS using Akzidenz Grotesk and Orator fonts.

Marcia Friedman designed the interior layout. Melanie Wang designed the template; Phyllis McKee adapted the template. The book was converted by Keith Fahlgren to FrameMaker 5.5.6 with a format conversion tool created by Erik Ray, Jason McIntosh, Neil Walls, and Mike Sierra that uses Perl and XML technologies. The text font is Adobe's Meridien; the heading font is ITC Bailey. The illustrations that appear in the book were produced by Robert Romano, Jessamyn Read, and Lesley Borash using Macromedia FreeHand MX and Adobe Photoshop CS.

Better than e-books

Buy *Essential Business Process Modeling* and access
the digital edition FREE on Safari for 45 days.

Go to www.oreilly.com/go/safarienabled
and type in coupon code TSDI-T3IC-7IGP-YZC8-NII8

Search
thousands of
top tech books

Download
whole chapters

Cut and Paste
code examples

Find
answers fast

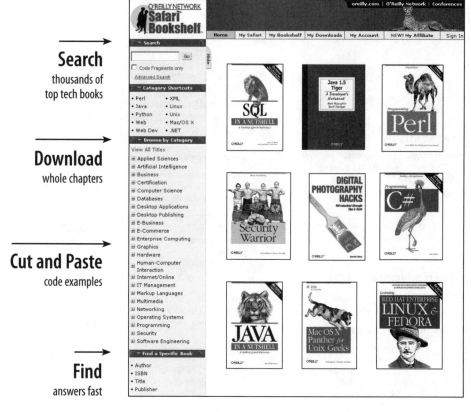

Search Safari! The premier electronic reference
library for programmers and IT professionals.

Keep in touch with O'Reilly

Download examples from our books

To find example files from a book, go to: *www.oreilly.com/catalog* select the book, and follow the "Examples" link.

Register your O'Reilly books

Register your book at *register.oreilly.com* Why register your books? Once you've registered your O'Reilly books you can:

- Win O'Reilly books, T-shirts or discount coupons in our monthly drawing.
- Get special offers available only to registered O'Reilly customers.
- Get catalogs announcing new books (US and UK only).
- Get email notification of new editions of the O'Reilly books you own.

Join our email lists

Sign up to get topic-specific email announcements of new books and conferences, special offers, and O'Reilly Network technology newsletters at:

elists.oreilly.com

It's easy to customize your free elists subscription so you'll get exactly the O'Reilly news you want.

Get the latest news, tips, and tools

www.oreilly.com

- "Top 100 Sites on the Web"—PC Magazine
- CIO Magazine's Web Business 50 Awards

Our web site contains a library of comprehensive product information (including book excerpts and tables of contents), downloadable software, background articles, interviews with technology leaders, links to relevant sites, book cover art, and more.

Work for O'Reilly

Check out our web site for current employment opportunities:

jobs.oreilly.com

Contact us

O'Reilly Media, Inc.
1005 Gravenstein Hwy North
Sebastopol, CA 95472 USA
Tel: 707-827-7000 or 800-998-9938
     (6am to 5pm PST)
Fax: 707-829-0104

Contact us by email

For answers to problems regarding your order or our products:
order@oreilly.com

To request a copy of our latest catalog:
catalog@oreilly.com

For book content technical questions or corrections: **booktech@oreilly.com**

For educational, library, government, and corporate sales: **corporate@oreilly.com**

To submit new book proposals to our editors and product managers:
proposals@oreilly.com

For information about our international distributors or translation queries:
international@oreilly.com

For information about academic use of O'Reilly books:
adoption@oreilly.com
or visit:
academic.oreilly.com

For a list of our distributors outside of North America check out:
international.oreilly.com/distributors.html

Order a book online

www.oreilly.com/order_new

 **O'REILLY®**

Our books are available at most retail and online bookstores.
To order direct: 1-800-998-9938 • order@oreilly.com • www.oreilly.com
Online editions of most O'Reilly titles are available by subscription at *safari.oreilly.com*